THE SEX GAME

THE SEX GAME

Jessie Bernard

ATHENEUM 1973 NEW YORK

Acknowledgment is made for permission to reprint excerpts from the following works:

Mistress to an Age, copyright © 1958, by J. Christopher Herold, reprinted by permission of the publisher, The Bobbs-Merrill Company, Inc.

And the Poor Get Children, by Lee Rainwater, copyright © 1960 by Social Research, Inc., reprinted by permission of Quadrangle Books, Inc.

The Age of Confidence, by Henry Seidel Canby, copyright 1934, © 1962, reprinted by permission of Holt, Rinehart and Winston, Inc.

"Playboy After Hours," *Playboy* Magazine, January 1965, copyright © 1964 by HMH Publishing Co., Inc.

War and Peace, by Leo Tolstoy, abridgment by Edmund Fuller, copyright © 1955 by Edmund Fuller and used with the permission of the publisher, Dell Publishing Co., Inc.

Wild Heritage, by Sally Carrighar, reprinted by permission of the publisher, Houghton Mifflin Company.

Love and Death in the American Novel, copyright © 1966, 1960 by Leslie Fiedler, reprinted with the permission of Stein and Day Publishers.

The Sociology of Child Development, by James H. S. Bossard, reprinted by permission of Harper & Row, Publishers, Inc.

Love in America, copyright 1943 by David L. Cohn, reprinted by permission of Curtis Brown, Ltd.

Cambridge History of English Literature, reprinted by permission of Cambridge University Press.

The Family: A Dynamic Interpretation, by Willard Waller, revised by Reuben Hill, copyright 1938, 1951, © 1966 by Holt, Rinehart and Winston, Inc., reprinted by permission of Holt, Rinehart and Winston, Inc.

Art Buchwald's Column, *Washington Post,* December 30, 1965, reprinted by permission of Art Buchwald.

On Aggression, by Konrad Lorenz, reprinted by permission of the publisher, Harcourt, Brace & World, Inc.

War Time Shipyard, by Katharine Archibald, reprinted by permission of University of California Press.

Sexual Behavior in the Human Male, by A. C. Kinsey and Associates, by permission of W. B. Saunders Company.

Sexual Behavior in the Human Female, by A. C. Kinsey and Associates, by permission of W. B. Saunders Company.

CONTENTS

Part Four. Mise-en-Scène

INTRODUCTION

Since this book first appeared in 1968, communication between the sexes, its major theme, has taken a most unexpected turn. Women have begun to transmit messages quite unheard-of in the past, in a language of words and deeds almost totally without precedent[1]. It is not so much the factual content of their message that is new. That, in fact, is quite old. Indeed, the contents of this book constitute a good share of the facts of their message. What is new is the interpretation given to these facts[2]. This book, in fact, constitutes in a way wholly unintended a portrait of the relations between the sexes which are the prime targets of these women. It is, par excellence, a statement of precisely what it is they wish to be liberated from.

I wrote in the Epilogue that I did not want to be like the television weatherman reading blithely from his script that the day was to be clear and fair while a blizzard raged outside (p. 328). But in a way that was roughly the case. I was forecasting continuing but not catastrophic change. "Old myths which served so well in the past [now] got in the way. . . . New ones have to be evolved" (330). "Despite the remnants of this [segregated] pattern . . . it appears to be on its way out. The conditions of modern life do not support it and the kind of women our times create do not like it" (330). But how little they liked it was just becoming evident.

As I wrote those bland statements, a furious storm was brewing. Not catastrophic or apocalyptic, to be sure, but not a light summer shower either. *The Sex Game* described with considerable accuracy what the relations between the sexes were like in a variety of life situations. But it did not prepare us for the attack on them then begininng to be launched by the angry women.

Yes, these women are saying, what you report is true: "women in task-oriented groups of mixed-sex composition often have a hard time getting the floor" (145); "women have a harder time getting the attention of the group; and they are more likely to lose it by successful interruption from men" (146); women "are not listened to" (283). The protesting women now complete the picture: it infuriates us that the men won't listen to us! that they do not hear us![3] I accept their correction. They are outraged but their outrage was never reported in the research literature on which this book was based.

And so all the way through. The pathos of the married woman's hunger for conversation with her husband remains (Chapter 10). The husband's reluctance to satisfy it has been interpreted as a power play.[4]

The analysis of communication between the sexes at work (Chapter 11) still retains its validity. But it is now being completed by the angry women. We are not willing to sacrifice our own achievement in order to preserve male sexuality! (285-286). Nor to use our sex as a competitive weapon! (279-280). We reject the use of sex in advertising! (281-283). Indeed, the members of NOW—the National Organization for Women—monitor advertising that exploits women and register protests against the most offensive. I asked at the end of Chapter 11 what would be the effect of the Civil Rights Act of 1964 which forbids discrimination in employment on the basis of sex (293). Regrettably, this question cannot even yet be answered. Revolutions these days, though numerous, are not fast.

In Chapter 12 the discussion of sex-as-fun also ended with an inconclusive "we'll have to wait and see" (308). The answers are only now beginning to come in. The newly emerging custom in some areas of "swinging" has as one of its rules that there is to be no love between partners, thus embodying the basic rule of sex-as-fun, namely, that love spoils the game (306)[5]. On the other hand, judged by the rule propounded in this book—"if they remain as lonely afterwards as before or if the experience leaves a bitter taste, it was not fun" (306)—sex-as-fun has not worked out well for women. One of the most poignant replies to the "let's-wait-and-see" stance of Chapter 12 was supplied in a "rap session" of women seeking liberation the very year, 1968, this book was published[6]. Sex-as-fun was not working out well for them.

The social apartheid documented in Chapter 13 remains; but the stultifying life-style which condemns married women to dullness (322)[7] is under attack. It is still true that "men . . . have the kind of feminine company they deserve" (324).

Aside from the impact of this momentous movement, there is, unfortunately, little about this book that has to be changed. The Commission on Obscenity and Pornography has updated some of the work of Kinsey and his associates on sex differences in response to sexual stimuli;[8] the suggestion (75) that the grammar and syntax of body language be formalized and codified has been followed;[9] but for the most part little needs alteration.

In light of the critiques of the women's liberation movement, this is regrettable. *The Sex Game* still stands as a picture of what these women are trying to change. We will know how successful they are by the amount of rewriting the next edition will call for. Hopefully, a total rewrite.

Jessie Bernard

Footnotes

[1]I say *almost* totally without precedent because there were some precedents in the woman's suffrage movement during the earliest cycle of feminism in this century during the first two decades. Both here and in England symbolic acts were used, including chaining themselves to the White House gates, to convey the message of angry women. A major difference is that at the present time electronic media make available a wider use of symbolic acts, provide more strategic targets, and give access to a wider audience. The contents of the message were, to a large extent, without precedent, especially those that dealt with sexual relations between men and women. Women had never written in this vein before.

[2]New also were the uses being made of the theory of communication. One of the most powerful techniques the women developed was one of blunting the messages of men by "calling their shots." Thus, for example, Beverly Jones analyzed for intimidated wives the techniques, both postural and verbal, used to intimidate them, thus arming the women against them. Pat Mainairdi interpreted all the excuses men gave for reneging on their share of household chores, thus deflating them of their validity. Dana Densmore verbalized all the subtleties of dating, of chivalry, of friendship, exposing the assumption of superiority and power by the men and the subservience and inferiority of women. See Jessie Bernard, *The Future of*

Marriage (World Publishing Company, 1972), Chapter 10, for further discussion of this point.

[3]To the complaint of one angry woman that even when a woman enters a discussion, it resumes "at the exact point from which she made her departure, as though she had never said anything at all" or that men leave the room while a woman is talking, or talk among themselves, one young man replied: "What they say just doesn't sound relevant. So we just go on, as they say, as though they hadn't said anything. So far as we can tell, they haven't." (See Jessie Bernard, *Women and the Public Interest, An Essay on Policy and Protest*, Aldine-Atherton, 1971, pp. 209-210). Men found it hard to believe that women were not listened to. Once it was called to their attention they were surprised to find it true. Brewster Smith, one of the most outstanding psychologists today, interpreted it in terms of the ongoing status competition among men. Since women had no place in the status hierarchy they could be ignored; they were not competitors. No matter, said the angry women. They would not take explanations as a substitute for change. We want in, they continued to cry.

[4]Dana Densmore, "On Communication," *Journal Female Liberation*, No. 5, July, 1971, pp. 66-82. Joseph Veroff and Sheila Feld have asked whether there is an intrinsic incompatibility between marital companionship and sexuality (*Marriage and Work in America*, Van Nostrand-Reinhold, 1970, pp. 118-119).

[5]For a discussion of the practice of swinging, see Jessie Bernard, *The Future of Marriage* (World Publishing Company, 1972), Chapter 9.

[6]Since "Notes from the First Year," which reports this rap session, is all but impossible to find, see *The Future of Marriage* (Chapter 10) for a resume.

[7]For a resume of the research literature on what housework does to women, see *The Future of Marriage*, Chapter 3.

[8]The Report of the Commission on Obscenity and Pornography, with an Introduction by Clives Barnes (The New York *Times*, 1971). The Commission found that "females are less responsive to male-oriented erotica but almost equally responsive to heterosexual action themes. Differences . . . appear to be essentially qualitative, rather than quantitative" (231-232). It is remarkable how well the findings of Kinsey and his associates have held up.

[9]A best-seller in 1970 was Julius Fast's *Body Language* (Lippincott, 1970).

A WORD ABOUT WORDS

This book is about the manifold and variegated relationships between the two great collectivities that we call the sexes. Both of these collectivities have peculiar and characteristic qualities which render their relationships—in the family, at work, at play, or in social life—unique, *sui generis* as compared with the relations between all other kinds of groups and collectivities. For the wide gamut of relations possible between these collectivities, the term here used is "sex relations," by analogy with, for example, "race relations" or "group relations." The emphasis is on the entities themselves. For the narrower conceptualization usually subsumed under the term "sex relations" the term here used is "sexual relations," by analogy with, for example, "racial," "international," "industrial," or "intergroup" relations; that is, the emphasis is on the fact that the relationship itself is sexual in nature.

The kinds of sex relations we are interested in here, out of the infinite variety possible, are those which are mainly, though not exclusively, mediated by words. They are interpersonal, for the most part face-to-face.

❖❖

Before the Curtain
Rose

❖❖❖❖❖

The sexes were communicating with one another millennia before Adam and Eve. The relations between them were therefore
social long before the sixth day. Sometimes, in fact, even more
social than sexual.

There was a time, to be sure, early in the fifth day, let us
say, when there were neither sexual nor social relationships
between the sexes. Female insects, for example, or fishes who
simply deposit eggs which then await fertilization can hardly
be said to have social, any more than sexual, relations with males
of their species.

But as the fifth day wore on, females whose eggs were
fertilized within their bodies did begin to have sexual relations
with the males of their species. And this change to within-body
fertilization necessitated at least a minimum amount of communication between the sexes. Since, unlike the human situation,
it was the female who controlled the whole sexual business, the
male somehow or other had to learn when his contribution was
needed, when the eggs were ready, when she would receive
him. A kind of protosociability was thus involved.

But it was not such a big deal. For among many preprimates,
"sex is a sometime thing, very intense while it lasts, but when

it subsides the whole business seems to go out of mind."[1] And for seasonally mating animals, the intense times may come but once a year. Between these intense times there is not much male-female sociability.[2] In fact, after the male has performed his fertilizing function he may even be destroyed. He is expendable. Who needs him? The social life of the species is organized to operate without him.

Somewhere along the line—say about twelve o'clock high— female birds and mammals whose eggs are fertilized within their bodies came to have warm, even tender, social as well as sexual relations with males. Sometimes even more social than sexual. One researcher, Konrad Lorenz, even finds love among some. He self-consciously rejects the use of quotation marks around the expression "falling in love" in describing the behavior of his experimental animals, Greylag Geese. Among them he finds, as among men, one kind of relationship between the sexes which is strictly and exclusively sexual and only minimally social; but he also finds one which, by way of contrast, is social with all the earmarks of love.

The "purest" love leads by way of the greatest tenderness to a physical approach which, however, is in no way the essential part of this bond; and conversely, those stimulus situations and partners which release the strongest copulatory drives are certainly not unconditionally the ones that produce the most intense falling in love. In the Greylag Goose, the two function cycles can dissociate themselves as completely from each other and make themselves as independent as they can in man, though they undoubtedly belong together "normally" and just relate to one and the same partner if they are to fulfill their survival value.[3]

Among these geese, Konrad Lorenz continues, "everything purely sexual plays a very subordinate role." Social rather than sexual ties characterize their relationship. "The bond that holds a goose pair together for life is . . . not the sexual relationship between mates." (Sometimes, to be sure, they do not live up to their high goose standards—they slip to the human level. Thus when Lorenz found so many cases which did not conform to the regular pattern, because of unusual circumstances, a co-worker, Helga Fischer, protested, "What do you expect? After all, geese are only human!")

Sometimes the sexes even have social *instead* of sexual relations with one another. The relationship may not even be a breeding one. Thus, "if two lonely geese are dependent on each other's company a nonbreeding association between a male and a female may occur. . . . There are true friendships between male and female which have nothing to do with love."[4]

In brief, sexuality as a primarily social phenomenon was present in the animal world long before the curtain rose on man. The relations between the sexes were not restricted to reproductive ends nor communication to signs of sexual readiness. The sexes were sociosexual beings long before they were human beings. And reproduction was not the only *raison d'être* of their relations.

✦✦✦✦✦

It was the transfer of fertilization from outside to inside of the female's body which demanded communication between the sexes. As compared with the nonsexual language of, say, the bee in communicating the location of honey to its hive-mates, the language of sex is elementary. Originally, the female's message was simple and straightforward: I am ready. Charles Darwin was only one among many who have reported on the sexual language of animals and Konrad Lorenz only one of the latest, though certainly not the last. Scientists could probably compile dictionaries of the languages of sex among lower animals.

Simple the language of sex may be but it must be unequivocal, especially among mammals with a mating season. For if the egg is not fertilized at the proper time, it cannot be fertilized at all. The female has to let her readiness be known; the male has to get her message.

In the case of the porcupine, for example, fertilization has to occur on a specific day in November. The female is in estrus only once a year and matures only one egg.[5] Frequent copulations are not needed; but when copulation *is* needed, she must give the signal and he must be ready. In July both sexes are relaxed and playful, wrestling and gently "horsing around" in a social but not a specifically sexual way. By August she has begun to show signs of tension and nervousness. In September they increase and reach a peak, and then in October she enters another phase, which is quiet and subdued. By November, she has chosen the male she wants for a mate and sits close to him most of the time. Then, at last, as though tolled by a bell:

... the moment for coupling arrives. ... She comes out of her waiting mood. She sniffs the male in significant ways. He responds. They touch noses, retreat a few steps, rise on their hind feet, walk toward each other, and, standing upright, touch noses again. This touch is the trigger. With the speed of a fire storm the female is down and the male is atop her. ... This embrace ... may last for as long as five minutes and be repeated, but only during a span of three to five hours. Then the female is through. She will no longer receive this male, or any other until a year from now. So perfectly has she timed the coupling, however, that her pregnancy almost certainly is assured.[6]

Timing is of the essence, for the female porcupine, according to this author, has "less than a day in which to ... reveal her willingness to the male, carry out with him their brief mating ritual, and then come together. Yesterday would have been too soon; tomorrow would be too late. Only today will do."[7] Three to five fertile hours in a whole year. The punch line in this story is that now the female will no longer receive this male, or any other, until a year from now.

Elephants, we are told, have somewhat different problems. For among them the male also has a kind of periodicity which has to be adjusted to. He is subject to attacks of a kind of madness known as "must," which renders him hostile. The degree of hostility can be gauged by the amount of a brown discharge from a gland near his eyes which accompanies the attack. The female has to learn to read this sign and steer clear of him.

When it is not present, however, she has no reason to fear him. His advances to her are gentle and unhurried. As with porcupines, there is a primarily social relation between the sexes.

... after he chews and swallows the root, the male stands still for a moment, watching her. ... He comes forward and gently runs the tip of his trunk down her back. She lifts her head, meets his eyes, and with the tip of her own trunk she touches his neck. This is all that will happen today. The two will resume their feeding, and when she returns to the swamp, he will go with her. He is willing to take his time, but something momentous has started.

From now on they spend all their days together, and their nearness seems almost enough. There are, however, more and more frequent caresses, a fondling which seems as yet to express no more than affection. The male's trunk will brush her side, a touch that she almost always returns. Or the forehead of one will give a little push on the side of the other. They nibble each other's cheeks—the play is growing a bit more stimulating. Tails swing and ears flip, and the pair are communicating with sounds. . . .

Weeks pass with such expressions of tenderness but no real excitement. When a more sensual stage is reached, their trunks show their true versatility. They are often entwined. They are tied in a lovers' knot over the elephants' heads. The tips are put into each other's mouths, an elephant's kiss.

The dalliance becomes more intense. Her motions are more inviting —so provocative that female elephants have been called the most sophisticated of all wild animals in their courtship. And finally they play with their trunks erotically. They tease. But when the climax is reached, even then in the male's embrace there is no coercion.[8]

There is less urgency among elephants than among porcupines because estrus occurs more often. Thus, coupling may occur again the next day, perhaps several times, and if she does not conceive during this estrus, it will occur again several weeks later.

But once pregnancy has begun, the female breaks away; she now prefers the herd to the male. For "although altruism . . . affects the quality of the elephant's male-female relationships, the physical cycle determines how long the pairs stay together. The male's fertility and desire are continuous; yet the female . . . removes herself from his company for three years at a time."[9] The male gives her up, "reluctantly," tries, in fact, to hold her. Then, failing this, he looks for another female. Punch line: she now prefers the herd to the male and he gives her up.

All is not, to be sure, so idyllic between the sexes in all mammals. In some of the so-called combative species, for example, such as some squirrels, weasels, and shrews, ovulation does not precede copulation but is induced by aggressive pre-coupling fracases. But in "even the species which seem so antagonistic, the male does not become really aggressive until the female indicates that she is ready."[10] Once the female is pregnant, the sexes part company. Males and females are neither enemies nor competitors.

The social relations between the sexes among preprimate mammals, then, is related to sexual seasonality, which, in turn, is regulated by the female's "inner bell," a term poetically applied by Sally Carrighar to the triggering effect of female estrus. Those whose periodicity is annual, having only one mating season during the year, devote only a relatively small part of their lives to sexual relations and a considerable part to uncomplicated social relations. The porcupine illustrates a situation in which the female has only one very brief period for conception; the elephant is an example of a species that has an annual mating season but one that is less restricted, so that there is less urgency about copulation. If at first they do not succeed, they can try, try again. There's time.

On logical grounds one might suppose that when estrus became monthly, as it did among primates, sexuality would have become less urgent. Nature might have argued that when conception could happen every month, there wasn't much need for frequent copulation. If one cycle was missed, there would be another soon. Among porcupines it could be argued that it was better to take a chance and copulate even when the female was not ready than not to copulate when she was; there could be nothing lost in the first case but a great deal in the second. But Nature did not seem to think along these lines. She arranged for only one copulation for the one-estrus-a-year porcupines. Among the thirteen-times-a-year primates, however, she arranged not a thirteen-copulations-a-year pattern but copulations any and every day of the year, wholly without regard to estrus. Whether or not seasonality is present in subhuman primates (it is still mooted among some biologists[11]), copulation can and does occur in or out of season.

Something crucial has occurred. The signs of female estrus are no longer scrupulously respected. Males approach females even when they are not in estrus, and the female receives the male, or even herself approaches him, when she is not actually in estrus. Nature's bell has fallen silent. Coupling ceases to be limited to times determined by the female's physiology. Sexual relations are no longer closely tied to reproduction; they are independent of seasonality.

Now that estrus occurs monthly, Sally Carrighar asks, "Will the constant association of males and females make it easier for them to live harmoniously, or otherwise?"[12] The answer is, yes —both.

The habit of engaging in sexual relations even when the female is not prepared for conception introduced confusion, or "chaos" as one writer calls it in the case of rhesus monkeys,[13] into the social relations between the sexes. The female no longer controlled her own sexual relations. Other messages came to occupy the communication system between the sexes: messages about status, in the form of dominance, or about property. All this even before the emergence of culture with its almost infinite complication of both messages and media.

Among Old World monkeys, the female still signals to the male when her estrus has come; there are other signs, too, like the scarlet coloring of her sitting pads. But, and this is the point, she is approached even when her estrus ebbs. The rhesus monkey evolved a "brutish and bestial" kind of relationship between the sexes. The male attacks the female and often actually injures her. They seem to one author, Sally Carrighar, to be "hypersexed." Hypersexed they may be when compared with other subhuman primates, but not necessarily when compared with human beings. One scientist reported seeing a male monkey copulate with fifty females in two months;[14] Kinsey and his associates reported males who copulate—if not with fifty females—at least fifty times with some female in one fourth that time.[15]

The chimpanzee, who tends to be rather unstable, shows various kinds of relationships, cruel and belligerent as well as friendly and loyal. And the female is not above exploiting the male as well as vice versa.[16]

The male baboon is dominant and he alone determines the time of copulation, entirely reversing the primitive pattern.

In these three cases—rhesus monkeys, chimpanzees, and baboons—the male-female relationship by human standards has deteriorated from that of the elephant, porcupine, or even—perhaps especially—the Greylag Goose. The male is a bully, the female coy and foxy.

But the American monkey is not belligerent, socially or sexually. And the stable gorillas even have a gentle relationship between the sexes. The tolerant and dominant male is a leader, not a despot. He is not jealous. The sexual act is not one of

[7]

mastery, for "gorillas do not confuse sex and dominance."[17] And the gibbons, we are told, are exceptionally tender in their relationships and capable of sympathy—even with human beings.[18] (Who are we to call animals "brutish" or "bestial"?)

> The sexual chaos of rhesus monkeys, the frequent viciousness in the baboon harems, the armed truce of the chimpanzee males and females, and the permissive paternalism of the gorillas: this is strangely diverse behavior for animals who all belong to the same primate order.[19]

Among those other primates, human beings—sexier and more social than the others—what did the silencing of the bell do to the relations of the sexes among them? But that, of course, is the theme of this whole book. . . .

❖❖❖❖❖

How Nature's bell was silenced is not altogether clear. Sally Carrighar suggests that both "lust" and "affection" played a part in the overruling of Nature's restriction of coupling to times determined by the female's reproductive readiness: "lust" as among the rhesus monkeys, chimpanzees, and baboons and "affection" as among American monkeys, gorillas, and gibbons.

> At some stage in their evolution, the males of some primate species began to adopt a demanding attitude. It was no longer enough that . . . the female . . . never would challenge his strength. Now she must bend to his will. . . . Those evolving males who found that they liked to intimidate mates were responsible for replacing joy and freedom in sex with fear and deviousness.[20]

> But their aggressiveness was not the sole reason why nature's bell became silent. . . . With increasing intelligence, obviously, the sexes became aware of each other more consciously, and then warmth of feeling may have become a motive as strong as lust. . . . The primate's evolving mind began to overrule nature's restrictions.[21]

It was not the male alone, whether through lust or affection, who contributed to the silencing of the bell. Among even the chimpanzees, the male is considerate of the female during estrus when she is sexually receptive and offers herself. But learning this, she takes advantage of his generosity by offering herself

[8]

even when she is not in estrus, slipping in for a bit of stolen food—a strategy, incidentally, that has been whimsically labeled a form of prostitution.

✦✦✦✦✦

Whatever the causes may have been, the effects of the silencing of the female bell constituted one of the most widely ramifying revolutions in the sexual history of life on this planet, as revolutionary as the transfer of fertilization to inside of the female's body. To emphasize its importance and put it into perspective, Sally Carrighar associates it with the very concept of original sin itself. Perhaps, she suggests, the real meaning of original sin was this "seeking of intercourse during nature's forbidden time."[22] If so, the "fall," in the sense of "disobeyed nature," occurred before the time of man.

Such a view presupposes a sinful view of sexual relations. The behavior of the rhesus monkey, chimpanzee, baboon, and some human beings supports such a view. But it might also be argued that the silencing of the bell was an upward step, permitting, as among the American monkeys, gorillas, gibbons, and some human beings a continuously affectionate relationship not dependent on estrus.

We need not accept either of these interpretations to recognize that the silencing of the female bell greatly complicated all the relations between the sexes. Receptivity in the female became more related to social than to biological influences, and they did not always reinforce one another. They might even be different. The whole drama of sex relations became subject to missed cues and fumbled responses.

Then one day—in the Genesis meaning of the term—males and females began to talk to one another. They discovered words and invented more. And either as cause or as effect or as both, they became human. Something new was added. Their relations became cultural as well as biological and social.[23] Because so much of human culture rests on words, it had to await the advent of a verbal language. With words communication becomes infinitely elaborated; only a small proportion

[9]

remains physiological. Culture introduced such complexity into the picture—for words make possible messages never dreamed of before—that not only do relations between the sexes become transformed but so, too, do the sexes themselves.

THE COMMUNICATORS

CHAPTER ONE

✦✦

What Do You Mean
"The Sexes"?

✦✦✦✦✦

. . . male and female created he them.

—Genesis 1:27

✦✦✦✦✦

The Creator was satisfied with two sexes; mankind has hardly ever been. Two have almost never seemed to be enough for all the things human beings wanted to use the sexes for. Some of the insects are better off than humans in this respect; they have at least warriors, workers, and queens. Short, therefore, of the wanted number of genetic sexes, human beings have created more: biologically when they could, culturally or socially if they could not.

Anatomy, as Freud insisted, may be destiny. If you are born with the anatomy (and physiology) of a woman you are destined—in whatever culture you are born—to have certain experiences and not to have others. And the same, of course, if you have a male body. Your anatomy will determine how people will treat you, how they approach you, and how they react to your approach. We have to start, therefore, by recognizing this fundamental biological cleavage in the human species. The subsexes emerge within these two collectivities.

If anatomy is destiny, so also is class. If you are born into a certain position in your society, you are destined to have certain experiences and not to have others. This position will also influence the way others treat you. The same can be said of race or nationality or culture. All of them "determine" one's destiny, as biological sex does. They combine to differentiate separate little sexes within the great collectivities.

❖❖❖❖❖❖

In creating new or special sexes, it is somehow or other usually considered better if it can be done by means of biological changes. The legendary warrior sex, the Amazons, for example, cut off one breast so they could use their bows and arrows more effectively. The traditional Chinese woman of leisure had her feet bound to distinguish her from women who belonged to the working female sex. The hourglass figure of the nineteenth-century lady served a somewhat similar function. Jewish matrons used to have their hair cut off at marriage, putting them in a different category from the unmarried. The almost disabling obesity of women in some African tribes marked them as a special sex. The woman who is kept constantly pregnant is, in effect, a different sex from the woman who never is, so far as her relations with men are concerned. The emaciation demanded of fashion models creates a kind of sex specialized for display. The body of the star ballerina, almost the epitome of feminine grace and beauty, may in real life be quite asexual. Sterilization, which irreversibly separates sex from reproduction, also creates a new sex, sociologically speaking. The eunuch and the castrato were among the most drastic experiments in extending the number of sexes on a biological basis. But the celibate too, male or female, is an attempt to create, in effect, new biological sexes so far as relations with others are concerned. The virgin belongs to a different sex from that of the sexually awakened woman, a difference recognized in the distinction some men make in their judgment of the rightness or wrongness of extramarital sexual relations. The unawakened girl misses cues, fails to catch a great many of the messages beamed in her direction, doesn't get the point of the risqué story. She may know all about sex, especially if she is a sophisticated modern, but not yet "addicted" to it, she is like the sleeping beauty so far as a vast amount of communication is concerned. In fact, because initiatory sexual experience is such a rite of passage, some cultures attempt to control it rigorously: young people are never left alone without chaperones.

Even without cultural intervention, the pretty woman, for all intents and purposes, is a different sex from the ugly one. She has more privileges and prerogatives; her relations with men are of a different order. Upward mobility based on beauty has a long history, as Esther and almost any current movie queen can illustrate. Biology, then, alone or with human assistance, is a great subsex differentiator.

So is class. It may be true, as Rudyard Kipling said, that Judy O'Grady and the Colonel's lady are sisters under the skin. But they will neither send nor receive the same messages. The heiress's chauffeur does not show any signs of the attraction he feels toward her; she, on her part, scarcely sees him as a man. If she does, it may become a cause célèbre. In general, the college boy puts the waitress in a different category from the prom girl, as far as communication is concerned. His message is different, and the signs, signals, and strategic language he uses are different for the two girls. Conversely, the attraction toward the blue-collar young man felt by the college girl may have the same appeal-of-the-exotic as attraction toward a young man of another race; he seems like a different sex from that of the college men she dates.

Kinsey and his associates have documented the differences in sexuality among men in the several classes, and studies of working-class wives and marriages have corroborated them. Upper- and lower-class females are, for all communicative intents and purposes, different sexes.

The incest taboo adds to the number of sexes in the sense that it places some females completely out of the range of a male's circle of communication. Mothers and sisters—as well as fathers and brothers, of course, and even in-laws—do not inhabit the same world of relationships as nonforbidden peers. Other kinship rules also differentiate special subsexes, prescribing the kinds of relations permitted or forbidden, such as the so-called joking relationship prescribed between men and their mothers-in-law in some societies.

The Greeks specialized women as companions, as sex partners, as breeders, as servants, and as slaves. Said Demosthenes, "We have hetaerae for pleasure, concubines for our daily needs; and wives to give us legitimate children and take care of the house." A concubine was, for all practical purposes, a quite different sex from the hetaera; as was, again, the slave from the wife. The fact that a modern woman has to perform so many of these different functions by herself has been cited as one of her major problems.[1] It is hard to be part of so many—often conflicting—subsexes. The much-advertised role-confusion today is as much a matter of confusion among intrasex roles as between male and female roles.

We seem to be fighting a losing battle in the modern world so far as functionally specialized subsexes are concerned. The homogenizing forces that shape our times tend to reduce the number of functionally differentiated subsexes, since we no longer socialize people for specialized sex-related roles to the same extent as in the past. We can see, though, what a disadvantage it is to have so few functional sexes. Life would be simpler if there were at least half a dozen different sexes, unequivocally specialized biologically (though not necessarily genetically) if possible, and culturally or sociologically if not, in order to accomplish all the different things the same woman has to do and hence to provide for all the different role-relationships she has with the male subsexes today.

As a parenthetical aside we note that so far from elaborating new specialized subsexes, modern young people seem to be attempting a convergence into a kind of uni-sex or mono-sex, a sort of all-purpose sex that can perform, almost indiscriminately, any kind of role. One of the most common sources of amusement in the press today is based on the difficulty outsiders have in distinguishing boys from girls. Their coiffures are the same; they both wear sandals; they both wear slacks or jeans; they execute identical steps when dancing.

The suffragettes and feminists of the nineteenth century also insisted on underplaying sex differences, maintaining that men and women were human beings first, and males and females only incidentally. They were also, in their own way, trying to reduce the number of sexes.

✧✧✧✧✧

Even with our present meager complement of functional subsexes there are at least two among women (whatever the gross biological facts may be), that have had a powerful, almost determinative, effect on the relations between men and women. They reflect a differentiation among females associated with Christian ideology—that between madonna and harlot. One was pure, or sexless; the other sinful, or sexually approachable. Good girls and bad girls. Nice girls and not-nice girls. In terms of the signals they were specialized (and socialized) to send and receive they were surely different sexes. From one emanated spirituality or refinement; from the other, carnality. Any examination of communication between the sexes has to take these differences into account.

Leslie Fiedler, the literary critic, analyzed the part played by these two subsexes in the mentality of American men. He based his discussion on the kinds of women portrayed in American novels by male authors. He found throughout nineteenth-century novels that there are White or Fair Maidens and Dark Ladies. The White Maiden is blond and blue-eyed. James Fenimore Cooper almost automatically provided his heroines with dazzling complexions, fair golden hair, and bright blue eyes. Hawthorne's special metaphor for the nice girl is the snow maiden. Melville pictured his Lucy, another sexless White Maiden, in the conventional color scheme, white and gold and blue.[2]

The Dark Lady was a brunette. In Melville's *Pierre* she accepted, though she bemoaned, the ineluctable fate that went with being dark. "Say, Pierre, doth not a funerealness invest me? Was ever hearse so plumed?—Oh, God! that I had been born with blue eyes, and fair hair! Those make the livery of heaven! Heard ye ever yet of a good angel with dark eyes, Pierre?—no, no, no—all blue, blue, blue. . . ." The Dark Lady was the "sinister embodiment of the sexuality denied the snow maiden."[3] She was a contemporary descendant of Lilith and Eve, original source of sin in our world and hence a more complex symbol than the White Maiden. There are few ways of being virtuous, and they are frequently negative, denying, nondoing. But there are many ways of being evil, most of them compellingly attractive. Fiedler suggests that the White Maiden was a male defense against the powerful attraction of the Dark Lady.

> The sentimental apotheosis of woman as immaculate savior had all along been in conflict with the older orthodox view of woman as temptress and witch. Indeed, the temporary exile of that older view to the unconscious had only proved to the American male that, banished from daylight, the terrible woman did not die but returned in nightmares; for it was she (he came to realize), in all her ravening sexuality, whom he really desired; though he led her white sister to the altar and the legitimate marriage bed.[4]

This interpretation, if valid, is a new twist. In the nineteenth century, the Dark Lady in the form of the prostitute was viewed by at least one scholar, W. E. H. Lecky, as a protection of the White Maiden. If it weren't for her, all that male sexuality would be wreaked on the White Maiden. And in the Old South, analogously, the Negro woman, by absorbing white male sexuality, protected the white woman from it. That this protection may have embittered her was beside the point.

Fiedler also noted that the Dark Lady was "typically Catholic or Jew, Latin or Oriental or Negro," suggesting that she represented not only Dionysian sexuality, but also a "surrogate for all the Otherness against which an Anglo-Saxon world attempts to define itself . . . the hunger of the Protestant, Anglo-Saxon male not only for the rich sexuality, the dangerous warmth he had rejected as unworthy of his wife, but also for the religions which he had disowned in fear, the racial groups he had excluded and despised." In brief, the Other, the Strange, the Forbidden.

At the end of the nineteenth century and beginning of the twentieth, the two subsexes were in transition; it was possible to have components of both subsexes in a single heroine, the Good Bad Girl. Sometimes as the prostitute-with-a-heart-of-gold and sometimes as a falsely impugned Maiden who, despite all her indiscreet behavior with men, is proved in the end to have retained her virginity, she became a stock character in the movies, "a living embodiment of the American faith that evil is appearance only." A way of having one's cake—the Fair Maiden; and eating it, too—her Dark Lady behavior.

By the 1920's the change had gone so far that there was a great switchover in roles. On a superficial level, the blond preferred by gentlemen became a golddigger; at a deeper level, Faulkner's Temple Drake showed that "the blond virgin is only a mask of the insatiable brunette." There were not two subsexes, one good and one bad. There were, rather, two sets of expectations "and a single imperfect kind of woman caught between them: only actual incomplete females, looking in vain for a satisfactory definition of their role in a land of artists who insist on treating them as goddesses or bitches. The dream role and the nightmare role alike deny the humanity of women, who, baffled, switch from playing out one to acting out the other."[5]

Fiedler's literary analysis has been corroborated by scientific observers of the transition, confusion, and reversal of the roles of the White Maiden and the Dark Lady in the twentieth century. Psychiatrists, for example, have shown how the sexuality of women has been changed,[6] and Kinsey and his associates documented the change.[7] Before the 1950's, anyone talking to an audience on the topic of, let us say, chastity in women or premarital virginity could take it for granted that, despite an occasional protester, most of his listeners accepted the current standards. They held to the traditional White Maiden as standard and they attempted to impose it on their sons and daughters: "Men may like to play around with loose girls (Dark Ladies) but they marry the virgins (Fair Maidens)." Little by little, though, audience support became less and less expectable, let alone certain. Those who believed in the White Maiden were clearly in the minority—and, finally, even on the defensive.

The White Maiden and the Dark Lady survive, though not in either the pristine or the reversed form. And men are still engaged in fighting them.

[19]

One transmogrification of the Dark Lady is the subsex called the bitch, who, according to some commentators, has been especially powerful in our society. D. H. Lawrence first articulated the so-called bitch theory of American society. His thesis was that women in America were the dominant sex: they had assumed, he said, so much power that men could hardly stand up to them, and as a result they had, in effect, castrated the men. James Thurber's name has come to stand for the same view of the battle of the sexes. The bitch is "a woman without heart, who . . . [loves] merely power over men and the momentary satisfaction to vanity or flesh which they . . . [can] give her."[8] They are the women who dominate men, who have power over them, who outmaneuver them, who successfully compete against them (especially if they make something of it). The bitch may take different forms at different times, but she retains her archetypical characteristics. At the time of the Renaissance, the bitch took the form of the witch who, by having sexual relations with the devil, acquired supernatural powers and could therefore do enormous damage, including the infliction of impotence on men. Today she is sometimes called the castrating female. She is powerful and therefore fearful.

Another form taken by the bitch in European if not in American literature is the Fatal Woman, described by Mario Praz. She was usually older than the man who loved her, more active, superior in status or in physical vigor. And deadly. She stood "in the same relation to him as do the female spider and the praying mantis to their respective males: sexual cannibalism is her monopoly."[9] The castrating female destroys only male sexuality; the Fatal Woman, the male himself.

Another myth of the overpowering female that Fiedler found in American literature was that of the mother. In the nineteenth century, "the alienation of mothers (then White Maidens) and sons" was blamed on the sons; they were therefore guilt-ridden. But in the twentieth century, the devil-Mom supplanted the saint-Mom and the counterattack by men began; the women were now the betrayers. However it originated, the effect of the mother-as-bitch conception, says Fiedler, left men incapable of an adult confrontation with an adult woman.[10]

It is, in a way, too bad that mothers and wives belong to the same female collectivity. The child is conditioned to an image of women as powerful and dominating characters. Some students of the subject believe that it is the mother-son relationship— supporting and disciplining at the same time—which determines all a man's later sex relations, including sexual relations. In some societies this inevitable circumstance is mitigated by taking boys from their mothers as early as possible. They are sent away to school or they are turned over to men. But the power of this sex of women probably can never be wholly compensated for. Grown men, even in Asian societies, cower before their mothers. We have been told in a horrendous literature that in our own society boys rarely escape these vipers until they are fairly grown, if even then.

The hatred most men feel toward the White Maiden in bitch form can be noted even among the most objective scientists. The Kinsey team, for example, had not a word or nuance of judgment when discussing bestiality or homosexuality or masturbation. Their antiseptic calm remained unruffled. Only in the case of the asexual woman was their guard down and then only for an instant.[11]

Strangely, sociologists have found little corroboration for the thesis of the hag-ridden male. When they study dominance in marriage to the extent of determining who makes the important decisions, they have found that men tend to make at least as many as the wives and that women prefer it that way.[12] Of course, it is always possible that the researcher's approach is too crude to lay open the "real" relationships between men and women. Members of the female collectivity surely do not see themselves as the powerful, let alone menacing, creatures that Lawrence, Thurber, and Fiedler see. They see themselves as put upon rather than as aggressors. Thus we have the situation— cosmically humorous—in which each collectivity views itself as the put-upon sex and the other as the exploiting one. The distinction between what is characteristic and what is typical is important. The scientist shows what is typical; the artist, what is characteristic.

Fiedler's analysis of the several subsexes in the female collectivity is impressive and evocative. What he found in American literature corresponds to much that many of us have ourselves found in the life it reflects. It gives us insights and understanding, but not necessarily knowledge. For knowledge, we have to look to the social scientists.

Lee Rainwater is one. On the basis of a hundred interviews among working-class people, the males under forty-five and the females under forty, he distinguished three female subsexes—as we use the term here—on the basis of where the emphasis on sex lay. He labeled them the Sexy Ones, the Rejecters, and the Loving Ones. The Sexy Ones are real-life analogues of Fiedler's Dark Lady; "they do not feel that they must be simply passive in order to be good women." Sexuality is important to them. The Rejecters correspond to the sexless White Maiden. Some, the Active Rejecters, feel disgust, fear, or anxiety, conscious or implicit, toward sex. An Active Rejecter "fears that if she were to enjoy sex she would be a bad woman." Some are Passive Rejecters, or repressive compromisers, who "seek to neutralize their negative feelings and to regard their wifely duty as simply another chore."

So far so good. Fiedler's analysis has at least this much basis. But Rainwater found a subsex that Fiedler did not, the Loving Ones. Sexual relations are important to this subsex, but intrinsically they are not nearly so important to her as the social relationship with her husband that accompanies them. These women "emphasize the non-physical aspects of intercourse and its after effects more than the orgasmic gratifications." It is the loving attention of the husband more than the sexual aspects that gratify her. The enjoyment these women find in sexual relations, which is considerable, results from the sense of closeness with their husbands more than from orgasmic experience as such. Whether or not she finds physical pleasure in sexual relations, "she accepts her duty and wants very much to make her husband happy; she is [therefore] able to find pleasure in sexual relations and to achieve a measure of mutuality in her relationship with him."[13]

Rainwater found that class makes a difference in the relative proportion of the several subsexes present. Thus there were three times as many Sexy Ones in the upper-lower class as in the lower-lower class (three-fourths versus one-fourth); and conversely, four times as many Rejecters in the lower-lower class as in the upper-lower class (forty versus ten percent). The middle category of women, largely in the lower-lower class, accepted their sexuality but feared pregnancy.[14]

No one has made a similar analysis of higher socioeconomic classes. But there is no reason to believe that these subsexes are not also present there, however different in relative proportions they might be. The statistics presented by Kinsey and his associates clearly reveal wide differences in frequency of sexual outlets among women, as among men; but they do not distinguish among women on the basis of the importance attached to sexual experience and therefore do not help us in delineating the several subsexes. Frequency of sexual intercourse in the case of women often tells us more about their husbands than about them.

Two new female subsexes are in process of being differentiated in the female collectivity, with reverberations in the intersexual world not yet fully understood. Both are "inconceivable" in the sense that they do not conceive, one because of reliable contraception and the other because of age. Their "inconceivability" is related both directly and tangentially to their sexuality and may further blur the Dark Lady–Fair Maiden anomaly.

Although on the basis of their midcentury data, Kinsey and his associates computed that perhaps only one in every thousand premarital coital experiences resulted in conception, those small odds were still enough to serve as brakes on the sexuality of women and to exert a powerful influence on the relations between the sexes. There was always a possibility, whatever the probability, and this was all that was needed to inhibit sexuality. For some women in all ages, sexuality had been free from reproductive concern. But not until after the middle of the twentieth century were so many women in a position to keep sexuality divorced from reproduction.

This "contracepted woman" was a new subsex so far as relationships with men are concerned. The consequences of sexual relations need be no more significant for her than for her partner. She does not have to think about a new life she might be responsible for or about the need for a father to share the responsibility of rearing such a child—concerns far removed from the immediacy of sexual relations. She can assume the same kind of hail-and-farewell stance as her partner can. Whether many will actually want to, we haven't yet had time to learn. In fact, all the consequences of this new subsex have not yet become apparent. That they will be profound can be accepted without qualification.

The other new "inconceivable" subsex is differentiated by age. Long before culture intervened, age differentiated members of both collectivities into basically different subsexes. Even among animals the aged constitute, in effect, a different sex from the young. And until recently the same was true for human beings, especially for those of the female collectivity. The sheer weight of the years desexed them. Even after biology no longer inflicted the stigmata of age on women, culture stepped in and did it anyway. Women beyond the reproductive age, or even earlier, were assigned a sexless role. The very idea of sexual interest among them was viewed with disapproval. They were to be neuter. Thus in the past, demographic and social circumstances combined to deprive women even in their late thirties and early forties of their sexual nature; women looked forward with dread to their fortieth birthday. In the lower socioeconomic classes, to be sure, their bodies really were old by forty, worn out by sheer physical labor and childbearing; institutions merely ratified biology. Not so, however, among the more comfortable classes. Even among them, however, no sexiness was permitted. "I said that the two sexes lost interest in each other because these people were old," said Henry Seidel Canby, recalling the social life of his childhood in the 1890's, "but they were not old, not even their glands were old; it was their imagination that had suffered from the restraint of something vital."[15] There was a missing ingredient and the result was stultifying:

> Leave out manganese (or is it magnesium) from the diet of a bitch and she will cease to nurse her puppies. An element, not necessarily the most important, was excluded from the daily diet of our relationships, with the result that society grew anemic as it grew older. Unrest or boredom hovered in the corners . . . , the friendship was real but the gaiety forced, and even with fine people had a note of the trivial and the commonplace. . . . In our town . . . a woman of thirty or forty . . . [was little] more than a domestic variety of man.[16]

A great deal is made nowadays of hormonal deprivation in the middle-aged woman's body and of the destructive effects it can have. We hear less of the social or recognition starvation she may suffer from, though, as Canby shows, it can be even more destructive. Advertisements promise rehabilitation of good marital relations if the wife covers that gray in her hair; she can again show her husband that she is still the exciting person she knows she is. Banishing the gray may not hurt; but banishing enforced sexlessness may be more important in restoring her appeal. And that depends on men. "How a little love and good company improves a woman!" said George Farquhar's early eighteenth-century Beau,[17] corroborating the point Canby was also making for the late nineteenth century.

A woman of twenty-three can no longer hope to stir romantic interest in men, said Jane Austen, who ought to have known but probably did not. The heroines of Racine, Shakespeare, Molière, Voltaire, Aristo, Byron, Lesage, and Scott were almost always sixteen or thereabouts. We had to wait for Honoré de Balzac in the nineteenth century to show us that even a woman of thirty could still stir romantic interest. Some of Tolstoy's heroines remained fascinating well beyond even this age. In 1965 the heroine in a woman's magazine story by Noel Coward was fifty. For nowadays women of almost any age can stir men. We smile in amusement at the quotation attributed to Oliver Wendell Holmes who, at ninety, when he saw an attractive woman, said, "Oh, to be seventy again." We were disbelieving at Colette's analogous comment, "Oh, to be fifty-five again, still desired." Both now seem equally credible. For sexual interest and responsiveness last, and more to the point, are permitted to last, far beyond the reproductive period.

Something new has been added in recent years. A genuinely new biological subsex has been added to the human stock of sexes. A new kind of woman. She is the result of cultural forces, technological as well as normative, and of advances in medicine, nutrition, and health care, especially obstetrical. She was not designed and shaped for a specific function, as some other manufactured subsexes were. She was, in fact, an unanticipated consequence of modern science.

In the past when we spoke of "the new woman" we were

likely to be thinking of women with new ideas and attitudes, new aspirations and new conceptions of themselves and of their relations to the world. But the new women today are new in a quite different way. Not in the sense that they are young, for they are not; they may be in their fifties and even, in some rare cases, their sixties. They are new in the sense that women like them have never existed on this planet until now. Their very existence is a brand-new human and therefore social phenomenon—as a whole generation, that is; there have always been such individuals.

A demographic revolution has extended sexuality into later years than in the past. The menopause comes later now than it used to. Not only do women live longer than preceding generations did; they also retain their youth and even beauty much longer. And those who do not do so naturally can be helped to do so by the new hormonal therapy.

If they were new only in this demographic sense they would not necessarily be new sociologically. They would just be more of the same—old women in larger numbers than before. And in fact, not all of these surviving women really are new. Many still are the same old kind of women as in the past— bitches, moms, Helen Hokinson types. But some are genuinely new.

They are attractive, though not in the youthful way. They are not trying to look young. As one woman in her mid-fifties commented, "I know I can't look young at my age, but I *can* look pretty." And she did. There was a time when the pretty clothes were designed only for the young. The styles for older women were drab and even ugly. Who was going to see them, anyway? Today there are attractive clothes designed for all ages. And the new women have the bodies to wear them. Not all, or even very many, new women look like Marlene Dietrich or Greer Garson or Claudette Colbert or Joan Crawford—still dazzling well into their fifties and sixties—or even like Mamie Eisenhower, youngish at seventy. But these women show what is possible. And what is possible for them will soon become possible for many more and, ultimately, for almost everyone.

The ability to be attractive is almost as much a cultural as a biological phenomenon. Even in the case of youngsters, beauty is becoming more and more widespread. Girls today are prettier than in the past, even taking into account changing tastes in beauty, and prettier even than those in the fairly recent past. Better health and nutrition are a big part of this change; but so also is the hygienic and beauty care that the skin, teeth, and the hair of modern girls receive from an early age. Any girl without a pockmarked face was considered a beauty before the eighteenth century. Facial deformities resulting from lack of orthodontic care—buck teeth and receding chins among the least of these—have become rarer. Deformed and rachitic bones are almost a thing of the past.

The same forces are at work to improve the beauty of the new women as well as of the young. In addition, however, social changes are in process which make it legitimate and proper for them to be attractive. Even to have sex appeal. When women in the middle years were treated as neuter and passé as women, as they were in the past, it was difficult for them to act like women, like sexual beings. They may now be viewed as sexual as well as human beings.

In effect, then, these cultural (technological and normative) changes mean that we really do have a new sex: women who are still women but, like the young contracepted woman, not susceptible to conception; women in whom reproduction and sexuality are truly separated; women who are still attractive and sexually responsive but whose maternal functions are completed; women with experience and, hopefully in some cases, wisdom; and, in addition, women with sex appeal.

A reviewer of a novel on sexual rejuvenation by Gertrude Atherton in the 1920's, *Black Oxen*, commented on the dire consequences to be expected if sixty-year-old women could be rejuvenated to the beauty of twenty. Imagine, he pointed out, how devastating a woman would be with the wisdom, knowledge, and experience of sixty and the beauty of twenty at her disposal. The idea is no longer a mere fantasy. We may, in fact, now be witnessing some of the possible reverberations of the creation of this new sex.

In the first half of the twentieth century, the disparity between young men and women in sexual desire—as measured in terms of average frequency of "sexual outlet per week"—was very high: 7.2 times higher in boys aged sixteen to twenty than in girls of the same ages. The disparity declined with age until it was only 1.6 times as high among men as among women in their early forties.[28] There was, in brief, a convergence with age. The sexuality of women increased with age and remained at a plateau through their fifties; that of the men, at a peak in the late teens and early twenties, declined thereafter.[19] If desire outlasted performance in the case of Falstaff, performance outlasted appeal in the case of women.

When almost everyone was young, at any rate under fifty, the picture of relative sexuality reflected in these findings could be interpreted as true for almost everyone. Practically all of our myths of male and female sexuality grew up when people were young, and they reflect the situation expectable in a young population: urgent, aggressive male sexuality, Apollonian female sexuality. With the advent of the new female subsex, however, the picture changes. The sexuality of the new subsex matches and may even exceed that of men. Is it possible that it is this new combination of circumstances—ancient stereotypes about male sexuality confronted with a new, sexually questing female sex—that is contributing to the modern man's "masculinity crisis"?

Other subsexes in the female collectivity could also be identified by a wide variety of other criteria than sheer sexuality or attitude toward sexuality. The nestlings, for example, and the non-nestlings might be differentiated, the first referring to women who are happy to be mothers and homemakers and nothing more, and the second, to those who are restless if they are nothing more. Some women in this subsex seem to be almost compulsive breeders.

As soon as one child leaves babyhood, I want another. . . . No amount of talking to from my husband or the commonsense half of myself can outweigh the urge to reproduce. . . . I get that broody feeling. . . . Some people say that women cannot separate sex from love, but I find it hard to separate sex from fertility. . . . I like to think of marital life as a sort of constant pagan spring rite, the aim of which is conception every time. . . . Giving birth . . . plays its part in this crazy notion I have of fulfilling my biological and emotional needs. . . .[20]

This is one subsex that may have to get lost.

Or one could distinguish four subsexes on the basis of "life styles," so called. This criterion gives us an individualistic subsex characterized by a life style which strives for autonomy; an influential subsex, characterized by a life style which tries to influence people and events; a supportive subsex, characterized by a desire to help people; and a subsex with a communal life style, one which desires to improve the community.[21] It is not too difficult to supply the categories into which bitches and Dark Ladies and Fair Maidens might comfortably fall.

Everyone could doubtless supply his own additional categorizations. Many are possible. But since our concern is directed toward the relations between the great collectivities, a criterion that is specifically sexual is most relevant. White Maidens and Dark Ladies in their several manifestations are enough.

(These two, by the way, are far from being peculiarly American. They are, in fact, versions of European literary types which Mario Praz has traced as the Persecuted Woman, epitomized by Richardson's Clarissa Harlow, the Fatal Woman, and La Belle Dame sans Merci. The Persecuted Woman was refurbished in the eighteenth century. She permitted the luxury of Dark Lady goings-on combined with White Maiden purity; both author and reader enjoyed her suffering.[22] It might also be noted in passing that in Japan another kind of solution was evolved for both having and eating one's cake. The geisha girl was essentially a compromise sex, the quintessence of feminine sexuality but not necessarily of physical sex.)

Before turning to the male collectivity, one other female subsex, a secret one, calls for attention. It is perhaps the most beloved of all. It includes the girl, never known on land or sea, who nevertheless has inhabited the minds of men in all places at all times. She is the tenderly voluptuous girl, the calendar girl who, until her tragic death, enchanted millions of men everywhere. In real life she was a sick girl, perhaps even a frigid girl. Yet through the camera's lens, she was a member of the secret sex that Everyman fantasies and adores. Her successors are found pinned up on the walls where men can see her morning and evening and bring her to life in their reveries. "Art" magazines, photography magazines, movie magazines, are full of her image. Real flesh-and-blood girls no doubt appear before the camera, but the girl who appears in the pinup in barracks and dormitories is as much a creation of the lens as any artist's model. This subsex exists nowhere among real people and yet in a way it is the realest of all the subsexes. And practically indestructible.

This secret subsex, according to one commentator, reflects an ancient cleavage in human sexuality between "full aggressive potency, demonic genitality" and the "elaborately developed life of the emotions which is our civilized heritage—and burden." The best evidence of this cleavage "is to be found in the fact that one part of our sexuality has been relegated to the world of fantasy and to the underground of civilization where, lamely, it continues to persist."[23] The innocent, spontaneous, uninhibited expression of sexuality which is no longer permitted by civilization lingers wistfully in the daydreams of modern men.

Men are doomed to disappointment in their search for this lovely wraith. They may find many women willing to "give" themselves, many women who can absorb seemingly exorbitant amounts of tender caressing and lovemaking, but they will never find in the flesh the fantasy that haunts their imagination. Some men finally come to terms with this fact and settle for reality. Others never give up. It doesn't matter that every real girl turns out to be a disappointment; somewhere, sometime, she will turn up. "The 'craving for variety,' common to so many of us, is always an admission of inadequacy—of the inadequacy of the partner for us, and probably of our inadequacy for her. Usually, it also testifies to our optimism: Somewhere, out there *she* is. The next woman, or the one after her, will be *the* woman for whom we have been searching."[24]

This universal male dream cannot be shared with real women because it represents a kind of disloyalty to them. But men are aware of her presence in one another's fantasy life and take it for granted. Although she is a standard furnishing in male mentality, the discovery of her existence and of the enormous part she plays in the life of the men about her is often astonishing to real women. Real women, with their usual sizes and shapes, even resent her and marvel that even the seemingly reconciled men still dream of her. She is rough competition.

For the most part, therefore, men do their best to keep her secret and to protect one another's secret.

❖❖❖❖❖❖

The male collectivity is no more homogeneous than the female. But the same criterion—acceptance of sexuality—cannot be used very meaningfully to distinguish subsexes within it, for practically all men accept it. Enthusiastically. One useful criterion has to do with the place assigned to women—not sexuality—in their lives. On the basis of this criterion, three general subsexes can be discerned: the Dionysian male, the Parallelist male, and the Assimilationist male. Dionysian males put great distance between themselves and women; Assimilationists, hardly any at all; and Parallelists, varying amounts from great to small.

The importance of distance as a criterion for classifying male subsexes derives from the fact that the masculine mystique depends on distance. A man is no hero to his valet because the valet sees him off guard, behind the scene, tired, at a loss, puzzled, perplexed, even defeated. The public's eyes will supply the emperor's clothes for him so that the emperor himself need never see his nakedness in their presence. The valet cannot always do the same for the hero, though a good one will try. Without the supporting cues from an admiring public, without his accoutrements, naked and alone—"backstage," to use Goffman's term[25]—the hero is not much different from the valet. The valet is superior in many of the nonheroic aspects of life—the daily coping with details that are the most trivial and nonheroic when everything is operating well, and the most important when it is not.[26] Sometimes he is, therefore, the one who is leaned upon, the one on whom the hero is dependent. If the valet is a good valet who loves his hero despite his weakness, who is careful not to force his hero to see himself as the valet sees him, or (if this ever happens) shows him that he knows the hero is still a hero, the relationship can be rewarding for both. The valet can share the public's acclaim of the hero because he knows how much he contributes to the hero's achievements; the hero can rest in the presence of the valet,

[31]

secure in the knowledge that he *is* a hero, even though it takes a good valet to make him one.

Many a girl has married thinking she could happily depend on her hero for the rest of her life only to discover, much to her shock, that she, not he, was the strong one in the relationship, that he, not she, was the dependent one. "The modern woman . . . may find it difficult to maintain . . . [the illusion of male strength and female dependency]. Such a state of affairs . . . almost invariably results in a secondary contempt for the disappointing hero whose normal weaknesses quickly become apparent."[27] The wife's awareness may come gradually or suddenly. If she is tender and loving, he will never know what has happened. If she cannot hide her consternation, the moment of her illumination (not, as Fiedler reported, of her sexual initiation) will mark her transmogrification from White Maiden to bitch. It is important to protect the masculine mystique by at least some distance.

The Dionysian subsex, apotheosized by Nietzsche, is a very old one, known among Romans, Arabs, Germans, Japanese. They were Homeric heroes; they were Vikings and Plains Indian braves; they were Kwakiutl potlatchers; they were fifteenth-century explorers; they are mountain climbers who climb mountains because mountains are there. Adventure and excitement, especially combat, are their meat and drink. Nietzsche almost caricatured the Dionysian male as the blond beast. "He has a strong body, good health, handsome features, noble bearing; he delights in the use of his strength in bodily combat, in the indulgence of all the fine gifts of enjoyment his lusty senses afford him."[28] Sexual excitement for the archetypical Dionysian male is just one kind among many, better than some, not so good as others. One takes it where one finds it. Wenching is part of the mystique, along with, let us say, dueling for the upper classes and brawling and fighting for the lower. One certainly never exchanges one's freedom for anything so trivial as the privilege of regular sexual relations. The Dionysian male takes women and leaves them. He lacks what Lewis Terman called marital aptitude; he has no taste for domesticity. He shies away from commitments; he does not want—cannot sustain—a permanent relationship with any one woman. He believes "it is base for a soldier to love."[29] He wants "some dish more sharply spiced than this/Milk-soup men call domestic bliss."[30] Women constitute far less than half of the population in the world he inhabits.

Fiedler found this subsex the most characteristic hero in American literature, from Rip Van Winkle on.

> The figure of Rip Van Winkle presides over the birth of the American imagination: and it is fitting that our first successful home-grown legend should memorialize, however playfully, the flight of the dreamer from the shrew—into the mountains and out of time, away from the drab duties of home and town toward the good companions and the magic keg of beer. Ever since, the typical male protagonist of our fiction has been a man on the run, harried into the forest, and out to sea, down the river or into combat—anywhere to avoid "civilization," which is to say, the confrontation of a man and woman which leads to the fall to sex, marriage and responsibility.[81]

This fleeing male, who rejects everything women stand for in the way of stability—order, discipline, civilization—looks instead for the "hieragamous," or sacred, marriage with another male, a relationship which is homoerotic but not grossly homosexual:

> There is an almost hysterical note to our insistence that the love of male and male does not compete with heterosexual passion but complements it; that it is not homosexuality in any crude meaning of the word, but a passionless passion, simple, utterly satisfying, yet immune to lust—physical only as a handshake is physical, this side of copulation. . . . There is at the sentimental center of our novels . . . nothing but the love of males![32]

Fiedler presents a rather dazzling array of evidence for his thesis. And it is certainly true that the fleeing male is well known to the female collectivity.

In the modern world this male subsex has many embodiments: the Cagney tough-guy type, the man's-man type, the James Bond type, the robber-baron or tycoon type, the Hell's Angels type, the Western-hero type, "the real gutsy guy," and until recently, the hobo as well.

The hobo was a man "in whom the wanderlust [was] the strongest lust. . . . Women and trifling other things . . . [didn't] bother him."[33] The same kind of restlessness characterizes the men Jack Kerouac has written about. They have to move, to go somewhere else. Narcotics, jazz, sexual experiments, are vehicles of escape. But not love. They have no conception of a giving relationship. When a woman in one book refers to a man as kind, a man who "at least . . . gives of himself," the Kerouac man (he certainly cannot be called a hero) replies, "What's all this giving of ourselves, what's there to give that'll help anybody?" And she replies, "You'll never know you're so wrapped up in yourself."[34] He hates even to give himself sexually; it makes him feel robbed:

. . . there's an awful paranoiac element sometimes in orgasm that suddenly releases not sweet genteel sympathy but some token venom that splits up in the body—I feel a great ghastly hatred of myself and everything, the empty feeling far from being the usual relief is now as though I've been robbed of my spinal power right down the middle on purpose in a great witching force—I feel evil forces gathering down all around me, from her, the kid. . . .[35]

The California motorcycle cultists known as Hell's Angels also illustrate the Dionysian attitude toward women. They distinguish "old ladies," "mamas," and "strange chicks," all of which are *things*. One Angel, out of beer money, auctioned off his mama at a bar for twelve cents. Another expressed astonishment when a gas-station attendant refused him a gallon of gas in exchange for a go at his mama.[36] These men are, of course, degraded specimens of the sex. James Bond shows far more finesse.

Perhaps because the Dionysian subsex inhabits a world so remote from that of most members of the female collectivity and because they are so different from most of them, they have become almost the archetype of masculinity. And if masculinity is defined in terms of strength, physical power, adventurousness, combativeness, and challenge-seeking, then this subsex is indeed masculine; on the other hand, if masculinity is defined in terms of sexual potency or virility, then this subsex is not necessarily very masculine. This kind of male spends a great deal of time in pursuits without women. He may have a girl in every port, but there are many days, even weeks and perhaps months between ports. Since he seeks women only when he wants them and does not subject himself to the demands of women, his self-image is one of tremendous virility, and there are no women to challenge it. He is the man-without-women who chooses to be a man-without-women—at least most of the time.

There have been women with an insatiable appetite for life, action, and excitement, too. Amelia Earhart, Babe Diedrickson, and the James Bond girl are representative.[37] On the frontier there were women who "held their liquor, rode like Comanches, dealt stud poker, packed guns, rustled cattle, and played road agent with great efficiency and picturesqueness."[38] If they were, in fact so competent in the Dionysian world, they illustrate the fact that women were admitted into it only on male terms; they had to be one of the boys. There are also women camp-followers among the Hell's Angels. But for most women such a roistering and adventurous life is not appealing; the excitement they enjoy is rather in the direction of combat with men. There were, thus, in addition to the gun-totin' girls, others who "possessed a cold courage whether they were using their sex to steal military secrets or holding up a stage coach. . . . They committed espionage as coolly as they sipped their tea, seduced men in high places. . . ."[39] If women want adventure they take it in male form or they take it in an ultra-female form.

Members of the Parallelist subsex admit women into their lives. They do not flee women. They want women around. But they keep them at a *varying* distance. They live with and among women but more or less separately. Their world is one thing; the world of women, another. The lives of these men and the women they live with run parallel; they do not intersect.

The Parallelists who put great distance between themselves and women may resemble Dionysian males; those who put little distance, the Assimilationists. They may look up to women as at least their moral superiors;[40] or they may look down on them as necessary evils. They are believers in *machismo*; they support the masculine mystique and upon occasion they may even revert to Dionysianism and "hell around with the boys." For the most part, though, they are satisfied with vicarious Dionysianism in the form of spectator sports, wrestling, prize-fights. All they insist on is that they be allowed their male separatism, that they be free from the intrusion of women into their world. They don't care how high women aspire, just so it is in their own world.

The Parallelists who put relatively little distance between themselves and women insist on their sexual autonomy. But they can take, even with pleasure, the presence of women. They never lose their awareness of sexuality, in themselves or in women, but they are not afraid of it. Some of their best friends, they will concede, are women.

The Assimilationist subsex is willing to live in a truly bisexual world. Sexuality may be played up or down in this world. Those who play it down may casually accept a girl as one of the boys. If sexuality is played up, women are viewed as identical with themselves. They are not necessarily homosexual; indeed, they probably are not. But if or when they are, they are likely to be the feminine kind. In extreme form they are the men who are uncomfortable with a male identity and are among those who ask to have their sex changed.

Women are said to be fatally attracted by the Dionysian subsex. Little good it does them, as their mothers could have told them. Not all women enjoy the Assimilationist pattern. Even those who are most insistent on equality all along the line may recoil at being deprived of their sexuality, an effect this pattern tends to have. Women want to live in a bisexual world—but as women, not as sexless companions and sometime-collaborators in the sexual act. It can be as frustrating not to have one's sexuality recognized and appreciated as to have it the only thing recognized and appreciated. By and large, women tend to prefer less distance between themselves and males than most males do. Different women prefer different degrees of distance between themselves and men. There is no distance which is optimum for all. Too much distance between men and women deprives women of male sexuality; too little distance deprives women of their own sexuality as women. The Dionysian subsex is too centripetal for most women, the Assimilationist, too centrifugal. There is a vital tension that the Parallelists can supply. Whatever the distance, though, women want it sufficiently small so that it does not render interaction too difficult.

So much, then, for intrasex differences. Whether or not one calls them subsexes, no one questions that members of the female collectivity differ greatly among themselves and that members of the male collectivity do also.

❖❖❖❖❖

It seems clear, then, that there cannot be any generalizations about sex, any more than about other categories of human beings. For every generalization made about men or women, there is always an authentic exception, and the generalization has to be hedged. In the relations between the sexes, "it all depends." Men and women show great qualitative diversity in subsex composition and wide quantitative variations even within the subsexes. Thus when men and women talk to one another about one another, for example, they may be talking about quite different people. "Women are always . . ." say the men. "Why, they never . . . !" reply the indignant women. Both may be at least within hailing distance of the truth, but they may be talking about quite different female subsexes—one, for example, of Dark Ladies, the other, of White Maidens.

Although intrasex heterogeneity among both males and females must be emphasized, it would be a mistake to imply that this is the whole story. All members of the female collectivity do have a great deal in common, as do all members of the male sex. Women are members of a great universal sisterhood, able to communicate with one another easily over vast cultural, racial, and even age differences. The most highly sophisticated modern woman can, as a wife and especially as a mother, find much in common with a wife and mother in the South Seas or the heart of Africa. Despite the cliché that pictures women as cats with one another—often accurate among women competing for men—the relations between and among most women are supportive. Women tend to have confidantes with whom they can discuss their problems. They enjoy one another's company (so much so, in fact, that lesbianism is often, quite erroneously in most cases, attributed to them). Even the successful professional woman enjoys occasional indulgence in "woman-talk." The same things could also be said, of course, of the male fraternity.

❖❖❖❖❖

There is universal consensus with respect to the anatomical signs of maleness and femaleness. If the normal newborn has a penis, no one doubts that he belongs in the male collectivity and if not, no one doubts that she is a member of the female collectivity. But anatomical maleness or femaleness is not the whole story, for "chromosomal sex, hormonal sex, gonadal sex, morphological sex, gender role sex, and behavioral sex do not fuse into a monolithic male or female but function as interacting and even conflicting systems."[41] Quite aside from those cases in which sex is indeterminate and quite aside from those cases in which transsexuality exists[42] (both extremely rare), a creature *assigned* to one collectivity or the other may not *belong* there in one way or another.

Thus, quite without regard to within-sex differences, taking each collectivity as more or less homogeneous, we find great overlappings between them: some in the female collectivity, for example, are taller than most males and some in the male collectivity are fatter than most females; some females are stronger than most males, some males more sedentary than most females. This is confusing and complicates the relationship between the two collectivities.

As a corrective to this nonsense on Nature's part and to tidy up her carelessness, concepts like masculinity and femininity evolve to show the two collectivities what to be like vis-à-vis one another, regardless of their heredity. A set of standards is set up: "This is feminine behavior; act this way with members of the male collectivity. It isn't natural for you? So what? We can't have all this rugged individualism. The other members of your collectivity manage all right, so why can't you? We based these standards on what a plurality of your fellow members in the female collectivity were comfortable with. Learn to live with them. They help to standardize your relations with males; they know what to expect. It's for your own good anyway; it helps you, too. You know what to expect from males. We don't care so much how 'masculine' you are in your relations within the female collectivity; it's in your relations with members of the male collectivity that you have to be feminine. . . ." (In recent years we have come to relent in extreme cases. We now permit surgical changes to bring conformity to conflicting components of sexuality, so that individuals can be admitted to the collectivity they feel more comfortable in.) Concepts like masculinity and femininity, in brief, are attempts to standardize primarily the relations between the collectivities and only secondarily, if at all, the relations within them.

In our society, femininity is defined in terms of overt behavior, feelings, wishes, motives, and attitudes. Vis-à-vis males, it is feminine to be nonaggressive, dependent, passive, conforming, and "nurturant," to be able to gratify a love object and to arouse males sexually, to have emotional capacity. Masculinity, in turn, is defined in complementary terms: independence, activity, aggressiveness.[43] If all female subsexes and all male subsexes conformed to the cultural patterns for femininity and masculinity, relationships between and among them would presumably be facilitated.

To achieve this goal and to minimize any potential waywardness that can result from a lack of consistency in the several components—hormonal, gonadal, and morphological—of sex, families go to work on infants at birth to impose masculinity on the one with the penis and femininity on the one without.

The recorded [table] conversations of all the [82] families in which there are children bear witness to these sex differences and the family's consciousness of them. "Little girls do not talk that way." "A lady never raises her voice." "He sounds like a boy all right." "Her voice will be a great asset to her." This sex distinction is evident at every turn—in the words used, habits of exclamation, intensity of expression, and stock phrases, as well as the subjects discussed. The child learns early and is reminded constantly that there is prestige in learning the sex-appropriate forms of expression.[44]

Discipline differs for those assigned to the two collectivities, girls being dealt with more affectionately, boys more punitively.[45] The aim is to produce feminine women and masculine men, as conceived in our culture, in order to simplify the relations between the collectivities.

Our success is quite phenomenal. Children learn at an early age that mothers are nurturant, fathers punitive but competent. They learn this from their own experience, but they learn also from the mass media, which describe mothers as loving, weak, and subordinate, and fathers as competent, aggressive, and powerful. This is how feminine people behave; this is how masculine people behave. Children must do likewise.

Because masculinity and femininity are cultural constructs, they vary in some aspects from place to place and from time to time. Anthropologists delight in highlighting the parochial nature of our own concepts. Thus one tells us that:

> In Iran . . . men are expected to show their emotions. . . . If they don't, Iranians suspect they are lacking a vital human trait and are not dependable. Iranian men read poetry; they are sensitive and have well-developed intuition and in many cases are not expected to be too logical. They are often seen embracing and holding hands. Women, on the other hand, are considered to be coldly practical. They exhibit many of the characteristics we associate with men in the United States. A very perceptive Foreign Service officer who had spent a number of years in Iran once observed, "If you think of the emotional and intellectual sex roles reversed from ours, you will do much better out here." . . . Fundamental beliefs like our concepts of masculinity and femininity are shown to vary widely from one culture to the next.[46]

Clifford Kirkpatrick, a sociologist, once described masculine-feminine role reversal. His *Men's Home Companion*

> gives helpful hints in regard to husband's work, and writes of a thousand ways to please a wife. A feature article shows how a husband got his wife a raise by devotion and manly guile. In Washington a Men's Bureau protects the frail male from overwork, late hours, and moral hazards. The statute books define the age of consent for boys. Rape is strictly forbidden and punishable by heavy sentences imposed on brutal females. Women take pride in punching other women who use foul language in the presence of men. Masculine intuition is contrasted with feminine pugnacity. The masculine touch about the home transforms it from a mere house to an agency for shaping healthy personalities. Many a woman is reformed in the movies by the influence of a good man. Soap operas reveal in sentimental detail how John finally gave up his job to make a satisfactory home for Mary. Men are warned against "becoming a Pop to your children." Women in the armed forces suffer from deprivation of father love. Psychiatrists deplore the silver cords holding daughters to a maturity level below that of the she-woman worthy of the Marine Corps.[47]

The most famous of the anthropological contributions to the study of cultural variability in standards of masculinity and femininity, so far as temperament is concerned, was by Margaret

Mead, who in 1935 reported on three South Sea societies. In one, the Arapesh, she told us that both men and women tended to have nurturant, that is, feminine temperaments; in one, the Mundugumor, both tended to have masculine temperaments—ruthless, aggressive, and positively sexed; and in the Tchambouli, the men had temperaments we would label feminine—emotionally dependent, less responsible—and the women had temperaments we would label masculine—dominant, impersonal, managing.[48]

Margaret Mead's book seemed to demonstrate unequivocally our own cultural parochialism. Whatever the author's intention may have been, the effect was to convince readers that all sex differences were matters of cultural pressures, and the sooner, some concluded, we got rid of them the better. No one, at any rate, could ever again say that women were thus and so, men so and thus. The success of the book was a triumph of Plato over Aristotle. The findings appeared, with approval, in the textbooks of all relevant fields of thought. It was a major cultural event.

The Mead thesis became doctrine with many people. If one wanted to believe that the differences between the collectivities were wholly cultural in nature, practically independent of biology, there was no denying it. There were always those Arapesh, Mundugumor, and Tchambouli.

Many psychologists have also accepted this thesis. Some years ago, L. M. Terman and his associate, C. C. Miles, devised an instrument to measure masculinity and femininity. It was based on interest items that differentiated the two collectivities in our society. A score of +220 represented extreme masculinity; —219, extreme femininity. There was a considerable overlapping of the collectivities between scores —99 and +60, but the average for members of the male collectivity was +62.6 and of the female collectivity, —70.7. (Male homosexuals averaged —20.) College athletes and engineers had high masculinity scores. But those with high femininity scores turned out to be a strange assortment: domestic servants, mothers of gifted children, and teachers. In fact, domestic workers scored highest.[49] (It is interesting to note that both "emasculated" and "effeminate" mean that the men so characterized are not masculine. Logically, "effeminate" ought to refer to women who are not feminine, but apparently femininity is so negative that there is nothing less than it.)

In 1966, however, Clark Vincent found that tests of masculinity and femininity were both time- and culture-bound. Items that had differentiated the two collectivities in the past no longer did.

> If today's female is to be "successful" in terms of current role expectations of the middle-class female, she will tend to score low on femininity as long as tradition-oriented items are included in the scale. Such items penalize today's female who is expected to assume leadership responsibilities in community, civic, political, and religious organizations, [and] to make noteworthy contributions in a variety of occupational and professional pursuits. . . .

> If today's male is to be "successful" in terms of current role expectations of the middle-class male, he will tend to score high on femininity when items are included which formerly described the more dependent, intuitive, sensitive, "peacemaking" role of the female in a tradition-oriented society, but which now tend to describe the "other-directed," "organization man" in-the-gray-flannel-suit whose success depends more on a psychological than on a physical manipulation of environment and people.[50]

There appears, in brief, to be more consensus about differences within than about differences between the two collectivities. Some observers, in fact, seem more willing to admit the differences within than between them.

If both sexes are just congeries of differing subsexes and if the differences between them are only superficial cultural impositions, just what *do* we mean by the sexes? Figments of our *cultural* imaginations? No, not really. Not, in fact, at all.

CHAPTER TWO

No Figments

"Women almost invariably behave thus," thought I. "What does the fact mean? Is it their nature? or is it, at last, the result of ages of compelled degradation? And, in either case, will it be possible ever to redeem them?"

—Nathaniel Hawthorne, *The Blithedale Romance*

Women don't mind your asserting that their psyches *are* different; they mind your asserting that their psyches *have* to be different.

—David V. Tiedeman and others, *Position Choices and Careers*

No wonder they mind. All too often sex differences have been used to justify, or at least to rationalize, discrimination against them. Women were, almost by definition, the weaker vessel, obviously inferior. Even if, as Hawthorne's hero was willing to concede, women were degraded by their history, they were in urgent need of redemption.

There is an enormous literature on sex differences.[1] Some of it, as one researcher has shown, is based only on inherited authority.[2] Some of it is mythical; it suits our needs. Some of it is valid. Some of it is trivial. Scarcely a week goes by that some popular journal or other does not augment it by expounding the nature of sex differences. People examine this voluminous literature and make of it what they will. Some—especially, let us say, the Assimilationists—study it and discounting what they find, coolly ask, *"What* difference?" Others, scrutinizing the same findings, react with *"Vive la difference!"*

Many of those who ask *"What* difference?" are usually idealists. It has seemed to them that to prove women worthy, they have had to prove that they were just like men. To be different from men would mean being inferior to them. Whatever anyone says about women, they insist, can be said about men also, only perhaps more—or less—so. And vice versa. If not, it can be explained away: it is a cultural artifact; it is a product of different socialization; but in any event, it is more or less fortuitous, accidental, extrinsic.

A second branch of the *What*-difference? school is willing to grant the existence of differences, but it insists that the similarities between men and women are much more important than the differences, which should be ignored, if not denied. To persons of this branch men and women are human beings first and sexual beings second. Women with this opinion tend to be White Maidens or Rejecters, active or passive, or for historical reasons, women who are trying to vindicate the rights of women. Men who hold this view tend to be Assimilationists.

The general tendency of those who belong to the first two branches of the *What*-difference? school is to minimize sex itself, to play it down, to mute its importance. They can do this because in their thinking they emphasize the body systems that the sexes have in common and leave out or ignore or minimize the major system, the reproductive, that differentiates the sexes.

It is certainly true that because both sexes share a common species heredity there is a vast inventory of similarities between them. All body systems in the members of both collectivities—except always, of course, the reproductive—consist of the same kinds of organs. They both have nervous systems, circulatory systems, digestive systems. There are differences, to be sure, but usually the differences are of distribution of traits, and there is such a wide overlap that only extremes are relevant. For the most part, they can be discounted. Both sexes see red when the retina is stimulated by a certain light wave, hear high C when the ear is presented with a certain sound wave, get stomachaches, suffer pain, laugh, and so on. Thus an enormous amount of the ordinary give-and-take between the sexes is matter-of-fact and unimpeded by barriers; it is between similarly equipped beings. If you leave sex out, there are irrelevant or no sex differences.

The third branch of the *What*-difference? school rests its case on an opposing view. Rather than disregard the sexual systems of the collectivities, it maximizes the importance of sex rather than minimizing it. Adherents of this view single out the sexual systems and highlight the similarities between them. To them the sexuality of men and women is the same. Women, in their opinion, experience sex exactly as men do; it is as urgent and persistent with them as with men. If women act differently sexually, it is part of a plot to exploit men.[3] The members of this school tend to be Dionysian males who do not wish to be beholden to women. There tends to be a cynical overtone to their asking *What* difference?

The Long-live-the-difference! school is not cheering all differences in common body systems, such as the greater susceptibility of males to hemophilia, color blindness, baldness, or their lower viability. On the other hand, they select only certain differences to emphasize. Usually they are men who have a specific kind of difference in mind. They do not think of men and women as fundamentally alike except for their anatomy and physiology, which were superimposed. They maintain that we are sexual beings through and through and would not have it any other way. They like being different and having their counterparts different. It's more fun that way.

For the most part there is no implication of superiority in one or the other sex. Parallelists tend to belong to this school, especially those who can tolerate intimacy with women at close range. By and large, in whatever subsex they fall, those who accept a wide range of sex differences tend to be men and women who are sure of themselves, of their sexuality, of their identity, and they have been successful with one another. In the higher socioeconomic classes they also tend to be clever, verbal people and men who enjoy encounters with women.

❖❖❖❖❖❖

Those who accept sex differences as more than cultural artifacts, as more than figments of our culturally created imagination, are not convinced by the evidence marshaled to rebut this view. They wonder, for example, about the fact that the feminine Arapesh recently had been headhunters and constantly on the verge of fighting one another. Or the fact that the masculine Tchambouli women devoted themselves so happily and efficiently to the care and feeding of children. Or that their cheerful working together to prepare a feast would fit equally well a group of women preparing a church social in the Middle West. Or the fact that the Arapesh men and the Tchambouli men, both presumably feminine, were so different—the Arapesh being gentle, unacquisitive, and cooperative and the Tchambouli quarrelsome, bickering, strained, and catty. Or the fact that the Mundugumor and the Tchambouli women, both presumably masculine, were also so different, the first nursing their babies willingly and generously, the second, grudgingly. Or why, if as Margaret Mead said, the Arapesh and the Mundugumor did not differentiate the sexes temperamentally, the women differed from the men. Or why the Mundugumor made little girls desirable to others, dressed them up and decorated them, protected them from hazing, did not use them for hostages. Or why married women had fewer affairs than men.[4] Or more to the point perhaps, why recent anthropological and social-psychological research with more refined techniques arrives at different conclusions. Why a number of studies find that by and large, among peoples as diverse as the lowly Pygmies of Africa and the highly literate Israeli in their kibbutzim, boys value aggression, competition, and dominance more than girls do, while girls value nurturance, stability, and order more than boys do.

They are willing to concede that a great deal that goes under the rubric of masculinity or femininity is indeed a cultural invention. Curls, ruffles, and lace were not considered unmasculine in the eighteenth century, as portraits, even of our own founding fathers, show. No one would dream of calling them effeminate. Nor are the cleverly tailored pants that women wear today masculine. The symbols of masculinity and femininity can change from age to age. They are by no means trivial, of course, for this reason. For to say that something is *only* cultural in no way denigrates its importance. It is sometimes easier to modify a biological trait than a cultural one.

But to concede that some masculine and feminine traits are cultural artifacts is not the same as saying that all are. Those who accept sex differences as something more than masculinity or femininity are not willing to write off all the evidence. They do not believe that the sexes are mere figments.

The effect a woman has on a man is different from the effect she has on a woman; and the effect a man has on a woman is different from the effect he has on a man. An ancient literary device is one in which an imposter of one sex masquerades as a member of the other. When he or she is unmasked, the whole situation is transformed. Everyone's relationship to the revealed character depends on his or her sex. If an ambi-sex name is misinterpreted and a receiver learns he has been communicating with a woman rather than, as he had supposed, with a man, their relationship changes. It can be argued that the change is a derivative one, based on role rather than on sex per se. This cannot be denied, but neither can it be denied that, quite aside from role, a pretty girl affects a young man in a way that her brother does not. And whether one labels it biological, psychological, or cultural, this difference in the effect each sex has on the other is itself a sex difference.

It is, then, impossible for either sex to have the same experiences as those the other has. No matter what a culture may prescribe, the sexes are not reacted to the same way. They are rejected differently; they are accepted differently; they are ignored differently. They are deprived differently; they are indulged differently. These are social phenomena and independent of culture. No culture can provide identical experiences to both collectivities. The timid man is treated differently from the way the timid woman is treated, the aggressive man from the aggressive woman. Since minds and hearts are shaped and formed by experiences, people with such different experiences have to be different.

Not all differences between the sexes are relevant for communication between or among them, so that they do not seriously influence relationships. Some *are* relevant, though even these may not have much influence on communication, or at most only minimal influence.

A linguist has noted that when people of different cultural backgrounds fail to understand one another, each tends to blame the other for his stupidity.[5] And so, often do people of different sex. What seems so clear and obvious to women may be unintelligible to men, and of course vice versa.

Psychologists have accumulated a vast literature documenting sex differences in a wide variety of areas. But in the area of intelligence they have found very little. When they first set up mental tests they started with the extraordinary assumption that the I.Q. of boys and girls must be equal. If any test gave an advantage to boys, it was discarded or compensated for by a test that gave an equivalent advantage to the girls and vice versa. The average I.Q. had to end up at one hundred for both sexes.

Actually, boys tend to do better in mathematical and mechanical tests. Girls tend to do better in verbal tests, a fact that may or may not be relevant for verbal communication between the sexes. Some researchers are of the opinion that these verbal sex differences are cultural in origin, resulting from differences in socialization and that they are declining as a result of changes in the way children are reared nowadays, underplaying, as it does, sex differences.[6] Yet in one recent study, girls still had surpassed the boys, certainly up to the age of eight.[7]

Some—puzzled Parallelists, perhaps, and nonplussed Assimilationists—fall back on differences in the way the sexes use their intelligence to explain differences. Margaret Mead has supplied them with support in her conclusion that women actually think differently from the way men think.[8] Yet in one study attempting to pin down the nature of this difference, the results were by no means convincing. The researcher, for example, had forty groups of four members each with varying sex composition discuss given topics, tape-recording what they had to say. When the records were transcribed, judges could identify the correct sex of the speakers at a level of accuracy just barely above chance, and this slight margin of accuracy could often be explained on the basis of kinds of words used and style of participation.[9]

To the extent that there really are differences in the way women think, they may be due to the fact that, having different muscles and glands at the disposal of their brains, they have different kinds of experiences.[10] The major differences may also be intrinsic but social in the sense that they lie in the effect each sex has on others. Women are different in part because they affect others differently than men do. Therefore, they have different experiences to supply their minds. This difference is not always cultural, but it is social.

The *What*-difference? school emphasized the fact that many scientifically documented sex differences were merely differences in the distribution of traits common to both sexes. Here the distinction between traits that are typical and those that are characteristic is relevant. Both sexes may be quite alike in a given trait but when or if they do differ, men differ in one direction and women in another. Thus, for example, one study of thirteen hundred subjects hypothesized that (1) masculine thinking was a less intense modification of feminine thinking; (2) masculine thinking was oriented more in terms of the self, while feminine thinking was oriented more toward the environment; (3) masculine thinking anticipated rewards and punishments as a result of the adequacy or inadequacy of the self, whereas feminine thinking anticipated rewards and punishments as a result of the friendship, love, or hostility of the environment; (4) masculine thinking was associated more with a desire for personal achievement and accomplishment, while feminine thinking was associated more with a desire for love and friendship; and (5) masculine thinking found value more in malevolent and hostile actions against a competitive society, while feminine thinking found value more in freedom from restraint in a friendly and pleasant environment.[11] After long, involved, and technical testing of these hypotheses, the authors concluded that "the basic factor which cannot be ignored is the extreme similarity between masculine and feminine thinking, with the feminine modes dominant for both groups. For men these modes are only partially overlaid by the jungle-like orientation."[12] The so-called feminine mode of thinking, in other words, was typical of both male and female subjects. But when they did differ it was in a certain characteristic way.

In any event, though, whatever the nature of sex differences in mentality may be, they are not great enough in and of themselves to interfere with communication between the sexes. If or when the sexes do not succeed in communicating with one another, the failure cannot be attributed to lack of the requisite intelligence. Whether or not it is true that women do, in fact, think differently from men, it is a strategic advantage to have men think they do.

Because of the common species heredity and the common body systems, especially the sensory systems, we can assume that all of us, regardless of sex, experience red when stimulated by the proper wave length, hear high C when the proper note is struck, taste sweetness when we eat sugar, smell fragrance in a rose garden, feel softness when touching silk. The same confidence in assuming similarity in all sensory experience, however, is not warranted, for some differences between the sexes in relevant areas of experience can influence communication and therefore the relations between them. Some of these differences are physiological, some anatomical. Some are culturally induced. And some are bio-socio-cultural.

Certainly, as to within-body sensory experience, physiology and anatomy contribute to differences. At any one time about 8½ percent of all females in the United States between ten and fifty are pregnant (as of 1960), and of the rest, a fourth, say, of those not breast-feeding their babies are menstruating. Perhaps another 10 percent are experiencing pre-menstrual symptoms of one kind or another. About half, in brief, and perhaps even more, are reacting in some way or other to stimuli not present in the male body at all. The young man can only observe from the outside the young woman's submission to the inner calendar which so profoundly influences her moods and her responsiveness to him. As to young males, most probably woke up with an erection and have been aware of sensations emanating from their organ off and on most of the day. The two sexes are thus constantly exposed to differing internal stimulation. Each sex is immersed in its own part of the sexual gestalt.

Anatomy makes for differences in kinesthetic experience. A heavy wet cape whose weight is carried by the shoulders feels different from a heavy wet skirt whose weight is borne by the hips. The relative distribution of weight by the male and female frames must similarly generate differing kinesthetic experiences. What effect such differences have on general kinesthetic sensations of women and of men is indeterminable since there are no people who have experienced both.

Erik Erikson has spoken of inner and outer space as related to boys and girls, boys tending to think in terms of open, and girls in terms of closed, space. If it were possible to think in terms of internal body sensations, might we also find sex differences? Quite aside from the fact that there are different organs present, do women experience different body sensations from men? Are they more aware of inner body sensations and is that why they seem to men to be fussier about their bodies? The constant attention which the bodies of women seem to need has been called narcissism. The aspect that has to do with adornment and exhibition women share with men, for males as well as females "on a public beach . . . receive some sexual gratification from displaying their anatomy. [But] in numerous instances the display is not a form of solicitation—they are not seeking sexual activity. . . . [They just] wish to enjoy the knowledge that they are sexually desirable."[18] But there seems—to men, at least—to be an increment which is beyond mere adornment or sex appeal and has to do with the serious care of the body.

The remarks of a group of young men during an informal discussion not too long ago went something like this: "The bodies of women seem always to require attention. They are always too hot or their feet hurt or they are cold. They are always aware of little aches and pains. They have a headache or they are hungry or thirsty or tired." In addition to these constraints, they included some narcissistic items in their bill of particulars which culture adds to biology: hairdo, makeup, stockings, heels, brassiere, girdle, hemline, and all the other accoutrements of the female body.

They have to fix their hair—always their hair—or their makeup. They have to stop to straighten the seams of their stockings. They say they look awful. Not the same girls for all these things. But all of them for some. They seem never to forget their body sensations. The excitement is out there, but when you want to run out to meet it, they pull at your sleeve to keep you back because their shoes hurt or they have to put on more eye shadow or powder their nose. Their bodies get in the way. They don't seem to enjoy movement for its own sake. You hate it when they are like that. But the girls who aren't like that aren't the kind you care for either. . . .[14]

It did not occur to these young men to wonder how it feels to carry around those encumbering breasts or to run with such awkward hips.

Each sex views the other from behind a wall of quite different kinesthetic experience. If each sees itself in the other, it will often see wrong. Each sends the kind of message it is equipped to send; each receives the kind of message it is equipped to receive. They may pass wide of the mark.

❖❖❖❖❖

Kinsey and his associates documented less speculative and more demonstrable sensory sex differences which may influence communication between men and women. They have to do not with sensations originating from stimuli within the body but with those originating outside the body, and specifically with stimuli which produce sexual arousal. They reported, for example, that women were less stimulable sexually than men. In only three areas of stimulation—watching motion pictures, reading romantic literature, and being bitten—did their female subjects approach or exceed males in stimulability. In twenty-nine out of thirty-three categories of outside stimuli, fewer females than males were sexually aroused.[15]

Both internal stimulation and constant stimulation from the outside world combine to keep the vulnerable young man at a fairly high level of sexual restlessness. If he does not find release in one outlet or another, he will be uncomfortable. Not so the young woman. The tensions that build up in her body have to do with ovulation, a process so little felt that she does not even know when it occurs.

In a fanciful mood, one could lodge charges of utter frivolity and irresponsibility against Nature in her ordering of female sexuality. She evolved a creature in whom orgasm was completely irrelevant so far as reproduction was concerned. At the same time she gave this creature a body with shorter refractory time after climax so that it had greater orgasmic capacity than the male's. She did not phase sexual desire in this creature with ovulation; she made no provision for signs to alert the male to female readiness. She seemed not at all interested in making this creature open to sexual stimulation. She seemed, in brief, to have planned this creature in an offhand manner, without attention to detail.

It can be taken for granted that women are just as "sexy" as men, as it can be taken for granted that they are just as intelligent. But not necessarily in the same way. They appear to have greater tolerance than men for long periods of sexual deprivation. "Some females, for example, may go for weeks or months or even years with very little outlet, or none at all. . . . [Such] discontinuities in total outlet are practically unknown in the histories of males."[16]

It is conceivable that the greater protection of women from sexual stimulation which Kinsey and his associates documented helps to explain her greater tolerance for abstinence. Even when she engages in sexual intercourse, though, her reactions seem far more variable than men's. She may reject it; she may accept but show no enjoyment in it; she may show boredom; she may show enjoyment without orgasm, or enjoyment with mild, strong, or extreme orgasm, physiologically identical to that of men. Psychologists warn us against making comparisons between the subjective feelings of individuals. We cannot make direct comparisons and say that one sex enjoys sexual relations more or less than the other. The comparisons must always be made between the relative preferences for two or more things. We then ask the question in this form: do men place sexual pleasure higher on their scale of values than women? If we base our reply on the record, we have to answer yes.

Kinsey and his associates could find no biological differences between men and women to account for the differences in sexuality they found between them. They concluded that there must be a difference in the cortex of the brain which made it easier for men than for women to be conditioned by their sexual experience. Thus they could be affected by psychological stimuli more easily than women. There is no evidence as yet, however, that men are more easily conditioned than women; nor have the posited cortical differences been demonstrated. Another explanation proposed has to do with the differences in erectile tissue. Although women may have as much erectile tissue throughout their bodies as men, if not even more, differences in its distribution and accessibility give it somewhat different significance. As a result of frequent penile erection almost from birth, the male infant may well become aware of genital responsiveness even before he can talk. No one has studied the analogous response of the clitoris in female infants.

The greater tolerance of women than of men for sexual abstinence is related to the peculiarly anomalous nature of female orgasm which, since it has nothing to do with conception, is a highly expendable luxury. Cultures can proscribe it—and have—without in any way affecting population growth.

The "sex act," so far as women are concerned, consists of the extrusion of an ovum into a tube. Thereafter, all she has to do is wait for a sperm to find it. There is no sensation of pleasure, let alone of ecstasy, associated with this female "sex act." Indeed, there is so little awareness of it that women have to do a considerable amount of research on themselves to determine exactly when they have so "acted." William James once commented on the great ecstasy a certain insect must experience when she found the one leaf that could stimulate her to release her eggs. This was a purely anthropomorphic male fancy. Certainly it is not relevant for human ovulation. Whatever insects may feel when they deposit their eggs, women do not feel pleasure when the ovum is released.

The "male sex act," ejaculation of sperm, is quite different in all respects. Orgasmic paroxysm, totally irrelevant in the female's extrusion of the ovum, is an important ingredient in ejaculation of the sperm. (Kinsey and his associates report orgasm without ejaculation but not the reverse.)

Perhaps because it is so irrelevant to reproduction, female sexuality as expressed in orgasm appears to be surprisingly amenable to cultural constraints.[17] The bodies of women can be practically desexed by cultural norms, even rendered frigid. Whole generations of women have lived without ever experiencing even sexual pleasure, let alone orgasm. In almost every generation there have been many who have lived practically sexless lives.

But the bodies of women can also be resexualized to high levels if the culture so permits. The fifteenth century happened to be one in which women's sexuality was assumed to be, if anything, more urgent than men's. It could be taken for granted, said Rabelais, that every husband would be a cuckold. Conversely, however, the nineteenth century happened to be one in which sexuality was not recognized, let alone encouraged, in women. Women, in fact, bragged of their sexual unresponsiveness, even frigidity. Submission to male sexuality was a prescribed but not a pleasurable response.

Because women can be both Dark Ladies and White Maidens, they have been pictured as evil sex-driven temptresses and as pure, sexless madonnas; men have attributed to them a sexuality identical with their own, rejecting it with horror at some times, welcoming it with joy at others. Partly as a result of these differences, the "real" nature of female sexuality as compared with male sexuality has not always been clear; quite opposite results could emerge from equally adequate research in different times and places.

❖❖❖❖❖

Male sexuality is far less susceptible than female sexuality to direct cultural—as distinguished from social—constraints. If cultural proscription of male orgasm were possible, the population would suffer severe attrition. Thus, with some rather minor exceptions related to religious proscriptions, age for age, men since Adam (assuming a certain kind of Eve) have had erections and ejaculations and orgasms with about the same frequency, subject more to nutrition and fatigue than to cultural constraints. The mores may command young men *not* to be sexually excited, *not* to have erections, *not* to have ejaculations, not even to have lewd thoughts. But to little avail. Whatever the cultural norms may be, male sexuality does not seem to be greatly affected. Heaven knows men have tried! In some centuries they have spent a great deal of time and energy trying to live up to cultural anti-sex imperatives, wrestling manfully with sin. But the wayward flesh went its own way, almost if not entirely oblivious to the threatening norms. No society (again, given a certain kind of woman) has had to cultivate sexuality in males. It was there. If anything, it had to be muted, played down. In some times and places, to be sure, male sexuality has been exalted; *machismo* has been much prized; aphrodisiacs have been avidly sought. It is doubtful if they ever greatly increased male outlets. No matter what the norms have been, repressive or stimulating, male sexuality seems to have its own laws. The direct impact of culture is minimal.

Because of it, the consensual picture of male sexuality, based on centuries of observation of and by generations mainly of young people, is simple and clear: men have strong sexual drives; they think and dream about sex a good deal of the time; they are always ready, or at least ready to be stimulated and excited. Male sexuality, or the myth of male sexuality, has been taken for granted. Because only the seeking, aggressive male got into the folk tradition, he became the archetype of maleness. And most men may have more or less fit the archetype during all the millennia when most men were young, when few lived beyond forty and when women granted men this sexuality.

In recent years, however, hints and cues have been accumulating in popular culture to the effect that male sexuality may not be all that robust—that it is, in fact, in a state of crisis. We hear more about hatred of women, about impotence, about rejection of sex. A psychiatrist reports that girls complain of boys who are not interested in sex, that there is a growing indifference to sex among men. All this looks new. Whether it is, in fact, new, we do not know, for only in this century have the circumstances arisen which would make such aberrations visible.

They may be related to the attrition of the *cichlid-effect*, to be described presently.

Resistant as male sexuality may be to cultural influences with respect to frequency of outlet, it is not equally so with respect to the nature of sexual relationships. It is possible, on evidence reflected in literary works, to distinguish long swells of change in the expression, if not in the strength, of sexuality. There can be delineated, for example, a long-time swell from, let us say, antiquity to modern times—a change from a biological kind of sexuality which stressed the sexual act itself, a body-centered kind, to a social kind which emphasizes the partner, a person-centered kind. As Freud put it, "The ancients glorified the instinct and were prepared on its account to honor even an inferior object; while we despise the instinctual activity in itself, and find excuses for it only in the merits of the object."[18] The archaic concept lives on, but at least since the beginning of the century, there has been emphasis on the importance of the partner, on the social aspect of the act.

And it is the social aspect which appeals especially to women. Female sexuality more than male, it appears, is person-centered. If they *had* to choose between a relationship of genital expression without social warmth and intimacy and one of social warmth and intimacy without genital expression, most women would undoubtedly choose the second.

❖❖❖❖❖

But person-centered sexuality is not necessarily benign. Like all social relationships, it can be negative as well as positive. If the relationship is one of male aggression and domination, it can become hostile, even sadistic. And it often does. The author of a nineteenth-century erotic autobiography, *My Secret Life*, for example, gives an illuminating insight into eighteenth- and early nineteenth-century male sexuality "as almost pure aggression." In this conception, woman is an object who must be dominated; she must be made by the male "to submit to his will in copulation." She should at first resist, and her resistance must be overcome by the impulsive power of the male and by the communication and installation of that lust in herself.[19]

[57]

Erotic writing of this time has to do with a kind of sexuality that is sheer domination, a kind "in which the aggressive and sadistic components almost exclusively prevail."[20] If this is what person-centered sexuality means, who wants it? Not most women, evidently.

Even in the nineteenth century this aggressive, sadistic style of male sexuality was on its way out.[21] In fact, there had been, at least as reflected in the literature, a kind of reversal. By the end of the century male sexuality was in a state of as much confusion as the female sexuality documented by Fiedler. At the beginning of the nineteenth century we are told it had been the Fatal Man or Byronic Hero who attracted and sacrificed the woman; by the end of the century it was the Fatal Woman, and the victim was a man.[22] "The male, who at first tends toward sadism, inclines at the end of the century, toward masochism."[23] (And, incidentally, also toward homosexuality, "a clear indication of a turbid confusion of function and ideal."[24])

However much or however little weight one assigns to the evidence of literature for a picture of the nature of sexual relations, the part played by aggressiveness does seem to make a difference in them. And that is a long and altogether complex story.

Confronted with confusion all around us, we sometimes feel how wonderful it would be if there existed somewhere a right way, a correct way, a natural way for the sexes to relate to one another. No matter how hard it would be to find, we could trust our scientists to dig it out for us in time. In answer to this quest for natural guides we sometimes turn to animals. There is, however, no single clear-cut pattern of relations between the sexes that prevails among all animals. The sexes among some animals relate to one another one way, among other animals, another. Females may be sexually recessive or they may show sexual initiative. No guidance there.

George Bernard Shaw had a merry time early in the century poking fun at both the Nietzschean concept of the glorious he-man and the conventional concept of the passive female; his play *Man and Superman* was a humorous elaboration of the popular bon mot which defined courtship as the process of chasing a woman until she caught you. But Shaw was not picturing a universal subhuman pattern. Males may rule the roost; males may be a means to an end and thereafter quite expendable. Matings may be monogamous or polygamous. We can find almost any kind of relationship between the sexes among animals somewhere at sometime. There is no single pattern of relations between the sexes even among the primates. They may be brutish and bestial among Old World or rhesus monkeys; aggressive on the part of males and gentle but crafty on the part of females among chimpanzees; peaceable and unthreatening among New World monkeys; mild and gentle among gorillas and gibbons.

If we want to advocate any particular pattern between the sexes, we can find some species somewhere that conforms to it. But so too, of course, can those who support an opposing pattern.

Sally Carrighar thinks that human beings are a good deal like animals. In a playful way it might be said that there are traces of rodent heredity in some human beings: they have to fight and the male has to conquer in order to enjoy the sexual encounter. There is certainly no fish heredity left in the human population, except in the embryonic stage, but one particular kind of fish, the cichlid, seems to be an interesting and suggestive prototype.

The cichlid is a peculiar animal. The two sexes have no identifying signs to differentiate them. It is difficult for biologists to distinguish one from the other, and it was something of a scientific achievement when one of them, B. Oehlert, finally did. The differentiation proved to be nothing as simple as a trait like color, size, shape, or even a combination of them. "Male and female are exactly alike, not only externally but also in their movement patterns, even those of the sexual act, fertilization, and oviposition, and it was therefore difficult to find out what mechanisms were at work to prevent homosexual pair formation."[25]

Both male and female cichlids are capable of aggression, of

fear, and of sexual response. So there are no distinguishing sex traits here. But these three kinds of behavior are not inter-related in the same way in the two sexes. The specimen in which sexual behavior is related to aggressive behavior is the male; the specimen in which it is related to fear is the female.

. . . in the male, the motivations of flight and of sexuality cannot be mixed. If the male has even the slightest fear of his partner, his sexual-ity is completely extinguished. In the female, there is the same relation between aggression and sexuality; if she is so little in awe of her partner that her aggression is not entirely suppressed, she does not react to him sexually at all. . . . [Thus] a male can only pair with an awe-inspired and therefore submissive female, and a female only with an awe-inspir-ing and therefore dominant male.[26]

There it is, spelled out in capital letters. The cichlid's masculin-ity depends on the female's awe; if she withholds it, his masculin-ity wilts, is extinguished. He must be dominant or, in effect, cease to be a male. She must defer to him or risk not conceiv-ing. The aggressive cichlid is, indeed, a "castrating female."

We cannot, as noted above, learn much from subhuman animals; and despite the slang epithet for pitiable men—"poor fish"—it would be fanciful to suppose that human beings are just like cichlids. Yet it is hard to ignore the evidence of the widely ramifying cichlid-effect in human societies. Human male sexuality, like the cichlid's, is vulnerable to female aggres-sion, or even to lack of subservience or awe. It is dependent on them. It can withstand cultural restrictions to a considerable extent. It can withstand body abuse. It cannot withstand the cichlid-effect. This vulnerability of male sexuality is social, based on relationships with women. The Achilles' heel of male sexuality is its inability to maintain itself in the face of the cichlid-effect.

Not only as the inhibition of aggression but also as the positive expression of subservience or awe, the cichlid-effect enters almost all relations between the collectivities. It takes the form of "stroking" in some situations. It takes the form of "emo-tional-expressive" behavior in others. It takes the form of a kind of pseudonurturance in still others. We are going to find this cichlid-effect almost everywhere, in the family, at work, at play, in social life.

It is not that women lack aggression. Women, like female

cichlids, have the physical equipment for most kinds of aggression. They have arms and muscles and fingernails and fists and teeth and enough energy to use them. They can master karate and jiu jitsu. In the Middle Ages and even as late as the fifteenth century they did a considerable amount of fighting, including fighting with men. Judy slugged Punch as much as he slugged her. And mothers of any century can be extremely aggressive against threats to their offspring.

Still, there is hardly any research-finding better established than the greater prevalence of aggression among boys than among girls, in our own society and throughout the world.[27] There are different interpretations and explanations of this finding but a fairly well established consensus about the fact itself.

The question might be raised: granted that individual women are denied the capacity to aggress sexually against individual men, why are they also denied other forms of aggression against men other than their sex partners? Why do they have to be the second sex outside of the bedroom as well as inside? Why does their role prescribe that they be appeasing and nurturant and stroking in other areas of life also? Why does the cichlid-effect have to ramify through all the relationships between the collectivities?

Again, it is understandable that a woman dependent on the sexuality of her husband might be willing to accept the cichlid-effect. But, asks the woman who is not involved with any man and not interested in preserving anyone's masculinity, why should she also be expected to? Why should such behavior be prescribed for the feminine role, applicable to all? In a quite different but analogous case—the surrender by superior workers of their competitive advantage by accepting flat union pay rates—the courts held that sometimes increased pay for the better individuals was purchased at the expense of some other values. "Individual advantage or favors will generally in practice go in as a contribution to the collective result."[28]

A distinction has to be made between initiating a sexual episode and sexual aggression. There is an endless parade of advertisements teaching women how to use their initiative. Provided she is catlike in her stalking of her prey, says Emily Post, it is permissible. (Most of this female stalking is for a husband,

[61]

not for an immediate sexual partner.) She must use strategy instead of a direct approach. And there is a substantial body of research documenting the sexual initiative practiced by females around the world.

When the statement is made, therefore, that men can aggress sexually against (or should the word be *toward*?) women, but that the reverse is not true, men often smile with condescending amusement and pleasure at the idea of being sexually pursued. But there is a difference. Female initiative is successful only when the male is willing. Her fatigue does not prevent the sexual encounter; his does. Even the towering, muscular female cannot rape an unwilling male, whether he is merely passive or actively resistant. He can take her; she must excite or incite him. If he does not become aroused, she cannot have him sexually.

More to the point, even if he is willing, not all women can succeed in winning him. It is not true, as George Bernard Shaw said, that any woman unless she were positively a monster could have any man. The ugly woman or the unattractive one or the older one cannot seize the sexual initiative, even by feminine wiles. She may have precisely the opposite effect. She becomes a stock comic character, laughed at for her self-delusion in supposing that a man would be attracted to her. Even if she is a run-of-mine girl, there may be annoyance at her interference with male sexual autonomy. She even makes him look ridiculous.

The only female of whatever subsex who has the privilege of the sexual initiative is the lovely young one who can arouse a man. Even then all she has is the privilege of enticing or exciting him to take her sexually. She must get by guile and strategy what he can simply take or, at worst, get by force. And sometimes even the beautiful girl does not succeed. The very act of sexual initiative may inhibit the man. Thus in Italian motion pictures of the 1960's the point sometimes lay in the inability of men to perform sexually according to traditional, perhaps mythical specifications. In *Bel' Antonio*, for example, the hero was adored because of his assumed sexual athleticism, and when he was unable to perform with his wife the family was disgraced; he was finally redeemed only when it became known that he was the father of a servant girl's illegitimate child. The family could breathe freely again, rescued from ignominy. *Gold of Naples* had a similar theme. So did *Casanova 70*, in which the hero found himself impotent in the presence of both aggressive and compliant women, the first because they made dominance too difficult, the second because they made it too easy and thus robbed it of its savor. He could perform only under dangerous circumstances; the last scene shows him crawling along a ledge outside the building instead of walking through a door to his wife's bed. If her compliance robbed him of dominance, he would supply it himself in the form of victory over danger. The 1967 motion picture, *The Family Way*, pictures an analogous situation in Lancashire, England. A young man finds himself impotent once his wife is no longer inaccessible. There is great shame and dismay on the part of the families involved and even on the part of the neighbors.

Having to wait for male initiative gives women a profound inferiority feeling. There is no agony like that of the wall-flower, or like that of the thousands of girls and women who sit waiting for the longed-for telephone call or watching anxiously for the letter. Or like the humiliation a girl or woman feels at the scores of makeshifts, ruses, and strategies she must invent to invite male initiative, or even aggression.

It is this having to wait for male initiative which makes her the second sex. Why does she tolerate it? Quite aside from considerations of expediency, which suggest that discretion is the better part of valor for a smaller animal facing a larger one, there is the inescapable fact that female sexual aggression in the human species, whatever it may do in others, defeats its own purpose. When culture permits or encourages sexual pleasure in women, it is derived not from her "sex act" of ovulation but from the male "sex act" of sperm ejaculation by way of erection. Her own sexual satisfaction as well as his thus depends on male potency. The human female who aggresses simply inhibits the male muscle. The conflict is not between male dominance and sex equality; it is primarily a female one, between behavior which facilitates and behavior which inhibits or suppresses male sexuality. Since it seems that the ability of males to perform well sexually depends on nonaggression in females, the

[63]

female cannot have it both ways—actions that inhibit and actions that facilitate male sexuality.

But if the dependence of sexual relations on male arousal forces a humiliating and subservient role on women, it has equally great impact on men. It puts them to a test—sometimes agonizing. A woman can pretend and deceive; an erection cannot be pretended. She can be unengaged and still participate; he must remain erotically stimulated in order to sustain the erection. Her success or failure is not, or need not be, observable; his, especially his failure, is highly visible, and according to one psychiatrist, highly publicized also.

. . . modern man literally lives in a sexual goldfish bowl, where he is constantly up for appraisal. His girl friend has usually read the latest psychiatric book on sexual behavior, in which practically anything he does is called "infantile"; his friends openly discuss frequency and duration of the sexual act; his family ridicules him if he escorts an unattractive female; and for years, he has heard the older females mocking the sexual prowess of their husbands. There is a constant aura of jokes about male sexual inadequacy in the atmosphere. Haunted by his dwindling stature, he may look for help to the marriage manuals, where he is reminded once again, that it is his responsibility to satisfy his wife.[29]

It was different in the past, in the days when sexuality was the prerogative of males, when women were pure, not only undemanding sexually but positively rejecting. It was the resexualization of the female body and the consequent demands by women for sexual "parity" which highlighted the dependence of sexual relations on male readiness.

The resexualization, or transformation, of the female body constitutes one of the major revolutions of this century. No one seemed to think of it as epochal or world-shaking when it came. The suffragettes were not the leaders in this revolution, nor even the great feminists. The women who spoke for free love may have had it in mind, but their target was primarily legal and other institutional controls which constrained the relations of the sexes. The real torchbearers were the marriage-manual writers and the schools of thought which they pioneered.

Under their tutelage the responsiveness of the female body became the responsibility of men. In the early years of the century, the relationship was still that of a benign master conferring a grace on a subservient. Sex was still a man's game. But little by little the news got around. Women could be sexually responsive. Even White Maidens. Later on it was bruited about that, further, she could experience orgasm. It seemed incredible. A spate of research studies confirmed the fact. In one generation—Kinsey and his associates pinpoint it in the 1920's—the sexually involved population potentially doubled.

As if this were not enough, it was now learned not only that the female body was capable of experiencing orgasm, but also that because of shorter refractory time, it had even greater orgasmic capacity than the male body. Women could outperform men. The fifteenth century had known this. Imperial Rome had undoubtedly known. Contributors to the great Hebrew library had known. But the nineteenth century had not known. Now the twentieth century did. The female body could tolerate abstinence better than the male body could; it could also outperform him. At both ends of the scale it did better. There was the added humiliation to men that the do-it-yourself female climax was quicker and physiologically more intense than the one he cooperated in. . . .[30]

All of this, conceivably, could have been absorbed without too much trauma, but, the twentieth century being what it is, the combination of resexualized bodies and an ambience of equality, there developed a veritable cult of orgasm. Women came to expect, even demand, sexual gratification on equal terms. It became practically a civil right.

Most western societies tend to give lip service to a single standard of sexual behavior: no sexual relations outside of marriage. In actual practice, however, they tend to be less permissive toward women than toward men and to give men the prerogative of initiating relations. A variety of reasons may be invoked to justify this double standard. Whatever they may be, whether valid or not, the double standard has the actual effect of protecting men against the greater potential sexuality which an emancipated female sex could demand. Just as marriage, however much men may rail against it, is a man's best friend (the man protected by marriage shows up better than his unmarried brother on almost every index), so also, in fact, is the double standard. The men of the nineteenth century put women in a pumpkin shell and there they kept them very well while they went about building empires and industrializing their world and otherwise tending to the really important things. It was useful to have women out of the way or at least in their place in order to free men to do these things. It also kept them from making undue sexual demands on men.

"I just don't get it," a boy from Seattle is quoted as saying. "I've shown this girl Audrey in every way that I'm not interested, but she still chases after me. Man, she must be sick!" And the counselor replies for the benefit of the girls that "teenage boys find boy-chasing girls unfeminine—in fact, frightening."[31] And a psychiatrist finds the increasing assertiveness and sexual demandingness of women "horrifying, a danger to the future of the human race."[32]

The aggressive cult of orgasm in women placed great burdens on men. When men had had the final decision about sexual relations and women had bodies trained for frigidity, there had been no occasion to measure either the quantity or the quality of their sexual capacities. If men were poor sex partners, no one was the wiser, not even the men themselves. The women expected little and that was what they got. With the inflation of women's demands, the sexual performance of men came to be measured by very exacting standards. Worst of all, it was the wife who did the measuring. Since the books taught that the entire responsibility for female responsiveness was his, any failure was attributed to him.

Women were not unscathed. The new outlook on female sexuality built an undue expectation in women, so that any experience short of what the books prescribed made them feel like failures, half-women, less than normal. The achievement of orgasm became almost as compulsive as the suppression of responsiveness had been in the Victorian nineteenth century. The woman who responded lovingly to her husband, who experienced profound joy and happiness in his ecstasy, who wanted nothing more than the satisfaction of having brought him sexual pleasure, was made to feel that this was not enough. Unless she herself experienced orgasm she was at best neurotic, at worst frigid. As if to increase her anxiety, she was told that she had to experience a certain kind of orgasm. Just any old kind would not do. To be normal, it had to be so-called vaginal orgasm; clitoral orgasm was infantile and would not count on her scorecard for normalness. Ironically, the books were wrong. There proved to be only one kind, the kind the books had been calling infantile.

Not all the problems the sexes face today are traceable to social or cultural changes. Some are demographic, related to the increased longevity which characterizes both men and women today and new only because they were masked in the past by youth. It has been found that the interests of the sexes tend to converge with age. It has been found also that sexuality does, too. Thus Kinsey and his associates found that in the early years male sexuality was more than seven times greater than female sexuality, but that in the later years the disparity was reduced to slightly more than a fraction; the women tended to catch up with the men. Conceivably, there may even be a reversal. The seeming greater sexual aggression on the part of women may therefore reflect only a changing age composition of the population. We retain in our folk imagery the myth of male sexuality as it was when people were all young. It does not fit a population when a large proportion of men are no longer young. Older men measure their sexuality on a scale no longer applicable to them. We have noted the new female sex which modern science has made possible. There may be a corresponding new subsex among men. Now that males live so much longer than in the past, male sexuality, beyond the prime years, may be more fragile than used to be supposed. The rapprochement in sexuality between men and women in the later years may interfere with good communication rather than facilitate it. Until new concepts of sex which are appropriate for these changes are substituted for old stereotypes which are appropriate only for the young, there may continue to be obstacles to mutual understanding between the sexes.

❖❖❖❖❖

Despite the similarities of men and women, despite their common species heredity, Kinsey and his associates concluded that they differed profoundly in crucial ways. They wrote that "the possibility of working out sexual adjustments in marriage, and the possibility of adjusting social concepts to allow for these differences between females and males, will depend upon our willingness to accept the realities which the available data seem to indicate."[33]

The sexes, that is, are certainly not figments of our culturally determined imagination. They are frighteningly real. To say that many sex differences are *merely* social or cultural in nature does not add much to the discussion if it is impossible to imagine a society in any culture in which sex differences are or can be ignored. What does it mean to say that if boys and girls were treated exactly alike, they would be alike, when it is impossible for a society to operate on such a principle? Further, it is impossible to understand communication between the sexes and the resulting relations between them if one categorically denies the existence of differences between them quite beyond those traceable to culture or social structure, which are important enough themselves.

These, then, are the communicators. Like the English and the Americans, just similar enough to expect more similarity, just different enough not to get it; just similar enough to be intolerant of differences, just different enough to guarantee their presence. Far more different from one another than any of the races, they are nevertheless bound together so inextricably that apartheid is an impossible solution; but still so different that apartheid is an inevitable one. The story of the man who complained to the gods that he could live neither with nor without his feminine companion is true, if not soberly factual. He could not. Nor could she. They have to live together. This means they have to communicate with one another. They have to learn one another's language. They have to get one another's message. At least enough to get along.

This is where we find the sexes today, this is where they are as we enter the last third of the twentieth century, caught up in a revolution they don't entirely understand, uncertain themselves of how much of their difficulties—at home, at work, at play, in social life—is intrinsic and inevitable and how much of it they can do something about, engaged with desperate earnestness in an effort to find the *modus vivendi* that fits the kind of people they are, the kind this day and age produces.

MEDIA AND BARRIERS

CHAPTER THREE

❖❖

Actions Do Speak, But Not Louder Than Words—to Women, at Any Rate

❖❖❖❖❖

Coquetry . . . depends upon giving and interpreting small indications of interest and small hints of erotic possibilities; in its subtler forms these indications may be very small indeed; an almost imperceptible gesture of the hand or body, a look, an intonation of the voice, or the accent of a single syllable.

—Willard Waller and Reuben Hill, *The Family, A Dynamic Interpretation*

Women . . . want to make love when they feel loving. But often a woman doesn't make it clear that she does, and a man can't be blamed for becoming confused. Particularly when she greases her face at bedtime, wearing curlers with or without a pink grandma-type net bonnet that ties under the chin, and a bed bra . . . , it's understandable if he reads or misreads all this as No Trespassing. He may assume, naturally enough, that if the lady were willing, she would have made herself more generally beddable.

—Peg Bracken, *I Try to Behave Myself*

Signs and signals have not disappeared as media of communication in the dialogue of the sexes. The introduction of words to mankind did not obviate the need, or at any rate, the actual use of signs and signals. In fact, they have proliferated, not only in relations between the sexes, but in other relations as well. A vast, if indeterminate, proportion of communication among human beings is still mediated by signs and signals.

For our purposes, signs are things that give us cues as to the state, nature, or character of another living thing—in our case, other human beings and more specifically members of the other sex. (The term *opposite* sex is rejected because the sexes are conceived of as complementary not opposite entities.) Signs, that is, tell us how others feel, what they are "like."

Signals here refer to more active cues; they are, in effect, cues for permitted, encouraged, even ordered, actions. Both signs and signals may become conventionalized into symbols. The distinction between signs and signals may be blurred at the edges. Thus a sign may easily become a signal. The smile is transformed by a wink. If weeping is a sign that a girl is hurt, batting eyelashes may become a signal—a command—for him to apologize. Tenderness in a wife may be a sign that she is receptive; touching him may be a signal to him to go ahead. The expression on the wife's face at the cocktail party may be a sign that she is jealous; taking his arm is a signal to leave the party. Sometimes, as we shall see presently, the sign and the signal give different messages. Nevertheless it is helpful to retain the distinction between signs which tell us the state or status of another being, and signals, which serve as invitations to action.[1]

If signs are to serve communication they have to be read. And the ability to read signs is a major component in any social interaction, at the prehuman as well as the human level. No one better exemplifies adeptness in reading signs than Sherlock Holmes. "In meeting a fellow-mortal," he tells us,

we learn at a glance to distinguish the history of the man and the trade or profession to which he belongs. Puerile as such an exercise may seem, it sharpens the faculties of observation and teaches one where to look and what to look for. By a man's finger-nails, by his coat-sleeves, by his boots, by his trouser-knees, by the callosities of his fore-finger and thumb, by his expression, by his shirtcuffs—by each of these things a man's calling is plainly revealed. That all united should fail to enlighten the competent inquirer in any case is almost inconceivable.[2]

Even more. A trained observer, he tells us, could read the inmost character of a man as well as the more obvious signs of calling, that is, occupation and class. Holmes claimed that he could "by a momentary expression, a twitch of a muscle or a glance of an eye . . . fathom a man's inmost thoughts."

Simple enough so that animals and infants can learn to do it too. A dog, for example, is waiting for his master. At last he hears the car in the driveway. He runs to the door. He sees the worry lines across his master's forehead and the weights pulling down the corners of his mouth. His master says not a word. In fact, eyes downcast, he has not even looked at the dog. But at once the dog knows he must keep out of the way. Even a mild kick is not wholly out of the question. He slinks away. For he, as well as Holmes, is adept at reading "momentary expression," "the twitch of a muscle," and the "glance of an eye." Perhaps one reason a dog is man's best friend is precisely because he becomes so skilled at reading the signs his master, consciously or unconsciously, gives him.

Sign-reading is subtle and complex enough to engage the serious efforts of scientists as well. For Sherlock Holmes was not the only one who reduced this kind of sign-reading to a science. The psychiatrist also knows that every little movement, however imperceptible, has a meaning all its own. He is trained in the syntax of the muscles. A great teaching psychiatrist used to devote an entire lecture to a detailed study, complete with slides, of the small muscles around the eyes; another, to the muscles around the mouth, which experiments have shown to be especially explicit in transmitting messages. "In the face . . . the emotions typical of the individual leave lasting traces . . . of permanent character . . . [so that] the face becomes the geometric locus . . . of the inner personality."[3] But the face is not the only medium of communication. The large body muscles can also serve, for carriage and posture can be as communicative as facial expression. One psychiatrist claimed that "with a proper technique it is possible to analyze a personality solely by a study of his muscular behavior."[4]

Relationships as well as individual personality can be read in these subtle nuances of postural language. An acute observer can tell the nature of the relationship between a man and a woman from the way they carry themselves when they talk to one another.

With this tool-kit of muscular cues, signs *of* almost everything may be sought and read. Among human beings there appear to be no limits to what we seek and transmit signs of—sexuality, health, character, attitudes, opinions, emotional state, social class, marital status and marital aptitude, relationships. . . . One has only to name it, and someone or other at some time or some place has looked for signs of it in someone.

Among human beings, one of the saddest facts of life is that the signs are all fouled up. A female's receptivity so far as desire is concerned does not at all coincide with her physiological readiness. The signs of sexuality among women are also frequently equivocal or even wrong. Men, for example, want very much to know the sexual temper of the women they meet. Does she or doesn't she? Which subsex is she? White Maiden? Dark Lady? A whole folklore has developed to guide in the search for signs, most of them wrong. There is no infallible way of knowing the capacity for sexual response in women from external or superficial signs. The girl who is most attractive, most appealing, may be the least sexually responsive physiologically. The love goddess, worshipped as the very epitome of lovely female sexuality, may be frigid. Contrariwise, the most responsive girl may not be at all attractive physically.

A modern diagnostician has a laboratory full of equipment to locate and interpret signs whose presence means that some kind of pathology is present in the body and scores of researchers are constantly at work to find earlier signs of illness. Clinicians and psychiatrists, similarly, seek to find early signs of emotional or mental illness.

Related to signs of emotional and mental health are signs of character, for lack of a better term. Here, also, scores of researchers are at work trying to find ways to "test"—that is, produce signs of—character. The personnel officer in industry wants such signs; so do the armed services. But most especially do families want them. Is this young man reliable? Will he take care of our daughter? Are his intentions honorable? Is this young woman a virgin? Is she stable? Will she remain loyal under pressure?

Signs of attitudes and opinions may also be sought. Political leaders scan the scene for signs of public attitudes and opinions at home and abroad. The successful ones are adept at reading the signs of disaffection; they have the knack or talent for reading all kinds of signs, unfavorable as well as favorable. Are the riots a sign of disaffection with the regime; or are they merely an emotional outbreak? But, girls and boys, women and men, also ask: what does he (she) think of me? Respect me? Look down on me? Admire me? Condemn me? Since we cannot always ask, we search for signs.

Signs of the emotional state of the other are among the most eagerly sought. Not only, as among animals, is she ready for me, but also, or rather, does she love me? When the signs are not forthcoming we turn to other tests, such as the petals of the flower: she loves me, she loves me not. Considering the almost fortuitous nature of so many youthful attractions, this seems about as pertinent a test as any other. In a girls' game in the early years of the century there was a chant which included the line: "Dressed in white and dressed in blue, That's a sign that he loves you." Tea leaves will do if there is nothing better. Sometimes even more urgent is the search for a sign of our own emotions: "Do I love her (him)?" And modern textbooks for college students in courses on marriage often include chapters on "how do you know it's love?" complete with a ten-item questionnaire to elicit the proper signs, positive or negative. Does she like me? dislike me? Is he jealous? afraid of me? The suspicious one wants signs to reassure him. The guilty one wants to know, does she suspect me? (This one may be especially important since the widespread sense of guilt, especially in men vis-à-vis women, is sometimes used by women as a strategic ploy, as illustrated by Chaucer's Wife of Bath.[5]) In brief, signs are sought which will tell us how the other feels toward us.

In addition to the signs dealing with the sexuality, health, character, opinions, attitudes, and feelings of people, we also look for signs of their social class. Sherlock Holmes referred to the stigmata of occupation (fingernails, callouses, clothing), but we also look for signs of education in the use of the voice, in enunciation, in accent, in grammar. We look for signs of income, also, in clothing and home address. We look for signs of social status in the school attended or in club membership. The message conveyed by a taste for chitlins and watermelon leads some Negroes to eschew them entirely; the message conveyed by a taste for exotic foods and wines leads some upwardly mobile to endure foods in public that they abhor; the message conveyed by adherence to dietary or ritualistic rules leads some to order ham and eggs and others meat on Friday. The use of so-called status symbols as signs of importance in industry has become a standard joke. But in our mobile, urbanized society, where most people meet as strangers, signs of social class seem especially important, and most especially in the search for mates.

We look most anxiously for signs of marital aptitude and of compatibility. A whole armory of tests has been devised to help the counselor look for signs of these "states" in the young people who come to him for help. A great deal of dating and courting behavior is dedicated to the same end. Girls especially are asking, will he make a good husband?—father to my children?

The relationships between people, as well as individual personality and states, can be read in the subtle nuances of postural and face-muscle language. A sensitive observer of the relationships between men and women can often tell the nature of their relationship from the way they enter a room together. It is a sign of one thing if they bear themselves with respect to one another as a common unit looking out upon the world together, shoulder to shoulder; it is a sign of something else if they stand as though they were unrelated to one another, like two separate, disparate individuals; it is a sign of still another relationship if they stand so as to give the impression of focusing on one another, either fiercely or absorbedly. Rivals for the same prey have to be especially good at reading such signs.

The *forms* signs take as media of communication are manifold. Even among animals, they may be on a rather complex level, but usually they are fairly simple and clear-cut. The porcupine sniffs the male in significant ways, the elephant uses her trunk erotically. The monkey presents herself.[6] Among human beings, too, signs may be simple and clear-cut. But the gamut runs infinitely wide. Signs may take the reflex form of the blushing and blanching of young lovers or, at the other extreme, the abstract form of indices based on graphs from laboratory drums or scores on a test. Stance and posture may be obvious signs; stiffness means one thing, relaxation, another. Sometimes a total act, or nonact, may serve as a sign.

Signs in the form of physiological and muscular reflexes may not be as accurately read by the layman as by the psychiatrist, but they are read. Boys and girls, men and women, even infants and children, do it all the time. It is easy to see why physiological behavior becomes significant. If loss of control of sphincter muscles always accompanies extreme fear, then the army researchers are justified in taking it as a sign of fear, just as the diagnostician is justified in taking the symptoms as a sign of the disease. Blanching and blushing, a cold sweat, a thumping heart, panting breath, tears, shivering or quivering, and a host of other reflexes are often taken to be signs of love, hate, fear, joy, or lust. Young men and women are especially sensitive to such signs in their own bodies. They are likely to read their own quickened pulse, the response of erectile tissue, and the panting breath as signs of love, what else?

The voice may be a sign. In an article on how to avoid being a flop, the author warns girls against "a 'too-crisp way of speaking' . . . , an authoritative attitude . . . , a voice that barks out orders like an army sergeant," and career girls are warned against showing such signs if they wish to be socially acceptable.[7]

Clothes are, of course, clear-cut signs of occupation or "calling," as Sherlock Holmes noted. We even speak of blue-collar and white-collar occupations (although with the transformation of the nature of work and the reduction of "dirty" work, it is not always easy to distinguish a blue-collar from a white-collar worker in the traditional sense). But clothes are much more than signs of calling only. They tell more than that. As a language, in fact, they are almost as conventionalized as verbal language. Thus, for example, casual clothes say "at your ease." Formal clothes demand decorum. The habit of the nun and the Mother Hubbard which the New England missionaries put on the native women of the South Seas say "no sex here."

Décolletage and bustle say "look at me!" The hippie says, "see, bourgeois conventions and mores mean nothing to me; I'm not in the rat race." The strictly tailored suit, severe shirtwaist, flat heels, have become stereotypes for the woman who does not know what her body is for, just as the frilly blouse, high heels, and sleek leg announce that the wearer is very much aware of her sex and hopes the observer is, too. The way the clothes are worn helps to interpret them and to translate them into signals. The swiveling hips or the mincing gait can revise the message of any kind of clothes.

Signs may also take the form of cosmetics. Emphasis on the mouth, we are told, highlights sex appeal; playing up the eyes, on the other hand, gives an ethereal or spiritual message.[8] "A man's face is his autobiography," Oscar Wilde has said, whereas "a woman's face is her work of fiction." Whatever the story she tells, it is the fact that she tells that one rather than some other, which renders it autobiographical.

Sometimes a total act serves as the sign. If a man sends the very best, according to the advertisement, it is a sign that he cares. If a man marries a woman, this is taken in our society as a sign that he loves her. If a man waves a gun at his wife, or vice versa, this is usually taken as a sign that the relationship is in trouble. Edith Wharton described a hostess who judged a young man's alcohol habits by the amount of sugar he took in his tea: if he took little or none, this was a sign that he probably drank too much.

There is even a kind of grammar in signs. An etiquette book for men interprets the brush-off signs which women may use. If she is "busy" three times in a row and/or breaks more than one date, the young man is to take this as a sign that she does not care for him. Similarly, if it is the man who wishes to communicate the brush-off sign, he should stop calling her or asking her out, and if she calls him, he should be busy, late, forgetful, or have urgent work to do. He should lie if necessary, but he should let her save face if possible and make her think she is the one breaking off. This book also summarizes the language of gifts.[9] Etiquette books are, in fact, dictionaries of sexual signs; they standardize the meaning of behavior.

Men and women are always demanding acts as signs from

one another. If you love me you'll: marry me, sleep with me, go with me to the ends of the earth, leave your wife, get a divorce, embezzle the money, give up your job. Refusal is taken as a sign that the reluctant one does not "really" love the importuning one. Sometimes a nonact is the sign: not telephoning, not asking for a date, not stopping by for a chat.

The search for signs in whatever form also goes on at an abstract level. The scientist devises many kinds of instruments to give him accurate signs, which he calls indexes, about people. If a child scores high on a test, for example, this is taken as a sign that he is bright or prejudiced or trusting or suspicious. Social psychologists and sociologists have for a generation sought signs that would indicate marital aptitude or a favorable or unfavorable prognosis for marriage. Some looked for such signs within the personalities of the partners themselves; some looked for them in the family and social background. Both sought signs of the characteristics, personal or background, which would make for successful marriages.

Some such signs are complex; they are composites of many related signs; they are gestalts, or patterns. Among the most interesting signs that a young man will make a successful husband, for example, reported by researchers, was conventionality or conformity to conventional norms: a steady work record, church attendance, thrift, and the like. Unconventional behavior, contrariwise, tended to be a sign of greater marital risk. By not conforming, we shout, in effect, "I'm a rebel, a beatnik, a dissenter, a direct-actionist, a nonbeliever in the status quo, a hippie, a teeny-bopper." If a girl accepts a young man's invitation to his apartment, the act is taken to be a sign that she is receptive to his advances. It may or may not be, according to the context in which it occurs. Or if it is assumed, as it used to be in Latin America, that no man could be alone in a room with a woman without making sexual advances to her, then if she permitted herself to violate this rule, her act was taken as a sign that she was approachable. Again, it might, or it might not.

In settled times, conformity and nonconformity may be taken as fairly good signs of the kinds of people we are. But when norms are in flux, they are equivocal signs at best. Should the girl's rejection of premarital sexual relations be interpreted as a sign of acceptance of a societal norm, or is it a sign that she is frigid? Is the young man's urging a sign that he loves her dearly or a sign of rejection of a societal norm? It isn't always easy to know for sure. The same sign may mean different things in different contexts.

❖❖❖❖❖

For this and other reasons the language of signs in whatever form is by no means unequivocal. And, contrary to Sherlock Holmes's dictum, deceit is possible—as possible as it is with words. Some signs tend to become standardized or convention-alized media. Actors learn the subtle muscle-language, so that when they want to convey an attitude or emotion or subjective state, they have a set of more or less conventionalized signs to work with. But imposters—and most of us are imposters in one form or another at some time or other—can learn to use the same language. People who want to make the right impression use it all the time. We smile to hide our hostility; we listen with rapt attention to the boring V.I.P.

Not even physiological signs and signals are infallible media. The shrewd criminal learns to control his reflexes and thus to fool the lie detector. The hysterical patient produces symptoms to order. Prostitutes become adept in the use of sexual signs to deceive; themselves unaroused, they nevertheless writhe and moan in simulated orgasmic ecstasy to convey to their customer the virtuoso nature of his performance. A young woman living in a Parisian pension was once admonished by the concierge to be less noisy when she entertained her gentleman friend; too much was, after all, too much; others were complaining; there was a decent limit. "But he's so old," replied the girl com-passionately, "he needs more encouragement than others." And with less skill, perhaps, but with the same intent, many ordinary wives go through the same performance regularly. Their will-ingness to do this to please their partners is meaningful, not the performance itself. And that is not deceitful.

Even if people are quite sincere in their intentions, this in itself is no guarantee of the accuracy of signs. The introduction by Freud of the unconscious into our thinking alerted us to a whole new order of complexity in signs. Sincerity was no longer proof of anything. For the Freudian legacy has made us humiliatingly aware that others may know or understand or read us better than we do ourselves. We may be unaware of the messages we are sending, or we may pick up messages from others that they do not know they are sending and would not send if they did. All the convenient forgetting, the unsent letters, the tardinesses, the sleepiness, the fatigue, the burned meals, the broken promises, the yawning, the bored expressions, the misremembered dates—even the illnesses—add up to an eloquent array of signs for those who can read them. Even more confusing, behavior may "mean" or be a sign of precisely the opposite of what it seems to be a sign of. The years of devotion to a spouse may be interpreted not as a sign of faithful love but, on the contrary, as compensatory for hatred or as a hostile control technique or as, somehow or other, a sinister fostering of dependency, and so on. Parlor psychoanalysts become adept at reading such signs. If, according to Holmes, deceiving a trained sign-reader is impossible, so also is sincerity discountable by him.

❖❖❖❖❖

Even if there is no deceit, intentional or unintentional, or any unconscious distortion, signs and signals may be equivocal because the message sent may not be the same as the message received. All language is subject to misinterpretation; no language guarantees perfect communication. But the language of signs and signals is especially vulnerable, for the message conveyed may not always mean the same to both parties.

Most men refuse to believe, or cannot believe, that the nubile young woman, luscious in her tennis shorts or bikini, is not deliberately signaling a come-on. But the signal is not necessarily the one the men pick up. She may be asking for admiration; the man hopes she is asking for him. Her body keeps signaling: I am a desirable woman. The men who see her reply, Don't be so damn provocative about it unless you want us to make something of it. The clothes, designed by knowing men, seem to signal clear and loud, Take me! The girl may actually mean nothing more than, Admire me.

Sometimes the help of a judge may be called for to interpret the girl's no, as in the case of one young man who chased a girl to her home and attempted to break open her locked door. When he was arrested for assault, his lawyer claimed that this was only "the classic problem of when you hear a girl say no, you don't know whether she means yes or no." To this the judge replied that her rebuff had been clear enough. "Even if we make allowance for what is commonly excused under the heading of masculine ego," he said, "one attempt to persuade her by pulling on her or pursuing her to her home would have been sufficient."[10] A girl who put up as much of a fight as this one had was certainly shouting no in a convincing enough manner. Anyone should be expected to get her message.

This misreading of even such unequivocal signs between the sex-appealing young woman and men is extremely old. It was well understood by the Church Fathers. Tertullian inveighed against the tinkling anklets the girls were wearing in Carthage. And St. John Chrysostom railed against the young women he indicted for making adulterers of men they did not want sexually, of men, in fact, they would not even consider meeting socially. "Are you not ashamed and do you not blush to be showing yourself off to these people and to be doing all this for men whom you do not consider worthy of a greeting?"[11]

And there is the society woman who, upon being reminded of a romp in bed by a young man just introduced to her, replied haughtily, since when does sleeping together constitute a proper social introduction? Ralph Waldo Emerson was as skeptical as most men with respect to the signals women seemed to be broadcasting. "The cultivated, high-thoughted, beauty-loving, saintly woman finds herself unconsciously desired for her sex, and even enhancing the appetite of her savage pursuers by these fine ornaments she has piously laid on herself. She finds with indignation that she is herself a snare. . . ."[12]

It comes as a surprise to some men that young women in the prime of their beauty and appeal are not always aware of the signs they are sending or the attraction they are exerting. Contrary to the male myth, they do not necessarily know how appealing they are. "I am told at reunions how popular I was as a coed years ago," says one woman. "If I was, I didn't know it. I was very uncertain of myself. I must have projected a good deal more assurance than I felt." Even older women may be unaware of their appeal: "A friend laughingly referred to the time several years ago when, he says, I had made such a big hit with a V.I.P. visiting our town. It was a surprise to me that I had." Another woman: "Several years after Jack had remarried, a friend of mine told me that he had wanted to marry me and would have asked me if I had given him the least hint. This was news to me. It had never occurred to me that I might appeal to him." Conversely, of course, other women may over-interpret; they read even a casual gesture as meaningful, the guiding arm as a caress, and they leave their date at the door convinced that he loves them. Not knowing or misinterpreting the signs they are sending is, of course, no monopoly of either sex; both are capable of it.

❖❖❖❖❖

Among human beings the drama between the sexes can be played out by the media of signs and signals alone, or with a minimum of words. Among inarticulate people it often is. And the interaction can be powerful. But when words were added to signs and signals at the human level, the impact of all kinds of signs and signals was compounded. Words transformed the drama. A wholly new dimension was added.

To highlight, underscore, and insist upon the importance of words—as this book does—is not the same as denigrating the continuing importance of signs and signals. Actions, as Emerson noted, can still speak very loud. They can, in fact, drown out the loudest words, harsh or gentle. The tender kiss or the refused invitation conveys more than a thousand words. Sometimes words can impede actions, as when one curses the darkness instead of lighting a candle. Sometimes, too, the more words there are the farther apart talkers become; the words get in the way of communication; a gentle caress conveys the true message. In the long run, for most people, no amount of beguiling talk takes the place of doing what has to be done. Eliza Doolittle is justified in demanding to be shown, in asking for proof in the form of deeds. Words, admittedly, are sometimes inadequate; emotions may be too deep for words.

Having said all this, however, and having paid our profoundest respects to actions of all kinds, from the flutter of the eyelashes to overt aggression, and admitting that without them communication would be all but fatally flawed, we have to recognize that there is an enormously important place for words as media of communication between the sexes, not only in lovemaking, where it is just short of magical, but also in the simple companionship of everyday life. The introduction of words into the communication process made possible, if it did not actually guarantee, a new, exciting and delightful relationship between the sexes. It opened up a world peculiarly congenial to women. If asked, most women would usually prefer Cyrano de Bergerac's emotions which were not only "deeply felt" but, in addition, "nobly told."

The strong, silent hero is a man's man. Women prefer the strong (or even the not-so-strong) man who can also—if not, like Cyrano de Bergerac, actually rhapsodize over them—at least tell them in words that they are lovely, desirable, that he wants them. If the epic poet sings of arms and the man, the dramatic or lyric poet sings of words and the woman. Christian and Miles Standish were great soldiers; arms were their stock-in-trade. John Alden and Cyrano de Bergerac were facile talkers; words came easily to them. Priscilla and Roxanne, like most women, preferred the men of words to the men of arms. "Speak of love in your own words," says Roxanne, "Improvise! Rhapsodize! Be eloquent!"[13]

Women do not always accept actions as an adequate substitute for words. Quite the contrary. Both the simple, inarticulate husband and the most sophisticated word-monger may think that their behavior speaks for itself. They could hardly be more wrong; for it doesn't. When the wife asks her husband, Do you love me, dear? he replies, Of course I do. Why don't you ever say so? Well, I support you, don't I? I bring home my paycheck, don't I? I don't hang around with the boys or run around with other women, do I? I don't get drunk, do I? Isn't

that enough? What more do you want? But the message embodied in fidelity or in sober and responsible actions is drowned
out by the thundering silence about his feelings.

Even with a sophisticated woman like Simone de Beauvoir:

> Sartre talked to me a great deal about M. . . . He evoked the weeks
> he had spent with her in New York with such gaiety that I grew un-
> easy; suddenly I wondered if M. was more important to him than I
> was. . . . One day . . . I asked, "Frankly, who means the most to you,
> M. or I?" He told me, "M. means an enormous amount to me, but I
> am with you." His answer took my breath away. . . . It was all I could
> do to shake hands, to smile, to eat. . . . That afternoon Sartre ex-
> plained. . . : we had always taken action to be more truthful than
> words, and that is why, instead of launching into a long explanation,
> he had invoked the evidence of a simple fact.[14]

Conversely, the loving words of a passive-dependent husband
can speak far louder than his exploitative behavior:

> *First woman:* I don't see how she tolerates him!
> *Second woman:* Neither do I! He has never supported her a day since
> they were married. She works all day at the office and slaves for him
> at home all evening while he sits around and pretends to paint. How
> can she bear it?
> *Third woman:* I know how. Have you ever seen them together? He
> appreciates her. More than that: he *tells* her that he does. He tells her
> how wonderful she is. He tells her how beautiful and brilliant and wise
> and gentle she is. He may not act like a man but he makes her feel like
> a woman. He not only sweet-talks her; he talks to her.

The talk does not even have to do with love. "With thee
conversing," says Milton's Eve, "I forget all time; all seasons and
their change, all please alike." The interesting conversation of
even the homosexual can be a welcome substitute for physical
sex: "I'm a healthy girl who happens to have one good friend
who's a homosexual guy. . . . I find this person charming and
companionable. He shares interests of mine that I've never
been able to get my regular boyfriends the least bit curious
about, and I can talk with him for hours on end on subjects
which my other friends find boring."[15]

❖❖❖❖❖

To converse: "to have sexual intercourse." This definition of
"to converse" from Webster's Third International is, to be sure,

labeled obsolete. But the implications are not necessarily so. One researcher is, in fact, of the opinion that talk may be as important as sex in marriage, or even more so.[16] In a mid-sixties play, *Help Stamp Out Marriage*, a man does not tell his wife about his talking relations with another woman because he is afraid she will laugh at him, considering him either impotent or queer. When he finally does tell her, she is angry because enjoying talk with another woman is perceived by her as a greater threat than his simply hopping into bed with another woman. The distance beween conversation and sexual intercourse may not be all that great. Words can be very powerful aids in the seduction of women.

Words can transform "raw sex" into idealized sexuality; they can individuate the relationship. There can hardly be anything less accurate than the statement attributed to George Bernard Shaw that love was based on a gross exaggeration of the difference between one girl and another. The implication was that potential partners were interchangeable, one about the same as the others. A coarser, less witty statement of the same idea is that "all women are the same in the dark." Whatever validity there is in this cynical aphorism pertains, at most, to only one of the two kinds of sexuality that Freud, among others, has distinguished. It is the kind that "glorifies" the instinct in contrast to the kind that lays emphasis on the object. Freud thought the first kind was characteristic of the ancients, but any issue of *Playboy* demonstrates that it is very much alive today, too. Contrariwise, sexuality that justifies itself "only in the merits of the object"[17] implies idealization—recognition of the sexual partner as a unique and individuated human being. It implies, in brief, a fairly high level of communication, verbal as well as muscular. And when "to have sexual intercourse" and "to converse" meant the same thing, a giant stride toward the civilizing of the relations between the sexes had been taken.

Women want to be made to feel like women, but not just any way. A simple answer to the question of how to achieve this goal would be by force: knock them over and drag them home by their hair, caveman style. (This was actually not the way cavemen acted at all; but it is a convenient cliché.) She is thereby relieved of responsibility. The man has mastered her.

If this technique ever worked, which is doubtful, it doesn't seem to anymore—at least not with modern, literate women. Women may like "masterful" men when the men take over responsibility for doing what the women want them to do. ". . . Don't ever ask a woman if you may kiss her. There's only one thing she can say, but there are several things she can do. Make a move, or don't, but don't have a lot of conversation about it."[18] This is acceptable. But women do not like "masterful" men who ride roughshod over them, treating them like things and doing what the women do not want them to do—like the many women who charge physical violence in divorce suits.[19] None of this makes them feel like women; rather like things.

In a literate, civilized society women can be made to feel like women most expeditiously by the use of words. Not just any words, of course, but the right ones. For words, as even preliterate people know, can be quite magical. Sweet nothings are anything but nothing. Beautiful. Ravishing. Sweet. Wonderful. Lovely. Desirable. Cool. On the ball. Hip. Even a casual *dear* or *sweetheart* or *honey*. Whatever the language used, the words mean: I approve of you, I am attracted to you. You are a desirable woman.

One of the interesting findings reported by Kinsey and his associates was that women responded to words more than to many other kinds of sexual stimulation. Unlike men, they were not likely to be excited erotically by nudity, by pornographic pictures, or by other kinds of stimuli which were exciting to men. They did find words stimulating—as much as men did. But not just any words. Not erotic stories, not sadomasochistic stories, not burlesque or floor-show stories. *Romantic* stories. Kinsey and his associates noted that other researchers had also recognized that the erotic stimulation women derived from romantic stories exceeded that derived by men.[20]

If men could be persuaded, they would find that ten minutes of tender words, loving words, gentle words, appreciative words, were worth twice as much as twice the amount of time spent in silent pawing. Indeed, without the words, the pawing may not even excite women. *Sweetheart, honey, darling,* even a plain but heartfelt *dear* can be the open sesame. It is so simple, so nearly foolproof, so effective, the wonder is that everyone does not know it.

But hardly anyone does. It is a major complaint of women that their husbands, once the honeymoon is over, rarely make verbal love to them. They scarcely even talk to them at all, let alone talk of love.

The importance of talk in the seduction of women is not a new discovery. "How a little love and good company improves a woman," said George Farquhar in 1706 in *The Beaux' Stratagem*. But predictions about the future currently reveal a new twist. In a playful picture of the dating scene of the future, if present trends continue, a writer in *Playboy* has prophesied a reversal of the relative functions of talk and sex. Until now, a young man has had to pay for sexual relations with talk; in the future he may have to pay for talk with sexual relations. There are, he notes, already signs of this reversal, for "although it takes less and less time to sleep with somebody, it takes longer and longer to get to know somebody well enough to really talk. . . . It's easier to sleep with someone than reveal your deepest feelings and hangups." If this situation continues, fifteen years from now "a guy will spend enormous amounts of time sleeping with a girl, just so he can get to talk to her."[21] Maybe the boys are as wistfully hungry for talk as the girls?

If the equation "conversation = sexual intercourse" is valid in one direction, it is equally so in the opposite direction. Words can be used by women for the prevention of seduction, as well as by men for facilitating it. Women who do not want to have sexual relations may, if they are clever, substitute words and get away with it. The Arabian Nights are the classic example. The technique still works. Thus, one writer on etiquette, in answer to a girl who wants to be popular though good, replies: "Men love to talk, and good listeners are usually popular. As long as he is engaged in an interesting conversation his mind is not likely to wander to other things. Don't talk too much about yourself, but make it easy for him to talk."[22]

It is not only women who find words seductive.[23] Men also can be won, as well as deterred, by them. For words can be as seductive as more physical charms. Madame de Staël is the archetype. "Germaine took conversation as a means to seduction so much for granted that she endowed her heroine, Delphine, with that power, even though she credits Delphine with physical charms that would have been sufficient by themselves. Describing a brilliant gathering at which her lover was present, Delphine writes: 'For a long time I made conversation with him, in front of him, for him.' And her lover reports on the occasion thus: 'I saw, I heard a woman such as there never was. She is an inspired being.' "[24]

As the character of society changes, making it possible for everyone to become literate and, hopefully, even articulate, the joys of such verbal intercourse may be shared more widely. Verbal sex relations, it is not unreasonable to anticipate, may contribute much to the leisure of the future. We might do worse than make provision for it in training young people. The inculcation of verbal skills and the development of a taste for, and a habit of, talking with the other sex are by no means contemptible goals. Why restrict such important skills? The ability to enjoy the pleasure of her company (as well as of her body) might be at least implicit in all aspects of the education of boys. Both boys and girls, it can be maintained, should learn at least to be comfortable with one another on a verbal level.

Words in sexual relationships are not limited to erotic uses. They may be extremely important in another form of relationship. Researchers have long since noted that emotional deprivation can have fatal consequences. We know that infants require a considerable amount of physical contact with mothers or mother-surrogates. The fondling that the human mother bestows on the infant is not something extra thrown in, an expendable item of care that could easily be dispensed with; it is not just something she does for fun. It is, apparently, a necessary, even essential, ingredient of infant care, not much less important than food. Without such nurturance, infants may waste away and die. This wasting death is called marasmus.

The need for affection, recognition, stroking, or nurturance, outlasts infancy. But the form it takes changes. It becomes verbal as well as physical. "By an extension of meaning, 'stroking' may be employed colloquially to denote any act implying recognition of another's presence. Hence a *stroke* may be used as the fundamental unit of social action."[25] And among adults a great deal of the stroking is in the form of words—words of recognition, of acceptance, of reassurance. Women are often assigned the stroking role. But they are also great consumers of stroking. They may often, in fact, much prefer a stroking relationship with a man to an erotic one.

Words can be used exploitatively as well as strokingly. If the tender words win acquiescence, so, too, do pejorative words, strategically used, win conquest. Increasingly among the complaints of girls and women is the charge that unless a girl yields to a man's request she is called frigid. "Any girl of twenty who is still a virgin," he flings at the resistant young woman, "is either foolish or frigid. She must have met *some* man by that time for whom she felt something genuine."[26] Or with patronizing surprise: "Don't tell me you are a stuffy old maid at heart! Surely you're not that kind of girl."[27] The implication is that she is frigid, neurotic, a potentially lousy wife, or if that doesn't work, too unattractive to appeal to a man. "I marvel at the vanity of the man who fancies, or alleges, that there must be something wrong with the girl who won't yield to him."[28] Rather than accept the self-image that the man's words are designed to foster, some young women capitulate. It is no overwhelming passion on her part. It is protection of her conception of herself. For nowadays a girl may consent in order to retain her self-respect, just as in the past she refused for the same reason. Others find it, in effect, just a new form of male dominance and fight back.

Words add another complication to the relations between the sexes. The fact that messages may use so many media—words as well as signs, signals, and total acts—means that there is more likelihood that they may conflict with one another. The signs may be sending one message, words another. A new form of equivocation is possible.

It has become a commonplace that at every formal meeting there are at least two sets of agenda, the formal and the hidden. The formal interactions get into the minutes; the hidden ones do not. Similarly in all kinds of relations between the sexes there is the possibility of at least two quite different conversations going on at the same time. One is the verbal, mediated by words; the other is nonverbal, mediated by signs. The boy and girl carry on a nervous dialogue about school, about the weather, about common friends. At the same time there is an anguished dialogue in terms of signs and signals.

Sometimes the two conversations coincide; at least they have the same general tenor. They are not contradicting one another. But sometimes they may be in opposition to one another. The words say one thing; the body says another. This kind of ambivalence has been labeled a "double-bind." It involves sending two contradictory messages at the same time.

The double-bind . . . deals essentially with the incongruity between the multiple messages involved in a communication and the ability of the sender to cover up or disguise the incongruity. This places the receiver in extreme difficulty in responding with appropriate action to the disparate communications. In a sense none of the logical alternatives are satisfactory. For example:

Mother: (Stiffens and draws away).
Child: (Draws away).
Mother: What's wrong, dear? Don't you love your mother?

In analyzing this interaction we see that mother has sent two kinds of messages in a single tone communication. One is verbal which says *come*, the other is nonverbal which says *don't come*. The second could further indicate (1) I didn't mean the verbal communication or (2) I don't want you near me. Since the child is dependent upon mother in a variety of other respects, he risks much if he leaves the field. He must respond to this situation yet cannot point out the contradiction in it for him. Mother may deny or ignore his interpretation of her metacommunication (which in fact she probably does not recognize). Thus the child in this situation learns a peculiar kind of communication pattern.[29]

Women are allegedly expert in the use of the double-bind. There are scores of folk generalizations to the effect that if she says *no* she means *maybe* or that if she says *maybe* she means *yes,* and the like; she is, in brief, sending one message through the medium of words, a quite different one through the media of signs and signals. Clever people learn both to use the double-bind themselves and to interpret it in others. But we are not to suppose that the duplicity is always deliberate or even conscious. Often the verbal message is a bow in the direction of conscience or the mores or convention and the body signs and signals carry the "real" message. This does not necessarily mean that she—usually a she, at any rate—is speaking with a "forked tongue." She believes her words.

❖❖❖❖❖

It is true, then, that actions speak, and very loud. No one could deny that they do. But words do, too. Whatever the complications they brought with them, they brought with them possibilities of relations between the sexes far beyond anything lower animals knew. Words are magic; they can sing. The troubador no less than the knight appealed to the lady. One need not be an anthropologist or a linguist or a semanticist to stand in great awe of words. One has only to watch the radiance or the despair pass through the face of lovers as the words work their spell or cast their hex.

CHAPTER FOUR

Communication, Without Mirrors and With

Therefore all things whatsoever ye would that men should do to you, do ye even so to them.

—Matthew 7:12

We should behave to friends as we would want friends to behave to us.

—Diogenes Laertius, *Aristotle*

Do as you would be done by is the surest method I know of pleasing.

—Lord Chesterfield, *Letters*

Don't do unto others as you would they should do unto you. Their taste may be different.

—George Bernard Shaw, "Maxims for Revolutionists"

The Golden Rule in either its positive form or its negative form, is a safe guide only among a close band of like-minded people, such, for example, as the tribal Israelites or the early Christians or Athenian or British aristocrats. It does not necessarily work among people who are very different in what they would like done unto them. The man who does to a girl what he would like to have her do unto him may end up in trouble. The girl who would like a man to pursue her will not necessarily please him by chasing him. The girl who refrains from kissing the man because she wishes he would refrain from kissing her may find herself left all alone. Other people are not reflections of ourselves; certainly the sexes are not reflections of one another.

Some kinds of relationships between the sexes do not depend on communication. The women stockholders in a corporation, for example, are related to its employees, but there is a minimum of communication between them. The women who buy mink coats are related to the men who trap them. And Ernest Hemingway long ago popularized John Donne's poetic statement of the basic human relationships: no man is an island to himself alone; we are all diminished by the death of any one of us. In this fundamental sense all the sexes are related to one another in a manner beyond communication. But for most day-by-day relationships, at home, at work, at play, in social life, in the ordinary sense, communication is of the essence. No communication, no relationship. Sometimes communication *is* the relationship.

Under the rubric "communication" one finds a range of processes that include simple social perception on the part of receivers at one end and, let us say, the programming of the Voice of America by skilled professionals at the other—from the simplest to the most sophisticated. The processes are not the same for receiver and for sender, nor are they the same among either senders or receivers. All are accommodated under the wide-spreading umbrella of the concept of communication. Communication is not, in fact, a single process. No simple model can cover the diversity involved in it.

There are quantitative aspects to communication as well as qualitative, that is, degrees as well as kinds. When, for example, can we say that communication has taken place? Sender and receiver may not always agree on the answer. If it does take place, is communication an all-or-nothing process? Or are there, rather, degrees of success in the achievement of communication? And if so, what are the tests or measures of such success?

❖❖❖❖❖

Different kinds of communication make different assumptions about both senders and receivers. In one, there is no assumption of similarity between the receiver and the sender of the message; communication in this model is based on information or knowledge, learned either individually by experience or by tuition from others. In the other, either a moderate or a high degree of similarity between sender and receiver is assumed; the self is more immediately involved. Sex differences are not important in the first; they are of major importance in the other.[1]

The way of sign-reading of a pet dog, Sherlock Holmes, and the psychiatrist is "scientific." The dog has no conception of what it feels like to be told that one's work is not satisfactory, that a competitor has won the promotion, that the application has been rejected, that the contract did not go through. All he knows is that whenever his master has this look about him, it means that he should keep out of the way. He is conditioned to associate the signs with the expected behavior. In its most sophisticated form this is essentially the scientific way of reading any sign, in man or in nature. In a naïve way, it is probably the oldest as well.

In a dog's case, the information which made possible the reception of his master's message was the result of his own individual experience; he might not be able to read someone else. Human beings can generalize and apply what they learn in one situation to other situations as well. Human beings can also be taught by others what to expect; they do not, like Wowser, have to acquire their information case by case. The medical students can learn from their professor. Or anyone can learn from books.

This model of communication might be called protocommunication since sometimes it is inadvertent, unintended, on the part of the sender, and a matter of inert social perception on the part of the receiver. It requires only the ability to associate or relate signs to concomitant and hence expectable behavior. We read the signs and signals emanating from others exactly as we read the signs of coming storms emanating from the atmosphere. Of course, it can also be a mutual process. Two fighters circling one another are attempting to size one another up before committing themselves to any particular kind of strategy. So, too, a boy and girl on a first date may figuratively circle one another, waiting for signs that will yield useful information.

Because this model of message-reception makes no assumptions about similarities between or among the communicators, human beings can read animals as well as animals human beings.[2]

Women, in fact, who have never experienced sexual desire themselves can learn to read the signs of desire in their husbands as, indeed, the wives of workingmen do. Asked if or how they knew when their husbands wanted intercourse, the women in one study replied: "I am very aware of his desires because he always starts loving me up and playing around"; "I always know he wants to do it"; "we can usually tell when we kiss each other good night"; "I can always tell what's on his mind"; "I can tell, believe me!" "I can tell as soon as he walks in the room when he wants it"; "I am quite aware of his desires; I couldn't help but be; he lets me know right away when he gets home"; "I know when my husband is hot"; "he lets me know he wants it in different ways, usually he begins pulling at me."[3]

Sex differences are therefore not critical in this model of communication. It is available for both sexes, though it is probably more common in women than in men. It is indispensable for prostitutes and entertainers. They are paid to read their customers in order to supply the right product. Many wives become proficient in it too. Men can use this model also; they can learn to read signs of sexual arousal in women as coldly and as expertly as an animal breeder would in a horse or a dog. (It would be better if they did not, though, for if or when they do, their cynicism may prevent an acceptable response.)

Nor does age make a difference. Children learn to read signs in adults; like animals, they come to know when they can and when they cannot. And what they do not learn by themselves, they are taught. If they laugh boisterously in the presence of signs of grief, they are reproved; next time they know they must show decorous solemnity when they see the signs. Mothers learn, too. Almost every conscientious young mother has gone through the trial-and-error process of trying to decipher the infant's message. His crying is not a sign that something hurts; no pins. It's not a sign that he's hungry; he refuses the bottle. It's not a sign that he's cold; he's comfortably warm. By eliminating all the things that the crying is not a sign of, she finally gets the message: he's bored and wants to be played with or stroked. Thereafter she knows what *that* kind of crying is a sign of.

Race is no bar to this kind of communication, either; given time, a Westerner can learn to read even the "inscrutable" Oriental. Nor are cultural differences. It may be strange to translate the signs, but it can be done. All of us, infants, dependents, subordinates, dogs, can and even more must learn to read signs of all kinds or suffer the consequences. All that is needed is information and knowledge. Among human beings a considerable amount of this needed information is inculcated in the socializing process.

What we do beyond sign-reading depends on the kind of people we are. Children are taught not only to read signs but also to give the appropriate or expected or proper response, like the child who learns to be quiet at a funeral. But much depends on the kind of people we are. If we read signs of anxiety we may withdraw quietly; or on the other hand, we may offer a drink. Wowser may slink away, or if the man is a stranger, bark ominously. The sign-reading woman may melt into her husband's arms or bargain for a mink coat.

The shared-experience models of communication, unlike the "Wowser-Holmes" model, or protocommunication model, do presuppose similarity, if not standardization, among the communicators, both in sending and in receiving messages. They emphasize the "common" in communication. The thing that is "common" may be the result either of species heredity or of culture or of socialization. It may be sensory, perceptual, conceptual, or emotional. It is the inference that others' experience —as senders or as receivers—is like ours and the assumption that ours is like theirs which constitute the essence of these models of communication. The validity of this assumption or of this inference varies according to the actual degree of similarity among the communicators. If they are in fact similar, the assumption or inference is valid. And if valid, we have communication; if not, miscommunication.

At the level of simple sensory experience based on vision, audition, olfaction, taste, and common sensitivity (heat, cold, pain, touch), the assumption or inference of similarity between the two sexes is usually fairly valid. There are variations in acuity, but not enough to interfere with communication. And for the kinesthetic sensations derived from common muscular systems, similarity can also be assumed or inferred. Both collectivities are warranted in inferring that everyone sees the same colors or shapes, hears the same sounds, smells the same odors as they; just as, conversely, both can assume that what they see, hear, smell is what the other senses.

Though we can't prove the shared experiences, still we have to believe in them. "It's positively frightening," said one young woman, "to imagine that other people aren't seeing the same thing I see or that I don't see the same thing they see. It leaves you so terribly *alone*. You *have* to believe that you share the same world with other people."

It is precisely belief in such shared experiences that gives us confidence in the existence of a world out there. We are terribly puzzled if others tell us they do not see, hear, smell—in general, sense—what we do, just as we are if we do not sense what they say they sense. Fortunately, because the sensory equipment of human beings of both collectivities *is* fairly standardized, we can safely believe in at least a shared sensory world, if no other.

There are, however, body systems that the two collectivities do not share. The bodies of men and of women are subject to differing internal stimuli simply because they have different organs and different physiques and different kinesthetic sensations. Men can never understand what it feels like to carry about the encumbering breasts and the awkward pelvic cradle; nor can women understand what it feels like to operate a body with mechanical properties quite different from their own.

The work of Kinsey and his associates shows that men are more susceptible to sexual stimulation than women, but there is less knowledge about the sensations associated with such sexual response. The evaluation of sensory experience is notoriously idiosyncratic and not at all standardized. Everyone may be seeing red; but not everyone may like it. If one posits similarities in taste he may go far awry—as in the case of the couple who lived together for fifty years, he always taking the white meat and she the dark because he preferred the dark and she the white. There are great individual differences in reactions to sense experience. Some people are profoundly moved by the sound of music; others can take it or leave it, even prefer to leave it. Some find the colors of a sunset excruciating; others glance up at them and return to their knitting. Some people enjoy the taste of food in an almost esthetic way; others simply eat to live. Some people find the fragrance of roses a meaningful experience; others never even notice it. And so with the sensations associated with sexual arousal.

It can be shown on graphs and charts that, with the exception of ejaculation, the physiology of orgasm is identical in males and females. But this tells us little about the relative pleasure experienced. To some, it is a violently convulsive, all-consuming experience; to others it is a gentle paroxysm, hardly discernible to the partner. To some it is a *summum bonum*, to others, just one among many equally pleasurable experiences. There is doubtless the whole range in both collectivities. It is doubtful, however, that orgasm is ever as mild in men as it is in some women who honestly do not even know whether or not they have ever experienced it. In any event, identical sensory sexual experience does not guarantee identical pleasure in it.

The differences in "sexiness," that is, in relative evaluation placed on sexual pleasure as compared to other values, may interpose a barrier to communication. The young man cannot understand why marriage means so much more to the young woman than immediate sexual satisfaction, why sexual intercourse now has such a low place on her scale of values.

When we come to the perceptual level, the situation is more complicated. Since perception involves the organization and interpretation of sensory experience, it is less standardized among human beings than is raw sensation. The assumption or inference of similarity between or among communicators of the two collectivities is less valid. It can be taken for granted that all with normal vision will see red when the appropriate wavelength is presented to them; but it cannot be taken for granted that all will see, let us say, a cardinal's hat or a chair. Introductory psychology textbooks illustrate the ambiguities present in even the simplest levels of perception by the use of optical illusions; one student sees a cornice, another, a profile in the same configuration, or the same student sees now a cornice, now a profile. Poor children perceive money as bigger than do children who are not poor. Projective tests, so called, are based on precisely these individual differences in social perception of identical pictures or stories of human beings. The sexes, because their experiences tend to be different, differ notoriously in their perceptions. Even as children, boys tend to perceive an aggressive world, girls, a nurturant one. College men were reported in one study to be significantly higher on sex responses than college women.[4] Men seem more prone than women to interpret what they see in sexual terms. The kiss is perceived as a lesbian gesture by the husband, as a casual salutation by the wife. The story produces a raucous laugh in the male hearer, a puzzled frown in his feminine companion.

At the conceptual level, communication becomes more abstract. Concepts are verbal, symbolic. They depend on consensus. Communication on the conceptual level is at once the easiest and the most difficult kind, depending on the degree of consensus. Scientists can communicate across cultures because their concepts are highly standardized; every scientist knows what he can expect from others in the way of shared conceptual experience. NaCl means precisely the same thing to all of them. Politicians, though, may find communication difficult because they suffer from lack of standardization in their concepts. They do not have the same referents in all countries; they are not standardized even within the same cultures. Democracy means one thing in one country, something else again in another. A meeting of minds is notoriously difficult under such circumstances. Men and women may have the same problems. Concepts like *love, honor,* and *cherish* may not have the same referent to both. Nor concepts like *virtue, chastity,* or *fidelity*.

Emotions are composite phenomena which may involve raw sensation, perception, conception, and a wide variety of physiological responses. Human beings of whatever sex appear everywhere to have the capacity to experience the reactions we call fear or hate or love. The inference that male anger is the same as female anger, or the assumption that female fear is the same as male fear is usually safe. Neither collectivity suffers impediments to understanding the other's emotions. Communication on this level is not difficult. The same reactions are not, however, always attached to the same objects in one sex as in the other. They may differ by culture, class, or group as well. It is only when the emotional responses are associated with the same objects that we can infer the experiences of others to be the same as ours or assume that our experiences will be the same as theirs.

Empathy is a name commonly given to a special way of sharing emotion, to a kind of immediate communication from the recipient's point of view. In a way, it recreates in the recipient his own past experiences. It is sometimes said that we can never learn anything we do not already know, or share another's experience unless we have already had that experience or a similar one. We may read the signs of another's emotion without understanding them. Never having experienced his emotion, we cannot really share it. But once we have experienced the other's emotion we can understand it. We can now, we say, empathize with the other.

A woman may, for example, *know* all about lesbianism for years. She can read the signs, even report them accurately. Then an unexpected attraction felt toward another woman, as in the case of Dorothy Thompson, may suddenly illuminate her knowledge and she *understands* much that she only *knew* before: *this* is how lesbians feel. The woman who has never experienced orgasm cannot empathize with someone who has; the woman who has never experienced sexual deprivation cannot empathize with someone who has. The wife who has never been in the professional rat race cannot empathize with her husband's anxiety about the wall-to-wall rug in his competitor's office. She may be able to read the signs, including the words, of his anxiety, or she may be able to sympathize by "catching it" and becoming equally anxious. But she does not, as we use the term here, empathize.

Sometimes empathy is not synchronous. For years one reads of victims of flood or fire with only casual and formal consternation. Then one's own house is flooded or burned. And now one *realizes*—empathizes—what all those people experienced: this is how it was with them. Or the man who finds himself unexpectedly broke or unemployed now finds it possible to empathize with others he formerly had only a "Wowser-Holmes" knowledge of. During any new experience we may find ourselves reminded of past readings of people: *this* is how they felt, we tell ourselves. We can now empathize with them. The jilted girl now has more than a protocommunication knowledge of the boy she jilted last year. The classic example of delayed empathy is that of the adult man or woman who says, "Now that I have become a parent myself I'm just beginning to understand my own parents." (At the same time, however, the adult may forget how he felt as an adolescent and find it difficult to empathize with his own son.) A nurse made this comment: "I worked in a hospital for alcoholics for years without understanding them. I could take good care of them but, as I see it now, as though they were things, just bodies. I knew the symptoms and what to expect next. Then once I was told I would have to take off fifty pounds. The dieting was agony. I was miserable, restless, irritable all the time until I took a snack. Only then did I see how it really felt to 'need' a drink. A drink would allay their misery as a snack would allay mine." A convalescent man, dependent on nurses in a hospital world with uncongenial rules, for the first time "realizes" what it is like to be a woman and can empathize with them.[5] It does, indeed, take one to know one; and it is only in an empathic relationship that the Golden Rule has validity.

We are likely to place a high premium on empathy; we tend to think it a good thing. But how *good* it is depends on the people involved. The story is told that when W. C. Fields was performing, the men in the audience responded extravagantly; they laughed and applauded with great enthusiasm; he was their man; they could empathize with him all the way. But, he used to say, if he needed a ten-dollar loan he would turn not to them but to the little old lady near the back who wondered what all the laughter was about. The person who cannot understand the villain may be kinder and more generous than the one who can. And the person who can understand the victim knows best how to hurt him. It is only between or among people of goodwill that empathy is likely to be benign.

The ability to empathize is considered so valuable that some industries try to train at least their managerial personnel to do so. By means of sociodrama or of role-playing they try to get people to understand those they have to deal with. Marriage counselors sometimes do the same with husbands and wives; by requiring each to perform in the other's role, a kind of vicarious experience is gained which can presumably be used to make empathy possible.

When men and women live lives segregated from one another, sharing few life experiences, empathy will be limited. Each will learn to read the signs in the other but that is about all. The more experiences they come to share, the larger the base on which empathy can rest. The girl who has earned her own living can empathize with her husband in connection with his career problems. The husband who has been confined to the house all day baby-sitting for his wife can then empathize with her when she complains of the frustrations of her life. *This* is how she feels, he says to himself, as for the *n*th time he separates the aggressive child from the bawling sibling, while at the same time trying to empty the clothes dryer, or snatches the bottle of aspirin from the exploring infant. . . . The aging wife whose sexuality has now reached or surpassed the level of her husband's can only then empathize with his frustrations in the past when she rejected him. To say that people *can* empathize does not, of course, mean that they necessarily will. Refusal to empathize may be a way to refuse communication.

✦✦✦✦✦

At the opposite extreme from protocommunication or simple sign-reading, in which similarities need not be present, is sympathetic communication, a shared-experience model in which similarities are very great; so great, in fact, that experiences can be shared immediately, without the mediation of signs or inferences or even empathy. A stimulus is applied to one person and both persons respond in the same way. The child has a needle thrust into its arm and both mother and child wince. One person eats the lemon and both grimace. Or more extreme, the wife is in labor and both she and the husband experience labor pains. The devout nun shows the same stigmata as those of the crucified Christ. The heroine on the stage is betrayed and the women in the audience weep with her. The hero on the television screen is attacked by the villain and we experience his fear.

Another form of sympathetic response is that in which the response of another becomes the stimulus for the same response in us; we "catch" the other's state rather than read or infer it. An animal in a herd, for example, bellows in fear. Presently the same emotion sweeps through the herd. Each animal, having associated the sound of fear with his own experience of fear, now responds to the sound of fear in another animal the same way he would respond to the fearful stimulus itself. This is communication in the most literal sense, the rendering common of an experience.

Human beings show similar reactions; emotions can run through a crowd in an analogous way. They are "communicated." They can run through a family, too, including the dog. Parents experience anxiety; presently the children catch it also. The young mother entertaining the boss wonders why the baby is so unsettled today; why is it that he is always at his worst on the days when she has least time for him? Infants, like animals, catch the emotions of those about them. They do not necessarily read signs or infer from behavior; they catch the emotion immediately, without the need for media.

Sexual arousal in women is easily caught by men; the reverse is also possible but it is not so easy. Sexual excitement in men may, indeed, leave women unmoved. Worse still, in fact, it may have precisely the opposite effect. Instead of catching the sexual arousal, the women may react with coldness, revolted rather than excited.

Up to now we have been looking primarily at the person receiving messages—reading, inferring, empathizing, and sympathizing. But he is only one part of the communication situation. The sender has problems, too, and they may vary according to the kind of communication going on.

The person being read in protocommunication may not be a purposive sender at all; he may not even want to reveal himself. He is not trying to communicate. He may, in fact, be trying to hide, to protect himself. And even if he is not, even if he is willing to communicate, even if he wants to be known and therefore is willing to cooperate to see that he will be known as accurately as possible, he may nevertheless object to the "Wowser-Holmes" approach. He may feel resentful because, in effect, he is being denigrated. Most women very much resent being made love to by the book, which instructs the husband how to read her. One woman is quoted as saying that she could tell when her husband was turning the page. Marriage manuals with their recipes for dealing with women sexually tend to encourage the "Wowser-Holmes" form of sign-reading and, in reality, denigrate the woman. The amateur parlor psychoanalyst who insists that he knows the subject better than he knows himself may be infuriating. So also may the clever, manipulative advertisers be. There is something patronizing in the reader who insists that one's behavior *means* whatever the reader says it means. And the picture of crafty, cunning researchers picking up all kinds of signs not intended for their eyes or ears can be intolerable.

We usually think of sympathetic responses as desirable. They may be consoling, but they may also be dysfunctional. "When I come home from work worried to death about my job," says one husband, "my wife worries more than I do and I have not one worrier on my hands, but two." It has been said that the late President Kennedy appreciated the fact that his wife never asked him about the problems that were troubling him; presumably for the same reason. Others consider sympathy insulting. It is, to them, too close to pity or feeling sorry for or compassion. They're tough guys; they don't want anyone's sympathy.

Most people most of the time, however, do want to communicate. They do want to get their message across. They are not reluctant communicators. Most of the enormous literature on communication, in fact, deals with the sending of messages. A vast industry rests on it; a sophisticated research establishment supports it. And even in the day-by-day relations of ordinary human beings, we are engaged, as one social psychologist picturesquely puts it, in presenting ourselves to others in such a way as to convey our message. The senders' problems center on making others get their message correctly.

The first step in communication on the sender's side is knowing the intended recipient. A great deal of knowledge can be taken for granted among similar people. Human beings are enough alike that most senders know a great deal about recipients from the start. It has been said of Trappist monks, for example, who are men vowed to silence, that they could be dropped anyplace in the world and make themselves understood by the natives. There is a basis of common species heredity large enough to supply the similarities needed for at least gross communication. Everywhere, the eye is the organ for seeing, so some gesture involving the eye will refer to seeing or to nonseeing; and so, too, the ear for hearing and the mouth for eating or drinking or talking. This is a kind of inferential communication. Children in our own society love the game of charades in which they attempt to communicate without the use of verbal language, depending on a common background to supply the meaning of their gestures. In any one society, what infants do not have in common by species heredity, they are soon supplied in the way of language—verbal, tonal, and gestural.

For protocommunication, the basic ingredient for the one who "gives" or "gives off" impressions, to use Goffman's terms, is, as it is for the reader, conditioning. Signs are associated with messages so that thereafter the sign serves to communicate the message. If the sign is a standardized one, the problem is simplified. If it is understood that if I look like this, I want you to think that I feel thus and so, that if I dress like this, I want you to think that I feel so and thus, and that if I act like this, I want you to think that I feel such and such, then communication is not a problem. And ordinarily it is not among people who have been socialized in the same milieu. The reader in these instances need never even have felt or thought as the sender is feeling or thinking. The clenched fist can be read by the pacifist and fighter alike.

If the recipient and the sender are not alike, then the sender has to learn all he can about the recipient. If Ego knows or has a great deal of information about Alter he has a good basis on which to communicate. The way he gets the knowledge or information need not be germane. He may have got it by spying, by scientific research, or by long familiarity. However he got it, he has material from which to learn how to transmit his message.

Even in verbal communication we have to know our hearer. We have to adapt our language to him. Kinsey and his associates found that they had to use different vocabularies when they interviewed different classes of men. They had to translate scientific terminology into the terminology of the gutter when interviewing their less well educated subjects. Children of immigrants report that they adapt their accents to that of their parents to reduce the distance between generations and achieve communication.

It is not always easy to adapt nonverbal communication to the receiver. We do not always know how our message will be received. My behavior may not mean the same to the recipient as it does to me. When I look at myself in the mirror, this outfit and this gesture look conventional enough; they may look outrageous, like signs of rebellion, to the ladies' sewing circle. The sender has to see himself through the eyes of the receiver, how he looks to the other, not how he looks to himself. We have to know the other person in order to know how to reach him. In fitting our words and actions to the other person we may, in Goffman's sense, be "presenting" ourselves or, in de Beauvoir's sense, acting, performing. But those who can see themselves as others see them may be freed, as Robert Burns mused long ago, from many a blunder. The man who sees himself as a woman sees him does not make the mistake Kinsey and his associates commented on of, let us say, exhibiting himself. He sees his message as one of resplendent male glory; she sees him from a different angle. For the same barriers that impede the receiving of messages operate to impede the sending of them.

If, in addition to being read, we want also to be empathized with, we have to find some experience in the other that is like ours. "Weren't you ever young?" the son hurls at his father who seems never to understand. The younger sister asks the mother empathizing with the newly engaged older daughter, "How does it feel to be in love?" The husband reminds the wife how she felt when she did not get the lead in the high-school play in order to communicate to her how he feels about not getting the promotion. "I know the meaning of all the words you use but I don't understand a thing you are saying," says the nonempathizing woman to a group of men discussing guns as a hobby and lobbying against controls. "How would you feel if there was a law controlling the sale of cosmetics?" replies one of the men. Sometimes the sender gives up. "What's the use of talking. You wouldn't understand."

The object of the sender may be more than the transmission of a message, more even than empathy or sympathy. It can be and often is manipulation or control of the receiver. It is, in fact, hard to draw a line between communication and control. We want to influence people. We may want to "engineer a convincing impression."[6]

❖❖❖❖❖

The sender of any message can judge the success of his efforts, whatever his object may be, only by the reaction or feedback he gets from the receiver. "If in terms of language, content, and emotional concomitants, the reply fits the initial statement, as a key does a keyhole, then the sender experiences pleasure and feels that he has been understood; however, if the reply does not fit, various degrees of tension are experienced."[7] In general, that is, the basic test of the degree of success one has achieved in communication is the appropriateness of the response. If it seems inappropriate to the sender he assumes he has not succeeded in reaching the other.

But the criterion of what is appropriate varies from person to person. If the message is an order, some people do not feel they have succeeded in communication until the order is obeyed. The animal trainer who, for example, can make his subjects obey his commands knows he has succeeded in communicating with them when they do what he tells them to do. Advertisers might be fired by their sponsors if people did not buy the deodorant they were ordered to buy.

If the message is a simple cognitive one, the communicator might feel he had succeeded if it could be repeated verbatim. The elementary-school teacher, for example, is grateful when her pupils can repeat the multiplication table. If the message involves an emotional response, then the appropriate response is likely to be the conventional one: pleasure and joy at news of a wedding, delight at news of a birth, and so on. If a well-bred adult does not give these conventional responses when a death or a wedding or a birth is reported, the communicator feels he has not succeeded in getting his message across. "I don't think you get what I said: John died yesterday." But it is not always that simple. What constitutes an appropriate response may vary widely among different communicators and each may impose different tests of success.

In perverse people like, for example, two-year-olds, we know we have achieved communication when a negative response is given. Appropriate or not, it is expectable. An amusing example of this appears in a tale from Finland of a man with a perverse wife. Whatever he wanted or requested, she did the opposite. So whatever he wanted, he asked for just the reverse. In this way he managed to get her to put on a lovely harvest party, complete with the best wines. But when she saw how much, despite all his protesting, he really enjoyed the feast, she realized he had played a trick on her and became furious. Later, when spring floods were high, he warned her while crossing a board across a stream; in her perversity she rejected his warning and fell into the water. He ran upstream to save her. When two fishermen asked why he was running upstream, he replied that his wife was so perverse that even in death she would surely go against the current.[8]

❖❖❖❖❖

If a communicator cannot reach the desired recipient, for whatever reason, he fails completely. Everyone would agree that there has been no communication. Or if deliberate, that there had been noncommunication. Censorship, isolating potential recipients, turning off the dial, leaving the country: these prevent any contact and hence represent the level of complete failure of communication. The deserting husband, the returned unopened letters, the hung-up telephone receiver, the sudden trip to Europe—these and scores of similar devices for heading off messages prevent contact between or among communicators and hence represent failure.

The communicator may locate the intended recipient but the intended recipient may ignore the message. He does not listen or watch. He turns off his hearing aid, he leaves the room. He, in effect, exercises censorship or isolates himself. Again, failure, as sender, if not as recipient.

At the next level there is the beginning of communication by the original communicator. The recipient hears the message and can even repeat it verbatim. The Western Union clerk reads back to the sender his cryptic ten-word message. He confirms her rendition. This might be called a rote level of communication. It is mechanical. It has surely not done anything to or for either party or to their relationship. The only thing rendered common between them is the sound of the words; they might even be nonsense syllables or in a foreign language, so far as meaning is concerned. For some purposes this is all that is needed. A very considerable share of all communication consists of such rote communication. The elementary-school teacher communicates the multiplication tables at this level or the capitals of the major nations of the world or the rules of grammar. In Edward Albee's play *The American Dream* Mommy stops every now and then to "test" Daddy, to see if he is listening by making him repeat what she has just said. A considerable part of small talk and conventional social conversation is of this nature. Anatol Rapoport urges the repetition of the communicator's message as a routine procedure in all discussions to be sure that at least this level of communication has been achieved as a first step in getting to know the other person's point of view.

Sometimes the communicator wants more than simply knowing that the other has heard his message. He might not feel he has "really" communicated if the recipient does not agree with him on how to evaluate or interpret or feel about what he has said. The distraught wife has just told the counselor of her husband's infidelity. The counselor listens, hears, repeats, and accepts but shows no revulsion. "He's been unfaithful to me!" repeats the anguished wife. "He has been unfaithful to you," says the counselor, "I see." "I don't think I've gotten through to you, Doctor. He's been *unfaithful!*" She does not feel that she has "really" communicated unless he has also accepted her feeling, her evaluation or interpretation. She wants him to be persuaded, to believe, to share, her feelings as well as the intellectual or factual contents of her message. She wants her feelings rendered "common" as well as the information. Unless he feels the same way she does, empathizes, he does not understand.

Others might demand an even higher level of communication. They add another test. The receiver must not only agree with them on their evaluation and interpretation but also on the implications. A different, more empathic counselor now *does* share the distraught wife's shock and horror at the husband's infidelity. He really feels bad about it. But she is not satisfied with even this level of communication because he does not share her interpretation of the implications. "He doesn't love me anymore!" The counselor shakes his head. "That doesn't follow. I think from what you say that he loves you very much." "You don't understand! He has been unfaithful. What else could it mean than that he doesn't love me anymore?" The counselor continues to challenge this implication of the husband's behavior; he is well aware from his own experience and observation that it is quite possible for a man to engage in infidelity but still love his wife very deeply. "I don't seem to be able to get through to you," repeats the disconsolate wife helplessly; she knows that if she were guilty of infidelity, that fact alone would mean, *ipso facto*, that she did not love her husband anymore. She infers his feelings from her own; she reads herself in his behavior. So does the counselor. But with quite different results.

A still higher level of communication may be demanded. A different counselor now accepts the message, agrees with the wife's evaluation and interpretation and with the implications she draws; but he does not agree with her reaction, namely that she must get a divorce. Again she argues that he does not understand, she has not got through to him; he does not share the logic of her reaction. If he really understood he would see that she could not go on living with her husband.

Only when the recipient has listened, heard, accepted, agreed on evaluation and interpretation, agreed on implications, and agreed on a course of action, do some people believe that communication has occurred. Words, evaluation, interpretation, implications, and reaction must all be shared before these communicators feel they have succeeded. (One husband adds another criterion imposed by his wife before he passes the test of communication: he has to add his own positive support to his wife's message and even go her one further.)

Before we criticize the wife for demanding so much, we might examine her criteria in greater detail. Suppose the Western Union message we mentioned above gives detailed instructions for the murder of a specific person. Is simple reproduction by the clerk enough as a test now? Has the customer communicated with her? If she does nothing and the police come finally to question her, can she plead that she did not understand the message; all she did was record it. If she can so plead, has communication taken place? Like the distraught wife, can the police accept the fact that communication had not taken place? And what of the Nazi functionary who received the ghastly messages dealing with transportation to the extermination camps? He could repeat and execute the orders conveyed by the messages. Did he understand the messages? What was an appropriate response here? Suppose we did not share with the sender the evaluation, interpretation, implication, and reaction? (The world still says it cannot understand those orders.)

The school of thought that holds conflict to be a result of lack of communication demands a high level of communication. One is reminded of the story told about the prisoner in a French court who pleaded extenuating circumstances. "I had to eat," said he. To which the judge replied coldly, "I don't see the necessity."

Petruchio in Shakespeare's *Taming of the Shrew* offers an amusing illustration of the several tests of communication. Of the sun, he says: "I say it is the moon." And, worn out and hungry, Katharina now repeats the absurd statement: "I know it is the moon." Then, as a further test, he says: "Nay, then you lie: it is the blessed sun. . . ." A bit further along he carries the test one more step: they meet an elderly man; Petruchio addresses him as "gentle mistress" and orders Katharina to embrace him. She does. Petruchio rebukes her; she accepts the rebuke and apologizes to the old man. . . . Of course the real message Petruchio is conveying has little to do with sun, moon, or the sex of the ancient stranger. It is simply: "I'm boss." And this is precisely the message Katharina receives, as she proves in the last act.

CHAPTER FIVE

Strangers in the Night, And in the Daytime, Too

It is remarkable that human communication works at all, for so much seems to be against it.

—Colin Cherry, *On Human Communication*

Love is so different with us men.

—Robert Browning, "In a Year"

It is because we do not put the communication aspect of sex on a more businesslike footing that we cause each other and ourselves needless anxiety.

—John Wilson, *Logic and Sexual Morality*

How does one go about putting the communication aspect of sex on a more businesslike footing? Well, for one thing, Wilson says, we must improve the conventions of communication, behavioral as well as verbal. "Neither the sex war, nor any of our other similes, would exist if there were proper communication." We have to standardize the meaning of all kinds of behavior. And we need a vastly extended vocabulary to refer to the almost infinite variety of feelings which we now have to express by the one word *love*. "The minor tragedies which are caused by the misunderstandings that arise when a man and a woman, for instance, both say 'I love you' would alone justify our working towards greater clarity."[1] An improved language would not only facilitate communication but also encourage it. But improving the language with which to communicate would not, says Wilson, be enough by itself. We have to provide the right setting also.

> . . . in the sex war there are few fruitful contexts of communication. . . . Women have their own coteries, and men theirs. . . . The reason why a man rarely knows what goes on in the mind of a woman is not solely that women are mysterious and puzzling creatures nor solely that the woman herself does not know: it is that he does not always ask, and she certainly hardly ever tells him. Men and women meet in different contexts: as potential lovers, or potential enemies; but they rarely meet in a context designed primarily for the exchange of information about each other.[2]

We noted above that neither culture, race, age, nor even sex was a necessary obstacle to protocommunication, that is, communication of the "Wowser-Holmes" type. Since sign-reading or protocommunication does not assume any necessary similarity between or among communicators, the absence of similarity does not preclude communication. Thus, animals and human beings can learn to engage in successful sign-reading, even mutual sign-reading, within limits. The animal cannot read abstract signs such as "conformity to norms" or "caring enough to send the very best." And no one can receive or send messages for which he has no equipment. But within these limits, cultural, racial, age-related, even sex differences need not impede protocommunication. Wilson's suggestions about improving the conventions of communication by extending and standardizing them would surely help here.

It is in shared-experience communication, involving inference, empathy, or sympathy, that differences in culture, race, age, and sex make themselves felt. It is understanding more than knowledge which is hard to achieve across these barriers. It is in this kind of communication that the differences between the sexes make themselves felt. It is here that Wilson's proposal for "imaginative instruction" and "enlargement of awareness" is relevant.

◇◇◇◇◇

Differences in culture, race, and age impose difficulties to shared-experience communication which are easy to see. Certain acts, including sounds, have certain meanings because they have been conventionalized to have these meanings. Quite different sounds (*chien, dog*) may have the same meaning in different cultures—or the same sounds, different meanings (*oui, we*). It is not quite so easy to see that certain actions also have certain meanings because the culture assigns them such meanings. "In addition to what we say with our verbal language we are constantly communicating our real feelings in our silent language—the sign language of behavior. Sometimes this is correctly interpreted by other nationalities, but more often it is not. Difficulties in intercultural communication are seldom seen for what they are."[3] If, for example, we see someone crying we think what it would mean in our own culture. It would be a sign that he was unhappy about something or other. Conversely, if we see someone laughing, we take this as a sign that he is amused, as it would be in our culture. For the most part, this works fairly well among peoples who are like us. But we do not understand people of a culture whose bodies have been conditioned differently from ours, who laugh when we would not, or vice versa. If we laughed at suffering—as people often have to do when suffering is omnipresent and unavoidable—it would be a sign that we were callous and heartless. If a traditional Chinese laughed at a funeral it would mean something else again. If a native American beats his wife, we take this to be a sign that he does not love her; yet social workers used to report of the immigrant generation in some ethnic groups that women complained their husbands no longer loved them because "he never beats me anymore the way he used to." This was taken as a sign of indifference.

Even within different subcultures of our own, behavior may be differently interpreted. The new boy in the community is abashed to learn that because he has taken Mary out three times, both she and the town take this to be a sign that he is seriously courting her; his behavior has no such significance in the town he came from. On one campus, exchanging Greek-letter pins is a sign that the relationship is almost as serious as an official engagement; on another, that they are just going steady, if even that.

Communication between the races in the United States has been until recently rendered all but impossible, especially in the area of sex, by generations of exploitation and fear. If a Negro man even looked at a white woman in the traditional South, it was taken as a sign that he coveted her. The elaborate codes of interracial behavior have been interpreted as signs of the white man's fear of the Negro's sexuality.

Age may also block communication. It comes as a surprise—and it is often the first hint that one is getting along in years—that casual references to the past bring only vacant stares from young listeners. The war—no matter which one—that was such a powerfully shared experience with one's own generation, is only a paragraph or page in a history book to the next generation. They may be able to read you when you talk to them about it, but they do not share it with you. Age also influences the interpretation of signs. The teen-ager, watching the middle-aged couple silently eating their dinner at a nearby table in the restaurant, exclaims at this clear sign of the absence of love: they don't even talk to one another anymore. The parents, viewing the same behavior, see the silence as an example of complete mutual understanding; they don't *have* to talk to be in communication with one another. Adults sometimes comment on how seriously they misinterpreted the behavior of their own parents when they were children. . . .

But more especially, it is sex differences that make a difference in shared-experience forms of communication.

"Why can girls always stop necking whenever they feel like it?" a tenth-grade boy wants to know. "Why is it so much harder for a boy to stop?" "Why do girls dress sexily and then freeze up on you?"[4] These are among the kinds of things that puzzle boys. We would do well to answer the boy's questions. Unless we do, many like him will grow up to be men who, incapable of seeing women as anything but copies of themselves, will view them as engaged in a massive conspiracy to use their sexuality to exploit men as this hostile, paranoid rake did:

. . . women depend upon men not only in the struggle for survival but . . . they also need them for the satisfaction of their own sexual instinct, which, for strategic reasons, they're in the habit of denying. . . . Deny it as they might, women simply aren't the hapless victims of pursuit by bestial males. Rather, they fortunately have sexual cravings as strong as those of men. Though men may think they're suffering alone when they're itching with a yen for possession of a passionate female, the women they're chasing may have a craving for possession of a man which they're obscuring by their shrewish attitude. The Battle of the Sexes is more a war of nerves to determine who can hold out longest and exact the price of surrender than a one-sided pursuit. The only reason that it is usually portrayed in an erroneous light is that this war of attrition is customarily decided in favor of the female; and so, she has the moral triumph of yielding with pleasure to an embrace which she herself would have to plead for, were it not for the pursuing male. . . . Women [have] managed to depict themselves as the helpless victims of male cupidity . . . [and] men [have been] taken in by her fiction.[5]

Or they will grow up to resemble the men who wrote Victorian erotic and pornographic literature, projecting in it their male sexual fantasies onto the female response, believing orgasm in women to be identical to theirs, including ejaculation, taking it for granted that women were ready at all times for sexual activity, and assuming the sexuality of women to be as impetuous as their own, if not more so.[6] Or they may become men who, like Herodotus, are convinced that no woman is ever abducted if she does not wish to be.[7] Or, in their unenlightened state, they will grow up to be like the men who are convinced that the nightclub stripper or the Playboy bunny is as agog as they are. They will be among the men who never understand women and who are therefore most vulnerable to exploitation by them. These men can be "taken in" by their own fictions as well as by women's.

Kinsey and his associates have supplied us with answers to the boy's questions, not only about differences between the collectivities, but also about differences within the collectivities. First, with respect to something as relatively simple as frequency of outlet. Kinsey and his associates made a big point of the fact that people tend to project their own sexuality on others and in so doing misinterpret and misunderstand them. The person with little sexual interest finds those with more to be perverted; those with much, find those with less unnaturally repressed or inhibited. We assume a sexuality in others like our own, as we assume sensory experience in others to be like ours. The person who finds chastity possible if not easy, assumes that everyone can, and if he does not, there is a defect of character somewhere. Almost all discussions of sex are flawed by the inability of differently endowed people of either sex to understand the other, even those of the same sex. The "highly sexed" individual who finds himself in a constant state of stimulability finds no help from the clergyman who, in his estimation, doesn't understand, read, empathize.

Some measure of the chasm that acts as a barrier to communication among men in this area is available from the Kinsey data. The total variation among men over a lifetime in number of outlets was of the order of 45,000 to one, a range greater than that of most individual differences. And these are differences that may occur between men living in the same neighborhood, engaging in the same kind of work, and belonging to the same clubs and who, for the most part, might be expected to have a firm basis of shared experience to facilitate communication. But despite all their similarities, differences in sexuality can make it almost impossible to understand—empathize with—one another in this area. Differences in degree of sexual interest and drive may constitute a major barrier.

The possibility of any individual engaging in sexual activity at a rate that is remarkably different from one's own, is one of the most difficult things for even professionally trained persons to understand. Meetings of educators who are discussing sex instruction and policies to be followed . . . may bring out extreme differences of opinion. . . . No other subject will start such open dissension in a group, and it is difficult for an observer to comprehend how objective reasoning can lead to such different conclusions among intelligent men and women. . . . On both sides of the argument, the extreme individuals may be totally unaware of the possibility of others in the group having histories that are so remote from their own.[8]

The same inability to understand others is also reported among women. Variation in sexual responsiveness among women is greater even than among men, and the ability of women to understand one another is even less than that among men. The White Maiden, that is, "the female who goes through life or for any long period of years with little or no experience in orgasm, finds it very difficult to comprehend the female who is capable of several orgasms every time she has sexual contact, and who may, on occasion, have a score or more orgasms in an hour.[9] Conversely, the Dark Lady may be as much at a loss as any male to understand the White Maiden.

If differences in sexuality make understanding so difficult within each sex, they make the barriers even more nearly insurmountable between the sexes. If a highly responsive woman cannot understand an unresponsive woman, even a normal man may find even normal women hard to understand. And when there is a selective factor involved in a man's contact with the other sex, understanding is doubly difficult. Kinsey and his associates correctly predicted the attitude of the hostile, paranoid rake quoted above on the great female conspiracy:

We may predict that the persons who will be most often incapable of accepting our description of American females will be some of the promiscuous males who have had the largest amount of sexual contact with females. Most of these males do not realize that it is only a select group of females, and usually the more responsive females, who will accept premarital or extra-marital relationships. Some of these males will find it difficult to believe that the incidences of extra-marital coitus are as low as our data indicate; some of them will not easily be persuaded that there is such a percentage of females who fail to reach orgasm in their coitus; some of them will find it difficult to believe that there is such a large proportion of the female population which is not aroused in anticipation of a sexual relationship, and which is not dependent upon having a regular sexual outlet. They will fail to take into account the large number of females who never make socio-sexual contacts, and never become involved in the sort of non-marital relationships from which these males have acquired most of their information about females.[10]

The White Maiden is a myth to these men and they enjoy destroying her image.

❖❖❖❖❖

We noted that men are more easily aroused than women by a wide variety of stimuli. Their organ is vulnerable to a constant bombardment. Kinsey and his associates reported that "the male more often shares, vicariously the sexual experiences of other persons, he more frequently responds sympathetically when he observes other individuals engage in sexual activities . . . and he may react to a great variety of objects which have been associated with his sexual activities. The data indicate that in all of these respects, fewer of the females have their sexual behavior affected by such psychologic factors."[11] The young man cannot therefore infer that women respond as he does to, let us say, a nude body, a risqué story, or a dozen other kinds of stimuli which trigger an immediate response in him. Women can learn to read the signs of arousal in men but at best and only with great effort can share the constant and insistent and urgent message running through the body of the young man. A reasonable conclusion from the data of Kinsey and his associates would be that women tend to become more versed than men in sign-reading, partly because the male signs are more obvious and clear-cut and therefore easier to read and partly because, as a general principle, it is to a dependent's advantage to be able to read signs well. But because women seem to be more protected than men from sexual stimulation, their skills in sexual empathy might be less highly developed.

The errors in social perception, in understanding, in communication, may have practical consequences when either sex acts on the basis of its own experience, assuming similarity on the part of the other. Again Kinsey and his associates:

It is difficult for most males to comprehend that females are not aroused by seeing male genitalia. Some males never come to comprehend this. Many a male is greatly disappointed when his wife fails to react to such a display, and concludes that she is no longer in love with him. On the contrary, many females feel that their husbands are vulgar, or perverted, or mentally disturbed, because they want to display their genitalia. We have seen difficulties develop in marital histories because of this failure of females to understand male psychology, and of males to understand female psychology. Divorces had grown out of some of these misunderstandings.

The male who exposes himself in a public place similarly secures erotic satisfaction primarily because he believes that the females who observe him are going to be aroused as he would be at seeing a genital exhibition.[12]

Female exhibition of the body is of a quite different order; it is used not for erotic stimulation of the woman herself in anticipation of male reaction, but rather coolly, manipulatively, knowingly, *coldly*, as an animal trainer might manipulate his animals:

> There are some females who will show their genitalia to the male partner because they intellectually realize that this may mean something to him. But only an occasional female among those who exhibit receives any erotic arousal from this anticipation of the male's responses. There are no cases in our sample, and practically none in the literature, of females publicly exhibiting their genitalia because they derived erotic satisfaction from such an exhibition.
>
> Stage, night club, burlesque and other commercial exhibitions of female nudity almost never, as far as our sample indicates, provide erotic stimulation for the exhibiting females. Our specific data provide no physiological evidence of arousal among the females staging such exhibitions, although some of them may acquire considerable facility in making body movements which are taken by many of the males in the audience to indicate that the exhibiting females are tremendously aroused. Most of the females in our histories who had been involved in such stage exhibitions, were highly disdainful of males who could so easily be misled into believing that there was any real eroticism in such a performance.[13]

One is reminded of the male television interviewer with a hutch of Playboy bunnies, whose own blatantly lascivious interest in them (they were in their uniforms) and their work contrasted sharply with their major interest, which was in the amount of money they made. They were not oblivious to the effect on the customers of the provocative displays; but they took it in their stride. It was not nearly so important to them as the amount of money it produced. As almost any experienced man knows, even the whitest Maiden can make a monkey out of a credulous male if she learns the language; she gets an enormous amount of help from him, and from his insistence on reading himself in her.

Despite the inability of men to understand the White Maiden, because of selective associations with Dark Ladies or whatever reason, they tend to think that they understand everything about sex and, in fact, that they own the subject, that their knowledge is the only authentic knowledge, and that if women do not accept their view, they are ignorant and naïve. Actually, a nun in her cloister with access to a good library can *know* more about the subject than even the most experienced street-corner boy who reads little beyond the pornography available under the counter, or even than the college boy who depends on regular reading of *Playboy* for his information. Even a frigid prostitute who reads only customers' signs could know more about male sexuality than any of the men she learned it from. The person who depends exclusively on his own experience knows only his own sexuality.

The disparity between the sexes which gives the White Maiden such a bargaining advantage vis-à-vis men is widely resented. Male hatred for the White Maiden is deep and widespread. Even Kinsey and his associates who were most insistent on an impartial, nonjudgmental approach to sexuality in all its forms, could not disguise their hostility to abstemious women. Bestiality, homosexuality, masturbation—nothing fazed them; they could take them in stride. But the White Maiden was something else again.

The existence of such a large group of females who are not having any sexual outlet poses a problem of some social importance. . . .These females . . . were limited in their understanding of the nature of sexual responses and orgasm. . . . They were particularly incapable of understanding the rates of response . . . for the males in the population. When such . . . females attempt to direct the behavior of other persons, they may do considerable damage. . . . Some of them had been responsible for some of the more extreme sex laws which state legislatures had passed. . . . Parents and particularly the males in the population might debate the wisdom of making such women responsible for the guidance of youth.[14]

By way of contrast, most of the unmarried females "were not living . . . blank or sexually frustrated lives" and therefore they were all right, for they "did understand the significance of sex."[15] Little wonder that the cult of orgasm among women achieved such wide adherence. Who wants to be considered a public menace?

The signs and signals men and women send and receive are, then, filtered through different apparatuses; they may come through in a form different from that in which they were fed in. Lack of sexual responsiveness in a young wife may mean—be a sign—only that she does not need orgasmic release as often as does her young husband. If he went so long without active genital desire for her it would mean—be a sign—that he no longer loved her or that he was getting satisfaction with another woman. He tends, therefore, to interpret her behavior in terms of what it would mean if he were the one involved.

Sexually based social differences between the sexes may also inhibit communication. In the past (the situation may be changing now), women could not be casual about sexual relations. If a woman, therefore, engaged in extramarital sexual relations, this fact was a sign that the man meant something to her, she was involved, she loved him. It was not a casual affair, a mere incident. She therefore interpreted the behavior of men in the same terms. If a man had sexual relations with another woman, this fact was a sign to her that the relationship must be meaningful to him, he loved the woman, there was a genuine bond involved. Otherwise he would not have engaged in sexual relations with her. That was what such behavior would mean if she engaged in it. She could not understand that actually the contact might really be casual, unimportant to him, insignificant, trivial. "It didn't mean a thing," he might protest in all sincerity. To no avail. His wife could interpret his behavior in terms only of what it would mean if she had engaged in it. (One always wonders about the other woman; was the relation only casual to her, too?)

When the tables are turned and the wife is the one who has the extramarital relations, the husband may interpret her behavior as a sign of either a casual affair or a serious involvement; both are possible to him—though usually intolerable.

If a husband forgets an important family anniversary—birthday or wedding day—it might be a sign of nothing at all; he was simply preoccupied. But the wife, knowing that she would forget such an important thing only if she no longer really cared, projects her own meaning into his lapse and interprets it as a sign that he no longer cares. Or if in a burst of tenderness, he buys a bunch of flowers to take home to his wife on no particular anniversary, she might interpret this in terms of what it would mean if *she* did it, as an apology for—and hence a sign of—some wrong he has done her.

❖❖❖❖❖

So far the discussion has been about interpersonal communication between the sexes. One by one men look for signs in the bodies and in the behavior, including verbal behavior, of women for cues of what they think or feel; and women, men, also. But there is another level of communication between the sexes, communication between men and women not individually but as collectivities, as entities. Some of the most important communication between them is not individual, interpersonal; it is at this collective level. Such communication may take several forms, and the message may vary from time to time. By a not-too-far-fetched analogy, societal norms may be viewed as a fundamental form of communication between the collectivities, as conveying to each sex what the other sex thinks or feels about it. Laws, customs, mores, conventions, constitute signs of the way the relations between the sexes are conceived. "You are women and therefore inferior to men" the laws of one age insist. From this the message may continue either as "Men are therefore obliged to protect and take care of you" or "Men are therefore entitled to your services and favors without return." Similar messages are embodied in the folkways, in the mores, in the conventions. They appear in folk tradition. The norms of another age may constitute a clear message that men are depraved animals who will always take advantage of women. The conventions of one age may reflect a "mentality" favorable to women, of another, one unfavorable to them.

One anthropologist sees all culture as, in effect, "a silent language," with complex "primary message systems" delineating its class and group structure, including its attitude toward bisexuality.[16] Not only cultural norms but also the arts serve as media of communication between the sexes. The literature of one age tells women they are evil temptresses; of another, that they are tender, ministering angels. A pamphlet focuses the message and makes it more direct. Men and women authors hurl tracts or articles or research reports at one another. "You are denying us our rights!" "Aw, pipe down!" Sometimes it is the public address rather than the written word which serves as the vehicle of communication.

It was against implicit restrictions on communication that Hawthorne's Zenobia—a Dark Lady—protested so passionately:

It is my belief—yes, and my prophecy . . .—that, when my sex shall achieve its rights, there will be ten eloquent women where there is now one eloquent man. Thus far, no woman in the world has ever once spoken out her whole heart and her whole mind. The mistrust and disapproval of the vast bulk of society throttles us, as with two gigantic hands at our throats! We mumble a few weak words, and leave a thousand better ones unsaid. You let us write a little, it is true, on a limited range of subjects. But the pen is not for woman. Her power is too natural and immediate. It is with the living voice alone that she can compel the world to recognize the light of her intellect and the depth of her heart.[17]

Since many women agree with Zenobia that most forms of communication tend to favor men, they have been known to resort to direct action to communicate their message. If there is no institutionalized way to communicate, people find another, non-institutionalized way. It may involve words also, but the essential power resides in the act. The women who went on a sexual strike against their husbands under the leadership of Lysistrata were using direct action to convey their message: Stop the war. The cry of "No taxation without representation" of the North American colonists was adumbrated centuries ago by Roman women who reacted against an edict of the Second Triumvirate, which appropriated money from fourteen hundred of the richest women in Rome to finance the war with Brutus and Cassius, by resorting to direct action. They went to the forum where their spokesman, Hortensia, herself the daughter of a great lawyer, said among other things: "Why should we pay taxes when we have no part in the honours, the commands, the statecraft for which you contend?"[18]

Women used direct action also to have repealed the so-called Oppian Law which, as a war measure during the Punic War, limited their clothing and other expenditures. It said that "no woman should possess more than half an ounce of gold, or wear a garment of various colours, or ride in a carriage drawn by horses, in a city, or any town, or any place nearer thereto than one mile; except on occasion of some public religious solemnity."[19] The women were not going to take that. Harking back to the good old days when women had modesty and dignity and restricted their communication with men to their own husbands, the horrified Cato reproached them.

It was not without painful emotions of shame, that I, just now, made my way into the forum through the midst of a band of women. Had I not been restrained by respect for the modesty and dignity of some individuals among them, rather than of the whole number, and been unwilling that they should be seen rebuked by a consul, I should have said to them, "What sort of practice is this, of running out into public, besetting the streets, and addressing other women's husbands? Could not each have made the same request to her husband at home? Are your blandishments more seducing in public than in private; and with other women's husbands, than with your own?"[20]

The twentieth-century suffragettes who chained themselves to their posts, who paraded with banners, who went on hunger strikes, were shouting that they did not accept the message embedded in our institutions that they were politically inferior to men.

The communication is not always so direct and straight-forward. At the present time we try to decode messages that take the form of symptoms, especially of psychosomatic symptoms. What, for example, are men and women trying to say with their illnesses? What accounts for the reversal of sex incidence of diabetes and peptic ulcer since the nineteenth century? Does the state of the relationships between the sexes today literally make them sick? What does the increasingly open, even defiant, practice of homosexuality *mean* about the relations of men and women? What does the increasing discussion of male impotence tell us about their relations with women? What do women want? Freud asked. If even he felt stumped, it is not surprising that many lesser men and women are puzzled too. At any rate, the messages are by no means always clear.

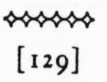

The wise man, we are told, is the man who knows when he knows not; the fool knows not when he knows not. Both the *What*-difference? and the Long-live-the-difference! schools may harbor those who know not when they know not.

"Here's this smart little cookie," says one graduate student, "who is writing a doctor's dissertation and quoting in seminar obscene expressions from her questionnaires that she doesn't even understand. It's embarrassing for the group. Not the quotations, but her not knowing what they mean." And another woman who learned the hard way:

> I had always assumed that I was on the inside of the gang in our office. Maybe not exactly one of the boys, but at least one of the bunch on our floor. At lunch one day, though, the men began to horse around. I was the only woman present and they seemed to have forgotten me. I saw from the outside the world they shared and which excluded me, as though I just wasn't there. It wasn't that they went out of their way to ignore me or to keep me out. I just wasn't "in." It was like watching while people tell "in" stories to one another. Or talked in a language I didn't understand.

And men sometimes playfully admit the same outsideness in the world of women. For there are ingroups and outsiders everywhere.

There are many ways of being an outsider. The new boy in the neighborhood, the Negro boy at the playground, the poor boy at the boarding school. Georg Simmel, the German sociologist, analyzed in more formal style the position of the stranger and what being in such a position did to the occupants. R. E. Park introduced the concept of the marginal man who was both inside and outside, a stranger who was not a stranger, a member who was not a member. Students of alienation, so called, have stretched that term to cover even this kind of nonbelonging, this *in* but not *of* state of being.

In these kinds of outsideness, the outsider knows that he is not in. Little has been said about the outsider who, like the "smart little cookie," does not know that he is not in. The dawning recognition by the adolescent that he has been an outsider in the adult world is a favorite topic of novelists. Children come in time to catch the sex cues of the adult world and presently wonder where they have been all their lives. The slow-maturing girl notes that there is now something more than meets the eye between her friend Mary and the boy down the street. There is some kind of communication going on between them which shuts her out. Soon enough the new language becomes understood by all the youngsters and gets translated on the walls everywhere: "John loves Mary." Now they are all members of the "adult" club. Or think they are.

But sometimes such recognition of outsideness does not take place. An eminent Jewish scholar has described the status and response of Jews in nineteenth-century Germany after the Emancipation. They embraced the culture of Germany with eager enthusiasm. They loved it as much as anyone born into it, if not more. They had no awareness of difference between themselves and others; they did not feel like outsiders.[21] Their descendants in the twentieth century were dumbfounded to find themselves viewed as such. Integrated Negroes have expressed the same surprise to learn that they are still viewed as outsiders after years of close association with the white world.

Men are often too gallant, too embarrassed, or too unskilled to let a woman know how *outré* she is in their world. Or she is incapable of reading the signs. She does not see how different she is; she does not feel strange, marginal, or alienated. She thinks she is in and may even brag about it. Maintaining her illusion may be rough on the men.

Neither the *What*-difference? nor the Long-live-the-difference! school is justified in claiming to understand what, if any, the differences between the collectivities in sexuality are. All we really understand is our own sexuality, how things look to us, with our own bodily equipment. The woman who claims that women have the same sexuality as men assumes that she understands the sexuality of men. The man who claims that the sexuality of women is different from that of men also assumes that he understands the sexuality of women. It is possible that both can be so dogmatic because they know not when they know not.

Everyone who puts his mind to it can get a sign-reading knowledge of the other sex. But that is not the same as understanding, as sharing their experiences.

There is no union so close and indissoluble as that possible between an individual man and an individual woman. They can become as one flesh, to use the insightful biblical way of saying it. Still, despite this unparalleled intimacy between individuals, taken as a whole, as collectivities rather than as individuals, men in a fundamental way are strangers to women and women to men.

PART THREE

THE MESSAGES

CHAPTER SIX

Talk, Conversation,
Listening, Silence

❖❖❖❖❖

A word spoken in due season, how good it is!

—Proverbs 15:23

Let your women keep silence in the churches: for it is not permitted unto them to speak; but they are commanded to be under obedience, as also saith the law. And if they will learn any thing, let them ask their husbands at home: for it is a shame for women to speak in the church.

—I Corinthians 14:34–35

A conversation is one of the commonest phenomena we encounter, yet it is one that raises very great scientific problems, many still unsolved. It is so often our commonest experiences, which we take for granted, that are most elusive of explanation and description.

—Colin Cherry, *On Human Communication*

These feminine institutions of civility were, for a long time, the greatest single influence in developing civilized social behavior.

—Mary Beard, *Woman as Force in History*

This degeneracy of conversation . . . hath been owing, among other causes, to the custom arisen, for some time past, of excluding women from any share in our society, further than in parties at play, or dancing, or in the pursuit of amour.

—Jonathan Swift, *Hints toward an Essay on Conversation*

❖❖❖❖❖

"To converse" originally meant, as we have noted in Chapter Three, to have sexual rather than social intercourse; but at least since 1615 it has had its current meaning of talk with. Talk means to discourse, speak of, discuss; it is a more or less formal or public oral interchange of views, opinions, or propositions; it has to do with conveying or exchanging ideas, information.[1] Talk is a more comprehensive term than converse. It can mean the same thing, but it can mean either more or less also. "We had talk enough," said Samuel Johnson, "but no conversation."[2] Talk can mean to rebuke, to scold, to reprimand. Thus when John says, "Mary, I'd like to talk to you," she has occasion to feel concern. What could it be?—the fender?—Billy's report card? Or if Henry says to Helen, "Let's talk about it first, before you go ahead," Helen knows that serious decisions are in the offing, probably a veto of what she planned to do. The same is not true of conversation.

Talk can be a medium for seduction by either sex or the other or, conversely, a way to deter it. But it is a great deal more than that. In fact, only a relatively small proportion of talk between or among the sexes is devoted to courting. Talk is used in many ways, performs many functions. A British social scientist of the nineteenth century, Walter Bagehot, taught us a long time ago that discussion was indispensable in the formation of public opinion.[3] "Word of mouth" has been widely researched in recent years and its contribution unequivocally documented in voting behavior and consumer choices. In written form, words are said to be mightier than the sword. Some talk is just for fun: jokes, puns, the play on words, conundrums, word games, wit, tall tales, repartee. Some talk is ritualistic, "small." Some talk is for self-expression; some for manipulation or control of others. Some is for therapy. Some for problem-solving. Some to convey information or emotion, some to conceal information or emotion.

❖❖❖❖❖

A great deal of what we know about talk in small face-to-face groups comes from research based on so-called task-oriented groups, that is, on small groups given a task to perform that requires them to talk a good deal. Especially useful is the distinction this research has highlighted between instrumental and expressive talk which such groups develop, the first having to do with orientation, facts, and information, and the second with feelings, positive or negative.[4]

One of the major functions of positive expressive talk is to raise the status of the other, to give help, to reward; in ordinary human relations, it performs the stroking function. As infants need physical caressing or stroking in order to live and grow, even to survive, so also do adults need emotional or psychological stroking or caressing to remain normal. Any one of us can waste away and die, like the infant from marasmus, without such stroking. Much of this stroking is done by way of signs and gestures or thoughtful acts, like reassuring smiles and silent applause, but much of it is done also by talking and by appreciative listening. Asking for clarification, for opinion, for suggestions, may also represent a kind of stroking.

Traditionally the cultural norms for femininity and womanliness have prescribed appreciatively expressive talk or stroking for women; they were to be generous in their strokes. They were to raise the status of the other, relieve tension, agree, concur, comply, understand, accept. Such behavior corresponds to the nurturance which psychologists find characteristic of women. In one study of fifty-six societies around the world, the expressive role was assigned to women in forty-six.[5] Simulated jury deliberations in the laboratory show the same kind of sex-role differentiation as families, that is, males take over the instrumental role and women, the emotional-expressive. "Men *pro-act*, that is, they initiate relatively long bursts of acts directed at the solution of the task problem, and women tend more to *react* to the contributions of others."[6] Almost twice as large a proportion of the women's talk as of the men's consisted of agreeing, concurring, complying, understanding, and passively accepting. Less than half as much of the women's talk as of the men's showed antagonism or deflated others' status. And although the men constituted only about two-thirds of the juries studied, they contributed almost four-fifths of the talk.

Sometimes women achieve stroking success by putting themselves in a subordinate position vis-à-vis their conversational partners. These women ask for suggestions or directions or opinions or expressions of feelings; they know how to "draw men out." Women who are successful in this are viewed as brilliant talkers. Even Madame de Staël, perhaps the best talker ever, used this method. "Her most remarkable talent," her biographer tells us, "consisted not so much in communicating her own ideas as in inspiring and helping others to formulate theirs. It was in this, rather than in her inspired flights, that her power resided, and she used it to its fullest extent."[7] This might be called aggressive listening.

The assignment of the expressive role to women is strongly reminiscent of the female cichlid's behavior. She, too, had to be appeasing; she, too, had to raise the male's status, comply, passively accept. She, too, performs a stroking function, if only by showing subservience. Like her, the human female also protects the male by conceding dominance even in nonsexual, merely talking, relationships.

That the relatively low rate of antagonism and status-deflation of others by women in the studies reported above was due to the cichlid-effect rather than to any intrinsic sex difference is evidenced by the fact that when one-sex groups of men were compared with one-sex groups of women, there was more disagreement interaction in the groups of women than in the groups of men.[8] Corroboration of this interpretation is available from another set of laboratory studies, this time of interaction in "games" rather than in task-oriented groups. These studies report that, overall, men tend to cooperate more than women, but that when the sexes "play" against one another, this sex difference disappears because "women are 'pulled up' when playing against men, that is, they play more cooperatively against men than against women. Men, on the contrary, are 'pulled down' when playing against women as compared with their performance against players of their own sex." These researchers find that initial differences do not explain these results. "We must look for the roots of the difference in the interaction effect."[9] Parenthetically, it may be noted that another set of studies, this time of children seven to eleven years of age, found that in same-sex groups older girls were less collaborative than younger ones but that the reverse was true for the boys,[10] suggesting, though by no means establishing, the fact that experience rather than intrinsic sex differences was involved.

To say that stroking has been assigned to women does not mean, of course, that it is their exclusive prerogative. Men engage in it also, among themselves and vis-à-vis women as well. Many men perform the expressive role as part of their professional work as psychiatrists, general practitioners, or counselors, and some women perform the instrumental role. Contrariwise, some men eschew the instrumental role as some women do the emotional-expressive. There is no evidence that either men or women are biologically better equipped to perform either role. Nor is either role in any way superior to the other. The instrumental role has to do with getting on with the job; it involves keeping the group at work; it means applying the whip if necessary. It tends, therefore, to engender stress in the members. The expressive role, contrariwise, tends to allay stress by emphasizing solidarity, by allaying anxiety, and by "accentuating the positive." There has to be just the right balance or tension between them, enough push in the direction of getting the job done, the task accomplished (even at the expense of creating stress), but also enough support to keep the stress from becoming disruptive.

❖❖❖❖❖

Task-oriented groups also show negative forms of expressive interaction. Some of these, such as disagreeing, rejecting, showing antagonism, and deflating the other's status, may be viewed as "striking" rather than as stroking in nature. Instead of stroking one another the participants now rain blows on one another. The words are barbed or cutting or steely.

In ordinary talk there may be a very fine line between stroking and striking. Instead of responding to a pleasant remark with appropriate recognition, Alter replies in a manner that has an unpleasant or negative effect. Thus, for example, although theoretically one kind of expressive behavior—that which agrees, shows acceptance, understands, concurs—is an emotionally positive type of reaction and hence, in a literal sense, a form of stroking, it actually can have nonstroking or antistroking effects. Ego tosses a conversational gambit; Alter catches it and it disappears. Thus, Ego: "Nice weather we're having." Alter: "Lovely." Ego: "Delightful party." Alter: "Yes, isn't it?" Ego: "Terrible news from Erewhon." Alter: "Yes, indeed it is." Technically Alter is agreeing, showing acceptance, understanding, concurring; but he is clearly not thereby stroking Ego. And since Ego has to supply all the balls and they all vanish (unless there is an infinite supply of them), he, or she, leaves at the first chance. For Alter is giving only a ritualistic stroke, hardly palpable. He (she) is saying, in effect, "I can't escape you; I'll give you the strokes demanded by good manners, but not a bit more. I hope you take the hint."

Good talk demands that listeners supply a large part of the speaker's message. They know what each other means without elaborate presentation, quite independently of the enormous load carried by tone, facial expression, and gestures. If the listener refuses to supply his share, the interchange becomes aborted. It is a once-over-lightly stroke with the impact of a light blow. Sometimes Alter is dumb; sometimes timid; sometimes taciturn; sometimes bashful; sometimes bored. But it is still true, as it was almost a hundred years ago, that it is considered rude to make the other person bear the entire burden in conversation.[11] And no concessions are made to sex. "An American lady does not expect to have conversation made to her. It is just as much her duty or pleasure to lead it as the man's is, and more often than not she takes the burden from him, darting along with a gay vivacity which puts to shame his slower wits."[12]

Other equivocal forms of stroking that turn into striking are the so-called *tangential*, or irrelevant, and *jumping* responses which one psychiatrist distinguishes. If a reply to an approach fits the initial statement, the sender experiences pleasure; he has been properly stroked. The less well the reply fits the initial statement, the greater the tension that develops. Perfect fit does not always occur with the statement; but if the listener is willing to continue the interchange, there finally emerges a reply that satisfies—that is, strokes—the sender. A receiver may, however, use the interchange to manipulate the sender. He may, that is, turn the talk into an unexpected direction; he "parries." The sender may accept the tangential reply, but there is no stroking; there is tension instead. Both sender and receiver may not even be aware that they are talking past one another. "Tension mounts and the unawareness of the participants as to what is going on prevents appropriate correction of behavior."[13] Sometimes the tangential response is deliberate, manipulative, or protective. But as between the sexes it may be wholly innocent. In Jean Kerr's play *Mary, Mary*, for example, the husband has often told his wife that he loves the way she looks. He intends this as a stroke, a way of telling her that he thinks her beautiful. But she interprets it as a tangential response, an evasion, a way of avoiding telling her that she is beautiful. One could love the way Carl Sandburg looks, she flings back at him; this would not be the same as saying that he is beautiful!

The tangential reply may have untoward effects. It interferes with feedback. It snowballs. "People . . . unduly exposed to tangential replies learn not to derive pleasure from enlightening communication. They conceive of communication as a means to achieve power over others, and by not giving appropriate replies themselves they in turn deny others the pleasure of feeling acknowledged [stroked]."[14]

The jumping response may look like a tangential response because the responding person jumps two or three intermediate steps in anticipation of statements to come.[15] But the two are not the same. The jumping response, although it may interfere with feedback just as effectively as the tangential response, is different in that it is, in effect, a way of seizing the initiative away from the original sender who may, in fact, now withdraw. As with the tangential response, so also with the jumping response—it may be either manipulative or inadvertent. In the first case, the receiver is suspicious. "What is he driving at?" he asks himself and then supplies his own answer. He replies to what he assumes the sender is driving at. He may be wrong. In any event, he has defeated the sender. But sometimes even the best-intentioned people may engage in jumping responses. Women are allegedly good at cutting through preliminary steps and arriving at the goal faster than men. The jumping response may be a form of anticipatory sign-reading. But, of course, as in all sign-reading, the reading may be wrong.

In some relationships the jumping response is benign. The secretary who can read her boss so well that she knows what he is driving at almost before he does, is a great asset. One form of the jumping response is supplying the words for the sender, or even completing his sentence for him. Some people find nothing more antistroking. "I just can't help doing it," cried one wife to a counselor. "I know it drives him crazy. I've tried to control myself. I'm not as bad as I used to be. But I'm always ten steps ahead of him and it's as hard for me to wait for him as it is for him to catch up with me." Another form, equally trying, is interrupting the sender, cutting him off, often to his great frustration.

The scientific categories for analyzing talk do not have room for the mild antistroking that takes the form of one-upmanship, of showing off in the exhibitionistic, name-dropping, or bragging manner. It can be as deadly as any. Ego: "Nice weather we're having, isn't it?" Alter: "Yeah. Reminds me of the summer I spent island-hopping in the Caribbean with the Vanderbilts. We. . . ." Ego: "Lovely party." Alter: "Sure is. It's like a party I once attended at the White House. . . ." Ego: "Terrible news from Erewhon." Alter: "Certainly is. Like when I was with the Kennedys in Alaska. . . ." This may be viewed perhaps as a masked form of the Bales category of showing antagonism by deflating the other's status. Instead of stroking Ego, Alter, in effect, strokes himself. This style might even be called masturbatory.

Very hard to take is the bludgeon style. The response is no longer even equivocally a stroke. Ego approaches Alter with "Nice weather we're having, isn't it?" Alter: "There must be something wrong with anyone who likes this kind of weather." Ego: "Lovely party." Alter: "For nuts and dumbbells, maybe." Ego: "Terrible news from Erewhon." Alter: "Anyone who sympathizes with those guys ought to have his head examined." The characteristic thing about the bludgeon style is that the bludgeoner reacts always by attacking the other person. The subject matter of the talk makes no difference. Whatever is said is interpreted as an opening for a strike that amounts to a blow. Unless Ego himself or herself relishes this kind of knock-down, drag-out encounter, he or she withdraws as soon as possible. The bludgeon pattern is expressive talk all right, but destructively so.

Expressive talk, then, covers a wide gamut, positive and negative, and takes a variety of forms. It includes purrs and snarls, stroking and striking. Words are the medium, but signs and signals supplement, complement, or controvert them.

Instrumental talk must orient, which often means convey information or facts or a cognitive message. Used this way it is pedestrian, cold, heavy. A task-oriented group depends on information to achieve its goal; however dull, it is indispensable. People have to have facts or information to perform the task. In a family budget-balancing session—a task-oriented group if ever there was one—a carefully kept record of expenditures and receipts is essential. "But what did you *do* with the money?" may receive only the vaguest reply. This may well lead to an explosion; it will certainly not advance the task.

Sometimes instrumental talk descends to the level of a lecture. Someone asks a simple question and gets a long discourse. It was to this bore that Sir William Cowper addressed his advice: "Tell not as new what every body knows; And, new or old, still hasten to a close."[16] It becomes impossible to cut the disquisition short. The lecturer does not get the ordinary cues which communicate boredom; he plows right on. The result may be disorientation rather than orientation. It seems to women that men suffer from this foible more than women do. Maybe it seems the other way round to men.

Instrumental talk may become argumentative in style. This style demands proof and evidence; it insists that everything be based on reason or logic. It can be as wearing as the lecture. Every statement, even the most casual, is a challenge to the argumentative talker. He will not let anything pass. He will argue any point, no matter how trivial. "Are you sure?" "You're wrong there." "You're wholly illogical." "That's just an inference." "It stands to reason. . . ." The argumentative style can be very boring. As long ago as 1883, the anonymous author of a *Handbook of Good Society: The Art of Conversation* noted that "a man who never risks a mere opinion, who always bases himself on a logical foundation, on reason and truth must be very annoying."[17]

Especially to women. "Men are much more given to 'argument' than women, and are far less sensible of its absurdity."[18] Good talk is based on an appreciation of differences. It encourages playing around with ideas, no matter how illogical or even unreasonable. Sometimes, as leaders of "think" or "idea" sessions have learned, the more playfully outrageous, the more exciting talk can be. It does not depend on reason and logic any more than on fact. The argumentative person will not concede this. He wants everything to be soberly rational.

This style is peculiarly inhibiting to women.

> Though syllogisms hang not on my tongue,
> I am not surely always in the wrong!
> 'Tis hard if all is false that I advance—
> A fool must now and then be right, by chance.[19]

Often the most interesting contributions are based on "intuition," that is, on unconsciously generalized observations. The argumentative man throws them out, freezing women themselves out in the process. The man who wants to enjoy the pleasure of their company does not argue with women; nor, of course, do women with men. They have learned that talk "which is suggestive rather than argumentative, which lets out the most of each talker's results of thought, is commonly the pleasantest and the most profitable. It is not easy, at the best, for the two persons talking together to make the most of each other's thoughts,"[20] but those who try usually conclude that it is worth the effort.

Equally difficult for many women is the debating style of talk, the style that views all talk as a competitive sport. If the argument is a fight in which one side tries to defeat the other, the debate is a competition for points. Just as among some North American Indians there was competition to outdo one another in, let us say, scalping, so does the debater try to outdo others in counting coups. The debater tries to back his opponent into a corner. Good talk thrives on mutual enhancement; you try to bring out the other person, to encourage him. Not so the debater. He is trying less to change the other person's point of view than to win a third person. Instead of viewing the relationship as one in which different people throw different ideas, points of view, and attitudes into the idea-hopper for the benefit of all, the debater insists on making points, on controverting the other person's point of view. He is competing for the outsider's accolade. Debate is a wonderful thing—in its place. But not in task-oriented groups and not in informal talk, especially with women.

Women tend to be less competitive than men. In laboratory experiments they use accommodative strategies; men use exploitative ones. Men are out to win; women want an equitable outcome. The psychologist who arrived at these findings concludes that "differences between the sexes may be accounted for by the fact that males are primarily concerned with winning, whereas females are more oriented towards working out an equitable outcome, as satisfactory as possible to all . . . participants."[21] Women also dislike to exert pressure. In a study of money-raising activities in a Canadian city, the men, accustomed to the rough-and-tumble of power, were reported to be more willing to use the same kind of pressure on potential donors; the women, unaccustomed to such a style of interaction, shrank from its use.[22] In debate, then, as in argument, in competitive as in conflict situations, women are at a disadvantage.

Women in task-oriented groups of mixed-sex composition often have a hard time getting the floor. An informal survey of television panel discussion programs showed that men outtalked the women by a considerable margin, as indeed they do also in laboratory studies. In another study of husbands and wives, husbands talked more in nineteen cases, wives, in fifteen.[23] Perhaps because their voices are less powerful, women have a harder time getting the attention of the group; and they are more likely to lose it by successful interruption from men. Unless someone in the group makes a special effort to give time to the women, they may sit for long periods contributing nothing.

When the talk is merely factual, without interpretation, there may be no sex differences at all in its acceptability by the hearers. The grade-school child will accept the multiplication tables as readily—or as reluctantly—from a woman as from a man. The board of directors will accept the purely technical report from the woman engineer as seriously as from the man. But beyond the sometimes-blurred boundaries between established or traditional fact and new knowledge, especially where differences of interpretation are still possible, there is a sex difference: the contributions of women are not taken as seriously as those of men.

One study of student reaction to lecturers of different sex concluded that identical words delivered by a man and a woman were received differently by listeners. Delivered by a man, they were apparently accepted as more authoritative than the same words delivered by a woman.[24] The ideas women throw into the task-oriented group's hopper are less likely to be followed up. Indeed, very often their ideas are almost ignored and the discussion continues along the same lines as before. What they say seems slightly out of focus to the men; it does not come clothed in their clichés, amenable to their empathic experiences. It may seep into their consciousness and become translated into a male idiom and be presented by a man a little later on in the discussion. It may even get attention from this source.

Conversation is almost the polar opposite of the kind of talk that goes on in task-oriented groups. In fact, one sociologist, Georg Simmel, was of the opinion that if conversation had a purpose it was no longer to be viewed as conversation. "Conversation . . . cannot allow any content to become significant in its own right. As soon as the discussion becomes objective, as soon as it makes the ascertainment of truth its *purpose* . . . , it ceases to be sociable and thus becomes untrue to its own nature."[25] Not that it should be trivial. On the contrary, it has to be interesting, fascinating, even important, but for its own sake. The idea may no longer be to have sexual relations, but neither is it to achieve any other goal. In good conversation, then, the positive expressive categories predominate. People build one another up.

The *con* in conversation implies that it is between or among equals or at least among people who accept themselves as equals. The inequalities that interfere with or prevent conversation may be subjective.

The first rule of communication is that communication will proceed smoothly as long as transactions are complementary; and its corollary is that as long as transactions are complementary, communication can, in principle, proceed indefinitely. It is irrelevant to the rule whether two people are engaging in critical gossip, . . . solving a problem, . . . or playing together. . . . The converse rule is that communication is broken off when a crossed transaction occurs.[26]

In the nineteenth century, Lord Bryce found American men more likely than European men to accept women as equals in conversation:

The average European man has usually a slight sense of condescension when he talks to a woman on serious subjects. Even if she is his superior in intellect, in character, in social rank, he thinks that as a man he is her superior, and consciously, or unconsciously, talks down to her. She is too much accustomed to this to resent it, unless it becomes tastelessly palpable. Such a notion does not cross an American's mind. He talks to a woman just as he would to a man, of course with more deference of manner, and with a proper regard to the topics likely to interest her, but giving her his intellectual best, addressing her as a person whose opinion is understood by both to be worth as much as his own.[27]

In view of all the evidence to the contrary, one wonders just what kinds of social circles Lord Bryce traveled in. For by and large, the position of women has tended to be in the direction of St. Paul's prescription rather than that of the civilizing hostesses of France.

Vocabulary, tone of voice, and inflection, as well as style, proclaim the relative position of each participant in a conversation. The inferior must show deference and respect; the superior may be permitted to condescend and patronize. Since women, by and large, are expected to engage in stroking, they may defer to men as one way to perform this role—unless, of course, they are very rich, very powerful, or very old. If they are rich *and* powerful *and* old they are above all rules! They need defer to no one. Or stroke anyone, either.

Age makes a difference in conversation also. One study of communication as related to age by a team of psychiatrists traced its development from the intra-uterine level through old age like this. In the 2 to 5 age bracket, the child learns one-at-a-time interpersonal communication. Between 6 and 12, group communication develops, especially in self-sex groups. During the 12 to 18 period, communication with the other sex takes a spurt. The 19 to 29 decade finds the communicator in a subservient role vis-à-vis his age superiors. The years 30 to 45 constitute a peak of communication with age inferiors and children; there is a switch from a role of receiver and transmitter to one of greater responsibility as sender. The 45 to 65 decades see output of information (in the form of teaching, governing, ruling, decision-making) displacing earlier intake of information. The years 65 to 80 prepare for the relinquishing of power. And from the age of 80 on, life becomes retrospective, with emphasis on early memories; communication is backward oriented.[28]

So far as intersex communication is concerned, the above schema is inadequate. It is especially so for one particular age grouping, that between, let us say, 18 and 25 or thereabouts. Just as the concept of childhood came in only about the sixteenth century and the concept of adolescence at the beginning of the twentieth, so there is need now for a new concept to refer to a new developmental stage which modern life inserts between adolescence and true adulthood. In the hiatus between adolescence and adult independence there appears to be intense need for validation of sexual identity. La Rochefoucauld commented that lovers often love one another because each allows the other to talk about himself. They are enthralled with each self-revelation. At the childhood level, they can ask about favorite singer, star, band, and find endless wonder at their agreement; they can tell one another about experiences with parents, school, adults in general, and marvel that they share so many. They can even find excitement in the differences, each finding the other an enthralled audience. Since they still share, as post-adolescents, enough background experience to find talking about themselves like talking about the other and vice versa, and the differences between them are not yet divisive (or they would not be in this all-but-symbiotic relationship in the first place), the all-engrossing self-other identity continues. "I've talked about myself too much," the girl in the cartoon can say; "why don't you talk about me now."

But as their life careers begin to diverge—his leading to concentration on the job and hers on domesticity and motherhood —talking about the self is not the same as talking about the other and differences become divisive rather than binding. Each has a competitor for the time and energy of the other. Conversation can become a casualty. Only those who keep growing can afford the mutual absorption in one another that is sought in this age period; others are left impoverished.[29]

✦✦✦✦✦

In task-oriented groups, the topics are given. They have to talk about anything that is relevant to the task. In conversation, though, there is more freedom. It may vary from desultory chitchat at one extreme to exciting "good talk" at the other; topics may vary from small talk and minor gossip to themes of the greatest import, including in mixed groups of lively-minded people the nature of the sexes and their relations to one another, one of the few topics both sexes are sure they know all about and pontificate on zestfully.

There are some areas of talk which interest men primarily and some that interest women. These differences are enough to keep most men and women from enjoying conversation about such sex-linked topics. Most women have only a tangential interest in the relative standings of pitchers or of quarterbacks; and most men can muster little concern about new hairdos or infant formulas. But there are areas, or ways of approaching them, that both can share. These areas lend themselves to interpretation, to personal response. Plays, books, music, art forms in general. They invite self-expression and they can be amusing. The kind of conversation about even these shareable topics that women enjoy is intimate, personal, having to do with how they think and feel. They are, as Erikson says, more interested in inner than in outer space. Even shoptalk can be good conversation-fodder when it is indulged in by people who see the shop in a wide rather than a narrow, technical, or personal perspective. In any event, the topic of conversation is merely a means to an end, the end being, ideally, "the purest and most sublimated form of two-way-ness."[30]

Style is the man. One man puts words together on a page in a way that shows compassion and tenderness. He strokes the reader. Another tells the same story with violence, bitterness, and hate. He frightens the reader. The "facts" are the same; the "truth" that comes through is different. And so it is with talk, too. One man speaks with a barbed wit, another with gentle humor. One uses mild irony, another abusive insults. Again, the "facts" are the same, the "truth" different. The words one talker uses delight and reassure or stroke us; those of the other leave us uneasy, disturbed, frightened. All this, independent of class differences in use of language and vocabulary.

Projective tests by psychologists are used as signs of the inner man. People respond to identical stimuli with characteristic and peculiar styles. Talk is, in a way, also a kind of projective test. It reveals us. The kind of person we "are" comes through.

Talking style is not necessarily a sex trait. It may be true, though, that one sex tends to find itself using one style more than some other kinds, for style emerges between or among, as well as inside of people. It is difficult for even the cleverest talker to engage in repartee with anyone who cannot hold up his side. And it is most difficult to be bland when talking to a violent person.

Conversation varies according to the sexual composition of the group. In mixed company, men, especially Parallelists, are likely to be more restrained, more inhibited. For "etiquette," the editors of *Esquire* remind men "is agin cussing in mixed company."[31] When men are by themselves, their langauge is freer. The topics discussed are also different. One may tell risqué stories (interestingly enough, usually called "dirty") to men who like them. All the studies of conversational topics among men place sex high on the list. They talk also about politics, baseball and other sports, the job, other men, and the like. But they talk about sex. Blue collar, white collar, executive, student, may talk at different levels, with varying degrees of sophistication. But they all talk about sex. It is a great big component of the world men carry about in their heads, and women are sometimes amazed how big a component when they catch a glimpse of it. Women seem not to talk about sex to one another as much as men.[32] But, again the editors of *Esquire:* "Remember . . . the woman who loves to talk sex to you alone may pretend Puritanism in the presence of other women."[33] Who are they trying to fool?

Individuals change also, as well as topics, in mixed groups. The quiet girl who has hardly said a word all evening becomes vivacious when an interesting man enters the group; a voluble man recedes into silence when a woman arrives. The girl who rarely talks when there are outsiders present thaws and talks freely among close friends and relatives.

Talking varies also from culture to culture. In reviewing a television program, one commentator noted that "most American officials simply are not adept in the cut-and-thrust style of public debating that is customary in many countries,"[34] especially where English parliamentary procedure prevails. In traditional Japan, etiquette required one always to denigrate oneself and build up the other. In some societies, it is alleged, people are told what the speaker thinks they want to hear. If they look tired, they are told that their destination is just a piece up the road, even though it is miles away. The physical stance may vary also. In Latin America, people lean toward one another when they talk; they are offended when a North American leans back. It looks to them like a kind of rejection.

Genuine conversation across sex, age, and culture is difficult to achieve. In fact, good conversation is difficult to achieve, period. It requires a happy concatenation of circumstances, but it can be the epitome of civilized relations.

Instrumental talk has little place in conversation. It may get in the way of the more fun-like aspects, hampering the free play of fancy. In ordinary conversation, the fact-bound talker can be very dull. Oliver Wendell Holmes found "men of facts" to be "formidable" and even "tyrannical." (The only use he had for facts was as a weapon against talkers who were flighty, empty, or paradoxical. Against them he recommended sticking "a fact into him like a stiletto."[35]) Instead of bare facts, some people prefer "truth" that is expressive, an emotional interpretation or coloring of facts. They have a dramatic style which is often delightful in conversation, however out of place in task-oriented groups. They see the world as literally a stage. We sometimes say they "ham it up." Recounting the simplest episode, they make it sound like a world-shattering event. If necessary they touch up reality to make it more interesting, for they would rather tell an interesting story than an accurate one.

One study of exaggeration concluded that "accuracy is not such an important concern to members of our culture that they routinely insist upon it at the appropriate occasions in their conversation."[36] But if any statement involves a quantity beyond what one might reasonably expect, some sort of device is called for to show that the speaker himself recognizes the exceptional nature of his statement; "I'm not kidding" is one such device.[37] Sometimes exaggeration is emotional-expressive in nature rather than instrumental. Sometimes it's an attention-getting device.[38] The whole nature and function of accuracy and exaggeration are amusingly highlighted in the television series in which Operator Smart bargains with his hearers over what they would accept in the way of exaggeration. "Would you believe . . . ?"

Exaggeration is allegedly more common in women than in men, but there is no firm evidence of this. Sometimes one spouse has such a style, and the other spends his time correcting the account. "It wasn't *exactly* like that," the husband breaks in as the wife recounts in harrowing detail the accident they had on the way over. "He wasn't knocked unconscious; he was just a bit dizzy. . . ." On the way home she turns to him in anger: "Why do you always make me out a liar whenever I say anything? It's downright humiliating." "But you exaggerate so!" "I don't either!"

Oliver Wendell Holmes was on her side:

. . . conversation must have its partial truths, its embellished truths, its exaggerated truths. It is in its higher forms an artistic product, and admits the ideal element as much as pictures or statues. One man who is a little too literal can spoil the talk of a whole tableful of men of *esprit*.[39]

Whether or not women play fast and loose with facts more than do men, they do tend to be handicapped in fact-anchored talk. In circles where conversation is most likely to occur, they are usually less well educated than the men, less likely to have a hard, factual background, less in contact with the world of knowledge. Personality is more important; personal opinion, attitudes, and observations give them a wider berth to move in and are therefore more important for them than facts.

The intellectual irresponsibility which she enjoys by consent, enables her to be paradoxical without losing credit and flippant without giving pain. To be brilliantly wrong and to submit gracefully to correction constitutes her greatest success. Her talk is not expected to inform but to stimulate.[40]

Unfortunately, modern life offers little opportunity for the conversational talents traditionally cultivated by the lady. "The modern lady is," therefore, "constantly tempted to leave her coign of vantage by the fact that life about her has often no social organization at all in which her special gifts can be brought into play."[41] Social life is no longer designed for this special kind of talk. More's the pity is the unspoken reaction to the bored company.

❖❖❖❖❖

Not instrumental talk, then, but positive expressive talk, is the burden of conversation. It is a stroking activity par excellence. It makes people pleased with themselves.

One kind of stroking is flattery. "I can't bear a man who tells me my faults," says the Wife of Bath, and in this she is certainly not unique. We all want our virtues equally, if not more, recognized along with our faults.

Francis Bacon distinguished several kinds of strokers who used flattery. The ordinary flatterer is, he says, indiscriminate; he uses the same flattery on everyone. The cunning flatterer, though, plays up the traits the victim considers himself good in, whether he actually is or not. The impudent flatterer, on the contrary, emphasizes the traits the victim feels himself weakest in. Waller and Hill add another kind, jesting flattery, which combines degradation and praise, leaving the recipient uncertain whether he should be pleased or feel insulted.[42] He is being praised for the wrong things. "What a lovely dress! Did you make it yourself?" "You sure know how to put things over on people!" "You can get away with murder, can't you?" "Some ladies' man, you are!"

Impudent flattery seems to be the kind most people prefer. The beautiful woman wants to be told she is intelligent and vice versa; the brilliant man wants to be told he is irresistible to the ladies. The difficulty with this kind of flattery as stroking, though, is that it may backfire. A beautiful but also brilliant young woman once complained that much as she enjoyed the compliments of men, after a while it became boring to have *all* of her conversation gambits answered with "how beautiful your eyes are!" Flattery may also be discounted. It is surprising, however, how rarely anyone recognizes flattery. No matter how extravagant, we always think it just short of the true facts. Women can probably get away with impudent flattery better than men. But apparently men do not think so.

The only limit to compliments to a woman is your imagination—and the only improper compliment to a woman is an absolutely incredible one. But your imagination will run out long before her credulity. . . . Needless to say, all common sense and etiquette bars are down when it comes to compliments and women. The only acknowledgement to a compliment *from* a woman is a much more lavish compliment *to* her.[43]

When it is a subordinate who applies the magic words we call it flattery; when it is a superordinate who does, we call it paying compliments. In general, convention permits women to flatter men; but men pay women compliments. If it is true, as de Tocqueville said, that European men flatter women, this fact is itself part of the flattery. They are thereby pretending to assume a subordinate position.

The tradition of courtly love found expression in the conventions of gallantry; today, or yesterday at any rate, it took the form known as the "line." The line was a stock set of compliments which a man evolved to help manage his relationships with a woman. The sophisticated woman was supposed to know how to accept them for just what they were worth, no more, no less. But she had to be able to assess their validity accurately. If she gave them more value than he intended them to have, she frightened him off; if she discounted them too much, she discouraged him; she wasn't playing the game right. She had to learn just what was being communicated by way of this form of stroking. Here is how it was once described:

> The object of the "line" is to entertain, amuse, and captivate the girl, but there is no deep emotional involvement; it is a game of skill. . . . To the extent that [the girl] falls for the line she is a loser in this intricate game; but if she discourages her partner so much that he does not request a subsequent date in the near future she is equally a loser. To remain a winner, she must make the nicest discrimination between yielding and rigidity. . . . The ideal date is one in which both partners are so popular, so skilled, and so self-assured that the result is a draw.[44]

The line was, in effect, institutionalized flattery. But the compliment, almost by definition, has to seem to be sincere. At least it has to be credible. It may be fun for the plain girl to be handed a bantering line about her golden tresses; she knows that the intention is playful. But if a man tries to pay her a serious compliment about her ravishing beauty, she may interpret it as a tactful gesture, as a recognition on his part that she needs this kind of support, of stroking. Or even that he feels sorry for her. This is the most humiliating, even degrading, thing of all. The genuinely tactful thing to do if he is serious in his stroking is to find something about the girl that he can pay a genuinely sincere, or credible, compliment about.

The girl's line usually consisted of appreciative listening with an occasional "terrific" or "wonderful" or "marvelous." But it may have been almost as elaborate as a man's, even if less aggressive. Simone de Beauvoir is of the opinion that the game of pleasant deceit is harder on women than on men.

The analysis of the line was made a generation ago and its discussion here has been put in the past tense, for whether or not this form of stroking holds for the current generation of daters is debatable. A degree of candor between the sexes seems to have developed which would practically outlaw the game between the sexes based on the line. Even a generation ago young women were beginning to have their doubts about it and suspecting that the young men did, too:

Part of me enjoys "putting something over" on the unsuspecting male. But this sense of superiority over him is mixed with feelings of guilt for my hypocrisy. Toward the "date" I feel some contempt because he is "taken in" by my technique, or if I like the boy, a kind of maternal condescension. At times I resent him! Why isn't he my superior in all ways in which a man should excel so that I could be my natural self? What am I doing here with him, anyhow? Slumming? And the funny part of it is that the man, I think, is not always so unsuspecting. He may sense the truth and becomes uneasy in the relation. . . . "Is she laughing up her sleeve or did she mean this praise?"[45]

But perhaps the young woman was inept? Perhaps only the vocabulary has changed?

Actions as well as words can flatter. There is, for example, the classic situation in which the girl deliberately misspells words or permits the boy to win at tennis.[46] The young woman does not want to seem better than the young man at anything. She does not want to suffer like the little girl in Whittier's poem who apologizes to the little boy for spelling the word because she hated to go above him. But even this kind of flattering or stroking has to be credible or it has the opposite effect to that intended.

❖❖❖❖❖

A very special kind of talk between the sexes takes the form of the verbal duel in which the ostensible blows are actually forms of stroking. This kind of interaction is common between men and women who are strongly attracted to one another. One man, immediately caught up in such a duel the moment after he was introduced to a woman, turned to a third person to ask, "Why am I fighting with her already?" The verbal duel is not a genuine fight. It may take the outward form of a fight, but there are controvening signs that betray its stroking nature. No matter what the words may be saying, all the other signs say there is a strong attraction here.

The verbal duel between the sexes has a long history.

Benedict and Beatrix in *Much Ado About Nothing*, much of the talk in Restoration Comedy (especially the so-called proviso scenes, one of the most famous of which is the one in Congreve's *Way of the World*, in which men and women bargain with one another item by item over the required safeguards of their freedom), represent only a few cases of the verbal sex duel. Because it is verbal interaction it tends to be the prerogative of the higher socioeconomic classes. It is off limits to the dull-witted even among them.

Sometimes the sex duel takes the form of complaints about the other sex. Women are accused of something or other and men are blamed or counterblamed. No one really expects to change anyone's mind, or even necessarily wants to. The object is to make clever points, to count coups, and to highlight sex differences. Sometimes the object is to find ways of twisting what the other says to make it sound foolish or absurd. The idea may be to misinterpret a simple statement as a double entendre. The talk may consist almost entirely of mutual, witty, but playful and sex-loaded, barbs and insults. Great fun, especially if all the signs and signals belie the words, as they often do.

One of the most soothing forms of stroking is simple listening. Almost everyone's idea of a perfect relationship is one in which the other person listens with rapt and appreciative attention to everything one has to say when one is talkative, or talks lovingly and tenderly when one is not, or remains solacingly quiet when only a physical presence is wanted. The understanding that requires no verbal communication is precious, too. Listening may go beyond stroking, in fact, and become a caress.

In actual life, listening may be of a quite token nature. A roomful of women—or men—can carry on a set of long monologues, each person chattering away, in effect, to herself (or himself). The stroking effect is present, but minimal. Still, it's better than talking to one's self at home alone. "Any social intercourse whatever has a biological advantage over no intercourse at all."[47] Sometimes, to be sure, they may be sharing a common topic; a bit of scandal or juicy gossip can pull them all into the same conversational system. Or a common "game" they are engaged in against their husbands. But a good deal of the time they merely take turns talking to themselves aloud, politely giving one another the floor from time to time as a matter of courtesy or fair exchange.

Listeners can have a strange effect on communication. Sometimes communication between two people is blocked by the presence of a third person listening in. The blocked message may be one of either love or hate. As soon as the two are alone again the message may come rushing. But the opposite may also be true. Sometimes, that is, communication between two people is facilitated by the presence of a third-party listener. Things are said that could not be said when the two were alone with one another. Protected from reprisal by the presence of the others listening in, the wife makes her bitter accusations. To avoid a scene in front of others, he refrains from answering back. The venting partner assumes support from the outside world listening in. It sometimes comes as a shock that old grievances, which the spouse had supposed long since amended, come out again in the protection of the listening other. The power of the listening third person can, when skilled, facilitate communication and can be therapeutic. It can, however, also be destructive.

The therapeutic uses of listening are widely exploited. Talk is sometimes a form of self-expression. This term has taken on a negative connotation. It became associated with a kind of defiance, especially in the case of the nineteenth-century woman. The implication was that the self could be expressed only, somehow or other, at the expense of the other. Wives like Ibsen's Nora walked out on their husbands; children defied their parents; all in the name of self-expression.

Expressing the self is not necessarily defiance. Talking to a person who listens may be self-expression of the profoundest kind. People may define themselves, tell themselves who and what they are, digest their own experiences by putting them into words and bouncing them on a listener or hearing them back from a human sounding board. The administrator or decision-maker has to tell someone who will listen about what he has done; he has to give it objective sanction this way. The sexes learn who they are by telling one another who they are. And the listeners learn who they themselves are as well as who the talkers are. The woman learns who she is both from what she tells the man and from what he tells her.

Talk to a hearing listener releases one from intolerable loneliness. The preoccupation of writers with contemporary loneliness has become almost a *reductio ad absurdum.* "If I were asked to sum in one word what it is that young Americans are chiefly writing about nowadays," said Christopher Isherwood as long ago as 1951, "I should answer 'loneliness.' "[48] Sentimentalizing about our alienation from the world we never made and all that, has become almost a national pastime. Each age seems to have its characteristic malaise. If melancholy is the fashionable illness of one century and *Weltschmerz* of another, loneliness or alienation seems to be the characteristic complaint of the twentieth. One of the luxuries that have come with the abundance of our society is the widespread privilege of individuality, of being independent persons in our own right. In the past this was a prerogative primarily of the privileged classes. The opportunity, not to say right, to have, on a relatively wide scale, a choice about even such relatively trivial things as luncheon menus is a recent achievement. But there is a price attached to this individuating privilege, this liberation from a fixed position. We pay for it with the pervasive loneliness that haunts so much modern literature and art. When people are organic parts of a clan or tribe or isolated community, they may not have much awareness of themselves as individuals; they may, indeed, have a hard time conceiving of themselves apart from the matrix of relationships in which they live. They are fixed in a certain position or status. They may from time to time be alone; but they are not likely to be lonely in the modern manner. Only an individuated person can be.

Because talking to a sympathetic and understanding listener seems to be one way to escape modern loneliness, listening has become a high-priced service. In California, people advertise that they will listen by the hour, and distraught people who "just have to talk to someone" pay them to do so. Listening is therapeutic for the talker. Professional listeners like doctors, especially psychiatrists, counselors, and ministers can command high fees for their listening time.

There was a time when it was one of the jobs of a woman to do this kind of listening—free. She was, par excellence, the great listening stroker. "Woman is the most admirable handiwork of God, in her true place and character. Her place is at man's side. Her office, that of the sympathizer; the unreserved, unquestioning believer."[49] She was the helper, rewarder, understander, roles that a highly individuated woman—herself requiring stroking, help, rewards, and understanding—might not be so willing or able to perform. The loss of the listening once freely supplied by women may be one of the contributing factors to modern loneliness.

❖❖❖❖❖

Sometimes the talk stops, and there is silence. Silences are of many kinds. Some are delightful. Sidney Smith spoke wistfully of "a few flashes of silence." They result from so much mutuality, so much understanding, so much identification with one another that words are superfluous. The man and woman have become, as the Bible has it, one flesh. They do not need words. They see something and know at once what the other's reaction is; the briefest glance is all that is needed to communicate this recognition. This is communication in the most basic sharing sense.

Some silences are pregnant. A great deal is being gestated by both parties. Such a silence may be the calm before a storm. Each is totting up the relationship, interpreting it, putting two and two together, getting new insights. When the process is complete the silence will be shattered with an explosion. But the pregnant silence may be gestating quite a different meaning —to be broken by a joyful communion: I love you! Whatever is being gestated during the silence is a prelude to powerful communication.

Some silences are discreet. It just seems best not to say anything. Since there is nothing to say, or since what there is to say would be better left unsaid, wise people decide to say nothing.

People of poise and wisdom do not find such discreet silences oppressive. Others, however, do.

Some silences are embarrassing if not downright uncomfortable. One of the commonest questions adolescents ask is what to talk about on a date. They are terrified at the thought of long, or for that matter momentary, silences. They feel they have to fill every moment with talk of some kind or other. Advice for daters usually includes suggestions of topics to talk about, ordinarily the boy's interest and activities. Among men and women the conventions of small talk solve the problem of awkward silences. They offer a more or less mechanical way of preventing silence which might involve a reassessment of the relationship. Without the protective shield of conventional small talk they would be obliged to observe one another as individual human beings and confront one another bare. Conventional small talk is a kind of pseudocommunication.

Some silences are sullen, some extremely painful. People may be struck dumb, stunned, or frightened into silence. Unlike the silence that results from having nothing to say, this kind of silence often results from having too much to say; so much, in fact, that the partners cannot trust themselves to talk at all. They are afraid that words might loose the floodgates; they might say more than they should; they might break into tears; they might strike physical blows. The wife who has been mulling over her grievances all day, rehearsing what she is going to tell her husband when he comes home, finds that, after all, she cannot say the words that have flooded her. Once she starts she doesn't know where she will end. She doesn't want to repeat the crisis of last year. Better keep quiet. To his repeated and increasingly irritated "What's the matter?" she can only reply petulantly, on the verge of tears, "Nothing's the matter!" Never were words and signs at greater odds. So they sit in hateful silence throughout the meal and he leaves for the bar as soon as he can.

The silence is not always so emotional. It may result from a consensual avoidance of sensitive topics. They can't talk about this, or that, or the other. They know from bitter past experience that these are hot topics, too fraught with dynamite to toy with. And so, finally, they sit in silence, blocking the other out, each pursuing his or her own train of thought. Such a situation is probably harder on Assimilationists than on others.

Sometimes this kind of silence is selective. The husband and wife can safely talk about some things but not others. His family is distinctly off limits as a topic of conversation; her cooking is out-of-bounds. Many husbands and wives—fewer nowadays than in the past, fewer among the educated than among the uneducated, fewer among the Assimilationists perhaps than among the Parallelists—find it impossible to talk about sex. All the manuals urge them to discuss freely what they like in the way of lovemaking, what they find exciting. But still for many this is an impossible subject to talk about, absolutely taboo, in or out of bed. In one study of Puerto Rican subjects, husband's work and children's discipline were never discussed by about a fourth of the couples; religion and plans for the future were never discussed by a third; birth control and sexual relations never by about half or more.[50] Modesty and respect were given as the barriers to the wife's communication with her husband. If too many topics are forbidden, the silences may become very long.

Silence does not necessarily mean, of course, that communication is not taking place. Some silences are eloquent. The silent woman may be looking daggers at the man; the silent man may be sending withering glances at the woman. Signs and signals may be causing a veritable din all around.

Although a low level of communication between husbands and wives is almost standard in our society, when it does become too extreme, the situation is considered serious. When the silence between husband and wife is the result of inability to talk, when it is the last resort short of violence, when they cannot discuss anything, when grievances pile up and cannot be ventilated, the relationship is generally viewed as a sick one. When such a complete breakdown in communication has occurred, so that neither can reach the other, strategic mediation may have to be invoked. Concessions which neither could make to the other face-to-face may be safely made to a third person. To achieve this end, the mediator must be skilled in intuiting the acceptable compromise, one that saves face on both sides, and makes communication possible again.

Marriage counselors tend to feel that the ability to engage in free and open communication is important, whether or not it is always strategic actually to practice it; at least it should, they think, be one of the options. A large literature has grown up on the treatment of communication disability on the theory that teaching people to communicate is salutary, even if all they have to communicate is resentment and hostility. Others challenge this viewpoint. Silence may not always be so golden, but neither, conversely, is talk in all cases. Nor does everyone have a silver tongue.

In a laboratory task-oriented group instrumental and expressive talk go on concurrently, alternately, or consecutively; in any event, there is no clear-cut demarcation or transition from one to the other. Between the sexes an awkward hiatus between the two kinds of talk may occur. It is not always easy to make the transition from informational-type talk and conversation. They may be reduced to devastating silences. In the following example, the young man was uncertain as to which of two alternative readings of signs and signals he should follow. Should he assume that the girl would welcome his advances or should he assume that she would not? Unable to assess the probabilities accurately, he chose the wrong one, the one with the worst payoff. If he had been able to make the transition from academic task-oriented discussion—on the best way to develop the talent of young writers—to conversation and expressive talk, he might have made a better choice. If the girl had had better communication skills she might have got her man. On the other hand, though, she may have been a White Maiden and communicated exactly the message she meant, intentionally or unintentionally. In any event, an instructive case.

I saw Jane often over a period of several years, and I spent many hours alone with her. I did not kiss her. I did not even try, formally and so that there could be no mistake about my intentions, but many times I tried to try. I remember one evening when we sat on her front porch and listened to the katydids and talked, as usual, about methods of teaching writing. It was a wonderful night to sit on a porch and make love, it was warm and there was a moon and the air was heavy with the conventional smell of magnolia blossoms and damp around us. We sat in the swing that missed the arc light behind some vines and talked about the best way to develop the talent of young writers. Both of us realized that the possibilities of this subject had nearly been exhausted. Neither of us wanted to talk about it, but we did not know how to stop talking about that and start talking about something else. Sometimes there would be a silence and expectancy would arise in cheer and slowly turn to pain. At each of these intervals I tried to make a graceful transition, but I managed no more than another remark about one of Browning's literary puzzles.

That night I wanted to do what I thought was expected of me. The slightest hint would have given me courage to go on. But when a woman has been talking about philology in the tone of mature scholarship, one cannot just begin making passes at her. The first steps must be taken gracefully and tentatively. When a woman is a colleague, one must consider the possibility that she may think of one thereafter as a victim of uncontrollable lust.

I sat with Jane and we rocked and talked and were silent a while and shifted our position. My hand brushed hers, as if by inadvertence. Nothing happened. I sat closer to her and she gave no sign of noticing it. A silence came again. I ran my hand through her hair; she said nothing and did nothing, her face and her body expressed no response. I drew my hand away hastily and thereafter whenever I have thought of the situation I have felt most inadequate. Possibly she wanted me to go on. Perhaps she did not know what to do when a man was sitting on her front porch and she would have liked him to make love to her.

Of course, as a teacher of English, I probably attached too much importance to a smooth transition. I should have made the break. Suppose she had slapped my face! My face had been slapped before, by women who meant it, by women who did not mean it, and by women who meant it then but did not mean it later. I have always thought that when a woman said "No!" she meant "No, not now" and sometimes "No, not you." . . . Jane should have helped me to get past that dead center. She should have been a little more responsive. Making love to an unresponsive woman is like making a speech over the radio, and it is difficult for the same reason. Jane gave me mike fright.[51]

CHAPTER SEVEN

Information . . . . Please!

This report presents . . . data on . . . age, race and color, State of birth, school enrollment, educational attainment, marital status, household relationship, size of family, . . . number of own children for women ever married, . . . employment status, hours worked, weeks worked in 1959, year last worked, industry, class of worker, and income in 1959, and, for household heads, the rent of the renter-occupied nonfarm housing unit. Some of these data are shown for urban and rural residence. . . . Data shown in this report can also be obtained for regions. . . . Requests for unpublished data . . . should be transmitted to the Bureau. . . .

—U.S. Bureau of the Census, 1960

If all this is not enough for you, other census volumes will tell you "whether married more than once, . . . nativity and parentage, country of origin, . . . age at first marriage" and average annual rates of first marriage. If you want even more, just write to the Census Bureau; they undoubtedly have it. Even so, businessmen and students of contemporary life continue to complain that there is too much we do *not* know about people; every ten years they flood the Census Bureau with additional questions to ask.

In a small, stable, intimate community, most people have enough information about one another to get along fairly well. They know the family background, the characteristic or expectable behavior, the status, and other kinds of facts needed for most of the decisions they may have to make about one another. And gossip keeps the information up to date.

A modern, complex, mobile community requires an enormous amount of additional information about people. The making and the administering of laws, the running of industry, the management of organizations of all kinds, including our own families, make inordinate demands for information. A vast information industry, including research, has grown up to help supply it, not to mention surveys, investigations, public and private, of one kind or another. We fill in dozens of forms every year, answer scores of questions, and, in one way or another, supply computers with their daily rations. A generation of computer-fodder has been reared that automatically fills in the dozens of questionnaires put before it and thinks nothing of being asked anything at all, from frequency of orgasm to political voting preferences. Never was so much known about so many. To what avail is sometimes debatable.

Undebatable, though, is the fact that personal relationships also require a great deal of information. "Getting to know you, getting to know all about you," in fact, is almost a full-time occupation. Whatever model of communication is involved, knowledge is needed. Much of it is already available to us when we first meet people in the form of signs of one kind or another. Clothes, stance, language, all convey their message. We do not, therefore, start altogether from scratch. Some people find it fun to read these signs; a puzzle is involved. All *aficionados* of the detective or mystery story enjoy figuring people out from signs, figuring out "who done it" from subtle hints. But some people find it endlessly confusing and they wish things were more scrutable.

Sometimes the information we need is fairly trivial: what would Mary like for Christmas? Sometimes this is enough. But for anything beyond casual contacts, considerably more is needed. How much does he know? Does she know anything? Is the man who knocks on the speakeasy's door really a customer or is he a plainclothesman? The secret agent has to identify who is the really authorized recipient of the information. Is the girl just leading him on? Or does she really care? And, increasingly, is she "contracepted"?

We have here a problem in what Thomas C. Schelling has called identification.[1] Identification is of especial strategic importance in the relations of men and women. The man wants to know which of the several women at the party or office is amenable to his advances. The woman would like the same information about the men. If a man approaches the wrong woman, his face will be slapped and, even worse, he may be reported to someone. But how can he get the necessary information in advance? As we have had occasion to note, a common preoccupation of men is precisely this problem: are there any signs by which one can infallibly determine which women will be sexually responsive and which will not? The difficulty is compounded by the fact that some extraordinarily attractive and appealing women who ought to match their responsiveness with their sex appeal are really not the ones most likely to be the responsive ones. The White Maidens are *not* all blue-eyed blonds nor the Dark Ladies all brunettes. More confusing, not all blonds are White Maidens or brunettes Dark Ladies.

In the workaday world it would protect career women against the prejudices of employers, who discount women's commitment to their work on the basis of actuarial experience with dropouts, if they could proclaim themselves as nonmarriers or as nonmothers, as safe bets for employment, therefore, as their male competitors. It would help college administrators who have to decide which unmarried students to give the pill to if they could identify "the immature students in need of protection from the 'bandwagon' effect to engage in sexual activity they are not ready for," those who need "elbow room to have experiences," and those "already engaged in sexual activity and should have protection against unwanted pregnancies."[2]

Identification is of even greater importance for women, especially when looking for potential husbands. The young woman prospecting for a husband, for example, has to know the marital status of her prospect: is he eligible in the first place? If not, she is wasting her time. If he is eligible, she has to know how serious his intentions are. If they are not serious, again, no matter how eligible he may be, she is wasting time that she could invest more profitably cultivating someone else.

The marital status of women is publicized by their names and often by a ring, so that men can easily identify those who are not available for serious courtship. All he has to do is say, "Miss or Mrs.?" when he is introduced. In 1965, incidentally, this advantage was taken from men in Sweden. In that year Sweden moved to equalize the sexes in regard to information about marital status. Stockholm newspapers announced on September 10 of that year that all mature women would thereafter be called "Mrs." regardless of marital status. They gave as their reasons that: (1) there was no reason to discriminate between married and unmarried women; (2) old maids felt inferior when addressed as "Miss"; (3) "the title 'Miss' implies innocence which is no longer the case in so far as most young women today are concerned; it is an outdated ideal"; and (4) it would free children of unwed mothers from stigma.[3] Said one editor, "It is absurd to label women as married or unmarried. It is an injustice long perpetrated by a man-made society." The change from *Miss* to *Mrs.* would come at the same age at which males become *Mr.* The change, understandably, was not favored by young women looking for husbands. It was to their advantage to have their marital status easily available.

It might be more useful if instead of erasing signs of marital status among women, signs were added among men. As it is, women have to explore and, for protective purposes, use artifice to determine which of the men they meet at work or play are fair game. A great deal of the introductory conversation is designed to elicit this information. Women have to find a natural way to inquire about a man's marital status. He may equivocate if he wants to protect himself. A popular motion picture was based on this strategy. An unmarried man who did not want to marry told the beautiful woman he loved that he was married and that his wife would not divorce him. This situation protected him from having to marry her. Conversely, a man might hide his married status in order to encourage the surrender of a woman, knowing that he was protected from having to marry her.

Even after information about marital status has been acquired, more is usually wanted. What sort of person is she? Is he? What are his (her) interests? The obvious rejects have to be winnowed out, the field narrowed. In our heterogeneous society, "one cannot count on a uniform subsoil of sociable resource: one must prospect for hidden resources, hoping to find a match which will permit the conversation to move rapidly away from the familiar to a level which combines surprise and mutual understanding."[4] Prospecting can help show up common or contrasting perspectives and whether or not there is enough of either one present to build a relationship on.

The need for a great deal of this and similar information is recognized by almost everyone as a prerequisite to marriage. The argument against elopements or hasty marriage is precisely that the couple have not had time to learn enough about one another to be sure of their commitment. Studies of marital success suggest that an engagement of at least, say, six months is usually necessary to acquire a minimum amount of information. Some young people argue in favor of premarital sexual relations on the logical, if not conventional, basis that they supply information needed for a lifelong commitment: how do we know that we are sexually compatible, they ask, unless we test ourselves in bed? And it is, in fact, interesting to note that the King James Version of the Bible uses the term "know" for having sexual relations.[5] Others argue that you can never really know people until you have lived with them, that there is no substitute.

When a person has to have information not readily available to base a decision on or for any other reason, he is, theoretically, a potential recipient of as-yet unsent messages embodied in signs, signals, or symbols. Short of the usual procedures, he has to go searching for the information, to create it if necessary. There is a considerable technical literature analyzing information problems, and like the African who never knew he was speaking grammatically until the anthropologist worked out the grammar of his language for him, we probably all follow the abstruse processes fairly closely in our groping way.

The garnering of information by direct questioning is by no means easy or simple. Different roles and status positions have different rights and privileges with respect to the asking of questions. Sometimes asking questions is a way of showing subservience; the questioner, by the very fact that he asks, admits his inferiority by showing his ignorance or need for answers. Women may use this technique as a form of stroking or as a way of proving they are not threats. Sometimes a question is used instead of a flat statement in a discussion to avoid the appearance of dogmatism or arrogance. This appeasing gesture is common among the English, who often end a firm statement with a mollifying "isn't it?" or "doesn't it?" Women use it, too.

Sometimes it is the person in a superior position who has the privilege of asking the questions. The interrogator can ask anything and no one can ask him anything. This whole matter of interrogation is hedged in with numerous safeguards in courts of law or in prisoner-of-war camps.

Sometimes asking questions is used by superiors to flatter subordinates: the chairman asks for expressions of opinion to build up the ego of the group members, to improve their morale. The teacher encourages her students to participate by asking questions. Usually this use of questions is not designed to elicit information.

In ordinary contacts, good manners forbid asking personal questions. The *Esquire Book of Etiquette* instructs its readers to respect the privacy of others and reserve some for themselves: never ask about anyone's marital status or children. A possible and permissible ploy is to mention one's own first, hoping thereby to elicit corresponding information from the other.[6]

Teen-agers sometimes resort to the good offices of friends for the information they need. Vicki asks Joanie to ask her brother to ask Steve if he really likes Vicki. But adults cannot be even this forthright. Sometimes gossip (Vicki's technique is a form of deliberately generated gossip) supplies important information. The description of any new person introduced into any group or set usually includes the basic relevant information about his occupation and marital status as of the moment. And thereafter gossip, again, keeps everyone *au courant* about changes. If you don't know that John and Mary are thinking of a divorce, you will make a *faux pas*. If you don't know that Helen and Jack are now married, you will go wrong if you make passes at her. There is often no other way than the channels of gossip to disseminate information vital to many relationships.

Gossip, in fact, is anything but idle. It is busy and important. Men in shop and office, women at home and at the bridge table engage in the exchange of personal news, transmitting information. Knowing professional gossip is an important component in a professional career; the person you know the gossip about is a measure of your own position. In informal social life, gossip is universally recognized as an indispensable source of information.[7]

When the signs are inadequate, when questions are not permitted, and when gossip does not supply the information we need to have, we must invent ways of ferreting out the information we want. The wife nags. Reads private letters. Eavesdrops. Ransacks drawers. Goes through pockets. Spies. Hires a private detective. Bribes informers. Interrogates. Grills. Threatens. Carries on an inquisition or third degree. Sets traps. Asks questions while he sleeps. Tries the *in vino veritas* bit. . . . The giving or withholding of information may be almost a life-or-death matter.

A perennial question that everyone asks in any kind of relationship at some time or other is: Why? Why did you say that? Why did you do that? Why don't you love me anymore? Why did you jilt me? Why do you laugh at me? Why do you avoid me? If only it were as simple as the advertisements say. Like body odor or bad breath. We could buy the answer at the corner drugstore.

It is safe to assume that no one really knows why he does anything. The body reacts as it has been trained or conditioned to react, on the basis of past experiences and present alternatives and a host of devious self-preserving devices, which only elaborate psychiatric analysis could reveal, and we, like those around us, observe what it does. We then find a logical or at least a reasonable explanation for what it has done—an explanation that looks logical or reasonable to us. It might not look logical or reasonable to someone in a different ethnic or class culture, but it does to us. If, for example, one asks a friend in our society why she sued for divorce, it would sound logical and reasonable to us if she replied, truthfully enough, that she and her husband did not love one another anymore. Such an explanation would not sound at all logical or reasonable to a traditional Chinese or French listener of the old school; what does love between spouses have to do with maintaining the stability of the family? Similarly, an explanation that sounds logical and reasonable to a woman may not sound that way to a man. Why did you buy a widget that we don't really need? asks the husband. Because it was such a bargain. The answer sounds logical to her; it does not, to him. Psychiatrists have familiarized us with the way we often substitute acceptable reasons for unacceptable ones in explaining our behavior to ourselves as much as to anyone else. This process has been called rationalization, that is, finding rational reasons for doing what we want—irrationally enough, perhaps—to do. It does happen, of course, that sometimes the rational reason is also the "real" or correct one. A properly nourished computer's are likely to be. We are reminded again how important information is in human relations.

Some people are delighted to supply both factual and motivational information about themselves, more in some cases than is called for or even wanted. They love to talk about themselves, and to be asked to do so is a delightful prospect. The research interviewer can hardly get away, the subjects so much enjoy talking to him. They gladly tell all, and even more than all, if the listener seems interested. Their likes and dislikes, their sins of omission and of commission, their successes and their failures are all happily exposed. Some people do not even wait to be asked before they reveal themselves. Confession is reputedly good for the soul. But people who *must* bare it, who cannot keep *any* of their sins to themselves, who are, so to speak, compulsive confessors, who *have* to tell all, are viewed by clinicians as not really well. "Too much or too little self-disclosure betokens disturbance in self and in interpersonal relationships."[8] A normal person learns to bear a good many of his sins with a minimum of malaise.

Not so the Ancient Mariner. Suffering from some great trauma, it will be remembered, Coleridge's poor character was racked "with a woeful agony" which forced him to begin his tales. "Since then, at an uncertain hour, That agony returns; And till my ghastly tale is told, This heart within me burns." So he, like many a descendant, had to travel about until he found a suitable victim, whose face he recognized immediately. "That moment that his face I see I know the man that must hear me: To him my tale I teach." Once he has finished his ghastly tale, he finds relief. His soul is no longer alone on a wide sea, "so lonely . . . that God himself scarce seemed there to be." He feels fine. Not the poor Wedding Guest, of course, who had not wanted to have to listen, but who could not choose but hear as the Ancient Mariner held him with his skinny hand. He now "went like one that hath been stunned," forlorn. The Ancient Mariner had transferred his own burden to the Wedding Guest. The Wedding Guest would gladly have foregone the Mariner's information. We usually flee the Ancient Mariners if we can. It isn't always easy.

Some people are willing to supply information about themselves but they really do not know the answers. To trivial questions no more than to weighty ones. "What do you want to do tonight?" the boy asks. "Oh, I don't know. What do *you* want to do?" Or "Do you love me?" (or, more likely, "Don't you love me?") the young man asks and she answers, again truthfully, "I don't know—I just don't." She really can't tell whether she loves him or not. Is what she feels the same thing that others mean when they speak of love? Not until one has actually been "in love" does one know; and not even then. One researcher, Carlfred Broderick, in studies of sociosexual development reports that young subjects commonly say that their current love is the real thing; all the previous ones were not. They were mistaken in the past, but not this time. They did not know what real love was until now. It always seems real while it is in process; until the next one hits them. No wonder the youngsters ask, how do you know when it's love.

Because our bodies are clear-cut entities, neatly encapsulated within our skins, we have the illusion that our selves are equally clear-cut entities. Everyone knows the color of his eyes, the size of his feet, his height and weight, at least approximately. But he may have no idea of what he wants, say, for Christmas. "Make up your mind!" is the final exasperated command of the husband trying to determine what his wife wants him to get. The truth of the matter is that we really do not know ourselves all that well. Not only in the relatively trivial examples just given, but basically as well. The currently—or at least until recently —fashionable expression for our groping is that we are in a "search for identity." We really do not know what or who we are. It is not that we are withholding information about ourselves; we do not have it to give.

Some people have no objection to disclosing themselves. They might even want to. But, let's face it, they cannot talk. They are inarticulate—ill at ease with words, especially about their feelings. If they are men, they can walk up to the most difficult mechanical or engineering problem, say, and solve it with their hands. But it would be impossible for them to tell anyone else how to do it or even to tell anyone else how they did it themselves. And very especially about how they feel— particularly how they feel about the other sex. Words are simply not their forte. "Yes, I have a sort of rough and ready soldier's tongue," says Rostand's Christian, "I know that. But with any woman—paralyzed, speechless, dumb. I can only look at them."[9] *Yep, nope, that's right* may be the extent of their conversational skills. If one needs information about them one has to read the signs; these are the people whose actions speak not only louder than words but often, in fact, instead of words.

The Dionysian subsex, men of action rather than of words, may be voluble with men; their inarticulateness with women is not, like Christian's, a friendly kind but rather, in effect, a contemptuous kind. They have nothing to say to women that cannot be said better by action in bed. They need no information from women and have none to give them. Among the Parallelists of both sexes, especially if the distance between them is great, there is sometimes an acceptance of inscrutability; they don't pretend to know anything about the other sex. Women are a mystery to men; why not just let it go at that. It is among the highly interactive Parallelists of both sexes that the quest for information may be keenest and where defenses against supplying it are highest.

Women tend to be less talkative in mixed company than men, all the clichés to the contrary notwithstanding. Studies show that in mixed company men talk more than women. Since women in one-sex groups talk as much as men in one-sex groups, and perhaps even more, this difference must undoubtedly be social in nature.

There may be any number of reasons for the plight of the inarticulate. If reared in a nontalking family they would not develop verbal skills. If reared in a very talkative family, on the other hand, they may have been outtalked and never given the opportunity to develop the talking skills.

Some people are inarticulate because they are "shy." They lack self-confidence, feel inferior. Why should anyone listen to poor little me? What do I have to say? Who am I, anyway? What can I say that would interest anyone else? Some are inarticulate because they get stage fright, like Christian in the presence of others. Some because they are intimidated. Some because they are modest. Some because they are hostile and cannot trust themselves to put their thoughts or feelings into words; it is safer not to communicate since what they have to communicate will antagonize others. Some because they are suspicious, self-protective, and hence secretive. For whatever reasons—many likely to apply to women more than to men—some people find it difficult if not impossible to use words with facility, let alone with grace, charm, or style.

Positive secrecy about oneself may be of many kinds. It may be passive and self-protective; it may be aggressive and belligerent; it may be strategic or manipulative. One author distinguishes "dark," "strategic," and "inside" kinds of secrecy.[10] Passive and self-protective secrecy is a form of shield of noncommunication painfully learned. It guards the innermost reaches of the self. Dreams and hurts, longings and fears, terrible disappointments and disillusionments, are involved. We learn finally to keep these to ourselves. We have to save our illusions, our self-images, from an un-understanding world. We dare not expose the deep recesses of our hearts. They are so uniquely our own that no one can share or even understand them. People would laugh. You're ridiculous. You're too old—too homely, too stupid, too dull, too anything at all—to do or think or feel like that. We shield ourselves by never exposing ourselves and thus continue to cherish illusions about ourselves. We correct the false image which we see reflected back from the outside world. This encapsulating noncommunication is not aggressive, not oriented so much toward others as toward ourselves. People may never even know what it is we are hugging to ourselves.

Some people are quite articulate; they have found their identity; they know what they think and feel; they are not withdrawing from others to protect a self-image. But they do not choose to reveal themselves. Theirs is the second kind of secrecy, belligerent, aggressive, an it's-none-of-your-business kind. They prize their privacy and resent any intrusion into it. They resent what looks to them like prying. They refuse to answer questionnaires; they slam the door in the face of the pollsters; they evade questions; they give tangential replies; they figuratively speaking "take the Fifth." They even resent being read by the tests and instruments devised by psychologists and psychiatrists and researchers. They are inscrutable and withhold even facial cues; they play it deadpan. They block such protocommunication as best they can. They recoil with abhorrence from the reading of signs by parlor psychoanalysts who insist they know more about people than the people do themselves. They object to sympathy that, to them, is insufferably patronizing. They do not want to be "understood." They protect their inner life. For just as there are people with an overpowering passion to communicate, so also are there people with an equally strong urge to *non*communicate.

Different people are secretive or noncommunicative about different things. Women are more noncommunicative about sex. "Neither younger girls nor older women discuss their sexual experience in the open way that males do. . . . Males are much more inclined and females less inclined to discuss sexual matters with other persons."[11] Actually, the contents of male sex talk is not necessarily self-revelatory.

The exchange of information about males in American culture is not sexually informative except in an indirect sense. The information comes as part of tales of sexual prowess or of humor in which emphasis is placed on heterosexual expertise or exploits. What evolves from this male-to-male interaction is an image of the sexual self rather than knowledge about sexuality.

The contents of female sex talk is not necessarily about sex, for "among females, . . . while a certain amount of sexual information is exchanged, by far the majority of discussion is related to affection and love."[12] Women are also allegedly less communicative about age. Men are reported to be more secretive about income. Pollsters report, for example, that men are far more willing to reply to questions about sex than about income; the latter are too "personal." Other people, both men and women, may be secretive about class or ethnic background, religion, or almost anything at all.

The third, or strategic form of noncommunication, is also protective but in an aggressive way; it is directed against others in a manipulative manner. The player with a poker face deliberately blots out his dismay or his gloating when he sees what he has been dealt in the way of cards; and each play leaves his face equally expressionless. If he showed any trace of his satisfaction with the cards in his hand his opponents would seize upon it at once and neutralize his advantage. They would then know how to play their own hands. In an analogous way, "keep them guessing" is a rule promulgated by some strategists in the game of love. Don't let him know how much you care; it would give him an advantage. "Clever women know how . . . to tell a little but not too much, to reveal enough to excite suspicion but never to establish a certainty, to meet the present crisis without quenching the springs of jealousy."[13] Women are also advised to maintain an aura of mystery, to leave a great deal to the lover's imagination, withholding enough to create illusion. Too much communication, revealing too much, may rob her of piquancy. The letdown that results when royalty or stars are permitted to talk without a script is analogous. Both sexes may feel they must protect their mystique by not revealing themselves. This is not, of course, a one-sex ploy. Any number of sexes can play. It works for one as well as for the other, for men as well as women have to maintain their mystique.

Sometimes all this strategic noncommunication, like passive noncommunication, is a necessary self-defense. We hide our feelings because we cannot afford to bare our real emotions, one way or another, hostile or friendly. Especially, we cannot take a chance on showing how much we care if the other person might take advantage of us.

There are persons in the courtship period who treat every courtship as tentative, and often attempt to remain mentally ready to accept its disruption: they want to be prepared to save face when the break occurs and to have the means of rationalizing the shock to their own egos. Therefore they commonly hide the extent of their own involvement from themselves and others in order that they may not suffer too keenly from a severance of the relations. They try not to show jealousy; they feign indifference until the other is committed. . . . One boy lectured a girl who had shown a jealous streak, in this manner: "You made a fool of yourself the other night. And now by going out with me again you have shown everybody else that you just can't get along without me."[14]

They're not, in brief, wearing hearts on the sleeve this season. Or any other season either.

Some people find it very hard to hide their feelings, hostile or friendly. If they love someone they want to shout it from the hilltops; if they dislike someone, they want to broadcast that, too. They do not accept the distinction attributed to Count Tarouca, personal adviser to the Empress Maria Theresa, between simulation, or pretense, and dissimulation, or the concealment of one's feelings. Or his rule that although the first is to be avoided, the other is to be cultivated as not only necessary but also virtuous.[15]

Any catalogue of forms of noncommunication must include the playfully sadistic form known as teasing. "Please tell me!" "What'll you give me if I do?" "Don't torment me; I have to know!" "Know what?" Juliet's nurse played this game. People of her ilk still do. It is a childish way of holding attention. I have something you want, information; what's it worth to you?

Sometimes noncommunication is protective of others, not of one's own self; it is tactful and meant to be kind. What he doesn't know won't hurt him. The kindest thing may be simply not to tell her. Why bother my wife with professional or business problems? Why bother my husband with junior's misbehavior? Sometimes the answer is simple; it really doesn't make all that much difference one way or the other. But sometimes it is not simple; it becomes involved in the most fundamental moral problems of human relationships. Among the most agonizing ethical problems we ever have to wrestle with are those which deal with how much or how little of certain kinds of information we should communicate or withhold. Should we report the cheating we saw? Should we publicize this sin? Should we tell all we know to the investigating agent, F.B.I.? Should we tell our friend we saw his wife out with another man? When is ignorance really bliss? When or what, in brief, should we tell?

It is surprising how many of the letters to the advice-giving sages in the daily press deal with problems of this kind. How much should I tell? It may be an anguished mother asking about what she should tell an adopted child or a disturbed child asking about what she or he should tell a parent. Or the prospective bride asking, should I tell my future husband that I had an abortion, a baby, or what-have-you before I met him? Should I tell my wife that I am the father of another woman's child? Or, even, should I tell my husband that I charged a new coat today? dented the fender? got a traffic ticket?

There appear to be two schools of thought about withholding this kind of information. One is the tell-all or come-clean school. It argues that the whole truth is a necessary foundation for any good relationship. Without it there may develop a credibility gap, fatal to its integrity. In addition, they note, there is a strong desire on the part of people who love one another to confess all, to share sins, to bare their souls. A desire for security, forgiveness, solidarity, all seem to be involved, especially between lovers:

There is sometimes a point where people desire to gain security in their love affairs and sometimes succeed in it, too, by telling the prospective mate all the bad things about themselves. . . . The lover's wish to explain himself, to reveal his short-comings and to receive forgiveness in advance for all the sins he will commit in later life—these things have their reason-for-being in this interaction of idealizations. Realizing that the girl he loves has idealized him, the lover is troubled, and he tries to persuade her that he is not what she thinks he is, but perhaps he never tries very sincerely. The girl assures him that he is not so bad, that his petty vices do not matter by comparison with his great and obvious virtues, and she recites a catalogue of her own evil deeds. But no one is an effective devil's advocate when he himself is to be canonized, and the result of this process is to bind the couple together. The scrupulous character of these mutual confessions indicates a nicety of moral feeling in the other, as the ready forgiveness bespeaks a magnanimous spirit. In other ways, as well, those who are in love try to bring their relationship into adjustment to reality; it is doubtless the realization that he is not what the woman thinks he is that prompts the lover's typical insistence that he wishes to be loved for himself alone (whatever that may mean) and not for this quality or that. The mutual interchange of confidences which takes place at this phase of the love affair is doubtless of great importance in cementing the relationship. There is ventilation of the soul and a resulting intense rapport established in these long rambling conversations of lovers who are never at a loss for something to say to each other.[16]

Samuel Johnson was not, like these young lovers, afraid that he would disillusion his bride; his candor with her was not an attempt to exonerate himself for everything that he might do or be forever after. It was a straightforward supplying of necessary information. When his mother raised questions about his marriage, he replied: "Mother, I have not deceived Mrs. Porter. I have told her the worst of me: that I am of mean extraction; that I have no money; and that I have had an uncle hanged." To this candor she had gallantly replied "that she valued no one more or less for his descent; that she had no more money than myself; and that, though she had not had a relation hanged, she had fifty who deserved hangings."[17]

The opposing point of view is that what the other doesn't know won't hurt him but might hurt you; therefore tell only what the other is likely to learn in any event. The groveling lovers look ludicrous to those of the let-well-enough-alone school of thought. They hold that "young men when they marry . . . must get over any habit of thinking that they must be frank and tell everything they know to their wives."[18] And their advice is against it.

"Let well enough alone" is a fine matrimonial slogan, and "as long as husband and wife are good actors it is the part of wisdom for their mates not to pry too deeply into the motives that inspire their conduct. . . . What we don't know doesn't hurt us in domestic life, and the wise do not try to find out too much." And again, "Nothing does more to preserve the illusions that a man and woman have about each other than the things they don't know."[19]

Confession, this school argues, may be good for the soul, but it is often very hard on the person who hears it. Now the hearer has to decide what to do with the information. Further, in the flush of young love, the girl may think she can forgive all. She may find it harder to take later on. But once having accepted it, the responsibility is hers. "You knew when you married me."

Still another point of view holds that one need not volunteer to tell, but that if one is asked, he is obliged to. This sharpens the decision. It may be morally acceptable not to offer information. But what if it is a choice between answering a question and not answering it?

The law takes a hand in some cases. Withholding some kinds of information—presence of disease, for example—may invalidate the marriage as well as positive miscommunication or deceit. But for the most part there is little formal guidance to help decide how much candor, how much secrecy, how much communication, how much noncommunication, how much information, how much withholding of information, there should be in any relationship.

❖❖❖❖❖

Sometimes tactful noncommunication is an attempt to protect both sender and receiver. It is the message that literally "hurts me as much as it hurts you." Rejection, for example, may hurt the rejecter as much as the rejected. Any rejection is painful. The author whose manuscript is returned with a formal slip, the athlete who doesn't make the team, the senior who is told that his application for admission to college has been turned down, the girl who does not make the sorority of her choice—all these know what it means to be hurt. But there is no hurt greater than the hurt of having the offer of one's very self rejected. It is such a terrible hurt that we do what we can to prevent it, for others as well as for ourselves. To make such a rejection tolerable to both persons involved, the rejecting one may resort to nonacts rather than to words. For once the rejection has been put into words—"I don't want you"—there is no place to hide. Rather than inflict such wounds, the rejecting one simply avoids contacts, is busy when asked for a date or when invited over. The message is not sent. Whether the motive is compassion or cowardice, the message would be cruel; words would not mitigate it. It is therefore noncommunicated.

The rejecting one is grateful if the other anticipates the possibility of rejection and makes his overtures playful, so that if they are unsuccessful he can deny them, even to himself. He was only joking. He didn't mean them. He was not rejected, not really. Both may sigh with relief if this charade is successful.

❖❖❖❖❖

There is a sex difference in noncommunication, men restorting to it more than women. "There appears to be a difference between the sexes in degree of reluctance to share worries and anxieties, with women generally more ready than men to

[182]

ventilate their concerns. . . . This may partly account for the fact that two-thirds of psychiatric clinic patients are females."[20] Another researcher concludes that it is not so much that men talk less, even about themselves, but that they reveal less.

Men do not disclose as much about themselves, generally, as women. . . . I am led to suspect that males are relatively unknown to and by anyone until they marry, while women are better known. In fact, it seems that women are both the givers and the receivers of subjective data. Women know more, and tell more, about people's selves than men do.[21]

Jourard does not attribute this reported difference to intrinsic sex differences per se but rather to the roles assigned to men and women in our society, instrumental for men, expressive for women. It is not manly to talk about one's worries. He concludes that women have at their disposal a stupendous store of private and personal data; he is, in fact, staggered by it. Men may know the facts of nature, "but women know the facts about men and women!"[22] The result, he believes, is that men are less insightful and empathic, less competent at loving, and more subject than women to demoralization.[23]

That male noncommunication is necessarily associated with the instrumental role may be mooted—at least within marriage. Another study of sixty married couples concluded that it was the social-emotional role that was the essence of the marital relationship and that it was mutual rather than specialized to the wife.[24] If anything, in fact, women were more likely to perform the instrumental role in marriage. One author explained the fact that women read the family attitudes of men better than men read those of women, and that they were themselves read better than the men were, in essentially instrumental terms. "For the female, accurate knowledge of attitudes of relatives is essential to immediate life-experiences. In short, her approach to family life is likely to be more rational and utilitarian than that of the male."[25] She has to catch signs and she has to make herself readable in order to keep the relationships functioning smoothly.

But that male noncommunication is related to the instrumental role that men perform in the work world may well be accepted. It is also related, no doubt, to the traditional norms of masculinity. These cultural norms of masculinity require that except with respect to sex, the self not be disclosed, that it be kept secret, often hidden from the self as well as from others. The Dionysian male in particular tends to be silent as well as strong.

In any event, whatever it is due to, self-concealment may be dysfunctional for mental health:

> I believe that self-disclosure is the obverse of repression and self-alienation. The man who is alienated from his fellows is alienated from himself. Alienated man is not known by his fellows, he doesn't know himself, and he doesn't know his fellows. . . . When we succeed too well in hiding our being from others, we tend to lose touch with our real selves, and this loss of self contributes to illness in its myriad forms.[26]

It is the refusal or inability to open one's self to others that, according to Jourard, helps to explain the lower longevity of men as compared to women. The women who, against male protest, insist on making their men tell them all about it may be doing them a great favor. Better to let it be said than to risk dropping dead.

❖❖❖❖❖

The noncommunication may be on the intended recipient's side as well as on the reluctant or refusing sender's side. We have noted that the recipient can produce noncommunication as well as the sender. The counterpart to the old question, does sound exist where there is no auditory mechanism to pick it up, is the analogous question, has communication taken place if the message is not understood, refused, or ignored? An unwilling intended recipient may use any of these techniques. The answer seems clear: there has been no communication. Better still, there has been positive noncommunication.

One of the most persistent clichés about women is that they are nonrational. You can't depend on their reactions, you can't predict what they'll do. Women behave unexpectedly, nonrationally. . . . To the extent that this is true, it may be because women are at least two entities, sexual beings and just simple human beings, sometimes operating in the same direction, but sometimes at cross-purposes, or taking turns in making decisions for the body. The behavior of each may be rational within its context, but appear nonrational to the observer. "Even the neurotic, with inconsistent values and no method of reconciling them, motivated to suppress rather than to reconcile his conflicting goals, may for some purposes be viewed as a *pair* of 'rational' entities with distinct value systems, reaching collective decisions through a voting process that has some haphazard or random element, asymmetrical communication, and so forth."[27]

But in addition, nonrationality, or better, the reputation for nonrationality, is a supremely valuable strategic chip. It is often very useful *not* to understand, *not* to be able to follow an argument, *not* to get a point. If one does not accept the logic of the credit system, one cannot be expected not to overdraw the checking account. The cute little bride who had no head for figures and therefore had to be forgiven her extravagance was considered adorable in nineteenth-century fiction; she is still with us, though our attitudes are different. "Darling, you just can't go on spending money like this; we can't afford it." Mary hears the words but she does not get the message; the words glance off. The bills are just as high the next month as the last. The child, the moron, the irrational, are often at a strategic advantage. They cannot be threatened or intimidated. They don't understand. They are beneficiaries of noncommunication.

Sometimes not understanding may be tactful and kind. It often involves not noticing something, not receiving the message, or not understanding it. It is tactful not to notice the *faux pas*, slip of the tongue, gross or even minor misinterpretation of a message by others. The kind woman begs her friends not to tell her the gossip about Mary; she does not want to hear it; she even wants to break the chain that is spreading it. In the 1920's there was a popular play on Broadway whose point was that a wife had to make strenuous efforts to keep her friends from telling her about her husband's affair; she did not want to receive that message.

Since how to say *no* in the kindest and most tactful manner is one of the important accomplishments of civilized man and one of the hardest to achieve, not getting the message that one must say *no* to, may be resorted to. The tactful man who gets all too clearly the girl's message, pretends he doesn't. Or he pretends she is only joking. Or he pretends he can't understand it. "If I weren't so modest, I might think you were actually leading me on," he says playfully and changes the subject. And one of the basic skills the girl has to learn is how to say *no* without crushing the ego of the importuning male. If she cannot prevent him from protesting his love, from offering himself— and if she is skillful, prevention is her best ploy—then she must at least pretend not to get the message or to interpret it playfully. A classic case of failure in this technique is the Reverend Mr. Collins's refusal to accept Elizabeth's declining of his offer of marriage in Jane Austen's *Pride and Prejudice*. She finally gave up.

Sometimes refusal to receive the message is strategic all right but not tactful or kind. "I won't discuss it!" "Let's not talk about it anymore." "I won't listen." "I won't hear of it." "I don't believe a word of it." The old man or woman who turns off the hearing aid is almost a cliché. Or the man who falls asleep during his wife's tirade. Or the woman who leaves the room. Or the man who grabs his hat and runs. Or the woman who refuses to answer the letter. Or in varying degrees, the hysteric who develops functional deafness toward anything he or she doesn't want to listen to or even hear.

Sometimes the message comes through, that is, is received but is not believed. The parents have proof positive that the young man is a heel, that he has a long history of brushes with the law, that he has been divorced for desertion by another woman, and so on and on and on. The daughter is not convinced. She does not get their message because she does not want to believe it.

There was a certain kind of logic in the old identification of ignorance with innocence in young women. Ignorance may be a protection of innocence if by ignorance is meant an inability to receive certain messages. There is a theory propounded by some criminologists that between the aggressor and his victim an understanding exists; they, in effect, speak the same language; each knows what to expect of the other. A certain kind of person, the theory implies, attracts aggression by expecting it and communicating this expectation. Carried to an extreme, such a conception is, of course, absurd. But it is certainly plausible that an aggressor, in choosing a victim, might show some selectivity; unless he is insanely compulsive he will not aggress at random. A girl who has no knowledge of the language of sexual communication would not understand the sexual advances of the wolf. The lascivious leer is lost on her. She does not know how to interpret it. "She fear'd no danger, for she knew no sin" is the way John Dryden put it in his poem "The Hind and the Panther."

Ignorance may be a stategic device. The husband who only wants peace and quiet ignores the taunts of his wife; he ignores the bait she wants him to rise to; he ignores her, period. Sometimes he may get away with it. But sometimes the aggressor may insist on at least a gesture or nod or sign that he or she is heard, like Mommy in Albee's *American Dream*. She stopped from time to time to make Daddy demonstrate his attention.

There are some messages that most sensitive people would agree no one should be asked to receive. We fight being told—by word or deed—certain truths about ourselves or about those we love. The importance of illusions about ourselves or those we love has become almost a standard theme in literature today. Destroying illusions often destroys the people themselves. The "this-hurts-me-more-than-it-does-you" kind of message is often the message no one should be asked to receive—so, often, is the "it's-for-your-own-good" message. The fact that a thing is true does not mean that it has to be either sent or received. People have a human right not to be told some truths about themselves. There are a great many things that are true that are nevertheless unfit messages to send or to receive. Some truths are insults to the self, wounds as mortal as the thrust of a sword.

Sometimes not receiving the message is neither a matter of self-defense, tact, nor yet a strategic move. Sometimes it is impossible for one or the other party to get the other's message. The noncommunication is not deliberate, purposive, or even wanted. "I just can't get through to her!" "I just can't make my husband understand!" The spouses may be willing, even eager, to understand; they may be trying to very hard. But the words just don't make sense. It is like trying to understand a foreign language or the ravings of an insane person. The original barriers of sex become bolstered by a thick layer of divergent experience in different roles. Noncommunication is the result.[28]

❖❖❖❖❖❖

The phenomena associated with not receiving messages have wider sociological ramifications also. Convention is an institutional permission to violate the mores, provided the violation is not so blatant that we have to notice it. So long as we can pretend not to know about the violation, can ignore it, we permit it.

> The basic institutionalizing norms for permitting . . . [violation of sex norms] might be summarized as: "keep your nonconformity as quiet as you can; don't openly flaunt the mores or the law; don't force us to take cognizance of your violations; don't be flagrant about them; show a decent respect for the conventions of our society." So long as these rules are obeyed, individual nonconformity is permitted. The legal and moral proscription of adultery is a universal norm; the law makes no provision for exceptions or exemptions. A large amount of violation goes on—Kinsey reported between 35 and 50 percent of his cases—and provided it is not flagrant it is accepted by general consensus. People either pretend they do not know about it or they act as though it did not exist. If gossips ferret out violations and attempt to bring sanctions against them, the community may punish them for their pains.[29]

One woman confided to another that she wished their mutual friend, Jane, would be more discreet in her affair with Jack. If they continued to be so open in their relationship, the community would no longer be able to ignore it, refuse to read the signs, and have to bring sanctions to bear against them. The community would much have preferred not to get any message at all.

The still tongue is not far removed from the forked tongue. The lie is a more aggressive technique than secrecy. The sending of no message may be the same as the sending of a false message. Deceiving by not telling may not be exactly the same as deceiving by telling a positive falsehood, but the effect may be the same. And the person who tells only part of the truth may be deceiving more than the person who tells nothing at all. The noncommunication we have been examining here may be not too different from miscommunication, to which we now turn.

CHAPTER EIGHT

Truth? Whole Truth? Nothing But the Truth? Anything But the Truth?

Confronting man, woman is always play-acting; she lies when she makes believe that she accepts her status as the inessential other, she lies when she presents to him an imaginary personage through mimicry, costumery, studied phrases. These histrionics require a constant tension: when with her husband, or with her lover, every woman is more or less conscious of the thought: "I am not being myself"; the male world is harsh, sharp-edged, its voices are too resounding, the lights are too crude, the contacts rough.

—Simone de Beauvoir, *The Second Sex*

There appears to be in the United States a singular mixture of respect and want of sincerity on the part of the men with regard to the women.

—Francis Joseph Grund, *Aristocracy in America*

Some kinds of miscommunication—that is of deceit or feigning —are, so to speak, just garden-variety; anyone may practice them on anyone else, and probably does. Buyer on seller, seller on buyer, guest on hostess, hostess on guest, and so on through all the roles in the social system. A powerful ethical argument in favor of always telling the truth or of never deceiving may well be made on the grounds that a firm grip on reality, however displeasing, is essential to normality and that if we deprive anyone of his anchor to reality by not telling him the truth or by deceiving him we do him a disservice. Although research has demonstrated the importance of trust in human relationships, lying still appears to perform some kind of function, and one student finds that sometimes it is a positive obligation.[1] At any rate, functional or dysfunctional, miscommunication is widely practiced.

Some kinds of deceit are peculiar to the sexes, *sui generis*. One need not go as far as John Masefield and say, as he does in *The Widow in the Bye Street*, that "women were liars since the world began," or as far as Simone de Beauvoir, as quoted above, and say that women are always play-acting, that they are never themselves with men. "Since the world began," "always," and "never" are pretty strong. It is, of course, quite true, as thoughtful observers have long since noted, that the whole tenor of a group of women changes when a man enters. We take this so much for granted that it rarely occurs to us to ask whether all are now play-acting. Still one must grant some occasions not characterized by deceit.

On the other hand, hardly anyone can deny that deceptions, large and small, are standard operating procedures in the relations between the sexes, well-known, accepted, almost institutionalized, and certainly not news to anyone over twenty.

There are several standard brands of such sex deception. There is, first of all, the age-old surprise expressed by post-honeymoon couples—the before-and-after branch of deception. During courtship it is expected that everyone will put his or her best foot forward. He is gallant, considerate; she is adoring, compliant. Once married and the honeymoon over, they show their "true colors." He is no longer the man she married; she is no longer the woman he married. Before we were married, she looked up to me; now she tries to boss me; she really had me fooled! Before we were married, he took me to concerts; now he says they bore him; why did I believe him! Older people simply shrug their shoulders at this. Of course, courting couples deceive one another. Why not? All's fair in love, *c'est la vie*, and all that.

The researcher might view the situation somewhat differently. He might ask, how do you know which are the true colors? Why do you think the posthoneymoon colors are any truer than the premarital colors? We are different in different situations and every one of the different *we*'s may be flying our true colors. The women Simone de Beauvoir says are play-acting may be different from those same women in one-sex groups; but that does not mean that one group is flying any truer colors than the other. The fact that we are different people in different situations may mean that we are not deceiving in any situation or, conversely, that we are deceiving in all of them. The disillusioned young couple reject this, of course, as casuistry. They know they were deceived then and disillusioned after.

A second standard-brand kind of deception between the sexes involves leading a man on, or leading a woman on, since this is a game both sexes can play, and do. Sometimes, to be sure, this deception is inadvertent, not deliberate. But sometimes it is done on purpose for exploitative or for psychiatric reasons.

A typical procedure of the college man is to give a coed a terrific rush, and then either drop her suddenly without any explanation whatever, or tell her that "Mary Jane Whosis, the girl he is engaged to at home, is coming up for Senior Ball," or something of that sort. If the coed has not learned the ways of the world, as typified by the State campus, she probably has fallen for this terrific build-up which the boy has given her, and when she shows that she is very much hurt, the boy is simply amazed. How could she for a moment have taken him seriously? He likes her an awful lot. He thinks she's a swell kid, but as far as being serious, why, he's in love with Mary Jane and always has been. He was only having fun. He's sorry if she's hurt, maybe for her sake he'd better not see her any more.[2]

In reversed form, that of the woman deceiving the man, this situation has been described by a psychiatrist under the rubric of a game which he calls "Rapo." At one level, a woman flirts with a man, signaling her availability to him; he reads her deceptive message correctly and pursues her through the evening. His pursuit is all she is after, and when he makes any further advances, she rejects him politely and moves to another conquest. At another level, the reward she is seeking by her deceitful maneuvers is punishment for him. She enjoys his discomfiture when she rejects him; that was what she was after. At the third-degree level, she leads him into a compromising advance and then makes criminal assault charges against him.[3] This is deception on a sick plane.

Most of the large proportion of men Kinsey and his associates reported as engaging at some time or other in adulterous relationships surely did not tell their wives, nor did most of the smaller proportion of wives who "cheated on their husbands" tell of their extramarital activities. This may be deception by noncommunication; but it is deception nonetheless.

Some standard-brand deception is loving. Husbands and wives pretend great enthusiasm for something because they know that will please their spouses. And one team of researchers reported that maintaining interspousal harmony by deliberately making incorrect statements was one of the major findings of their study of the responses of married couples to disagreement.[4] From a practical point of view, this gentle deception was probably justified. Assumed or perceived agreement or consensus, whether or not it is correct, has been found to be related to marital satisfaction. In fact, perceived consensus with respect to the importance of companionship in marriage was reported to be more important so far as the couple's marital satisfaction was concerned than objective or actual consensus.[5] Perhaps some of the assumed or perceived agreement was the result of Beauvoir-type deception?

The girl who tells the obstetrician she is married when she is not; the girl who tells her boss she is not married when she is; the fifteen-year-old girl who tells the young man she is eighteen; the forty-two-year-old woman who tells her lover she is thirty-five—these are a few of the many other stock characters in drama and fiction who engage in standard-brand deception. It would surely be elaborating the obvious to go on.

It is clear that neither sex has a monopoly on the practice of deceit. A study of male freshmen at Lehigh University found that these men attributed about as much "gilding," or deceit, to themselves in relation to girls as to girls in relation to themselves.[6] The Wife of Bath knew that "God has given lies, tears, and spinning by nature to all women" and that "there's no man who can lie and perjure half so boldly as a woman." It was Shakespeare himself who, referring no doubt to the Dionysian subsex, warned women that men were deceivers ever:

> Sigh no more, ladies, sigh no more,
> Men were deceivers ever,
> One foot in sea and one on shore,
> To one thing constant never.
> Then sigh not so, but let them go,
> And be you blithe and bonny,
> Converting all your sounds of woe
> Into Hey nonny nonny. . . .
> The fraud of men was ever so,
> Since summer first was leafy.
> Then sigh not so. . . .[7]

There is, however, one kind of deception—standard-brand among women—of which men are not capable. It is, indeed, true that men can deceive women about love, as women can deceive men. But although men can feign love as easily as women, they cannot feign intromission. They cannot feign orgasm. If they try, the end result may be disastrous, for nothing is more humiliating than to have one's bluff called. The man who flirts indiscriminately, conveying the impression that if only there weren't so many constraints in the way, what sweet music they could make together, may be nonplussed if a woman removes the constraints. The aging Romeo may learn that he was deceiving himself.

Women's bluff is not easily called—or, at least, hasn't been so far in human history. Only now that Masters and Johnson have published their findings is it becoming possible. For millennia prostitutes have engaged in this kind of deception, simulating great sexual ecstasy, to please their customers. Loving and well-meaning wives had been doing the same. Lee Rainwater has documented it convincingly. ". . . Even if I'm not happy I put on a good act. . . . When I'm tired it's no good, but I never let him know that; that's no good for his ego," says a sexy wife. "I always act interested; I don't know how he could know," says even the rejecting one.[8] This kind of deceit, if not all others, is encompassed in the dictionary definition which includes a quotation from Horatio Smith: "Deception—a principal ingredient of happiness."[9]

Still there undoubtedly are many men who resent being thus deceived by women sexually, especially since they are incapable of similarly deceiving women. The Mona Lisa smile has been interpreted as the patronizing look of a woman who successfully fools her husband, not with respect to a love affair but with respect to her sexual response to him. How much of the extensive discussion and research in the field of female orgasm had as its unrecognized and unadmitted purpose to learn how to "catch" women in such deception is indeterminable; but no doubt some of it was. The implicit condescension and even in some cases contempt inherent in such one-sided deception may be galling to sensitive men.

The work of Masters and Johnson now makes it possible for men to read the signs of orgasm and discount any attempt by women to pretend. "With the specific anatomy of orgasmic-phase physiology reasonably established, the age-old practice of the human female of dissimulating has been made pointless. The . . . [signs] remove any doubt as to whether the woman is pretending or experiencing orgasm."[10] Come to think of it, though, one wonders about the men who will take time out to study the signs of "orgasmic-phase physiology" of their partners to document the occurrence of orgasm, or to call their bluff. If the woman loves the man enough to pretend, isn't this truly a case where ignorance is bliss and wisdom folly?

✦✦✦✦✦

Deceit is commonly strategic in nature. In fact, the feint and the bluff have been strategic techniques from time immemorial. Strategic deceit may take many forms. "It is to your lover you must never say you disbelieve in God," a young French woman is quoted by the Goncourts as saying, "but to your husband it does not matter at all, because with your lover you must leave yourself a way of exit." For if you want to get out of a relationship with a lover it is convenient to be able to invoke religious scruples, since "religious scruples and devotion cut everything short."[11] This is a form of what Thomas C.

Schelling has called "first-move" strategy; it is the man who tells a woman he is married when he is not, so she won't insist on marriage herself, or the man who tells her he is not married when he is, so she will have an affair with him are also engaging in strategic deceit.

If not actually strategic, some things are interpreted as such. When men are told about women who can live happy and fulfilled lives without orgasm or even without sexual relations, they are incredulous. The women are deceiving the men. Some even accuse women of a monstrous conspiracy to propagate this canard in order to put them at a strategic advantage vis-à-vis men. It is interesting to note that if women act differently from men, they must be deceiving; if they act as men do—pretending, for example, that they experience orgasm—they are behaving honestly, sincerely. It is a nice question: who's deceiving whom? The Oklahoma girl who can't say *no* is not necessarily a nymphomaniac; she may just be a compassionate woman. It would be impossible to convince her partners, though.

A considerable amount of deception is built into civilized life for both sexes. No matter how they feel, people have to put up a civilized front. A deceptive calm pervades the hostile breakfast table; a deceptive smile masks the wife's resentment; a deceptively calm voice masks the husband's anger. The amenities prescribed by convention demand a high-level performance of deception: boredom masked by flattery, annoyance masked by attention, the whole repertoire of propriety and good breeding.

Then there is the deception imposed by role specifications. The norms of masculinity and femininity demand that impulses and tastes which go counter to them be hidden, kept from view, even denied. The man who would enjoy knitting or needlepoint—why not?—hides this damaging fact; and the woman who would like to roister with the boys smiles demurely instead at the cocktail lounge.

Almost as humiliating for one sex as the other is the requirement of pretended inferiority in the feminine role. "One of the nicest techniques," Mirra Komarovsky quoted one college girl as saying, "is to spell long words incorrectly once in a while. My boy friend seems to get a great kick out of it and writes back, 'Honey, you certainly don't know how to spell!' "[12] This is a lesson girls learn fairly young, as John Greenleaf Whittier's schoolmate shows. " 'I'm sorry that I spelt the word; I hate to go above you, Because,'—the brown eyes lower fell—'Because you see, I love you!' "[13] Girls play down their abilities, especially those that boys are supposed to be more proficient in; they allow boys to explain things to them, no matter how tediously; they let boys beat them at athletic sports. One wonders how different this kind of deceit is from the simulated orgasm. It is no doubt this kind of role-related deception that Simone de Beauvoir had in mind when she protested that women presented "an imaginary personage" to men.

But men must also present an imaginary personage that may be as poor a fit in his case as in a woman's. He must appear physically brave and courageous, unafraid of danger; he may be as sensibly frightened as she.

The expressive or stroking role, usually assigned to women, obligates a performer to engage in a certain amount of deception. It involves building people up, encouraging them, giving them self-confidence, whatever the woman as a woman may feel. She must appear compassionate and accepting; actually she may feel as justifiably resentful as a man.

Quite beyond the exigencies of the amenities and of role requirements, though, many people love all kinds of deception almost for its own sake, as observers, if not as participants, at play, if not in other aspects of life. Cinderella, Red Riding Hood's wolf, the distinguished prince, Snow White's stepmother, all the mistaken identities in Shakespeare, misinterpreted heroines—the cases are legion. A very considerable part of literature would disappear if all kinds of miscommunication—lies and deceptions on the part of the sender, misunderstanding and misinterpretation on the part of the receiver—were to be deleted. The denouement in many a play consists of clearing up precisely such misunderstandings. And of course, there is the whole genre of the detective story. Masquerade parties, practical jokes, teasing, kidding, playful disguises of all kinds, the masked voice over the telephone, the sly, misleading preparations for the surprise party, all testify to the delight people take in miscommunication in one form or another.

✦✦✦✦✦

Miscommunication is protean in form. On the part of the sender, it may be inadvertent, even accidental.

Dear Jeanie,

I arrived home safe and sound despite the bad weather and am back once more in the groove. Everything was in shipshape. . . . It was lovely to be your houseguest and I enjoyed every moment of it. . . . Now I wonder if I can ask you to do something for me? It has to do with your father who, I fear, has become much too serious about me. He completely misinterpreted my appreciation of the lovely times we had together. He is such a sweet person I hate to hurt him. But I was frightened to hear him talk of moving up here, how he would miss me. . . . And, now, when I got home there were flowers he had wired. . . . Please make clear to him that our relationship is extremely casual on my side. It would be calamitous if he pulled up his roots, leaving his friends and, yes, even the mementoes of your mother, to move up here. I would have little time to devote to him and he would have no one else. Don't be aggressively discouraging. Just enough to make clear that I was being kind and appreciative, not encouraging him or leading him on, if you know what I mean. . . . The men I associate with professionally are more sophisticated and it never occurred to me he would take me so seriously. . . .

Fondly,
Anne

If the man in this case had acted as Anne acted, it would have meant that he was in love; he therefore inferred that she loved him. Her behavior had no such significance for her. The deception was wholly accidental.

Like noncommunication, miscommunication may be tactful and kind or it may be hostile and exploitative. It may involve a kernel of truth which is either exaggerated or understated; it may involve equivocation, partial truths, or complete falsification. It may be defensive or aggressive.

On the part of the receiver of the miscommunication, it may also be inadvertent or deliberate. It may involve misinterpretation of a bona fide, true message or a misunderstanding of it; or a misinterpretation or misunderstanding of a false message. He may be misled, misinformed, or simply mistaken.

❖❖❖❖❖

Public relations specialists have accustomed us to the idea that corporations try to project a specific kind of image of themselves on the public. No matter how harsh and exploitative their actual policies may be, their advertising and personnel that have contact with the public give the impression that it is dealing with an organization overflowing with loving kindness. These images vary among different firms. Some images, for example, are staid and establishmentarian, like IBM or GE; others are playful and amusing, like VW or Avis. Celebrities also try to project a certain kind of image that may or may not have any basis in fact. At one time stars tried to project an image of the boy or the girl next door, cosily domestic; at another, of exotic glamor.

And so, too, do young men and women often try to project an image on one another. They want to make an impression. They want to seem to be a particular kind of somebody. He assumes a tweedy pose, complete with pipe; she assumes the young-sophisticate pose, complete with a nothing-surprises-me expression. "I wish it didn't seem so old-fashioned to have high moral values," one coed commented. "So many girls would just love to be able to say out loud that they think too much is being made of the importance of sex. The silly thing is that it's sort of embarrassing to admit that you disapprove. It's 'the thing' to sound modern and blasé even if you aren't."[14] Such images may be completely phony, but it is usually a fairly innocent deception; they are, from an adult vantage point, just preposterous imposters. For this reason we may view this as only quasi- rather than genuine miscommunication.

Among older people, however, such quasi-miscommunication often appears to be serious enough and genuine enough to be criminal. Newspapers report, for example, elderly women bilked of their savings by men who were convincing enough in their image-projection to win the women's confidence and trust. Their image-projection is genuine deception.

Another form of quasi-miscommunication is that of illusions, especially about ourselves, which writers have taught us are as essential for our well-being as food. We have to think well of ourselves or life is just not worth living. Cosmetics, falsies, padded shoulders and fannies, false eyelashes, hair coloring, toiletries of all kinds help us foster illusions about our looks; they are probably more successful in deceiving the user than the beholder. In any event, they are fairly harmless.

The white lies and polite deceptions which serve a legitimate stroking function might also be considered to be only quasi-miscommunication. No one except the hopelessly inexperienced or naïve is actually deceived. Among people who have the same background they do not really miscommunicate. They consitute a pleasant deceit between the sexes, institutionalized and benign. They become genuine miscommunication only when the receiver misinterprets or misunderstands them. The woman who was just being kind finds that the man has misinterpreted her behavior to mean that she was really interested in him. The polite boy who did not want to hurt the girl's feelings is dumbfounded to learn that she has mistaken his pleasant words for expressions of real interest.

Exaggeration is a simple and sometimes amusing form of miscommunication. It was simply *enormous*, the wife tells her husband about a friend's new diamond ring. What a *terrible* thing! the girl exclaims about a broken date. I'll *never* speak to you again! He dances better than anyone I *ever* knew! Aside from the emotional wear and tear that such miscommunication produces in the listener, it is probably not very serious. Exaggeration of income or of prospects or of attachment and love, on the other hand, might be serious, especially if the girl were using this information to base a decision on: shall I marry him or not?

Some people deceive by undue modesty. It is not only the college girls stroking the boys by pretended inferiority who underplay their qualities or their achievements in a sort of negative exaggeration. Some people underdress and drive cheaper cars than they can afford. Others deceive by overdoing. They inflate their qualities and their achievements; they brag and boast and dress better than they can afford and drive Cadillacs when they can afford only a VW. Newspapers sometimes report relief recipients who are found dead with thousands of dollars stashed away in mattresses or high-spending celebrities who die bankrupt. Each, in his own way and for his own purposes, practiced deception by exaggeration, negative or positive. And there is the old joke about the man who got his signals crossed; thinking he was talking to a prospective father-in-law, let us say, he discovered he was talking to an internal revenue agent.

Flattery as a benign conversational gambit has been discussed where its stroking nature was emphasized. It can also be more sinister, exploitative, manipulative. In Proverbs 2:12–19 we are warned against the way of the evil *man*, whose evil seemed to consist mainly of aggressiveness, that is, of "froward" behavior, deviance, or leaving the paths of uprightness and walking in darkness. But when we are warned against the strange *woman*, it is because she is such a flatterer. "Keep thee from the evil woman, the flattery of the tongue of a strange woman" (6:24). Men should seek for wisdom and understanding so "that they may keep . . . from the strange woman, from the stranger which flattereth with her words" (7:5). The prostitute accosts a man and "with her much fair speech she causes him to yield, with the flattering of her lips she forces him. . . . He goeth after her straightway, as an ox goeth to the slaughter . . ." (7:21–22). You just can't trust these women. "For the lips of a strange woman drop as an honeycomb, and her mouth is smoother than oil; but her end is bitter as wormwood, sharp as a two-edged sword" (5:3–4). One becomes extremely curious about these strange women. What was all this flattery *for?* Were they *all* prostitutes?

Hints and innuendo, by communicating less than the whole truth, may be in effect forms of miscommunication. Something is implied but not expressed. Iago hints at Desdemona's unfaithfulness but never really affirms it. Hints and innuendo may be ways of protecting oneself in case the reaction of the other person becomes threatening. "I never said that!" Of course, he had not, in so many words, but he supplied the basis on which a conclusion could legitimately and logically rest. The girl hints that she will be receptive to advances but does not commit herself because she is ready only if he is. An escape hatch is needed in case he is not.

Equivocation is another way of communicating a false message; it is a kind of double-bind in that it says several things at the same time. Like the hint, it leaves an escape hatch. "Oh, *that* isn't what I meant!" Or "*That* didn't mean you could . . . !" Or she neither consents nor refuses; she doesn't say yes or no.

The fact that a message is objectively true in the sense that it is factual does not mean that it may not be miscommunicating. The brutal truth is hardly ever accurate; it may transmit a false message of worthlessness or rejection or alienation. The sender of even factual messages who does not take into account the impact on the receiver may be guilty of miscommunication. "I had no idea she would take it so hard," says the young man who has just told the young woman her appearance was unkempt without telling her at the same time that her skin was lovely. The man who reports that the barrel is already half empty may be more guilty of miscommunication than the man who reports that it is still half full. In one case the message spells discouragement; in the other, encouragement. The latter may be more justified than the former. Twisting facts, or even the truth, to make them tell a different story is an old technique of deception.

Later we shall discuss the nature of threats and promises that depend on clear and unequivocal communication; there is no deception involved. More familiar are threats and promises that involve some form of deception, threats that are really feints and give wrong cues, or bluffs that trip others into wrong decisions and promises that are "empty." They achieve their goal by communicating false messages and work only when the receiver is actually deceived. It is in connection with these forms of miscommunication that information is especially important. One has to know the target of the threat or the promise.

"If you divorce me, I'll kill myself," says the wife, and the distraught husband believes the chances are great enough that she just might. He believes her enough, at any rate, not to sue for divorce. Actually the chances that she would commit suicide might be very slight, and if a psychiatrist convinced the husband that she would not, he might call her bluff. His information on her is inadequate; hers on him is not.

"If you'll just marry me I'll give up all this drinking with the boys," the young man promises. The girl believes him just enough to say yes. But when she confronts him with his promise six months later he chides her for throwing it up at him. His information regarding her was correct; he knew she would accept his deceitful promise at face value. Her information regarding him was wrong; she believed his promise. Promise her anything, but give her . . . whatever you please.

✧✧✧✧✧

Just as refusing to receive a message may be a strategic form of noncommunication, so also may misinterpreting or misunderstanding or mistaking a message by the receiver be a strategic form of miscommunication. "I distinctly told you it was a formal party," says the boy when he comes to pick up his date and finds her in stretch-pants and T-shirt. "But you didn't!" replies the girl who did not want to go with him in the first place. "I *can't* get ready *now!* My dress! Why didn't you *tell* me it was formal?"

Or, "Can I tell mother?" cries the girl joyfully. "Tell her what?" asks the mystified boy. "That we're engaged!" What in the world gave her *that* idea, he wonders. He has said nothing about being engaged. All he said was something about hoping they would still be going together at the time of the prom.

A classic case of coercion by enforced face-saving is the one presented in Tolstoy's *War and Peace*. By deliberately misunderstanding the situation, Ellen's parents put themselves and her in a situation that would be extremely embarrassing unless Pierre saves their faces. The Vassily's knew their man. Pierre just couldn't humiliate them by telling them he did not want to marry Ellen; he couldn't let them down; he had to save their face. He did.

On Ellen's name day, Prince Vassily was giving a little supper party of just their own people. . . . Pierre and Ellen sat mutely side by side almost at the bottom of the table. . . . The whole attention of all the party was really concentrated simply on that pair. . . .

"So it is all over!" he thought. "And how has it all been done? So quickly! Now I know that not for her sake, nor for my sake alone, but for everyone *it* must inevitably come to pass. They all expect it so, they are all so convinced that it will be, that I cannot, I cannot, disappoint them. But how will it be? I don't know, but it will be infallibly, it will be!"

Now he felt that this was inevitable, but he could not make up his mind to this final step. . . . "I must inevitably cross the barrier, but I can't, I can't," thought Pierre, and he began again speaking of extraneous subjects. . . .

Meanwhile Ellen's parents, Prince and Princess Vassily, were waiting restlessly for some progress to be made. When it was not, Prince Vassily shook himself, got up, flung his head back, and with resolute steps passed the ladies and crossed over to the little drawing-room. He walked quickly, joyfully up to Pierre. The Prince's face was so extraordinarily solemn that Pierre got up in alarm on seeing him.

"Thank God!" he said. "My wife has told me all about it." He put one arm round Pierre, the other round his daughter. "My dear boy! Ellen! I am very, very glad." His voice quavered. "I loved your father . . . and she will make you a good wife. . . . God's blessing on you!"[15]

Pierre was no match for this strategem. He had fought long if not cleverly against just such a contingency. Now he threw in the sponge.

"You twisted my words; you took me too literally; I was only joking and you knew it," says the young man. Here again information is important. Bona fide miscommunication *can* occur; how does one know if it did in any particular case or not? Did she really misunderstand? he wonders. "Or is she putting me on?" It may be quite awhile before enough evidence turns up for him to judge. As a rough-and-ready rule, *Esquire* magazine suggests that if something like this misinterpretation happens three times in a row, the miscommunication is communicating a message: she is saying *no*, loud and clear.

Sometimes accepting a false message is kind and tactful. Pretending to believe a bluff may, in fact, be a form of stroking. And nothing could be more cruel than calling it. The man who must make such mad love to the girl is nonplussed when she says, "OK, let's go to your apartment," and humiliated when he has to back down. It is often kindness on the part of the girl to pretend that it is her scruples, not her knowledge of his inadequacies, that protects them from making a fateful mistake.

❖❖❖❖❖

To round out the discussion of variations on the communication theme, a word about pseudocommunication. It is communication that assumes the form of communication but carries no message. It is talk that only pretends to communicate. It is a way of going through the motions of interaction without actually giving or receiving a message. We talk without saying anything. Words pass back and forth but not ideas or emotion or even simple information. In miscommunication the process is genuine enough; it is the message that is false. In pseudocommunication it is the process which is false.

Conventional small talk is the archetype of pseudocommunication. It really does not make too much difference who it is we are talking with. What is said is almost ritualistic. Almost anything is suitable for almost anybody. The participants are almost interchangeable parts. Exactly the same words spoken by those in the receiving line would be equally suitable for all those passing before them. Individuals as such are hardly present. Our real selves may be miles away. We talk to one another about the weather, the garden, the wedding, the dog. It really does not matter. We don't care what the other person thinks about anything. If he agrees with us, just fine; if he does not, well that's just fine, too.

Some people become quite adept at talking without actually communicating anything. They may even be vivacious. They may look as though they were really saying something. One comes away from such talk with only the vaguest idea, if any, what the person is like. They are articulate all right, but completely noncommittal. Sometimes, of course, such pseudocommunication is really a form of noncommunication. People go through the act of talking for the sake of appearances. Or they talk to cover up, in order not to communicate. They cannot or do not want, for any one of many possible reasons, to communicate.

If, of course, the small talk or ritualistic interchange is, in fact, personalized, it may be a form of stroking, and to this extent a form of genuine communication. In pseudocommunication proper, however, the process is itself false because there is no genuine confrontation of selves; it is not really communication or even, necessarily, a reasonable facsimile thereof.

❖❖❖❖❖

In real life, pseudocommunication, noncommunication, and miscommunication—in all their forms—can all take place together. In any one group, some people may be engaged in pseudocommunication, others in noncommunication, and still others in miscommunication. And sometimes the same person may be doing all three at the same time. Evasion, for example, is a kind of refusal to accept a message; it may also be a kind of pseudocommunication, and indeed a kind of miscommunication too. The wife never really answers the question; the husband never really discusses the issue. The wife changes the subject; the husband laughs off her statements. Somehow or other one or both find ways not to come to grips with whatever it is the other wants discussed.

Joking or kidding or teasing or playful insulting may involve noncommunication, pseudocommunication, and miscommunication all at the same time. A false statement is made. "You can't mean it!" or "You've just got to be kidding!" "No, I mean it." "Really?" The victim is uncertain. She doesn't know how much to believe, how seriously she should take him. "I can't believe it." "Ask Jack." Jack, of course, is in on the game and he corroborates the statement. Only after she has become convinced, do they tell her that they were only fooling. Great fun, enjoying her embarrassment.

CHAPTER NINE

Shrew and
Strategist

✦✦✦✦✦

... women are shrews, both short and tall.

—Shakespeare, *Henry the Fourth*, Part 2

A donkey, a dog, a wife, all three; the more you beat them the better they be.

—Popular adage

There is a difference between taking what you want and making someone give it to you, between fending off assault and making somone afraid to assault you, between holding what people are trying to take and making them afraid to take it, between losing what someone can forcibly take and giving it up to avoid risk or damage. It is the difference between defense and deterrence, between brute force and intimidation, between conquest and blackmail, between action and threats. It is the difference between the unilateral "undiplomatic" recourse to strength, and coercive diplomacy based on the power to hurt.

—Thomas C. Schelling, *Arms and Influence*

✦✦✦✦✦

Although it is certainly true that the sexes are not, either as collectivities or as individuals, enemies of one another, still it does happen that they are in conflict with one another often enough to popularize the battle-of-the-sexes fantasy.

Schelling's analysis of arms and influence as related to war has piquant analogies for the relations between the sexes. He shows the relative importance of influence—diplomacy, strategy —and force in dealing with an opponent.[1] He is concerned primarily with combatants who have a choice of either one. But sometimes one combatant has no choice. For a smaller or weaker combatant up against a larger one, discretion, as with Falstaff, is the better part of valor. Women are at a disadvantage with men in terms of brute force; influence has had to be their mainstay.

One of the major strategic achievements of women has been the disarming of men. The superior physical power available to men does them little good if they are not permitted to use it. It is an amusing, even fanciful, concept to think of sex relations in terms of Dionysian men aggressing and fighting and exploring and Parallelist women deterring and domesticating. (It does not detract from the insight to concede to the Assimilationists that there doubtless were also Parallelist men deterring and domesticating Dionysian women; assuming there to be many such, the preponderance of cases was in the opposite direction.) Delilah deprived Samson of his major power, his superior physical strength. Nuclear power is of no help at all against even, or especially a little country like North Vietnam. Women, not having the power, had to use influence. And influence requires communication.

When men and women confronted one another as physical combatants, the odds favored men. Before we became squeamish on the subject, they used their strength to their advantage. In the literature of the Middle Ages, husbands and wives sometimes literally fought to see who would control.

In the Middle Ages . . . anarchy often took the form of a fight for the breeches. In Germany, the city magistrates even recognized and sanctioned a duel between the partners for life. The *Towneley* and *Chester Mysteries* represented brawls between Noah and his wife. In the 16th century, this view of the relationship between husband and wife took the form of a *Merry Jeste of a Shrewde and Curste Wyfe Lapped in Morelles Skin.* . . . This version of the domestic battle tells how a young farmer, apparently kind-hearted and honourable, marries the elder daughter of a man of substance. The bride soon shows that she intends to rule her new home, but the yeoman strips her, flogs her till she faints and sews her up in the salted hide of an old horse [certainly a fate far worse than Mrs. Peter Pumpkineater's.] In this plight she capitulates, and peace reigns in place of discord.[2]

From Italy comes the story of Pisardo and Fiorella. When Pisardo married Fiorella, he proposed a tug-of-war with sticks, the winner to be boss: "Fiorella, you see here this pair of men's breeches. Now you take hold of one of these sticks and I will take hold of the other, and we will have a struggle over the breeches as to who shall wear them. Which one of us shall get the better of the other in this trial shall be the wearer, and the one who loses shall henceforth yield to the winner." But Fiorella was too clever to fall for such an obvious setup. She refused to fight. She used influence instead. He was the husband and she the wife and a wife should always "bear herself obediently toward her husband. . . . Wear the breeches yourself," she said, "for assuredly they will become you much better than they will become me."[3] It is not at all hard to guess who probably made most of the decisions in this marriage between dull-witted Pisardo and bright-witted Fiorella. (On the other hand, Fiorella reminds us of Petruchio's Katharina after she has been tamed; perhaps Pisardo had already cut her down to size?)

In the literary genre known as Satires against Women, women of the lower classes were by no means at a physical disadvantage vis-à-vis men. In the popular Punch-and-Judy type of comedy, for example, "the good man is invariably worsted by his muscular and shrewish helpmeet."[4] The mystery plays often included brawling scenes "as when the hen-pecked husband is sent flying from his door, only to discover his doleful neighbour in a similar plight." A sharp tongue was thus often an auxiliary rather than a substitute for physical force. Nevertheless women probably relied even then on other than physical means to have their way. A kind of woman's culture arose and was transmitted from generation to generation. In *The Scholehouse of Women*, the elder woman, "out of the storehouse of her experience, counsels the younger the best way to domesticate her consort, especially when he takes to beating."[5]

By the twentieth century, however, except in lower socioeconomic circles, men were no longer permitted to use their physical superiority over women. Beatings were out. In a modern Schoolhouse of Women, the curriculum includes no course on how to protect against beating. From time to time a movie character might indulge in it—often to the cathartic delight of the male audience—but for the most part striking a woman is taboo. (Except, again in some circles, in the form of sexual play such as wife-spanking which, apparently, both participants greatly enjoy.[6]) The physical superiority of men has thus been neutralized. One muscle, the tongue, has done it. Strategist and shrew have exploited it, the first with finesse, the second, not always. Not all women are clever strategists. Not all are even in situations where they can use strategy. Not all have good enough cards to play. Some have almost nothing going for them. What they have lacked in the way of other resources, including superior muscular strength, they have had to make up for in the venomous use of the tongue. And they have succeeded, as even some of the biblical proverbs attest: "It is better to dwell in a corner of the housetop than with a brawling woman in a wide house" (Proverbs 21:9); or "it is better to dwell in the wilderness than with a contentious and an angry woman" (Proverbs 21:19).

✦✦✦✦✦

It might be true, as the child's chant says, that sticks and stones can break one's bones, but it is not true that names can never hurt. They can hurt. They can even break the spirit. Sexual delinquency may have always been considered the first of the major sins of women; but almost without doubt, shrewishness has been considered the second. Complaints about the "subtlety, loquacity, hypocrisy and versatility of the female mind" and "the perversity, garrulousness and vanity of women,"[7] which pervaded writing in the sixteenth century, lasted a long time.[8]

The shrew—as scold, nag, virago, termagant—is a very old archetype. She is the woman who rejects the cichlid pattern of subservience. She is less malevolent than the true bitch, as delineated in Fiedler's analysis, but just as annoying, if not more so. She talks a man to death, nags him, defies him, disobeys him, manipulates him. Even women suffer from her. Here is one female victim of a pair of shrews:

I flee women not only because the company of men is more interesting but also and especially because women are so bossy. I can well understand why men find the company of women difficult. Women act as though they should manage everyone's life. They give advice freely. And more, expect you to follow it. Police you to see that you do. Two women I know especially drive me crazy. One tells me what color to use on my hair, what kind of drapes to have on my windows, what kind of house I ought to live in. The other is always advising me about my yard. . . . The men I know don't take my reformation in their image so seriously.

Still one can see that the shrew really recognizes her own inferiority, that her shrewishness is compensatory. You may have to escape from her, but you don't necessarily feel like killing her, as you do the bitch all too often.

Sometimes the talkativeness of women is not a weapon in conflict. It may be compulsive. Some people are inarticulate. Words do not come easily to them. They live in a world where words do not loom large. Words may even embarrass them. Some may not mind the words of others; they can listen. Others retreat from words even of others. Such inability to talk is a serious symptom. But inability to stop talking is too. Some people are almost pathologically articulate. They suffer from logorrhea. At one extreme are those whose words are almost mindless, not even part of the communicative process. If no one is around to hear them they talk anyway. They talk to themselves, to their cats, to their flowers. But at the other extreme are those who are highly articulate, who have to put things into words, no matter what. No nuance of a relationship can be left unverbalized. What did you mean by that? Why did you say that? What's the idea of doing that? They are communicating all right and demanding that others communicate, but almost compulsively. They cannot let anything just happen. Most people learn to take a good deal of their communication in the form of signs—facial expression, gesture, the exchange of glances—but the compulsively verbal do not.

Some of what is labeled nagging in women seems to them to be the minimum of prodding necessary for the domestication of men. They feel they have to keep after men to do certain things. Be sure to wear your rubbers; don't forget to shave; change your shirt before you go out; you didn't fix the faucet; why don't you ever. . . . In addition to the day-by-day nagging to get things done, there is also the scolding that serves to ventilate grievances. Since women are often at a disadvantage in aggression involving physical or muscular strength, much of their aggression takes on the form of verbal assault. In its most refined form, it may become strategic.

Folk tales are filled with stories about shrews. From Iraq, for example, comes the story of the woman of the well. A man and his wife were very poor:

To add to his misery, his wife was a very shaitan, whose tongue afflicted him from morning to night. For his misfortunes she had nothing but railing, and for his poverty she did nothing but upbraid him.

One day it happened that they had nothing in the house to eat or to sell, and as soon as the day dawned she began to scold and abuse him. "Here we are starving, and you look for no work! Never was a woman cursed with such a vagabond as you!"

By her stinging words she forced him to rise and go out to seek employment . . . but no man would employ him, for the harvest was over and work was scant. . . . His wife . . . began to scream and abuse him. . . . He answered nothing, for his conscience accused him [for wanting to desert her], and they sat together on the edge of the well, she reviling and he listening, until, losing patience he struck her with his elbow and she fell into the well below.[9]

Frightened but happy to be free again, he continued on his way. Presently a jinni descended upon him to kill him for throwing into his well "a woman whose tongue is a plague and her screaming like the screaming of peacocks." But, said the old man, just think of this: you have had to suffer her for only two hours, I have had to listen to her for forty years. So be merciful. They made a pact and wandered the world together. After a particularly severe quarrel, the jinni threatened to enter the old man's body and torment him to the end of his life. But the old man was a strategist (with the jinni if not with his wife). My wife, he said, has escaped from the well and is waiting for me outside. "What!" shrieked the jinni, "live beside thy wife and listen to her revilings? Never, never!" Rather than suffer such a fate, worse, obviously, than death, "he flew out and disappeared forever."[10]

The shrew appears in literature, as well as in folk form. One of the earliest fragments of English literature—before A.D. 886, in fact—is *The Wife's Complaint*, which is about a woman "who bewails the ever-increasing troubles with which she is beset. . . . She sits in solitude bewailing her troubles the whole day long. She has no friends at hand, and all the vows of lasting love which she and her husband had exchanged in the past, have come to nothing."[11]

Chaucer's Wife of Bath was an archetype of the shrew who was also a strategist. Her first two husbands were rich and old and she made great sexual demands on them. "How glad they were when I spoke to them nicely, for God knew how viciously I scolded." This is, in simple form, the technique of alternating punishments and rewards allegedly used in prisoner-of-war camps in World War II. (An unhappy husband might well feel like a prisoner of war.) "I'd bite one moment and whinny to be petted the next," the Wife admits. The recipients of any form of gentleness are so grateful for the crumbs of kindness that they repay with acquiescence. "This is the way to talk to them and put them in the wrong. For there's no man who can lie and perjure half so boldly as a woman. . . . A really clever wife who knows her business can make her husband believe that black is white." She got the drop on her husbands by manipulating the almost universally experienced sense of guilt that characterizes husbands. "I made my old husbands firmly believe they talked when they were drunk; it was all lies. . . . Lord! the trouble and grief I gave them! And they quite innocent." She acted on the theory that offense was the best defense: "I'd scold even when I was in the wrong; or I'd have been done for often as not. . . . I'd get in first with my reproaches and so put a stop to our strife. They were glad enough to find a quick excuse for things they'd never in their lives been guilty of." She was not above the exploitation of sex: "To get what I wanted, I'd put up with all his lust and even pretend an appetite for it, though I never had much taste for old bacon; and that's really what turned me into a scold." She had great endurance. "I paid them out word for word I tell you." And she sometimes won by outlasting her husbands. "I managed it so cleverly they found it best to give up; otherwise we'd never have had any rest." (We are reminded again of Petruchio's taming of Katharina; he didn't let her sleep or rest either. None of the Wife's techniques were the monopoly of one sex.) She used the allegedly greater rationality of men against them: "No doubt one of us must knuckle under," she would say, "and since a man is more rational than a woman is, you ought to be the one to give way."[12] The Wife of Bath, of course, reflects a man's conception of a woman's behavior.

The story of the reformed shrew is also a widely distributed staple of folklore. It developed probably in Italy in the Middle Ages and was revived in the sixteenth century. "Whether from these literary forms or others, it was popular in the folklore of the Baltic states and Scandinavia. It has also been reported from Scotland, Ireland, Spain, and Russia, and has been heard from a Zuñi Indian in New Mexico."[13] If the men could not control women in real life, they could at least control them in tale or play. The audience at the Globe Theater probably felt the same vicarious pleasure as that experienced by audiences when a tough guy on the screen wallops the heroine.

Fiedler, as we noted, has found the shrew a pervasive character in American literature, a character from whom men are constantly fleeing. And even today a man can write to a columnist in the daily press: ". . . I am writing about the lonely unmarried lady. . . . My own solution was to get a good dog as a companion. It makes all the difference, as I learned, after my marriage broke up. . . . Better a tail-wagging canine pal than a tonguelashing wife, in my book."[14]

✦✦✦✦✦

It might be argued that the shrew is really not communicating; she is trying to control. Actually, it is not always easy to distinguish between the desire to communicate and the desire to control. Control by physical force does not have to involve communication, but control by influence or by strategy always does. A man can pick a woman up and deposit her where he likes, as he might a sack of grain. Communication need be involved no more in one case than in the other. But "there is a difference between taking what you want and making someone give it to you."[15] It is the distinction between rape and seduction. And in seduction communication is of the essence.

The relations between the sexes may be viewed as a strategic "game." In a strategic game all decisions are made in the light of their effect on the other players. Ego has control over his decisions but not over Alter's; but their decisions are interdependent. As in poker, chance plays a part in the distribution of cards at one's disposal; but skill, including strategy or knowing how to play them, does also.

It so happens that although women have been dealt the best cards so far as some life "games" are concerned, they are at a great disadvantage so far as others are concerned. First, the poor cards. The dependency of women during the years while they bear, nurse, and rear children is one of the fundamental facts of life. They may be taken care of by their own mothers, or by mothers-in-law; by sisters or by sisters-in-law; by their own clan or by their husbands'; the woman's tribe or his. She may be taken care of by a commune. No matter. The important thing is that she be freed for the care and responsibility of children. She is not, of course, expected to be idle. She does contribute to her keep; but her first responsibility is to her children.

In our society it so happens that this care of mothers of young children has traditionally been assigned to husbands. They are held responsible for the support of their wives while they bear, nurse, and rear children. The implications for the relationship between men and women, husbands and wives, are profound. She is dependent, and dependency is one of the subtlest of all influences on personality. A person in a dependent position has poorer cards in his hand. He has to play those he has with greater skill. The dependent person has fewer prerogatives and even those he has may be at the whim of the person he is dependent on. Although the dependency of women is becoming attenuated in our day and age, there was a time when it was so almost completely absolute that divorce was out of the question. Women suffered anything at the hands of their husbands because there was practically no alternative. This is no longer true. But even today, it is still true that during their children's early years, women do depend on husbands for support.

The dependent person is likely to be the underdog. He isn't strong enough or powerful enough to enforce his wishes on others. But if he is clever, he soon learns how to manipulate others for his own purposes, especially if he has some good cards. Women have two such cards. They have greater orgasmic capacity than men and they also have greater capacity to tolerate sexual abstinence. The first of these advantages is available to women only in ages when sexuality is permitted to them. Perhaps because it is such a powerful and humiliating card, sexuality in women has been discouraged in many eras. Like the greater physical force of men, this greater orgasmic capacity of women has been held in check. But the second of her advantages she has played to the hilt. Much more than men, women can take sexual relations or leave them. Men rarely go very long without ejaculation. Most women can, if necessary, or if prescribed by their culture, go for years without orgasmic, or even any, sexual experience. This all adds up to a big difference in strategic resources, socially as well as psychologically and biologically. Not only does the greater urgency of genital sexuality in men give women a strategic advantage in a confrontation with men, it is ultimately the most valuable card a woman, especially a young woman, holds. (It is interesting to speculate about the White Maiden as a personification of the ability women have to tolerate abstinence and the Dark Lady as a personification of their greater orgasmic capacity.)

Men have their own strategic disadvantages, their own dependencies. The fact that they are less able than women to bear sexual abstinence for long periods of time strengthens the hands of women at their expense, especially if the institutional framework forbids other women to supply the relationships they withhold. The bargaining situation is not, therefore, all that one-sided.

Thinking in the field of strategy used to posit a relationship between the parties involved in which there was little or nothing in common. It was an either-or matter. They or we, us or them. The advent of nuclear war, however, created a new kind of situation and hence a new kind of thinking and forced strategists to rethink the whole problem. Now no matter how many opposing interests the parties have, they have one overriding interest in common and that is to prevent a nuclear war. This fact has produced new ways of thinking.[16]

They are lines of thinking that, quite aside from the situations that stimulated them in the first place, are especially applicable to the relations between the sexes. No matter how many opposing interests men and women, husbands and wives, have, they usually have an overriding common interest. They need one another. As collectivities they cannot live without one another. As pairs they have overriding dependencies. They do not want their relationship to break up; they want to preserve it. They are in a "mixed-motive" or cooperative, rather than a "zero-sum," game in which what one gains the other must lose. If they were not, they would almost certainly have gone their separate ways long ago. The opposing and the common interests between the sexes are in a delicate balance and hold them in orbit only so long as they remain so. It is a love-hate relationship of very long standing.

✦✦✦✦✦

The fact that men and women are bound to one another by such powerful ties means that the strategies available to them have to be of a specific kind. Strategies in a situation where the parties love one another or have much in common differ from the traditional strategy in the fact that the aggressor can depend on love or mercy on the part of the other person; that is one of the "rules of the game." He, or she, knows that the other "just can't" or "just couldn't" or "simply wouldn't" do such and so and therefore feels confident in taking certain chances, just as Gandhi's followers knew that the railroad engineers "just couldn't" run over them and therefore felt free to chain themselves to the tracks. The wife knows that her husband "just won't" make a scene at the party, so she saves her aggressions against him for just such an occasion. It goes without saying that this choice of strategies depends on accurate information about the spouse. There may come a turning point, a last straw; he might just fool her.

Traditional and modern approaches to strategy differ in several ways. Secrecy and surprise are major components in traditional strategy. You don't tip your hand or give yourself away by manner or deed. Or you communicate false messages: you feint, bluff, mislead, deceive. But clear, unequivocal, unmistakable communication is often important in current strategic thinking. You have to convince the other side that you really mean it; you have to prevent your opponent from misunderstanding you and doing something that will force you, for whatever reason, to do something neither you nor he wants you to do. War by misinterpretation is just as bad as war by correct interpretation. Traditional strategy presupposed rationality in both parties. Modern strategic thinking challenges this tenet and shows how great an advantage *not* being rational can often be, at least a reputation for not being rational, as the Wife of Bath knew so well. Flexibility in a bargaining or negotiating situation used to be viewed as important in traditional strategic thinking. Precisely the opposite—unequivocal commitment—is sometimes an advantage according to modern strategic thinking.

Women, it appears, have always known intuitively how to use the strategies which modern thinkers have now found scientific reasons for. The classic illustration is Mrs. Day who had to live with Father. Any successful wife knows how to manipulate her husband strategically. If she is really successful, of course, the husband never knows. Saving face is one of the things she knows best how to do. If she outfoxes him and gloats over it—an inexcusable mistake of judgment—she is almost by definition a shrew rather than a strategist.

✦✦✦✦✦

Strategic moves or actions are a special kind of total-act signs or signals—special because they are manipulative, coercive, and designed to produce a given result. "A strategic move is one that influences the other person's choice, in a manner favorable to one's self, by affecting the other person's expectations of how one's self will behave. One constrains the partner's choice by constraining one's own behavior." Strategic moves may be either tacit or explicit and verbal. If signs convey information and if signals invite action, moves force or coerce or manipulate.

Strategic actions constitute a whole communication system in themselves. Sometimes, for example, we burn our bridges behind us. This conveys the message that we are determined not to retreat; it is designed to convince someone or other that we mean what we say and won't back down. Sometimes we present our opposite number with a *fait accompli*. Sometimes we go on a long visit so that we cannot be reached. Sometimes we have an affair with John to show Tom. Sometimes we hire a lawyer to discuss a divorce with our husband to protect ourselves against any pressure he may exert on us. Sometimes we submit to the young man's advances because he asks us to prove our love. Sometimes the husband engages in what W. J. Goode has called the strategy of divorce, deliberately maneuvering his wife into asking for a divorce, leaving her no alternative except one with a payoff even worse than divorce—rejection, neglect, contempt, humiliation. These and dozens of other kinds of acts are strategic in nature, designed to convey a clear-cut message or to protect us from receiving unwanted messages. There are also, of course, strategic moves designed for purposes of feint or bluff, to confuse and confound.

If some kinds of strategies depend on miscommunication of one sort or another or on a break-off of communication, there are others that depend, then, on clear and unequivocal and successful communication. The message has to come through. Ego has to make it clear that there are no *if*'s, *and*'s, or *but*'s; this is a no-nonsense matter. No secrecy-and-surprise, no bluffing, no feints. But rather clear, emphatic, and especially *convincing* communication. Since Alter's prediction of Ego's behavior involves an assessment of the likelihood of his pursuing course A, B, or C, Ego has to convince Alter that the probability is 100 percent that he will follow A. Ego does not keep Alter guessing; he does not try to mislead him. He makes his intentions unmistakably clear in advance. It is of the essence in this kind of strategy that communication be not misleading or defective but rather that it be absolutely unequivocal and convincing.

Since it is so important for the success of this kind of strategy that Ego's message be accepted at face value he has, somehow or other, to convince Alter of its authenticity and validity. The way he does this is by a commitment of some kind. To prove that he "really means it," that he will not renege on his commitment, he has to do something that makes reneging either impossible or more costly than carrying out the commitment would be. If he says he is going to do A, he has to make A the best alternative available to him, including the alternative of any non-A course of action. We shall call these strategies based on commitment. Three forms—"first-move," promise, and strategic threat—are of special relevance.

A second kind of strategy may be called the passing-the-buck type. This may take the form of relinquishing the initiative or of delegating to someone else one's right to make decisions. This type is especially suitable to women who shun the rough-and tumble of bargaining or working things out.

Still a third kind carries the "face-saving" brand. It depends largely on love, goodwill, compassion, or unwillingness to hurt anyone. The underdog can use this. So can women, especially if they have projected the "little woman" image.

First-move as a strategy seems to fly in the face of much that we have believed about strategy in the past. A wide variety of options has traditionally been viewed as an important asset in a bargaining situation. If you had many alternatives, you could maneuver—that is, fall back or advance—with greater freedom. Otherwise there was always the danger of a stalemate or breakdown in the relationship. But sometimes, especially if a breakdown in the relationship is the worst possible outcome for both parties, it is to the advantage of at least one of the partners *not* to be free. It is an advantage *not* to be able to do something. It is an advantage *not* to be able to renege. If you have already committed yourself in an irrevocable way, or in a way costly to undo, the other party can no longer expect to make you do, or not do, what you have made clear you cannot, or must not do.

Thus the party who enters a bargaining or negotiating session with a clear-cut position that cannot be changed without some kind of penalty has practically won. Laws which put a ceiling over prices or a floor under them, protect buyers from sellers in the first instance and sellers from buyers, in the second. "I'd be willing to pay more," the buyer can say to the extortionist, "but the government would be on my trail if I did." "I'd be willing to sell for less," the seller can say to the buyer, "but the government would get me if I did." In such cases one of the parties has first-move.

Strict mores regulating the relations of the sexes function in a similar fashion. "I'd love to go with you," the girl could say, "but I'd be expelled from school if I did." "I'd love to marry you, dear," the man could say, "but my wife won't divorce me and I'd lose my job if I divorced her." Or the husband says, "The exchequer is low this month, dear. Let's just go to the cabin instead of taking the trip." "Of course, darling," replies the wife; "I'd be perfectly delighted to. But I already ordered the tickets at the travel agency and there's no refund." She may be bluffing; she may not have gotten around to buying the tickets yet. But if her husband accepts her word, there is no room for further bargaining. She has committed them and reneging will be expensive. If she *was* bluffing, she would better hurry down next day and make the down payment with a pre-dated receipt to make the commitment credible because true. A commitment has no strategic value unless it can be communicated, proved beyond a shadow of a doubt.

Promises in the strategic sense also depend on commitment to be effective. Promises constitute a considerable part of general talk. "Keep in touch." "I will." "Come to see us soon." "Sure will." "Let's get together next week." "Love to." "If you'll be good, I'll give you an extra dessert." Some promises are just chatter; promises in form only. Some are variant forms of stroking. Others are not intended to influence behavior, but just to be pleasant. The last one in the series, though, does try to influence behavior. And the mother will have a very good boy if she backs up her promise with an extra serving specially for him tucked away in the refrigerator.

A strategic promise tries to control behavior. Ego changes

Alter's behavior by changing his own. It is a sort of payment-in-advance. Ego commits himself to do something—serve an extra dessert—and in return Alter does something beneficial to Ego. It is like a bargaining situation in which one party pays now and one pays later. But the one who pays later has to add some guarantee that he will.

"Hop into bed with me!" says the lover. "Oh, I couldn't!" replies the adored one. "But I promise I'll marry you!" Still, she notes, he has not committed himself. What if he reneges? "You really mean it?" "I sure do!" "Good! I'll announce our engagement right away!" If he accepts a public announcement, his promise is valid; if the prospect of a public announcement cools his ardor, his promise is worthless and becomes a valid bit of information against him. She may use it, too, someday.

The most important promise anyone ever makes in a whole lifetime—the promise to love, honor, and cherish—is buttressed by such powerful commitments that it is almost impossible to renege. Even if a couple finds that they are not at all suited to one another, the publicity of the announcement makes it difficult to break even an engagement. So far as the seriousness of the commitment is concerned, the betrothal in Sweden is taken as of major significance. Sexual relations after betrothal are therefore common. Such relations are premarital but not pre-betrothal. The commitment has been made.

Promises have to be credible, just as threats do. The promise of a husband to buy his wife a mink coat if she will cook pizza for breakfast might not turn the trick if she preferred to sleep late; but if he promises to bring flowers home every day for a month and commits himself by placing a standing order with the florist, she might be willing to take the trouble. Assuming, of course, that she is a flower-lover.

The value of even a commitment depends on the information available about the promiser as well as about the promised. Even the banker and the credit man rely on "character" as much as on technical security. The husband who buttresses a promise with a worthless commitment won't find it very effective.

Threats, like promises, are commonplace in talk between and among young people. "If you don't stop flirting with Helen, I'll never speak to you again!" "Unless you take me to the shore, I'll just stay home." Or—this one told by an outstanding sociologist, Albion W. Small—"if you don't stop whistling on Sunday," says the Scottish lass, "I'll not fornicate with you anymore."

A strategic threat is distinguished from a simple warning. A warning is a straightforward communication which tells Alter what Ego will do, and has motivation or incentive to do, if Alter does such and so. It is useful information, like any information. It helps Alter make up his mind. But it may or may not be effective. If Alter knows that there is a probability that Ego will really not do what he says he will do; if, in fact, there are attractive alternatives to doing what he says he will do, Alter may take his chances on doing what he is warned against doing. He "calls Ego's bluff."

To transform a simple warning into a strategic threat Ego has to commit himself to do what he says he will do even if it is something he would rather not do. Reneging on his threat has to be harder than not. The strategic threat is in a way a technique for forestalling or neutralizing first-move by an opponent. It is a sort of second-move before the first-move. In the case of the couple referred to above, if he really wanted to stay home, he should have prevented her from buying the tickets in the first place. The day before he should have said: "Please don't buy the tickets yet." "But, darling. . . ." "If you do, I'll cut off your checking account." So far this is only a warning or an "idle" threat. She knows he doesn't really want to do this and it is quite possible that he won't. So he has to put the idle threat to work. He has to prove to her that he will do what he says he will. He has to do something that commits him to cutting off her account. "I called the bank to tell them that if or when a check made out to the travel agency comes through, they are not to cash it and they are to cut off your account." This is terribly unimaginative and gauche. But it has the effect he wanted. The threat is no longer idle, a mere warning. It is very industrious, a real threat. He is not bluffing. He has made it difficult to let her get away with the first-move strategy. It would be harder to call the bank to rescind his order than not to. Now if she buys the ticket, it is the same as stopping her checking account, as well as embarrassing herself with the agency. His threat to stop her account is made credible by his commitment. It puts her behavior squarely up to her.

A strategic threat, in addition to being credible, has to be reasonable. It cannot be so extreme as to trigger retaliation. A wife's threat to sue for divorce may be quite credible, but rather than bringing the husband to terms, it may give him incentive to sue her first.

A strategic threat should also take into account the alternatives open to the threatened person "who, if he is not to react like a trapped lion, must be left some tolerable recourse."[17] If my account is going to be cut off if I write a check to the travel agency, I'll go out and spend twice as much at the department store! If she's going to divorce me, I'll really go out on the town! If one is going to suffer, it might as well be for something big as for something small. Might as well be punished for a big sin as a little one. So if Alter is to be deterred from one course of action by Ego's threats, there must be some tolerable alternative he can substitute for it that is not calamitous for either or both.

Buck-passing must surely be one of the oldest indoor sports in the world. One of the common forms has been called relinquishing the initiative. This strategic ploy puts the final decision up to the other party. It can be very effective against people with strong consciences. It may fail utterly against cynical or hard-boiled opponents. Again, a matter of good information. The girl who puts up no resistance to the man's sexual aggression may find herself violated; but if she knows her man, this nonresistance strategy may be her best protection. It puts the responsibility squarely up to him; he feels he *has* to protect her. The wife who says passively, "It's up to you, dear," may, with one husband, find herself making all the concessions. With another husband, on the other hand, she may find herself winning all the time, as little Fiorella probably did. It is like the person who passes the cookies around; if he were placing them on the guests' plates, he would leave the smallest and least desirable for himself; but by relinquishing the initiative, all the guests are moved to take the least desirable, leaving the best ones for him. (We are reminded of the father who rebuked his son for taking the largest piece of cake. "If I were serving the cake," he said to the boy, "I would have taken the smallest piece for myself." "Well," the boy is alleged to have replied, "You got the smallest piece, didn't you?")

Delegating decision-making to another is another buck-passing strategy. The strategic advantage in delegating the final decision to someone else is that it protects the party against pressure. Many a housewife saves herself from the salesman by saying sweetly, "Yes, it's a wonderful widget, and I'd love to buy one, but of course my husband makes all those decisions." So does the husband. "It sounds like a swell idea, Jack, but you know that Mary decides where we go for our vacation." By delegating certain decisions to the other, each protects himself (herself) from pressures by outsiders.

Both parents can protect themselves against pressures from children by, "Ask your mother" or "Ask your father." In a breakdown of the relationship between spouses, the wife may delegate all contacts to a lawyer. The husband can then no longer put pressures on her. "Talk to my lawyer," she can always say.

Both relinquishing the initiative and delegation of decision-making are, in effect, forms of noncommunication. People who use them simply drop out of the communication network and substitute someone else.

Sometimes one party in a difficult situation would like to concede, would like to renege on a commitment, would like to accept defeat without seeming to, without humiliation. A way must be found to save his face. One way is to reinterpret his commitment or reinterpret his position. Touchstone in *As You Like It* (Act V, Sc. iv)—a fool who used his folly to convey wit and wisdom—shows how seven justices, unable to settle a quarrel among themselves, finally did so by reinterpreting their several positions. When they met, "one of them thought but of an If, as, 'If you said so, then I said so'; and they shook hands and swore brothers. Your If is the only peace-maker; much virtue in If." Now anyone could change his original position without losing face.

The husband knows he was wrong in the quarrel this morning, but he is too proud to admit it. The wife knows that if she rubs in his errors he will have to defend them; if she gloats, he will withdraw. But if she can let him "explain" she can let him off the hook. He can prove that "what he really meant" was quite different from what he seemed to mean. So she lets him explain. "Oh, if that was what you meant, of course! I couldn't agree more!" Your If may not be the only peace-maker; still, as Touchstone had it, there is much virtue in If.

A brace of experimental studies have shown that: ". . . when spouses were faced with apparent discrepancies between [their] answers, they tended to reinterpret their answers" in order to demonstrate that there was "really" no disagreement. "The apparent popularity of denying disagreements may be deplorable but has, as far as present data reveals, no untoward effects."[18]

There are other forms of face-saving. The wife deliberately gets herself into an embarrassing position from which only her husband can extricate her and he only by doing something she wants him to do. She has told the Joneses, for example, that her husband gave her a mink stole for Christmas; now Mrs. Jones insists on seeing it.

The girl who allows herself to become pregnant before marriage may be foolhardy in the extreme. On the other hand, she may be strategically clever. If she knows her man and can accurately assess the payoff, this may be the best or only way to get him to marry her. He feels he has to save her from shame. (Some girls are so quixotic that they refuse to tell the father of the child precisely because they fear he will interpret the message as a strategic ploy.)

The wife who makes an engagement or an appointment in the presence of other people knows her husband cannot make a scene in public by forbidding it, though she knows he objects; he has to save her face. The girl who can be seen socially with a young man often enough to make the relationship look serious may force the young man to make it serious in order to save her face. A great deal of strategic success depends on the milk of human kindness, or fear of human unkindness.

"All courtship systems," an outstanding sociologist tells us, "are market systems, in which role bargains are struck. They differ from one another with respect to commodities which are more or less valuable in that market (beauty, personality, kinship position, family prestige, wealth) and who has the authority to do the marketing."[19] The conception of the relationship between the sexes as a bargaining one is quite old, and very explicit where parents arrange marriages for their children. "How big a dowry for their daughter," the young man's parents ask of the go-between. "A thousand *pecunia*," he replies. "Only a thousand for such a plain girl?" or, "The Alters offer more dowry than that and their girl is even prettier." "This girl is a good cook. . . ."

Even when courtship was a major preoccupation among men and women themselves, as in Restoration comedy, bargaining was quite explicit, especially in the so-called proviso scenes, such as the famous one in Congreve's *Way of the World* in which each specifies the terms—rights and privileges—demanded in the marriage. The bargaining concept is still accepted when, for example, people say at the announcement of an engagement, "She could have done better than that."

"The man's desire is for the woman; but the woman's desire is rarely other than for the desire of the man,"[20] especially if it will lead to marriage. Men in love want women; women in love want marriage, a commitment from men to care for them and protect them while they bear children. The rewards of marriage may be equally great to both men and women—they are, in fact, documentably greater for men than for women as measured in terms of mental health[21]—but aside from sexual security, they may not always seem very great to young men, especially of the Dionysian subsex. Marriage may seem considerably less desirable to them than bachelorhood. The young woman is thus asking for something he is not always willing to give. If during the courting period, women made it plain that they wanted marriage and children more than, or even rather than, sex partners, it might frighten the young men. The men want the woman, but often marriage and children are secondary.

One sociologist who has analyzed the complexities of the courtship process concludes that women are better at it than men. Knowing her man pays off for a woman: this is what information is for. It is usually a gentle kind of deception the young women practice in the courtship process, and they are deceiving themselves as much as they are the men.

... perhaps it is not inaccurate to believe that women are more clever than men in taking advantage of courtship processes. A girl may pretend to be extremely involved, to be the person wholly dominated by the relationship; this she does in order to lead the young man to fasten his emotions upon her and prepare the way for the conventional denouement of marriage, for, in the end, while protesting her love, she makes herself unattainable except in marriage; this is certainly not an unusual feminine tactic and is executed with subtlety which makes the man's crude attempts at guile seem sophomoric. Women understand the intricacies of courtship interaction better than men do.[22]

Not all games are strategic. Some are sick. A great deal of the communication between some people is mean, destructive, and hostile; it is meant to hurt. And does. We have already noted that words open up a vista of delightful relationships between the sexes but that they also add powerful weapons to their armories to hurt one another as well.

The psychiatrist is likely to see the painful use of words, and one of them has come up with a set of stock situations dealing with the way people get psychic rewards by hurting one another.[23] He lists, for example, five sexual games whose titles are enough to indicate their nature: Let's You and Him Fight, Perversion, Rapo, The Stocking Game, and Uproar; and seven marital games: Corner, Courtroom, Frigid Woman, Harried, If It Weren't for You, Look How Hard I've Tried, and Sweetheart.

Rapo has already been described. The marital game which the psychiatrist calls Corner hinges on deliberate misreading of one another's messages, on taking them literally, at face value, instead of interpreting them as they know they should be interpreted. There are two versions: one rewards the wife, one the husband. The wife "unconsciously" does or says something that annoys the husband. She knows very well that she should not take his annoyance seriously but she does; if that's the way you feel you can go to the movies by yourself. He does, full of resentment. She remains home, ostensibly hurt, but with a secret feeling of triumph. Or the husband takes the wife's pique at face value, knowing well that all she wants is to be coaxed; so he goes to the movies cheerfully, leaving her disappointed and resentful at home. In both cases, one of the partners has been "cornered." In the game called Frigid Woman, a wife repeatedly repulses her husband. When he stops making sexual advances to her, she "carelessly" sends "unwitting" messages in the form of seductive deshabille; but when he responds to her provocative signals, she again repulses him. She repeats the charade, this time even making overt advances to him. When he responds she does not repulse him at first. But at the critical point she retreats from him with a cry that all she wanted was affection and all he is interested in is sexual intercourse. The psychiatrist notes that both husband and wife may be afraid of sexual intimacy and play out this game to protect themselves.

Some of these sick games are also played by normal people in their day-to-day relationships; but they are exaggerated to pathological levels among the clinical cases. Spouses are used exploitatively to help fight inner battles. In extreme form, two sick people need one another desperately, to punish or to be punished. They prefer to be miserable together rather than self-embattled alone.

Communication between and among all the sexes and sub-sexes, by way of all the media—signs, signals, strategic moves, words—using all the models—protocommunication, inferential, empathic, sympathetic—carrying all kinds of messages—instrumental, expressive, strategic—may occur in all kinds of settings, on all kinds of stages. The cast varies. Some media and models are more appropriate for some settings than for others. Some messages are forbidden in some settings; some are prescribed. In any event, communication between and among the sexes is not the same everywhere and under all circumstances, in the family, for example, or at work or at play or in social life generally. Let's watch them on these four stages.

PART FOUR

MISE-EN-SCÈNE

CHAPTER TEN

En Famille

... in God's intention a meet and happy conversation is the chiefest and the noblest end of marriage.

—John Milton, *The Doctrine and the Discipline of Divorce*

Companionship based on "a meet and happy conversation" was not new even when Milton wrote about it in the seventeenth century. It had existed no doubt among many men and women in many times and places. It had been institutionalized in salons of the hetaerae in Greece. But it was not considered essential for marriage, at least by men, whatever God's intention may have been. Only fairly recently has companionship been viewed as an important ingredient for marriage. And even now it is not so viewed by everyone or in all classes. By and large, women prize it more than men. In the great ongoing war between the sexes, one major battle has to do with precisely this issue: women want Milton's version of marriage, they want meet and happy conversation. Eve may, in fact, have used the apple gambit primarily as an attention-getting device, to get Adam to talk to

[231]

her, for when conversing with him she found all seasons pleasing. Even without work to distract him, he may have enjoyed just lying around thinking or inviting his soul, preoccupations he did not share with her. Without concupiscence to appeal to for attention, what else did Eve have except new experience?

So far the success of women in their search for companionship in marriage has been greatest in the higher socioeconomic classes. Among them, in fact, one researcher, Harold Feldman, concludes that "communication between husband and wife on a verbal medium may be considered a significant index of the total relationship, as significant [as] or perhaps more so than the quality of the sexual relationship."[1] His conclusion is corroborated by an earlier study by Burgess and Wallin of 666 couples which reported correlations between sexual satisfaction and happiness or general satisfaction in marriage about the same as correlations between companionship and general satisfaction.[2] In other words, happiness in marriage and general satisfaction with it were as closely related to companionship as to sexual satisfaction.

Subjective corroboration of the relative value placed by couples on sexual adjustment and on companionship has been reported by George Levinger, who found that all of the class groupings in a sample of 49 couples ranked companionship ahead of sexual adjustment as marital goals.[3] And Boyd C. Rollins found among 480 middle-class couples that "highly valuing companionship in marriage by both husband and wife is important for marital satisfaction."[4]

One woman, explaining why her marriage did not last, illustrates the relatively greater weight assigned to companionship as contrasted to sexual adjustment:

Jack and I had at least two essentials that everyone says are necessary for a good marriage; mutual admiration and respect and a good sexual adjustment. That, according to theory, should have been enough. But that whole stretch in between was missing. None of that delightful intimacy, self-revelation, gaiety, joyful playfulness. And, no matter what the experts say, neither respectful admiration nor good sex nor even both combined is enough. It was no go. I have more rapport, fun, and sheer pleasure with Tom, whom I have never gone to bed with than with Jack.

Jack's version, to be sure, is not available; his version might be different.

Still, the high importance assigned to verbal communication by Feldman, as quoted above, is not really surprising, since there is doubtless a close relationship between good communication and good sexual relationships. In general, as one psychologist notes:

> Sex deteriorates with deterioration of the capacity of a person to establish a close, confiding, communicative, loving, non-sexual relationship with another person. . . . Openness before a person renders one open to . . . the riches of one's own feelings. The person who effectively guards himself against pain from the outside just as effectively ensures virtual sexual anesthesia.[5]

The importance now assigned to meet and happy conversation between spouses reflects a profound change in the very nature of marriage which has been in process in this century. It was articulated in 1945 in an outstanding textbook on the family which had as its central theme the transition from "an institutional to a companionship form" of marriage, resulting from major social changes which had created "situations in which impersonal, secondary associations predominate," so that "the small-family unit becomes the major area of intimate, affectional association." As a consequence, there had been a "growth of the companionship family, characterized by the mutual affection, sympathetic understanding, and comradeship of its members."[6] The institutional pattern may be viewed as a parallel one; the companionship pattern, as an interactional one.

In the parallel pattern the husbands and wives go their separate—close or distant—ways with a minimum of interaction. Each has his or her own sphere, performs whatever duties are called for, assuming that the other is performing similarly in his or her sphere. There is only a minimum amount of talk, and what there is, is likely to be instrumental. Little talk is needed. Role performance dovetails the relationship; that is enough to make it function.

The interactional model is one in which husbands and wives are expected not only to talk to one another but to converse with one another also, to share, to live integrated rather than segregated lives, to offer companionship. Merely earning the family living on the part of the husband or keeping a comfortable home on the part of the wife is not considered enough. Thus in one study of the relative importance assigned to nine marriage goals by a sample of sixty couples, "economic security" was ranked eighth by the wives and "attractive home" was ranked seventh by the husbands, but companionship and affection were ranked first by the husbands and wives respectively.[7]

The parallel or segregated pattern was characteristic of the traditional, especially rural, family. In the backwoods of Appalachia, for example, husbands and wives until recently did not even refer to one another by name. "He," "she," "the old lady," "the old man," were among the circumlocutions used to avoid even implied intimacy or personal interaction. The parallel pattern still persists among lower socioeconomic classes even in cities.

Both the parallel and the interactional pattern are, theoretically, expected to be affectively positive. That is, whether or not companionship is expected to be present in a marriage, it is universally hoped that the partners will not actively dislike one another. In both patterns in actual practice, however, relations may be either affectionate or hostile. Between the spouses going about their separate business there may be an understanding too deep for words; there may, conversely, be a sullen resentment also too deep for words. The interaction between husband and wife, similarly, may be warm and supportive; but it may also be lethal.

There is an impressive research literature documenting the association of good communication between spouses and happy marriages. It shows rather conclusively that good talk is an excellent marital bargain.[8] Much of the knowledge this research yields has long been in the folk wisdom. But not all. Some of it is in a contrary direction; it is different from the tenor of many current assumptions. Such, for example, is the finding, reported above, that companionship is as highly valued by marriage partners as a good sexual relationship is, as Burgess and

Wallin, in their study of 666 couples found. They reported that happiness in marriage or general satisfaction was as closely correlated with companionship as with sexual satisfaction.[9] Levinger corroborated this finding for wives, if not for husbands; that is, although "for husbands, sexual satisfaction was more related to general satisfaction, . . . for wives, marital communication was of greater importance."[10] And even Levinger's couples ranked companionship ahead of sexual adjustment as marital *goals.*[11]

The close relationship between at least some kinds of communication and sexuality was adumbrated by the old definition of conversation, "to have sexual relations," cited earlier. Jourard explains it by noting that "sex deteriorates with deterioration of the capacity of a person to establish a close, confiding, communicative, loving, non-sexual relationship with another person."[12] One might cavil at this interpretation, at least with the extent of its applicability; Dionysian men may divorce sexuality from other relationships. But for run-of-mine husbands and wives, especially those in marriages of the interactional or non-segregated type, Jourard's interpretation is probably right. Perhaps all we need to explain the relationship between companionship and sexual adjustment is Feldman's finding that highly satisfied couples feel closer to each other after discussions;[13] the way is thus open to sexual intimacy.

It may be, of course, that husbands and wives have good communication because the marital relationship is good to begin with; or they may achieve a good marital relationship because they have good communication; or both. A considerable amount of marriage counseling and therapy rests on the second viewpoint. Other students of the subject lean toward the first. Jourard notes that "a healthy relationship between two loving people is characterized by mutual knowledge, openness of communication, freedom to be oneself in the presence of the other without contrivance, and respect" and since the amount of mutual disclosure is so great, people incapable of such close communication avoid marriage like the plague.[14]

Whatever the direction of the association, however, there are few conclusions in the social sciences better buttressed than the close relationship between marital success and good communication between the spouses. The consistency of research in this area is very convincing. It seems almost completely beyond doubt that good verbal relationships between husbands and wives are related, as cause or as effect, or as both, to good marital relationships. The conclusion by Feldman that good communication in marriage may be even more important than a good sexual relationship can be well documented.

Whatever the nature of the relationship between good talk and good marital relationships may be, and however important it may be for both partners, it seems to be especially important for wives. For wives, as Levinger found, good communication was more related to general satisfaction with the marriage than was sexual satisfaction.[15] A similar finding was reported by Roland G. Tharp.[16] And Locke and Thomes, on the basis of a careful scrutiny of the literature, concluded that at least "in the American culture husband-wife communication may be more important for the adjustment of wives than for husbands.[17] Levinger found, further, that although the happiness of husbands was not related to talking about a bad day, that of wives was; not only talking about their own bad day—which is quite understandable—but also their husbands' talking about theirs.[18] Apparently, just to be talking. Research thus supports Charlotte Brontë's insight into women. When she wanted to supply a happy ending to her novel *Jane Eyre*, she supplied it in the form of a good conversational relationship between Jane and her husband. "We are ever together. . . . We talk . . . all day long. . . ." Modern women might find this a bit excessive; togetherness does, after all, have some limits. But the limits for women are far broader than for men.

❖❖❖❖❖

The psychologically deserted wife, that is, the wife who is denied the comfort of discussing her problems with her husband, is likely to turn elsewhere for such support, especially to her relatives.[19] One study reported that six out of ten wives had such sources of support. The net effect is doubtless a strengthening of blood ties at the expense, perhaps, of the conjugal tie. Middle-class wives tended to be less exclusively dependent on relatives; they tended to confide in friends as well as in relatives. Husbands were reported to be much less likely to have confidants; only two out of ten did.[20]

Despite the unequivocal evidence in favor of marital talk and despite the wives' great need and longing for it, good talk between husbands and wives is not nearly so common as one would suppose. Not nearly common enough for the wives, at any rate, even in the lower socioeconomic classes where the companionship model of marriage has not as yet permeated and justified the wife's longing. Many wives face a silent spring—summer, fall, and winter, too.

Contrary to the old adage, talk—by husbands—does not seem to be cheap, at least in the sense that it is copious, free, and abundantly offered. There is a long and melancholy re-search documentation, indeed, of the fact that husbands and wives do not talk to one another very much. Quite aside from the fleeing Dionysian male described by Fiedler, there is the grim evidence presented by observers of the American scene for over a century. In 1839, a German visitor to the United States had noted that an American woman is seldom "the inti-mate friend of her husband, the repository of his secrets, his true and faithful counsellor."[21] Less than a hundred years later, the Lynds noted in Middletown that "in general a high degree of companionship is not regarded as essential for marriage."[22] The wives minded this. They were lonely. They enjoyed talk-ing even to the research interviewers. "In a number of cases, after the interviewer had succeeded in breaking through an apparently impenetrable wall of reserve or of embarrassed fear, the housewife would say at the close of the talk, 'I wish you could come often. I never have anyone to talk to,' or 'My husband never goes any place and never does anything but work. You can talk to him, but he never says anything. In the evenings, he comes home and sits down and says nothing. I like to talk and be sociable, but I can hardly ever get anything out of him.' "[23]

The same lack of talk between husbands and wives was noted again in the 1940's:

It would appear . . . that there is . . . too little intimacy in marriage, as the word is here understood. It is the rare husband and wife who pull up the chairs and spend an hour talking for their own pleasure about non-utilitarian things. The husband has his business, the wife her "cultural interest," and never the twain shall meet. Their intellectual and spiritual lives remain personal and separate, with the result that while their marriage is a physical union and an economic organization it involves no spiritual communion and no completion of minds. This is a large factor in the loneliness of the people and their all-too-common feeling of frustration in marriage.[24]

The same refrain was echoed once more in the 1960's. "Wives often lament, 'He never *talks* to me!' " an author in a popular women's magazine tells us.[25] And the syndicated agony-columns in the press continue to include letters from wives with the old lament that their husband's "only interest is dinner, a look at the news and off to bed," leaving them "with nobody around to share a discussion of books and articles."[26]

Since the interactional pattern of marriage has not yet succeeded the parallel pattern in the working or blue-collar class, the wives in such marriages should not expect much in the way of meet and happy conversation. But they long for it anyway. In fact, their longing for it may mark the transition from the old to the new conception of marriage. Research shows that even in working-class or blue-collar marriages wives feel bereft. One study of workingmen's wives, for example, found that they "often wish for more intimate interaction with their husbands, and a chance to share his experience away from home with him. More often than not, their experience is along the following line: 'I wish he'd let me take an interest in his work. But he doesn't want to talk to me about it at all. He just grunts when I ask him about it. He never has wanted to discuss it with me.' "[27] And the meagerness of talk between husbands and wives in blue-collar marriages was further documented in a study by Mirra Komarovsky. She found that husbands and wives pursued their own separate lives, amicably or not, but with a minimum of talk, a situation that was more troubling to the wives than to the husbands. Three times as many wives as husbands, in fact, complained that their mates did not talk enough or listen enough to their concerns. None of the wives reported that their spouses criticized them for not talking enough; but about a seventh of the husbands did. And probably many of the wives felt like criticizing their husbands for not talking to them enough, whether they actually did or not.[28]

But a dearth of conversation is not limited to working-class marriages, where it is expectable. It can be found at any level, even in those in which the interactional pattern of marriage is supposed to prevail. Women in higher socioeconomic classes may be less tolerant of marital separateness, but even among families at these levels, a sizeable proportion have fallen into the parallel or segregated pattern rather than achieved the interactional or companionship pattern, and are characterized by a minimum of talk. John Cuber interviewed 437 upper middle-class persons in the 35 to 55 age bracket, all white, all non-clinical, all urban, including widowed, divorced, and unmarried individuals in the appropriate proportions. People with these characteristics constitute only a small proportion—about 9 percent—of the total population, but they are socially important beyond their size. They are educated, traveled, sophisticated, emancipated, and articulate. If good talking relationships did not prevail here, where conditions were auspicious, something must indeed be wrong. They did not, in three out of five of the categories Cuber uncovered. In the first, or "conflict-habituated" relationship, there was a good deal of interaction, but it was of a hostile and quarreling type, sometimes genteel, sometimes not. In the second, or "devitalized" relationship, there was no active conflict present, but what interplay there was between spouses was apathetic and lifeless. The "passive-congenial" relationship was comfortably adequate but not really engaging. The "vital" was a really engrossing relationship, and the "total" was not only engrossing but multifaceted, the partners having many vital involvements with one another. The last two—the vital and the total—would presumably be characterized by good and abundant talk. But he found "good relationships . . . the exception rather than the rule" and concluded that "if there is a core problem in handling the world of men and women, the nub of it is the impasse in communication between the married and otherwise related man and woman who would be presumed *a priori*, because intimate, to be in good rapport. These impasses persist despite the fact that this is a highly educated, articulate group, highly adept in social skills."[29] If inarticulateness is a handicap to good communication in the lower socioeconomic levels, articulateness is not a guarantee of good communication in the higher. Where there is little talk in the higher socio-economic classes, the lack is due to personal and conjugal factors; in the lower, more likely to class-cultural ones.

There is interesting corroborative, though tangential, evidence of a low degree of communication between the sexes in a study of value-convergence among spouses. If there were a high level of communication between spouses, one would expect them to tend to converge in their values with time. Not, apparently, so. One study of thirty-four college-student couples, for example, found that although the spouses did tend to agree more than randomly selected matched pairs did, still there was no relationship between length of marriage, frequency of interaction, and "togetherness" on one side and agreement on values on the other. The authors concluded that "marriage partners may select one another on the basis of the agreement they perceived . . . but the level of agreement does not seem to be affected in any way by their interaction."[30] It is an idle dream, it seems, to hope that one can change a person's values by marrying him. If one wants agreement on values in a spouse, it is easier to marry with the agreement than to achieve it by communication later on.

The reluctance, refusal, or inability on the part of husbands to talk with their wives has personal, social, cultural, and societal roots. Everything said about noncommunication applies, of course, to husbands as well as to wives. In the case of the "weak, silent" type, silence may be self-protective. "Anyone who is reluctant to be known by another person and to know another person—sexually and cognitively—will find the . . . intimacy of marriage somewhat terrifying."[31] Men—especially Dionysian men—may be more reluctant than women. In some cases, lack of talk has strategic reasons; if you talk too much you give yourself away and surrender the strategic advantage of secrecy and surprise; you give her something to use against you. In blue-collar marriages, Mirra Komarovsky reported cases in which the husband withdrew to protect himself against emotional demands which he could not meet; he kept his distance.[32] In Middletown, the husbands simply felt that communication between the sexes was impossible; they conceded that women were "purer and morally better than men" but otherwise not suitable for companionship. "You simply cannot criticize or talk in general terms to a woman," they insisted, because "there's something about the female mind that always short-circuits a general statement into a personal criticism."[33]

Then there is just sheer boredom. When a wife initiates conversation, Feldman reported, it is likely to be about "her work, the children's problems and accomplishments, her parents and personal feelings, cultural topics," topics about which he couldn't care less. This boredom is even more characteristic in blue-collar than in other marriages. Mirra Komarovsky illustrates in great detail the boredom husbands express with their wives' talk. In part, she believes, this results from the exclusion of women from their husbands' work world, which deprives the wife of a sympathetic basis for understanding the topics he might be interested in.[34]

Wives complain not only of the meagerness but also of the quality of the talk in their marriage. Mirra Komarovsky found more women than men bored with marital talk—a third of the women, but only a fifth of the men.[35] Still these women wanted more talk from their husbands. So boredom couldn't be all that important. They probably preferred more interesting talk than they were likely to get, but boring or not, they wanted more. They would probably settle for whatever they could get if they had a choice between boredom and silence.

Perhaps a major reason for the paucity of good marital talk, despite its documentable relation to marital success and despite the deep longing for it which wives feel, is the relative recency of the new form of marriage which calls for it. It is hard to realize how new the idea is that husbands and wives should have a companionship relation to one another. Men and women have always been sexually attracted to one another, and there is an enormous literature on sexual relations between spouses. But there is as yet little precedent for emphasis on good social relations between the sexes in marriage.

There tends to be great inertia in cultural change, an inertia which impedes accommodation to the new demands being made on marriage. Thus, although modern marriage is called upon to supply intimate, affectional companionship, there is little in the education of young people to prepare them for it. Neither boys nor girls have been socialized into this kind of sex relationship. Indeed, almost everything in their training militates against it. The whole weight of the marital relationship is made to rest on a coital relationship. Evelyn Duvall in a personal letter has commented on the fact that

parents and children do little real talking with one another; children thus get little experience in good person-to-person conversation, listening, responding, empathizing with another person in face-to-face contact. Courtship tends to be based upon catching and being caught in a romantic game that relies upon sex appeal and attraction, sex stimulation and response with but a minimal intellectual and social contact between the dating and courting pairs. As a result the husband-wife relationship is not entered with a basis of conversation and companionship and the circle is repeated in their families.

Mirra Komarovsky goes even further. There is not only a negative lack of training but, in addition, in her words, "a trained incapacity" to share; boys are socialized into a role which positively inhibits expressiveness as effeminate. A masculine man does not talk about his feelings. And if the husband should be tempted to capitulate to his wife, his male associates keep him from it.[36]

It is conceivable that the time may yet come when we will all recognize the importance of a meet and happy conversation in marriage and try to prepare young people for it. The dividends in the form of successful marriages will be enormous.

It is just barely possible, though, that our society has not wanted husbands and wives to achieve too much social autonomy, to find themselves self-sufficient and hence too independent of the outside world.[37]

One class of wives is in an especially bad spot. Although marital communication is related to education—the more the better—differences in education between husbands and wives have a blighting effect if it is the wife who is superior. Such marriages are far from uncommon. Among once-married white husband-wife families, married between 1950 and 1960, more than a fourth (27.4 percent) were marriages in which wives had more years of schooling than their husbands, according to the 1960 census of population. Feldman found that in his sample even a difference of only a year or two of schooling in favor of the wife made for a marked decline in her satisfaction with her husband's companionship. It tended also to have a negative effect on love and her total marital satisfaction. Understandably the husband's position was not enviable either, for "when a man marries such a woman he is likely to be in for considerable criticism from her about his uncouth ways. . . . And the strain of incompatible outlooks is compounded by his inability to measure up to her expectations."[38] Alas, the shrew again, or even, perhaps, the bitch, and once more the reverberations of feminine superiority. Differences in the husband's favor do not have these untoward effects.

There doesn't seem to be much that wives can do to gain the kind of companionship they would like to have in marriage. Would it help if they tried more interesting, less boring, topics of conversation? Would they succeed better if they talked about, let us say, the odds on the current heavy-weight match? or who was going to win the game today? or who was the best pitcher this year?

Probably not. For although wives are increasingly encouraged to take the initiative in sexual relations, initiative in verbal relations do not seem to be rewarded and, in fact, may be punished. Feldman's description of marriages in which wives made the verbal overtures is depressing. Initiation of discussion by the wife was found to be negatively related to the amount of time spent talking with one another daily. The less he talked, the more she tried to get him to talk; or, equally probable, the more she tried to get him to talk, the less likely he was to want to talk. Understandably, therefore, such wife-initiated discussion left a negative effect. Feldman concluded that couples in which "the wife tends to initiate conversations find their conversations and their marriage less rewarding. Since they talk less with each other, it may be that the wife attempts to provoke a response from her husband; she also tends to be more dominant in general. . . . His passivity or her aggression, or both, are likely to be related to their dissatisfaction."[39] Again the blighting—cichlid—effect of feminine "aggression" on fragile masculinity.

In any event, whatever the reasons why husbands, especially in the lower socioeconomic classes, are reluctant to engage their wives in conversation, the wife must, apparently, wait until he is ready. If she attempts to seize the initiative, to make him talk, or even listen, the net effect will be disagreeable. She loses the war even if she wins a particular battle.

❖❖❖❖❖

Whatever the disappointments and complaints of wives in lower socioeconomic classes and despite the glum situation in Cuber's upper-class world, the picture among marriages in Feldman's sample is really not all bad. These couples averaged an hour and a half in conversation every day. In addition, they laughed together daily and had a stimulating exchange of ideas several times a week. They had arguments once a month, to be sure, but they also had gay times away from home with the same frequency. True, there were times when they felt resentful and misunderstood, but not often. They felt unneeded and too angry to talk to one another, but only once or twice a year.

There were, of course, individual differences among the couples which this overall inventory obscures. Some couples did better; some worse. Class, as we have already noted, made a difference. So did religion. Protestants, for example, as compared with Catholic couples or couples with mixed or no religion, spent more time talking with each other every day. Jewish and Catholic couples spent about the same amount of time talking to each other. One such differentiating factor may warrant more than a mere passing note. Couples without children, Feldman found, had more verbal communication with one another than did couples with children at home. They talked more about their own parents and about conventional topics. "But conversations are more reinforcing for the childless, who feel closer to each other after discussion."[40]

The stage in the family cycle, as well as class factors, seem to be related to talk between husbands and wives. The Locke-Sabagh-Thomes study of 126 urban couples, for example, reported that "primary communication of younger husbands and wives was significantly greater than that of older husbands and wives."[41] Blood and Wolfe found that informative companionship was high during the honeymoon stage and declined thereafter, more for childless couples than for those with children. During the preadolescent and adolescent years of children, however, there was not much difference between families with and without children. In the later years, when the children were older or had left home, informative companionship fell drastically, to a low in the retired years.[42] Feldman found that marital discussions tended to be at their maximum at the beginning of the marriage; they declined as time went on. Children seemed to have a blighting effect on marital talk in Feldman's sample. Talk between husbands and wives tended to decline as the children appeared and reached its nadir when the children were in their teens. Thereafter, however, it recovered somewhat. "Children," Feldman concluded, "appear to be . . . disruptive to marital communication and to marital satisfaction."[43] Unlike Blood and Wolfe, though, Feldman found an increase in verbal communication among the older couples whose children had left home. He suggests several interpretations for the original downward trend in marital talk: "the couple may not need to communicate verbally with each other since they may understand the other without being verbal, they may find each other less interesting, or have less to talk about."[44]

The total character of the verbal relationship, that is, of topics and affective nature, as well as the amount of talk, seems to change over time. Objective and conventional topics, Feldman found, increased in importance; discussion about the house, parents, and children tended to decline. Time seemed to mollify the nature of marital conflict also. Responses became less punitive. Husbands and wives talked about their troubles more calmly and forgot them rather than criticized one another and slammed the door.

Data with respect to the later stages of marriage are especially significant because of the new marital relationship now emerging. In the past, a wife was still living in a home with unmarried children when her husband died; there never was a time after the first year or two of marriage when the husband and wife were living alone. Nowadays, however, a woman is fairly young —under fifty—when her last child is married and she is not going to be widowed for another ten to fifteen years. A new kind of marriage, one in which the parental function is completed, is therefore possible. Men and women still youthful and vigorous, now have over a decade of companionship left to them without the distractions of parenthood. It is a relationship never known before. The potentials are only as limited as the imagination of the spouses themselves. Not the delicious and exciting intimacy of the honeymoon, but the warm and comfortable adventure of maturity is in store for those who have the imagination to take advantage of it.

The topics families talk about seem to be remarkably limited. One study of conversations in eighty-two families found a rich variety in the total sample, but a limited range within individual families. "In other words, most families talk habitually about a few things. One cannot escape the conviction that the range is determined not so much by the intellectual capacities of the persons involved as by their predilections. For example, some of the highly intelligent families devote their conversational prowess to a very limited number of topics which are discussed both *ad infinitum* and *ad nauseam*."[45] A narrow range might not be so boring if it included stimulating topics; but when the talk is constantly about the neighbors' children, the boss, or the movies, as it sometimes is, it can be deadly.

The Lynds found the topics people talked about to center on such things as plans for an addition to the house, normal school for the children, automobiles, lodge affairs, or the movies. In very poor families, where "the necessities of shelter and food overshadow other plans, such conversation as there is may be of a bickering sort, or may lapse into apathetic silence."[46]

Bossard found that some families talked mainly about themselves, their experiences, their achievements, their misfortunes, and their problems. Others talked about outside matters. Some talked about other people—friends, relatives, work associates, enemies, or public figures; others about things—airplanes, taxes, automobiles, books, and the like. Some merely recounted or described; others analyzed, judged, imputed motives, evaluated purposes and results. In his sample, the judgments and evaluations were usually depreciatory. It is interesting to speculate on the specific effects such depreciatory talk has on the socialization of children.

The commonest topic discussed by Feldman's couples was the husband's work. Money management was in the middle of the list of twenty-eight topics. And sex was fourth from the bottom, indicating a frequency of discussion of only once or twice a month.[47] The low salience of sex talk in marriage has been explained by John H. Gagnon as related to the different roles assigned to the sexes, roles "learned by and large through the exchange of cues and gestures rather than through discussion."[48] As a result, it is "quite possible for extensive and long-term sexual relationships . . . to work out to the apparent satisfaction of the two persons involved without a word being spoken about sexual behavior and its consequent pleasure or pain."[49]

Although Feldman did not find significant class differences in amount of time spent in talk, he did find differences in topics discussed. The white-collar couples expectedly had a wider variety of topics; the blue-collar couples were more male-oriented in their talk. The white-collar couples talked more about such objective topics as the news and cultural events and less about the husband's work and sports; they placed more value on intellectual stimulation; the blue-collar, on companionship.

Feldman wondered if the topics discussed differed in their effects on marital cohesiveness. He even anticipated that some might have a negative effect, might be threatening rather than contributory to marital unity. Not so, in his sample. If it were possible for husbands and wives to talk to one another at all, they could bear to talk about almost anything without injuring the cohesiveness of their relationship.

It might have been expected that couples would have some topics which were quite sensitive ones and would be indicative of disintegration in the relationship. In general, our data support the opposite conclusion—discussions with the spouse about most topics seem to have a cohesive effect. However, there were differences by topics in the extent of their cohesiveness. Discussions about the intrafamilial topics—children's problems, personal feelings, and sex—seemed to have the most cohesive effects while the management of finances, parents, cultural topics, work, and religion were less cohesive. The finding about money management as a potential source of conflict is borne out by several studies.[50]

We have already noted it in Middletown. The fact that talking about sex brought the husbands and wives somewhat closer together suggests that in these families there were few inhibitions. Talk may have been an acceptable substitute for or an erotic prelude to coitus.

Different topics, Feldman found, had different effects on the marital relationship at different times. Talking about impersonal topics, at least in the early years of marriage, did not leave the couple feeling closer together; discussion of values apparently did. Later on, however, talking about values did not have this effect,[51] but discussions about religion and culture did. Levinger found, not unexpectedly, that wives were happier when their husbands talked about outside frustrations than when they talked about the wives' own defects.[52]

❖❖❖❖❖

No matter what the topic of conversation may be, the message conveyed may include any of the forms we have already explored: simple information, threats, promises, strategies, moves —the works. It may be affectionate or hostile. Some families habitually snarl at one another; some purr, as Bossard found in his analysis of the tonal quality of family conversation:

At one extreme are conversations which abound with "snarl words," and much of the talk consists of spasmodically throwing verbal bites at each other as one throws sticks at a dog. There are loud noises, yelling, wrangling, constant interruptions, so that the whole performance partakes of the nature of static on the radio. At the other extreme are the family conversations which suggest, by way of contrast, the Sunday afternoon symphony. A quiet and polite exchange of ideas goes on, "purr words" dominate, there is politeness and consideration when disagreement arises. People are allowed to finish a sentence. Even the children are accorded these courtesies.[53]

The use of purr words does not, to be sure, mean that the message is friendly or affectionate. It is possible to deliver the most lethal verbal blows in the most dulcet tones, as almost anyone can testify from his own observation.

We noted that words add not only to the resources of the lover but also to the armory of the combatant. Because family members know one another's weaknesses, they know how to hurt one another. In some families, Goode has noted, though to the casual visitor the members seem insensitive to one another, close observation shows that they are sensitive enough to one another to know their weaknesses and guilts and therefore how to hurt most painfully.[54] Bossard's study corroborates the conclusion that no matter what people are talking about, the message they convey can be a hostile one. Wisecracks, smart-alecky comments, sadistic phrases, cutting speech, stinging remarks, no matter what the tonal quality of the voice or the specific words used, find the jugular vein and leave the victim bleeding.

In some families only superficial or instrumental talk is possible. Just enough is communicated to coordinate family activities: I won't be home for dinner, I need money for books, I'll let you know if I'll be here this afternoon, you can reach me at this number . . . but no more. There is no open quarreling; but neither is there fun or gaiety. The atmosphere is gloomy. "Members do not discuss their problems or experiences with each other and communication is kept to a minimum."[55] What arguments there are in this type of relationship are about little things; facing the big issues would destroy the relationship.

Again, let's not overdo the negative. The messages may also be of love, affection, and tenderness, of support and understanding. Blood and Wolfe studied such verbal stroking in marriage under the rubric of "the mental-hygiene or therapeutic function in marriage." To wives who turned to their husbands when they felt troubled (about half of those questioned, and more in the higher socioeconomic levels), the husbands gave sympathy and affection (28 percent), help toward solution (6 percent), or withdrawing from the situation (3 percent). Even just listening (18 percent) helped. Some (20 percent) offered help in the way of advice which, of course, may or may not have been welcome. But only a very small proportion were critical and rejecting (6 percent) or pooh-poohing (7 percent).[56]

✦✦✦✦✦

People who know one another well supply a great deal to the talk of others. They may not always be right, but they know in general what the others mean without having to have it all spelled out. This is true of work groups, roommates, fraternity brothers, college girls. It is preeminently true of families, especially of husbands and wives. Clark Vincent calls this ability to supply what is missing a kind of shorthand, and he illustrates it with this case:[57]

COMMENT	TRANSLATION OR TOTAL MESSAGE
Wife: You never care for me.	When you are ill I am with you 24 hours a day to look after and nurse you, giving you everything you want, including your meals in bed. But when I am ill you go on to work and my mother or someone else comes in to help. I struggle along and you have to work late or have other meetings at night.
Husband: I do too but you don't appreciate it.	I'm the breadwinner and I have to work. I can't afford to stay home with you all day when by working I can afford to hire someone full time to stay with you if that were needed. You don't appreciate my hiring someone to look after you as something I do for you.

Wife: You don't even know what I am talking about.	I'm lonely when I am sick and I hurt. I want you to comfort me, read to me, tell me you love me. I want to feel I am more important. I want to think you are worrying more about my being ill than about whether or not you get another contract or business deal.
Husband: Yes, I do! What about last night?	I know you want me to drop everything and give my individual attention to you, but the world still goes on and I have to make a living. Last night I was dead tired when I came home late, but I bathed the youngsters and put them to bed for you.
Wife: You don't believe I'm sick.	You expected me to put the kids to bed when I can hardly hold my head up?
Husband: Who argued that you go see the doctor?	If I didn't really care for you I wouldn't have been so concerned that you see the physician. I know more about how sick you are than you do.
Wife: Men have all the advantages.	When you are sick, I'm your nurse and the company gives you sick leave with pay. I have no nurse, no sick leave or pay, and have to keep running the house.

Men and women differ in every cell of their bodies. No society has ever been able to ignore this fact. Because they are so different, as noted in Chapter Two, it is impossible for them to have the same experiences; social differences in experience thus reenforce culturally defined differences. At the bare biological level, then, they are strangers to one another. All right, concedes the *What*-difference? school of thought. For the most part men and women respond like human beings rather than as sexually differentiated beings. They are not strangers outside of the bedroom.

Still one of the most thought-provoking results of a not inconsiderable research effort in the area of husband-wife interaction is how little they really do know or understand one another in even the human-being (as distinguished from the sexual-being) realm. "I know him like a book," brags a wife. Yet, under laboratory or experimental conditions, neither husband nor wife can come up with the right answers about the other even half of the time, let alone all the time.

Even in the simplest kind of predictions of one another's behavior they are usually wrong. One experimenter, for example, asked young husbands and wives which one of them would tend to talk more during a decision-making session dealing with how they should spend a hypothetical windfall of three hundred dollars. The session was taped so that the actual amount of talking done by each was on record and could be measured. Only seventeen out of fifty individuals correctly predicted who would do more talking. Even more surprising, after the session was over and the subjects were again asked who had talked more, over half still judged incorrectly. " . . . Only 11 persons were accurate both on the basis of the pre-session and post-session responses. Over half of those who judged accurately before the session failed to judge accurately immediately after the session."[58]

This experiment was paper-and-pencil in nature. A later study presented actual rewards for successful prediction of spouse's behavior. The subjects were highly motivated to show that they knew how their spouses would act. Husbands and wives in separate rooms were shown an array of twenty Christmas-type gifts—lingerie, gloves, scarves, belts, wallets—ten suitable for men, ten for women. If, without communication, they could successfully coordinate their choices, they would receive the gifts as rewards. They all failed. Not one of the twenty-five couples succeeded in reading or predicting one another's choices on as many as five items. (Among these twenty-five young couples, both husbands and wives tended to predict that the other would select the feminine gifts; that is, both gave priority to gifts that would please the wife.[59] This was variously explained by the experimenter and the subjects. The husbands, being graduate students, were poor, and their generosity was interpreted by some as compensation for the sacrifices the wife was obliged to make. Others interpreted the preference by both spouses for the feminine gifts as the result of the coordinating effect of custom; both spouses, that is, were following the prescribed custom, which would tend to favor women.)

In still another study, this time of thirty-nine couples, each partner was asked separately to give the names of persons considered by both spouses to be close mutual friends, not counting relatives. Only three couples were in complete agreement in listing mutual close friends, while one couple completely failed to agree.[60]

Although spouses know one another so little that they cannot predict one another's behavior, they can predict fairly well what their spouses will *say* about themselves. When asked, for example, what they thought their mates would say was true about themselves on such statements as "I assume responsibility readily" or "I am critical of others" or "I try to be boss" or "I worry over minor items," three-fourths of all the subjects in one study did very well.[61] They could, that is, predict what their spouses would say about themselves (whether what they said was correct or not is another question) but not what they would actually do, or how they would actually behave.

Happily married spouses, understandably, predict what each will say of the other better than unhappily married spouses. One study of eighty-two satisfactorily adjusted and eighty unsatisfactorily adjusted couples found that three-fourths of the first set, but only about half of the second, agreed in their checking of 128 traits of self and spouse.[62] And another, based on an elaborate sixty-item questionnaire which asked not only how the subject himself or herself felt and how the spouse felt, but also how the subject thought the spouse would answer, reported a high degree of agreement among ten nondisturbed couples and a significantly lower level of agreement among twelve disturbed couples.[63]

An Elmo Roper survey of 456 couples found that "Americans are often mistaken about the values that they believe their mates see in them. . . . Wives tended to overrate the importance to their husbands of their homemaking skills and sexual attractiveness, while husbands underrate intelligence, common interests and the same religion as qualities their wives most appreciate in them."[64]

Almost amusing was the lack of agreement between husbands and wives in Feldman's sample. They differed with respect to what topics they talked about, the amount of time spent talking, the one who initiated the conversation, and who made the decisions. "The low level of consensus and the number of disparities in perception," Feldman thought, "may indicate a serious lack of communication between spouses about what does occur. Projection in terms of one's needs may be distorting simple everyday events. If these sex differences can occur so often among these generally well satisfied couples, it would not be surprising to find even less consensus and more distortion in other less satisfied couples. The level of occurrence, however, in the present sample might indicate a low level of communication between spouses."[65]

Women seem to be better than men in the ability to predict what the attitude of other family members will be with respect to family ideology. They seem also to be themselves more readable or predictable.

At the opposite pole, so far as scientific seriousness is concerned, were the results during the first few days of a television program, "Newlywed Game," in which young wives had to predict what their husbands would say in reply to four questions about one or the other of the couple, and the husbands, similarly, had to predict the wives' answers in reply to another set of questions. The average level of success was slightly over two out of four questions. This was considerably above chance, however, since some of the questions were completely open and even the multiple-choice questions gave two, three or four alternatives.[66] And one husband has commemorated in verse, far from deathless, his ability to read what his wife has on her mind before she has a chance to say it:

> Spare the details!
> It's enough to make the merest
> Mention of your problem, dearest.
> For me you needn't diagram it
> Since the chances are I am it![67]

One of the most amusing sidelights to this whole matter of spousal communication is the fact that the better people think they are at reading their spouses, the less well they really are at it. In one study, again of married college students, it was reported that "the higher males rated their own empathic communication, the less able were they to predict their wives' responses to the Burgess-Wallin self-rating items. . . . Likewise the higher females rated their own empathic communication, the less able they were to predict their husbands' marital role opinions."[68]

❖❖❖❖❖

Before talking about the specifically sexual forms of communication, we have to remind ourselves that there is almost nothing more idiosyncratic than sexual experience. Even the idiosyncratic differences in taste buds which make the same chemical taste sweet to one subject and bitter to another, or the visual anomaly which causes color blindness, do not exceed the idiosyncratic differences among human beings in their sexual experiences. Kinsey and his associates told us long ago that "even the scientific discussions of sex show little understanding of the range of variation in human behavior. More often the conclusions are limited by the personal experience of the author." And they were talking of something as relatively simple as mere frequency. Individuals at one extreme or the other of any continuum dealing with sexuality "may be totally unaware of the possibility of others . . . having histories that are . . . remote from [their] own."[69]

Such idiosyncracies do not mean that shared-experience models are not possible. They do mean that everyone—husbands, wives, and scientists, too—has to be careful not to infer or take it for granted that the sexual experience of others is the same as his or her own or that his or her own is the same as that of others.

The inability of husbands and wives to read one another in the specifically sexual sphere finds striking confirmation in a considerable research literature. Kinsey and his associates attempted to validate some of their findings by comparing responses of husbands and wives in 231 marriages. For some of the items—number of children, for example—identical responses were forthcoming for all couples. Three-fifths gave identical responses on length of premarital acquaintance and length of engagement. Age at marriage and time between marriage and first birth were agreed upon by about two-thirds of the couples. But identical responses were given by only a third of the couples on maximum frequency of marital coitus or average frequency of coitus in early marriage. Responses on average frequency of coitus and on percentage of coitus with orgasm for the wife agreed in only a little over half of the couples.[70]

The Kinsey group invokes selective perception to explain its results. Since wives often complain about their husband's desire for more coitus than he has and husbands complain about lack of enough, "the females may be overestimating the actual frequencies" and "the husbands . . . are probably underestimating the frequencies with which they do have it."[71] These husbands and wives do not see the same red. Other researchers agree; they also invoke cultural expectations as well as own sexual satisfaction as explanatory of such distortions.

Levinger adds another facet to the picture. He compared spouse's own reported preference with respect to frequency of coitus with estimate of mate's preference, and found that "regardless of the spouses' actual preference, our respondents tended to overestimate the husband's preference and to underestimate the wife's preferences. This occurred even in the . . . group where the expressed preferences of the wife were clearly greater."[72] He interprets this tendency for both husbands and wives to reply in terms of the cultural expectations for each sex in terms of a theory of "cognitive consistency." "For example, to attribute a higher sexual desire to the female spouse would be dissonant with one's adherence to the cultural norm. Thus respondents are inclined to deny instances of the wife's higher relative desire."[73]

It is possible, too, that the tendency to assign preference for greater coital frequency to husbands and preference for less frequency to wives may be a residual from the probable situation early in marriage. The desired frequency of sexual outlet, as measured in terms of masturbation by single men and women in their late teens and early twenties was about six or seven times greater among men than among women.[74] This difference may become so impressed on the spouses that it remains in their minds even after the difference itself has disappeared or been reversed.

In any event, the impediments to clear communication in the area of sex come not only from sex differences which make the reading of signs and signals equivocal, but also from the cultural stereotypes which interpose themselves between us and the world we live in. Husbands or wives *are* that way because the cultural stereotype says they are; my own observations and experience can't possibly be right if they contradict the stereotype.

With respect to one critical item—proportion of times wife experiences orgasm—another interpretation is pertinent. Kinsey and his associates explained the low proportion of his couples who agreed on this item—slightly over half—in terms of the gentle deception practiced by wives. "The male believes that his female partner experiences orgasm more often than she herself reports; but it is to be noted that the wife sometimes deceives her husband deliberately on that point."[75] A considerable amount of space in the literature of marital sex is devoted to the unhappy wife who is denied orgasm by either an inconsiderate or an unskilled husband. Very little is said of the loving wife who practices thoughtful deceit to please her husband.

❖❖❖❖❖

It has become a cliché that the sexual act, or acts, can be used to convey a wide gamut of messages, all the way from contempt or hatred to tenderness and love; that it, or they, can be used to build up or to tear down. To confer pleasure or to deny it. To punish or to reward. To alienate or to reconcile. To repel or to attract.

Modern, especially educated, white-collar men and women want more than "raw sex." The quickie in the car or on the run is for them no longer enough, if, in fact, it ever was, especially for women. Women want more personal responsiveness than their forebears. Men want more than mere acquiescence. Both sexes want to be told that they are desirable, desired. He wants the message that only she can send; she wants the same message from him.

It was once supposed that long sexual foreplay was required for women to expedite response. Kinsey and his associates showed that this is not the case. Women can arrive at climax as quickly as men. They prolong the foreplay not necessarily as a prerequisite for orgasm but because it is this kind of psycho-social sexual relationship that they crave. The "insatiable women" sometimes referred to in the literature of sex—when they are not a figment of the male imagination—are probably women with insatiable desire for such psychological and social intimacy, rather than women with insatiable desire for orgasm. Even moderate craving for such psychological closeness on the part of a woman might make her seem insatiable to a man who did not share it or who even rejected it.

As media of communication, sexual acts are subject to the same kind of influences as any other and they may take the same form as any other. Any model—inferential or "Wowser-Holmes," sympathetic, empathic—of reading may be used by the receiver. There may be strategic reasons among senders for not conveying messages or for conveying false ones. And strategic reasons among receivers for not accepting them. Signs, including words, signals, symbols may all combine to reinforce a single message, hostile or loving. But they may also act separately, at cross purposes, and confound any message, rendering it both hostile and loving, as in the so-called double-bind, which can frustrate if not actually paralyze. No less in the coital act than in any other. And although human beings are unique among living creatures in having words available for sexual communication, they are far from having exploited this invaluable resource to the best advantage. Despite the fact that words can enormously expand and enhance the sexual message, they are often misused, used negatively, or not used at all.

Verbal communication in the area of sex suffers from peculiar handicaps which are almost unique. In the first place there is not a suitable vocabulary to use. The cold language of science communicates only information, and information alone is not the total message. People might know what you were talking about but they would not understand what you meant. Kinsey and his associates had to translate their questions into the vernacular before many of their informants understood what was meant by them. The common taboo words are too loaded for communication between the sexes. In addition, they are themselves stimulating, exciting. The mere vocalizing of them becomes a sexual act itself. Most intersexual communication is therefore mediated by signs and signals.

An examination of the specific sexual adjustments of pairs of persons reveals that it is quite possible for extensive and long-term sexual relationships—even, and possibly especially, in marriage—to work out to the apparent satisfaction of the two persons involved without a word being spoken about sexual behavior and its consequent pleasure or pain. This seems to be primarily a function of the character of the male and female roles brought to the marriage. . . . The male is cast in the role of the technical expert, and this expertise is related to his masculine role. Even if he is not expert, there is a substantial constraint on the female not to point this out and not to help in the sexual adjustment, because there is always the problem of revealing to the male how she acquired her knowledge and arousing his anxiety about her ability to make invidious comparisons. Consequently the sexual relation is learned by and large through the exchange of cues and gestures rather than through discussion or direct experimentation. When there is gestural silence, no affectional move toward one another, the anguish may be intolerable.[76]

Clark Vincent has made a perceptive analysis of "the difficulties in marital communication about sex." He views them as symptoms of (1) failure of the recipient to recognize cues of an unfavorable self-image or inadequate self-love in the sender; (2) failure to respect impressions as very real; and (3) underestimating the negative ideas and attitudes which hang over from childhood. An unfavorable self-image tends to make for defensiveness to keep others from seeing us as we really are and hence reject us. If we are ashamed of ourselves, think poorly of ourselves, or in other ways reject ourselves, we will not be willing to communicate freely. We do not want to give ourselves away. Unless the partners read one another's cues they will misinterpret the message, and the barriers to sexual union will be insurmountable.

The second difficulty, according to Vincent, arises because one or both of the partners do not recognize the lack of congruence between what each conceives of as reality. The classic spousal argument usually begins or ends in a dialogue which denies the reality of the other's individual impressions, thereby forcing the participants to establish which one was right, whose impression was real. "I said this!" "No, you didn't! You said that!" Neither is trying to deceive the other; both are reporting their genuine impression of what happened and both are correct. We are reminded of Levinger's finding that it was the illusion of agreement, not the fact of agreement, that made for marital satisfaction in his couples; and the assumption of disagreement rather than actual disagreement that militated against it.

The third difficulty in marital communication, says Vincent, results from defective sex education in childhood, especially in the case of men. Because so much is left undefined, unclarified, relatively empty, "there is a potential flow of aggression into this area that has never been made explicit or handled in a rational way."[77] Another outcome of defective socialization in the area of sex is that knowledge becomes equated with masculinity, and any implication of lack of knowledge or know-how about sex is somehow or other indicative of lack of masculinity. Clark Vincent supplies this example:

Suppose that the wife asks her husband to scratch her back. As he does so she may say "not so hard, a little to the left, under the shoulder blade, a little harder, now up between the shoulder blades," and so on. The husband follows her instructions [with no sense of humiliation whatever but, rather] with a feeling of dignity and perhaps a feeling of love mixed with the knowledge that on other occasions she will reciprocate.

Now consider this same couple involved in attempting to achieve some or increased sexual satisfaction for the wife. During lovemaking some of her comments are quite comparable to those made when she was [simply] requesting that her back be scratched. But this time the husband's reactions may be quite different. After the first few comments he may begin to feel threatened on the basis of *his impression* (which is reality for him) that her instructions imply he does not know how to make love to her or that he is not a good lover (which for him, questions his masculinity). Thus, he may quickly become quite defensive and may even make a few comments to her in self-defense or protection of himself. If she is defensive about her inability to achieve sexual satisfaction it will not take very many of his rebuttal comments before she will suggest or insist in her own defense that they forget about lovemaking for the night.[78]

It does not damage a young man's masculinity to learn the sexual ropes from an older woman or from a prostitute. Some societies, in fact, make explicit provision for precisely this kind of learning experience. Polly Adler reported the cases of fathers who brought their sons to her house for this purpose. Even in our society, and even among young women who believe in a single standard, many say—inconsistently enough—that they want to marry men who have had some experience. Husbands are, in fact, the major source of sex education of wives. There is, therefore, at least this much justification for the sensitivity of Vincent's young husband. If, furthermore, she makes even a tactful suggestion, he may conclude that she is implying an unfavorable comparison with some other partner or just another bossy female trying to tell him what to do. An infinite amount of tact is called for in coital communication on both sides.

A childhood hangover may have the effect of producing bashfulness in the girl. One man complains: "My wife is a good partner in every way except she never *looks* at me during sexual relations. She insists on keeping her eyes closed. If I am giving her pleasure, why won't she let me have the satisfaction of seeing it in her eyes, even if she can't say so in words."

The use of words is not common in lower socioeconomic levels. They may be used in many ways among the more articulate. Clark Vincent notes that husbands and wives evolve their own shorthand and he gives an example of how it may work:[79]

Husband:

How about it?

Wife's alternatives:	Love to
	Why aren't you more artful? (You spoil it by asking)
	I've a splitting headache
	How about what? (teasing or hostility)
	It's only been two days
	Let's go out for dinner (bargaining)
	It's about time!

Even among articulate mates, by far the largest part of sexual communication is by way of signs and signals. Instead of, as above, "how about it?" he caresses her—or she, him—and accompanies the gesture with a tender smile. And among inarticulate mates—as Lee Rainwater and John Gagnon have shown—the whole dialogue may be in terms of acts only.

We noted that the psychiatrist learns to read all kinds of muscles. Men learn to read one fundamental muscle, the vagina which, according to one psychiatrist, has its own message. He refers to "the vagina's ability to communicate meaning, independent of what the woman's behavior and her body communicate." He accepts the fact that:

There are men who declare that they "know" the woman immediately upon intromission and there is a wide difference among vaginas. One man classified them in this way: the "glad" or loving vagina, receptive and friendly, "a nice cozy retreat"; the indifferent vagina; the vagina that is frightened and "inhospitable"; the "sinister" or frightened vagina. . . . I would be inclined to dismiss it as more fancy than fact were it not for similar statements by other men. What seems to be true is the ability to distinguish between the extremes of nurturant and the hostile vagina.[80]

It is doubtful if the vagina by itself can communicate so much; but who can deny it? And it is certainly true that some women do learn to use the vaginal muscles to caress the intruding male organ, to communicate complete acceptance of it, welcome, appreciation. It is one of the more reassuring forms of stroking.

The importance of sexual intercourse as a medium of communication grows. As compared with the nineteenth century, standards with respect to the coital act have risen greatly. Not only is more physical responsiveness expected, but also more social, more psychological, responsiveness. Husbands and wives want more than a physiological reflex. Increasingly they want also an esthetic experience. Auguste Rodin was one of the first modern sculptors to show us the beauty of two bodies in a sexual embrace. More recently, perceptive cinema photographers, too, have given us visual insights into its beauty. Modern ballet and modern dance have also idealized and glorified it. Knowledge that the coital act can be beautiful and graceful adds an esthetic dimension to it; it ceases to be something ugly that one must hide even from oneself and get over with fast, or too ludicrous to take seriously. But it is esthetically beautiful only when it is as communicative as a dance.

CHAPTER ELEVEN

At Work

❖❖❖❖❖

When I was very young, maybe fifteen years old, six men and six women cut weeds together. The men and women quarreled. In the evenings after the older women went to fetch wood, the younger people used pea-stalk clubs with which to fight. Women pulled the men's legs and the men pulled the women's. Our bodies were sore. The men said, "Another time we shall continue." I was one of the men fighting. Another time there were about forty men and women working together in three fields. Toward evening the men said it was time to continue the fight. . . . The first time we fought it was because the men and women worked separately. The field was divided between them. The men raced the women in clearing weeds and beat them. . . . The women were angry with the men for making them ashamed, so they fought. After the quarrel the men said, "We mustn't work separately any more. We have to work together, men and women, so that we shan't quarrel." Once forty of us were working together. In one day twenty of us cleared Malemani's field and twenty of us cleared Tilemau's. That night five young men fought with five young women. . . . After this fight we said, "It is better that men and women work separately."

—Cora Dubois, *The People of Alors*

❖❖❖❖❖

This little experiment in industrial sociology took place on an East Indian Island, Alors, in the twentieth century. It could hardly have been unique in human history. Whether men or women worked together or separately, the result was the same —contention. Prototypes doubtless occurred many times and in many places all over the world. The lesson it taught has been universally assimilated. Most of the work of the world has been distributed between—or among, for age makes a difference— the sexes according to ancient traditions. Adam dug, we are told, and Eve span. (Actually, Eve was probably the first digger; it was only after the plow replaced the digging stick that cultivation of the soil was taken over by men.)

The specific work assigned to each sex might be different in different societies, but whatever it was, it was likely to be different for the two sexes. In some societies, for example, taking care of the cattle might be women's work; in another, women might not be permitted even to go near the cattle. Similarly, working in leather or preparing soil and planting might be done either by men or women exclusively or by both indifferently. But by far the largest number of industrial activities have tended to be either men's work or women's. One anthropologist, after summarizing the division of labor in 224 societies around the world, concluded that "while a number of occupations are universally masculine, none is everywhere feminine: men have, here and there, taken to themselves even such predominantly feminine activities as cooking, the making of clothes, water carrying, and grain grinding."[1] Feminine work can be done by men if they want to, but apparently at least some masculine work cannot be done by women, even if they want to. And in general, the work of men, whatever it is, has more prestige than the work of women. It is not that men choose the more prestigious work but rather that the work men do has more prestige, regardless.

In some cases, the basis for the sexual division of labor is understandable; any industrial activity that depends on muscular strength or body speed will be done better by men than by women. Hunting, for example, or lumbering, or quarrying. But why should work in wood and bark be exclusively or predominantly man's work in 124 out of 131 societies? or making musical instruments? or work in bone, horn, and shell? or even, for that matter, metalworking?

Despite the fact that modern technologies erase most of the physical bases for a sexual division of labor and despite many efforts to open all kinds of work to women—most recently by legislation that forbids discrimination on the basis of sex—there is still a strong tendency for certain kinds of work to be done by men and certain kinds by women. One sociologist has noted that in our society the kinds of work done by women—teaching, social work, nursing, secretarial, entertaining—tend to be those characterized by the expressive role that they tend to perform also in the family, and that they tend to be supportive to masculine roles.[2] Another sociologist notes that the division of labor has little or nothing to do with competence. "Women are barred from four out of every five occupational functions, not because of incapacity or technical unsuitability, but because the attitudes which govern interpersonal relationships in our culture sanction only a few working relationships between men and women, and prohibit all the others on grounds that have nothing to do with technology."[3] If not with incapacity or technical unsuitability, what *do* these attitudes have to do with?

So far as older women are concerned, this author offers as partial explanation the drive men in our culture have to free themselves from childhood controls by women. In rejecting the morality fostered by women, they develop an insistence on excluding them from their working lives.

Especially in the male group, which tends to reject overtly, if superficially, the official morality sponsored by women in the family, there is a culturally recognized atmosphere which symbolizes the exclusion of women. The use of tabooed words, the fostering of sports and other interests which women do not share, and participation in activities which women are intended to disapprove of—hard drinking, gambling, practical jokes, and sexual essays of various kinds—all suggest that the adult male group is to a large extent engaged in a reaction *against* feminine influence, and therefore cannot tolerate the presence of women without changing its character entirely.[4]

These women are the mothers—or bitches—who must be escaped at all costs, the moral disciplinarians who make them self-conscious about their masculine exuberance.

With regard to the younger women there is the obverse hazard: attraction toward, rather than revulsion against, what they stand for. In general, it is believed that any intimate group, "except those based on family or sexual ties, should be composed of either sex but never of both,"[5] and a stable work group does tend to become at least quasi-intimate. The insistence on sexual segregation has therefore been protective, for "practically speaking, it may be predicted that sexual or quasi-sexual relationships of some importance will develop in most mixed working groups. Insofar as this introduces extraneous conflicts, it represents a direct threat to the group. . . . It poses an additional threat and disturbs the carefully guarded separation between home and work which figures so largely in the psychic economy of the modern breadwinner."[6] The enemy is now a Dark Lady.

After World War II it came as a surprise to at least one shoe firm that girls could actually work with men without disrupting discipline. Thus:

> One shoe firm . . . explained that these departments "had always been 100 percent men and the introduction of one or two girls into a room of 100 to 150 men would have had an undesirable effect upon discipline. . . . During the last two years, however, . . . we are able to use a few girls in a large department of men without causing any comment or being considered an unusual thing."[7]

Both of these attitudes—revulsion toward the older woman and attraction toward the younger—have powerful, if indirect, relevance for the concept of competence. Even if men and women were, in fact, identical so far as talents and skills for Job A were concerned, there might still be preference for one or the other sex in filling it. It would still be theoretically classifiable under the Help Wanted–Male or Help Wanted–Female rubric, rather than under the Help Wanted–Male or Female rubric, even if forbidden by law.

For an important ingredient in competence for any job is social, having to do with the effect one has on others. Negro actors have been reported as resenting failure to be cast for roles they are well qualified for. By every technical or objective test they are the most talented among the applicants. On radio they would be perfect in the role. They are rejected not at all because of their deficiencies in skill or talent but because of the response to them by the audience. They are not credible. Even within both sexes, casting must take credibility into account. The most superb elderly actress cannot play Juliet, not because she lacks talent but because she does not have the appropriate impact on the audience. And the chairman of the board has to look the part, affect people in a certain way. Men and women are rejected for certain jobs for which they have superlative qualifications, not because they cannot do them well, but because they do not have the proper impact on others. In the case of the Negro actor, we are told to change the attitudes of the audience so that they ignore the performer's race and accept him as a man. After all, everything the actor does is make-believe; the actor is not really a murderer, magician, or what-have-you. If or when it does become possible to accept the actor on these terms, many job barriers will fall. But it is not likely that the messages broadcast by a woman's body, young or old, will ever be completely silenced. For a long time, the members of most work groups, therefore, will tend to have most of their communication with others of the same sex rather than with those of the other. The Alors experiment is still relevant.

In the earlier years of industrialization, the women who worked outside the home were overwhelmingly from the lower socioeconomic classes. A major exception were the so-called Lowell girls who came from good farm families to work in the first mills in New England. They established a kind of academy, spending their evening hours when they were not working in study, like girls in a college dormitory. They had no problems with men. The early "working girl" was, furthermore, young and therefore vulnerable. The penny dreadfuls had focused on the "Heaven-help-the-working-girl" theme and this was not a humorous cliché then; it was a legitimate attitude of the concerned. She was extremely exploitable by men. If a young woman worked as a domestic, she was in danger of being seduced by a man in the house; if she worked in a factory, by her boss. "Disrespect for the working girl sometimes led to sexual advances by supervisors or male workers. Girls complained of stolen embraces, pinches, and vulgar remarks."[8] For most of the girls this was not a welcome form of expressive communication.

Although a Bureau of Labor report in 1887 exonerated factory and sales girls from the charge of furnishing the chief supply of prostitutes, "nevertheless, whatever lesser breaches of propriety did occur were likely to be taken very seriously by any girl who shared the extreme sensitivity of polite society toward questions of sex."[9] Girls were reported to become ill rather than engage in even the instrumental communication involved in asking permission of their male boss to leave the floor to go to the toilet room, or even to let men see them enter it.[10]

The scene has changed so drastically since those days that it looks like a totally different drama being played on a totally different stage and by a totally different cast. The characters of the play, the labor force, have changed almost completely. The proportion of workers in blue-collar occupations has dropped spectacularly until now it constitutes less than half of all non-agricultural workers, and of these an increasing proportion are in the skilled, especially word-type, occupations. The living-in domestic has departed the scene. (Almost every domestic has.) The office girl has come to outnumber the factory girl. The women in the labor force today are more likely to be married and they are older, on the average, than in the past.

At the turn of the century, the average girl left school at, let us say, about the age of fourteen. If she entered the labor force she worked until she married at, let us say, around twenty-two. All told, then, she spent roughly eight years in the labor force, all of them before marriage. At the present time girls stay in school until the age of about eighteen; they remain in the labor force only until their first child is born. They drop out of the labor force while they bear their children. Then, when their last-born enters school, they begin to return to the labor force. The net effect is that a modern woman will spend about a quarter of a century in the labor force, but most of it will be after rather than before marriage.

Thus the women men meet at work nowadays are likely to be

married; only 23 percent were single in 1964. In addition, 6 percent were divorced. And they are not very young. The average age of women in the labor force rose from twenty-six in 1900 to forty-one in 1965; fewer than a fourth were under twenty-five in that year; about two-fifths were forty-five or over.

All these changes mean that the men and women who confront one another at work today are not communicating with one another under the same circumstances as in the past, nor are they, as a matter of fact, the same kind of people. The woman a man has to contend with at work today is more likely to be the mother he is fleeing from than the lovely wraith he is attracted to.

✦✦✦✦✦

Even if the sexes are performing different kinds of work, they are often performing them on the same stage. In some kinds of enterprise the talents of men and women dovetail very nicely. Under the preindustrial domestic or cottage system of organizing production, one sex might spin, another weave. The family farm is an ancient way of organizing work, the man in the fields, and the woman at the hearth and in the garden. The petty bourgeois shop also has a long history: the man usually assuming responsibility for the "foreign relations" of the enterprise, that is, contact with suppliers, revenue agents, and bureaucrats, and the woman for the "internal relations." In such work situations, communication need not be voluminous. Each knew pretty well what had to be done; communication could therefore be minimal, and usually instrumental. Since the enterprise was a family affair, the interjection of sex was not subversive.

Increasingly, however, the work of the world is done outside of the home, and the workers themselves are not members of the same family. This change makes a difference. One has to do with the mystique-enhancing function of work.

For a long time there was, understandably, strong resistance by men toward the movement of women outside the home as they followed their ancient occupations into factory and mill, not only because it made women more independent, but also because it changed the relationship between the sexes.

"Danger, Men at Work," says the sign. The danger is not to the observer so much as to the men themselves. Seeing men at work—most work—is disillusioning. The heroic firemen or the fabulously skilled handicraft worker may win kudos from an admiring audience, but most workers do pedestrian chores not at all designed to make them look heroic or larger than life. We spoke of the importance of distance in protecting the male mystique. Even in the world of work, distance lends mystery, if not enchantment, to the view of men at work. A close view, such as the co-worker gets, destroys illusions. The masculine mystique may be one of the casualties. When the male world of work is separated from the world of women, it is possible for men in their relations with women to project an image of importance, even of power. Where women have no contact with men's work world they can excuse or overlook his bumbling around the house. At work, at least, he is competent, capable, masterful. The distance between work and family which protects him from scrutiny invests him with an aura. He may be the veriest milquetoast at work; but he can be a hero at home.

When women share the work world of men, whether as subordinates or as co-workers, the aura vanishes. Women find no special masculine virtu in the men they observe at work. At work, as at home or anywhere else, they are, like women themselves, just ordinary beings. They are not powerful creatures engaged in world-shaking deeds. They are just the same men as those around the house—not bigger than life and as bumbling or as competent in one sphere as in the other. A man can no longer come home from work, as from a foreign land, and expect the special attention due an honored visitor. His wife has probably just come home from the same land and she knows it for what it is, without illusions. The entrance of women in the man's work world stripped him of the protection of the mystique conferred by a masculine work world.

Another problem introduced by the removal of work from the home has to do with status relationships. Students of status have found that if people have, let us say, a lot of money but little education, or, again, a prestigious occupation but little money, or if they have both money and education but are members of a low-status minority group, this inconsistency in the criteria of status introduces anomalies into their relationships. People who suffer from status inconsistency or "low status-crystallization" are less likely to participate in voluntary relationships. For example, they are less likely to remain active in organizations, and tend to have nonsociable rather than sociable motivations for establishing and maintaining voluntary ties, and so on.[11]

Women tend to be among those who have status inconsistency and it shows up in the workaday world. When and where their status as women takes precedence and when and where their status as workers does may be puzzling.[12] Industry has been organized on a hierarchical basis for a long time. It is taken for granted that there are bosses who give orders and workers who take them. In general, men are in the higher-status positions in a work situation. Not so in a social situation away from work. Social life is also stratified, of course, but within any one level, at least in "polite society," the myth of equality is at least minimally honored; or there are even vestiges of the chivalric tradition of special favors for women. Thus the relative status of the sexes in a work situation is often diametrically opposite to that in a social situation away from work.

In the office there is little difficulty in recognizing status relationships. But how about office parties? And how about lunch? The *Esquire Book of Etiquette* noted in 1953 that one's job, not one's age or sex, determined one's status.[13] But in 1964, Helen Gurley Brown noted that "regardless of the positions you and your [male] companion occupy back at the office, at lunch a girl is a sex equal. Democracy fairly gleams."[14] Well, which is it, hierarchy or democracy? It makes a difference in the communication pattern.

Either way the problems are complex. If it is a hierarchy, the men are likely to be the superordinates. If a democracy, the men are at a disadvantage because, says Caplow, "occupational competition between men and women is complicated by the feelings of guilt aroused in the men, and the fact that both sexes have been systematically trained to avoid [such] competition."[15] (The lesson from Alors again?) But if it is unavoidably a competitive situation, women may use their sexual advantage against their male competitors. ". . . Try in your ladylike way to interest people who are in power in your scheme. You may also get a crack at some of these men unofficially through dates, affairs, friendships. Smart girls sometimes get to be confidantes of important men. No reason not to talk about business when you're on his yacht."[16] Despite the absurdity of this advice, so far as most women competing with men are concerned, the point the author is trying to make bears thinking about.

A central theme in the male mystique, Caplow tells us, is that "it is disgraceful for a man to be directly subordinated to a woman, except in family or sexual relationships."[17] Since proprietors, managers, and officials are twice as likely to be men as women, most women, like most men, have men as bosses. This kind of situation does not make for status inconsistency. Both as woman and as worker she conforms to Caplow's central theme. Not so, however, when she is boss. The idea that it is disgraceful for men to be subordinate to women vastly complicates such a work situation. Now her status as a woman does not conform to her status as a worker.

But the difficulties do not seem to be as serious or as common as the clichés would have it. One study of women executives, for example, reporting on "what some men and some women were willing to say" found that it was the *idea* of working for women rather than the fact of working for them that the man objected to. "In the spirit of an anti-Semite who says, 'I don't like Jews, but some of my best friends are Jews,' male subordinates might say that ordinarily they didn't like to work for women but *this* one was different."[18] The most successful women executives, this study found, had had long years of practice working with men. And, interestingly, the higher the woman's status the more cordial were her relationships with her male subordinates.[19] That it was the idea of working for women rather than the actual practice itself that men objected to was documented in a study in the *Harvard Business Review*, which reported that "older men and those who had had some experience working with women were generally more favorably inclined" to working with them.[20]

The complications of sex-related versus work-related status may occur even in horizontal relationships. One of the most interesting studies of communication between the sexes in a work setting had to do with waitresses and countermen in a restaurant. It was found that when waitresses called in their orders to countermen who then filled them, the situation was rife with tensions. The men could not bear to seem to be taking orders from women. One solution was to have waitresses place their orders on a spindle and let the countermen fill them in the most convenient order. Even so, it was preferable to have some sort of buffer between the waitresses and the countermen to protect the men from even seeming to take orders from the women. There are constant wrangling and blowups between countermen and waitresses if waitresses call in their orders; the men consider being subjected to such a setup an "ordeal to which no man should be subjected."[21] Sometimes only a procedural barrier is enough to protect the men: all orders must be written. Even this may not be enough. Sometimes men at a bar will refuse to fill a waitress's written orders until she has stopped pressuring him and turned away; sometimes they collect the orders from a number of waitresses and fill them in their own sequence. They are thus protected from taking orders from individual women; they are, in effect, their own boss. Sometimes more than social insulation is needed; a physical barrier is interposed to protect the men from the status denigration involved in taking even written orders from a woman. Alas, how fragile masculinity.

Another status anomaly is the power that sometimes accrues to a good secretary.[22] She is not only what used to be called an "office wife" or, as now, a "Girl Friday," but also in effect an alter ego. A good secretary can read all the signs, catch all the signals, carry out all the strategic moves. She can answer her boss's telephone calls, take care of his correspondence, screen his callers. She can tell in advance what his reactions will be. She doesn't have to wait to be told what to do about Jones or Smith; an incipient gesture will do. For some men, dependence on a good secretary is the only kind they can tolerate. Since she often acts as mediator between the public and her boss, or even as his surrogate, she may wield great influence if not actual power. Making a good impression on the secretary often makes the difference between success and failure with the boss himself. This anomalous situation puts the secretary actually, if not theoretically, in a superordinate position with respect to, let us say, the junior executives.

Theoretically the logic of industry and the logic of the family and of social life are quite different. In the family no one has to deserve anything; it is enough that there are blood bonds or conjugal ties. One even has a right to stroking. One may, to be sure, be disciplined, even punished; but never fired. Similarly, in social life a host of conventions are enforced to build up the ego and smooth over rough surfaces; there are even prescribed stroking obligations.

When work was transferred from home to factory, shop, or office, there was no ready-made code to guide work relationships. In Japan, the employer-employee relationship has tended to retain a modified kind of family pattern; hiring implies a lifelong commitment. Not so in the United States, at least in theory. The employer-employee relationship was originally modeled on the master-servant common law. It tended to be hard-boiled and tough; workers had to meet standards of efficiency and productivity or get fired. Sentiment was not to get in the way of profit. It took almost a century and a half for new codes to be threshed out for regulating the new kind of work ties that came with industrialization. The men developed theirs by means of militant unions; women were protected, when they were, by legislation.

Since work is task-oriented, a great deal of the communication connected with it is of necessity instrumental in character. In order to do a good job, people of whatever sex, have to know what, where, when, and how, and sometimes even why certain things have to be done. Information up and down and across has to be clear and its flow unimpeded by intersex or intrasex obstacles. A vast amount of research in the field of industrial engineering and industrial psychology has been devoted to such instrumental communication goals.

Recognition of the contribution of expressive communication, even stroking, came later. It came from management, not from the workers. Industrial psychologists and "human-nature-in-industry" researchers taught management that workers needed expressive communication—stroking—as well as instrumental communication. With it their work was performed more efficiently, without it, less so. As a result of a spate of research studies, the human-relations-in-industry school of thought developed the theory that more attention should be paid to workers' social and psychological needs; they were not to be viewed as engineering details but as human beings in their own right. A vast apparatus of "personnel work" was instituted to provide some of the stroking needed, and let workers talk their problems out to counselors.

In addition, some firms encouraged the "all-one-big-happy-family" ideology, which tended to render contacts familiar and intimate. And since "human relations," in industry or outside of it, include sex relations—again in industry or outside of it—the impact of the changing scene was felt on the relations between the sexes also. It had the effect of lowering the bars between the sexes, of expanding the opportunities for expressive communication. After a few months of working together, "employees frequently know more about each other's current problems than members of their respective families know."[23] Little wonder, then, that "within this context, Christmas parties at the office are sometimes anticipated with more enthusiasm and preparation than are those at home," we are told.[24] (With, incidentally, almost catastrophic results both for office workers themselves and for their families at home. It is not hard to understand why such occasions are on their way out as a tribal custom in business.)

The messages conveyed by this expressive communication between the sexes vary widely, of course, not only according to the sex composition of the work group and the status of the communicators involved, but also according to the job itself. They are different in a cocktail lounge and in a factory; in a typists' pool and in a Madison Avenue office; in a library and in a hospital; in a computer center and in a boutique; in a court and in a social-work agency; in a faculty club and in a theater. And within any kind of occupation or industry, they may also vary enormously.

❖❖❖❖❖

As late as World War II, traditional taboos were still operating powerfully among blue-collar workers. Here is the situation as reported by a woman working in a shipyard, traditionally an all-male stronghold:

Sex attitudes made up the tangled background of the male worker's point of view. Sex was his great avocational interest; whether bounded by the proprieties of marriage or unconstrained in the reaches of bachelor fancy, it was the spice of his existence, the principal joy of his social life. In the largest part, shipyard conversation beyond the routine of the day's necessities, was occupied with some aspect of the pleasures or the problems of sex; and shipyard jokes were broad and racy in the extreme. Emphasized in this interest was the sexual role of women, which influenced every association between the sexes and surrounded with an atmosphere of obscure emotionality each area of unfamiliar and unusual cooperation. The emphasis upon sex, moreover, as it evoked the biological distinctions between men and women, also reinforced the lines of social demarcation. Traditions supposedly governing the proper division of labor between men and women were linked with even more profoundly rooted traditions concerning divisions in biological function, and change in the structure of the former might seem to imply a threat to the latter's sacrosanct stability. . . .

Thus, on my first day of work in the yards, I was warned by the superintendent of my craft that any flirting with the men in the yards would result in dire consequences for me. "Remember what I told you," he called after me as I left his office; "give a man an inch and he'll take a mile, and if there's any funny business on the job, it'll be you who goes out like a light."[25]

It is often just the sheer pleasure of word play that is reflected in the all-male sex talk of blue-collar workers. They enjoy the free use of words taboo in the presence of women. Under these circumstances blasphemy and the four-letter words are fun. They underscore the sex camaraderie which men, liberated from the inhibitions of the presence of women, enjoy. Sometimes the talk is just the telling of off-color stories. Sex is funny, amusing, a joke; but again, in this sense, forbidden in the presence of women. Again, half the fun in this kind of talk is the understanding which the sharing of such jokes implies: the male world against the restrictions of the female world. Much of the talk is about male sexual prowess. Virility, potency, organ size become topics of bragging, usually in a jocular vein. If the thing being bragged about is success in "making" women, the competition will center around how many conquests have been made or the speed with which they were made. Sometimes the talk may include the passing on of information about the availability of such women. But some topics are taboo even in the all-male work group. It is not good form to complain about sexual difficulties with one's own wife. Among very close friends, in an intimate personal discussion, such ventilating of difficulties might be permitted and a more experienced man might offer advice. But in the ordinary work or play group, such discussion would be taboo.[26]

Times, it should be noted, are in process of change. Thus in 1966 when a foreman forbade a woman worker in a plywood mill to wear tight pants, three hundred fellow men-workers went out on strike. "The men are all behind me," she was quoted as saying.[27]

Even though the sexes are doing different work in a white-collar setting, they are likely to be doing it together. There is not likely to be a woman on or near the assembly line, anywhere around the foundry or steel mill or rubber plant, or for that matter, the construction job. But there are a great many women in offices and stores, however similar or dissimilar the work they are doing may be from men's. White-collar jobs have burgeoned as blue-collar jobs have receded for both men and women. Most women workers are in white-collar jobs; by far the largest category is that of clerical and sales workers.

When women workers first moved into the white-collar occupations in force, the picture of sexual vulnerability characteristic of the factory girl remained. The seduction theme was standard in fiction, according to C. W. Mills, who noted that it persisted long after it had, in his opinion, become passé, at least in its traditional form. The fictional stereotype was of a girl who "learns how to handle the male element in the office, begins to believe that all men are after only one thing. . . ."[28]

Mills noted that the personal secretary or one-man stenographer was being superseded by the dictating machine and the typists' pool and that the old-fashioned office girl had become just a white-collar factory girl. There was little of the old interpersonal relationship between the girls in the typists' pool and the men whose work they did almost anonymously. Etiquette books advised the office girls to be neither coyly and insistently feminine nor one of the boys, neither to use nor to deny their femininity.[29]

With the denigration of the old-fashioned office girl came the inrush of a new kind. The types of jobs open to women, like those now open to men, had changed dramatically by the 1960's. Professions in which words were important—especially the communications professions—had waxed enormously. Women had for a long time been in charge of words—taking them in dictation, typing them, recording them, filing them, retrieving them—but now women were doing more: they were putting words together themselves, in conferences, on paper. They were in publishing, advertising, public relations. They were women who had clients to or for whom they did publicity, sold words, researched. They were enormously word-wise. Verbal communication was their métier. In this world of words they were competitors of men and often more successful than men.

The rules governing talk between men and these new women had to be more complex, subtle, and sophisticated. Helen Gurley Brown, patron saint of these working—now career—girls, was issuing some of the same kinds of instructions as those proclaimed by old etiquette books, but the underlying point of view was totally different. Stroking, yes, but now it was to be manipulative, strategic. Miss Brown added guidance even on how to conduct an affair, how to win a man, how to use any advantage derived from sex to compete successfully with men. It was no longer Heaven-help-the-working-girl but, in effect,

Heaven-help-the-*office*-workingman. He would have to be very sharp, very sharp, indeed, to cope with the office girls Miss Brown was advising. Sharper than a woman boss. One study explained the rejection of women bosses by women themselves as the result of a feeling that in such a situation they were deprived of their most effective weapons, for, as a woman in a professional magazine *Personality Journal* says: ". . . their underlying and unspoken reasoning is that one woman cannot exploit another woman the way she can almost always exploit a man. . . . The average female bitterly resents this stalemate of her feminine prerogative to beguile and to bewitch her way through life."[30]

The beguiling and bewitching need not be blatant. Listening was bracketed by Helen Gurley Brown with babying and flirting, but it should be done with style. Whether or not to sleep with a man in order to get ahead was a personal decision; but there was nothing wrong with *talking* to him. And "long, probing, business-friendship talks are delicious," whether or not they improved one's professional position.[31] No ordinary date can compare in sexiness and excitement with a business lunch between attractive co-workers. Body contacts act like cow-prodders. Hands brush, eyes meet, knees touch, but are quickly withdrawn. "It's all exciting . . . and puzzling. Was it an accident? Was it an invitation? Did he or didn't he do it on purpose?"[32] For once *not* knowing how to interpret signs and signals is fun; it adds to the excitement. Still, along with all this advice about expressive communication and how to use it looking for the "main chance," she tells her readers to do their jobs "fiendishly well." As a model, she cites a woman who applied for a stepping-stone job, saying: "I will work like a robin redbreast as a secretary and make this a smooth-functioning department. Then in return I hope you will let me have a whack at writing publicity releases some time. I won't badger you about it night and day or consider that *that's* my job and not secretarial work, but perhaps you'll give me some extra ones you're too busy to do."[33] Part of the advice to young women using this ploy was "to do *more* than your share to get them to do any of theirs" and to "pitch in and do the dirty work with enthusiasm as though that were all that mattered."[34]

Despite all the twentieth-century fancy sex work, then, are we right back at Horatio Alger's creed? It looks that way. Women are always telling themselves that they have to be better than the male competition to achieve the same rewards.

Not all the women interested in careers measure up. The story of those who do not has been reported also. The archetype here is a college graduate, very likely an Ivy League girl. She is bright and, for a leisure-class girl, well educated, with a good background in literature and even, perhaps, talented in writing in a small way. The first advertisement one such girl answered led to a job which ended in a tragedy of errors; the employer lost his temper at what seemed to him the pretensions of the girl; all he wanted was a secretary. She could not understand why he became so angry. Never having read Helen Gurley Brown, she was terrorized, but also indignant. When she finally did get a job as secretary to a magazine editor, the miscommunication was chronic. He called her by her first name, as befit his superordinate position in the office. Yet he insisted on maintaining a separation beween his work and hers. He seemed indifferent to her opinions. He stroked for the wrong things, the most ordinary tasks, but scolded for the important ones, including her efforts to go beyond what seemed to her her trivial obligations. The employer and the employee were surely not seeing the same red. So when she had been at this job for a year, she was turned over to a new boss. Now the problems were reversed. Instead of not permitting her much initiative, he expected more than she could deliver. She asked for simple instrumental information and he snapped back at her. She argued with him and sometimes burst into tears.[35]

In view of the large literature and commentary on advertising in our day, there is little left to say about this kind of communication between the sexes in the market. When the advertiser is beaming his message to a male market he puts it in the mouth of a pretty girl, preferably in a bikini. When he aims at a female market, he may also exploit the bikini; but he uses an attractive young man also. The kind of salesmanship involved in advertising depends so largely on good communication that the advertising industry has become almost synonymous with the communications industry. The reading of signs and signals—feedback—has itself become a separate industry in which the cleverest research brains are engaged.

The how-to-do-it literature on face-to-face salesmanship is also extensive. But C. W. Mills was one of the first to point out the exploitation of personality in the face-to-face market, especially the exploitation of sex appeal by young women.[36] The picture here, as elsewhere, is in process of change. With sales personnel in such short supply that department stores canvass apartment buildings hoping to find *anyone* that they can hire able to spell well enough to make out a sales slip, there is little need for the tactics of sex appeal. As a matter of fact, there are few young salesgirls left. Nor does the employer have to advise or instruct the old-timer on ways to sell. The customer comes begging for someone just to take his order.

The women in the stores are not necessarily customers. Many lonely housewives come to department stores just to break down their feeling of loneliness and isolation. Mainly they want to feel they are *au courant*. And a great department store can be as educational to them as a library. If, in addition, someone will *talk* to them, that is frosting on the cake, and, of course, if he is an attentive man, that is whipped cream on the frosting.

Even at the supermarket there is little face-to-face communication between buyer and seller. Dozens of isolated, encapsulated individuals, alone with their shopping lists and unaware of the other zombies milling around them, march up and down aisles, selecting goods, crossing items off their list, and finally checking out, scarcely having uttered a word or heard one. Selling, once the most talkative of occupations, has become one of the least.

Even the hardworking consumer who wants instrumental talk, who wants to know why the price of one brand is higher than that of another, what one should look for in this kind of product, what are the maintenance problems of this appliance or that—the bare minimum of information—finds that the pleasant young man she asks (one could hardly say he *waits* on her; if anything she *waits for* him), just does not know and could hardly care less. Hard sell? Not nowadays. More likely, hard buy.

A very considerable proportion of modern white-collar and professional work is talk. Not only giving instructions, as in old kinds of work, but much more. Discussing problems, exploring ideas, arriving at decisions, making plans, reviewing reports, stimulating innovations. Conferences, meetings, committees, boards, think sessions, constitute the work group and the work setting for this new kind of work.

Women seem to feel at a disadvantage in this kind of group when it has a mixed-sex composition. They feel that men resist their contributions; that they are not listened to. "Men dread the prospect of having a woman around. Their worst fear is that she will talk too much and often irrelevantly, that she may get emotional in seeking to have her own way."[37] In industry women believe they have to give men credit for their own ideas; they say they have to be oh-so-careful not to injure the men's egos. Or they learn how to use strategy to be sure they get credit for their own ideas. If the casually tossed-in idea which the woman has contributed to the idea-hopper is indeed The Answer, it will not, according to Helen Gurley Brown, be recognized as such because it came from a woman. But to prevent anyone else from appropriating it later on as his own, one makes something of it, for "if you make enough of a federal case out of your plans, it's at least harder for three other people to say it was *their* idea."[38]

The rules for success in business and professional organizations addressed to women are very much like those addressed to men in such books, for example, as those of Dale Carnegie.

They consist of a well-balanced mix of competence and hard work (instrumental task-activities) and stroking (expressive activity). It is in the nature of the stroking that what differences there are come through.

The assumption basic in these rules is that the woman worker really is seeking success in her work, not a husband. Actually, the job is not a good place to find a husband. One study reported that only about 6 or 7 percent of couples found one another in a business setting.[39] The emphasis on stroking is not, therefore, intended as a part of a how-to-win-a-husband campaign; it is, rather, part of a how-to-succeed-in-business-by-trying-awfully-hard campaign.

Through all the changes that have taken place, there has remained remarkable unanimity in the emphasis placed upon the woman worker's stroking obligations vis-à-vis her male employer, or even fellow employees. In 1935 the etiquette books were advising the office girl to be a model of tact. She was not to point out her employer's mistakes, or if she did, she was to do it indirectly, in a memorandum, for example, rather than verbally in a face-to-face confrontation; she was never to be blunt; she was never to gloat; she was to make it appear that he had found the mistake himself. She was never to puncture his vanity. She was not to argue.[40] She was, in brief, to be a model of the morale-booster, the male-ego builder-upper, a specialist, let's face it, in stroking. In 1956 she was told to "adapt herself to her employer's unexplained silences or other idiosyncrasies without taking them as a personal affront."[41] In 1965 she was to be helpful, admiring, to "let him know you think he's destined to soar to the top"; she was to be smart but never to "allow him to find you're brighter than he is."[42] In 1967, she was definitely to "hide her light under a bushel of modesty," and "not win the battle and lose the war."[43]

Successful women appear to follow precisely these lines. One such confides in a researcher that, after doing all the groundwork for a program, she turns it over to the district manager to harvest the glory and herself stays in the background. "A woman," she felt, "should not try to go ahead of the men." If she does, they will buck her. Another successful woman executive always tried to remember that she is in a man's world.

At important meetings she works things in such a way that "first thing I know they're telling *me* their ideas," which just happen to be the ideas she has been feeding them.[44] The researcher herself, commenting on these devious maneuverings to let men imagine themselves the leaders, comments laconically, "it sounds suspiciously like a kindergarten teacher using 'democracy' in planning the next classroom project."[45]

Indeed, taken at face value, the insistence on the necessity to protect the male ego constitutes the most humiliating insult to men. It is just another aspect of the picture presented in popular culture of the simpleton male, the bumbling husband, the outwitted father. This is a bitter *revanche* wholly out of proportion to any legitimate grievance women may have had against men in the past. The stupid little boy who happens to be chairman of the board and who must be protected by a patient, condescending, patronizing mother without his knowing what she is doing, is the modern vengeance for the old stereotype of the emotional woman, unfit for the discipline of a career, who also must be protected. The punishment more than fits the crime.

The fact of the matter is that both men and women have dependencies; they both need stroking; they both need, on occasion, a certain amount of prodding. Here the *What-difference?* school seems to be right. There is no justification for the implicit contempt of the woman stroking men, as there was none for the condescension to the "little woman" of the past. It may be true that the stroking function is more commonly assigned to women, and if it is natural, well and good. But "women have no monopoly on the virtue compassion; many professions are filled with compassionate men" also.[46] Deliberately to use stroking manipulatively in a patronizing and condescending manner is insulting. Better Helen Gurley Brown's feisty little competitor fighting for recognition of her own contribution than Margaret Cussler's kindergarten-teacher executive.

Yet lurking in the background of one's mind, there is always that cichlid. Freud implied that women had paid with the company of men for skyscrapers and bridges and atom bombs and all the other great achievements of modern civilization. The time, energy, and attention needed to create modern civilization could not be at the same time devoted to women. In an analogous way it might be said that women pay for male sexuality by "sacrificing" (in quotation marks because most of them do not view it as a sacrifice) their own potential achievements. If women had invested themselves as completely as men have done in creative work, if they had developed the competitive and aggressive drive required for such activity and used them against men, it might well have wilted male potency. At least in the past, men have needed sexual dominance as a protection of their masculinity. The sexual subordination of the female has been the price paid to protect male sexuality. Or conversely, male sexuality has been purchased at the price of female aggression. Whole social systems have been structured to this end. The well-nigh universal subordination of the female collectivity to the male, traced here in the world of work, seems therefore to be a protection of the indispensable male sexual aggression required to maintain the species. Maleness has, in effect, been conferred on men by women by their acceptance of a subordinate position. Left with the choice, male sexuality or their own achievement, most women have tended to choose the first.

The woman who is willing to go along with the need for male dominance is the woman who, by this willingness, shows a scale of values which places sexuality—his as well as hers—above, let us say, professional success. She is willing to confer masculinity on men because she needs it for her own fulfillment. She preserves his sexuality, for her own as well as for his satisfaction.

Women to whom male sexuality is not important, who neither need nor want it, often express resentment and indignation at the norms and prescriptions which protect it at their expense. They would like as good a chance to reach the top of a male world as their male peers. They do not empathize the damage they can inflict on men, or if they do, they feel only contempt for a sexuality so fragile that it has to be protected at their expense.

The figure of speech "castrating female" is such a violent one, conjuring up, as it does, leather, boots, whips, and other sadistic fetishes, that men and women of goodwill try to reject the whole idea. Actually, the castrating female need not even know what her effect is. She is interested in her work, she is excited by it, she is dedicated to it, as a man might be. She is not thinking of the men about her. She is not coveting their organ. She has no envy of them or hostility toward them. They are people, like anyone else. She is not attempting to outdo them, to outperform them. Her castrating effect is not one of positive and punitive and hostile aggression against men; it is an unanticipated—to her—consequence of her actions, an incidental rather than a purposive thing. If she "castrates" the men and robs them of virility, it is not by anything she does but by something she does not do, that is, by not taking a subservient position.

The cichlid-effect is certainly understandable. If millions of women are willing to do this, no one can deny them their right. But the question raised by the women who do not make this choice is also understandable: are the people they work with fish or are they men?

❖❖❖❖❖❖

A good deal of white-collar, especially professional, work is not performed in an organizational or bureaucratic setting. It is less involved with communication among co-workers, peers, superiors, and subordinates, than with audiences, patients, clients, and the public in general. Many professionals are listeners; many are talkers.

The usual status situation in an organization is one in which the employer is in a superordinate position vis-à-vis the employed person. But there are anomalies. (One of the phoniest is the pretense that the electorate is the employer and the official its employee, even "servant.") In the kinds of work situation which are outside of bureaucratic settings, the "employer" is in a subordinate position and the "employed" in a superordinate position. The patient "hires" the doctor but the doctor is in charge; so, similarly, the lawyer and his client, so, also, the housewife and the service or repair man she engages.

❖❖❖❖❖

A large proportion of the people who daily fill the doctor's office are suffering from psychosomatic or stress illnesses, often mild anxiety states, and need only the soothing reassurance, the stroking, of a sympathetic listener. So the workday of many physicians is filled with listening and talking to patients, men and women. Since women physicians tend to specialize in diseases of women and children, they are less likely to be talking and listening to men than men physicians are to be talking and listening to women.

"Society doctor" and "bedside manner" have become pejorative terms, implying a kind of parasitical practice. But the kind of treatment implied in the term "bedside manner" and the kind of patient referred to in the term "society doctor" are both very real phenomena. The bored, dissatisfied "society" woman is indeed sick, however normal all the laboratory test results may be, and her need for the "bedside manner" treatment and ministration is very real.

The communication between physicians and women has developed a kind of protection in the form of rigorous rules of professional conduct. When Queen Victoria introduced men to obstetrics by using a man for her own deliveries, there was a hue and cry at the immorality of it all. Even today the youngish physician protects himself, if not his patient, by having a nurse witness all but the most formal communication between them. If the physician is a psychiatrist, it is well recognized that the communication itself constitutes the treatment.

Interestingly, in view of the fact that the physician is in a position to have such intimate contacts with his patients, it has been only recently that the training of physicians has included the social and psychological aspects of the relations between the sexes.

The relationships between doctor and nurse in the hospital is also rigorously regulated by a powerful set of rules, both explicit and implicit. As professionals, the nurse is subordinate to the doctor, takes orders, shows deference. Actually, it has been pointed out, the women who administer hospitals often make the basic decisions which determine the limits of the doctor's powers. The close relationship that sometimes grows up in the hospital between a nurse and a doctor results in marriage with a frequency beyond chance.

Lawyers also spend a considerable amount of time listening

and talking to women. The women may be a rather selected sample. Elderly widows whose estates they supervise, perhaps, or distraught women in marital trouble. Although a certain amount of stroking is probably necessary for success in dealing with these women, still the major burden of the communication is undoubtedly instrumental in nature. What the women need is rather specialized information and advice. Although the lawyer is a favorite character in fiction and television soap operas as candidates for marriage, comparatively little is made of his relations with his clients.

Men teachers are in a rather vulnerable position. At the high-school level if they are young and moderately attractive, they may become the target of schoolgirl crushes. At the college level, the conditions are ideal for seduction, either by or of him. In one women's college some years back, the professor's door had to be kept ajar whenever he was alone with a student. The protection was for him more than for her. The student needs the professor; he has something to give in the way of grades. She can pay either in the form of verbal stroking or in any other form. The reverse situation, between a woman professor and a male student, rarely tempts either one.[47]

The minister's work has its own peculiar communication hazards. As counselor he has many of the same kinds as the doctor does. As head of an enterprise he has many of the problems that plague any administrator. As preacher his words must be instrumental; he must teach. As pastor his words must often be expressive, consoling, stroking. His role as guardian of sexual mores has made him a focus of fascinated interest from Arthur Dimmesdale down to the most recent marrying Catholic priests.

The work of the traditional engineer had fewer contacts with women than that of almost any other professional. He was, archetypically, viewed as "a man's man." He spent his time building military and civil installations, often far from the centers of civilization and away from women. As the nature of engineering has changed, however, so also has the setting of the engineer's work. The industrial engineer may have to know a considerable amount about women in order to make appropriate designs; the chemical engineer or the atomic engineer or the medical engineer may find a girl from M.I.T. on his team. He has to learn to live with women as well as with ideas and machines and instruments. They seem to do all right. Their divorce rates are low.

The newest professionals—computer caretakers and feeders—are a happy breed. There is as yet no tradition of their profession as belonging either to men or to women. And with talent in such short supply, there is no immediate tendency for either sex to take it over. Both are technicians in instrumental communication, and anyone skilled in communicating with a computer can, presumably, communicate with a member of the other sex.

Most professional women are in occupations that do not bring them into a great deal of contact with men. They are elementary-school teachers, for the most part, or nurses, social workers, librarians, and the like. As physicians they tend to be in specialties dealing primarily with women and children; as lawyers, they tend to have clerical positions in the firm. Nurses have an almost ritualistic subordination to doctors, but this is easily reversed. Vis-à-vis the male patient the nurse is in an anomalous position: she is the one in charge, he is subordinate. But she finds him in a particularly vulnerable situation; stroking may bring rewards far beyond expectable limits. Vis-à-vis the doctor, though the nurse is subordinate, she may actually prove to be superordinate.

The librarian has a great deal of communication with men. It has been said that the librarian is one of the few service professionals who do not demand a tip or command a large fee. She seems to love her work; she will spend hours chasing down a reference. In one great laboratory, the retirement of a longtime librarian all but wrecked the efficiency of the staff. She had read the men in the laboratory until she could anticipate their needs, routed material to them, called their attention to items they may have overlooked. She was all but indispensable and communication was her profession. But indispensable as the librarian is and is increasingly becoming, she is almost archetypical of the mousy woman. She has all the admirable qualities desirable in women; and, in addition, she is intelligent. But she is bypassed when the top positions are being filled; her devoted services are taken for granted by those she works for. The marriage rate is—or has been—low.

The world of the theater and entertainment, "show biz," is one in which sex is of the essence. It might have been true in Shakespeare's day that the roles of women were played by boys, but today they must be played not only by women but by supremely talented and attractive women. This is a world in which sex has to be recognized in hiring, a world in which the more nearly one resembles the masculine and feminine archetype or stereotype the better. Even in, let us say, a tap and soft-shoe dance routine, in which both men and women do the same steps, the sex differences have to come through. The audience has to get the message. The successful actor or actress "projects," makes intimate contact with the audience. The audience "catches" their emotions. And actors appear to need the stroking or love of the audience as expressed by applause in return. It is a peculiar kind of communication; fan mail and fan clubs have a distinctly idolatrous flavor. The communication between performers and teen-agers has become one of the characterizing phenomena of the current scene. It is distinctly an "in" phenomenon; adults do not seem to get the message.

The world of fashion has a peculiar communication pattern, quite apart from the elaborate press coverage it garners. Most of the great designers are men. It has been alleged that they are women-haters and therefore do all they can to make women look ridiculous. This would certainly be a defensible thesis on the basis of what they really do produce. Not at all debatable is their supreme knowledge of how to clothe the body of women in the subtlest way. Whether bosoms are exposed or covered, whether skirts are short or long, whether sleeves are present or absent, really makes no difference. The message is conveyed. The shift, for example, which on the face of it was simply a shapeless sack, after coming from the cutting board of a master, was a perfect setting for rolling buttocks and an amusing cover for a guessing game about the breasts. It is sometimes stated that the designers "dictate" fashions, that the order is given and women obey. Not so. At least not quite so. There has to be a feedback. There are limits to the control designers exert over the clothes of women.[48] Of the several "feelers" put out by the designers, some catch on and others do not. The designer who cannot read the signs loses out to those who can. As in other seeming dictatorships, the consent of the governed is necessary for success.

❖❖❖❖❖

The census rubric "proprietors, officials, and managers" does not include home managers. Thus only a small proportion of all those in this census category are women. If home management were included, the proportion would be far greater. There has been some talk of including "housewife" as an occupation in future occupational censuses. Its economic value is often recognized only when it has to be hired. Its contribution to the gross national product has been imponderable and hence indeterminate and discounted. But, in any event, it is impressive.

The men in the working lives of women whose work is homemaking tend to a large extent to be artisans of one kind or another. One of the oldest jokes has to do with the iceman or milkman and the amorous housewife. It is rarely heard anymore; it seems to have gone the way of the traveling salesman and the farmer's daughter. The men in the lives of a modern housewife, say repairmen, who, upon her urgent, even tearful if necessary, opportuning, have condescended to come and look at the washing machine, the dryer, the plumbing, the television set, the refrigerator, the dishwasher, the air-conditioner, the garbage disposal, or any of the dozen other things that can go wrong around a house and usually do—these young Lochinvars are too busy to spend much time talking to her, let alone making passes. They are on a fast-paced schedule. They are enormously self-assured, know how indispensable they are, are polite and courteous, but patronizing. Definitely in a position of superordination. Not employees. The housewife who tries to engage them in conversation will find them attentive; she will be addressed as "ma'am" or "lady." But she will not extract much talk from them. And with a charge of ten dollars for ten minutes of time changing a washer in a faucet or replacing a fifty-cent pane of glass, any talk that distracted him from the job would be expensive to her. The men themselves certainly do not consider anything but a minimum of instrumental talk with the housewives as part of their job.

There has been some talk that work may return to the home, but not in the form of the old domestic system nor in the form of sweated industries. Quite the reverse. The possibilities now are that computers may make it possible for much routine office work to be done at home. There is no need, it is argued, for people to come to their work; the work can easily go to them. It is doubtful, though, that many women working in a large, pleasant, modern office today would welcome a return to the isolation of work at home. Whatever the difficulties may be, it is too much fun to get away from home and mingle with other men and women. There are drawbacks, but a large proportion of women undoubtedly prefer to cope with them than with the boredom of work at home. People may cluck their lips in disapproval of them, but Betty Friedan certainly documented their existence. And seeing men is certainly one of the attractions of participation in the labor force.

In 1964, a Civil Rights Act was passed which forbade any discrimination in employment on the basis of sex. Employers were not to be permitted to specify sex when advertising for help. Only a few exemptions were permitted and then only when the specifications of the job clearly demanded one sex or the other. Many men had a merry time with this. What kinds of job did call for women? Playboy bunnies? Turkish bath massaging personnel? Actresses, obviously, and opera singers. How about airline hostesses? It is going to be interesting to see what this legislation does to the prejudices of men.

CHAPTER TWELVE

❖❖

At Play

❖❖❖❖❖

This upcoming weekend will probably be the loneliest weekend of the year for American wives and sweethearts. There are eight football games scheduled for the next three days and they are all being shown on television, much to the consternation of American husbands who would rather spend the time with their families and loved ones.

But the American man has no choice. He had nothing to do with the television football schedule or the escalation of the various bowl games by the networks.

"I don't like it any more than my wife," my friend Ben said, "but the sponsors are putting up a lot of money to telecast these games and I owe it to them to watch as much football as I can."

His wife was philosophical about it. . . . [But] my friend Phil's wife seemed to take it harder. She was crying when I called. "Every year it's the same thing. He goes into the library on Friday afternoon for the East-West Shriners game and I don't see him until the NFL pro championship game is over on Sunday."

"It's a lie," Phil said on the extension phone. "I always come out at midnight to wish her a happy New Year." . . .

I called a third friend, Larry, who said, "I think the women have a point. The New Year's weekend is no fun for them any more. So I've given it up."

"Given what up?" I asked him.

"I've given up the Gater Bowl game on Friday afternoon. I'll only watch seven games this year."

"You've got a lot of heart, Larry," I said.

"Well," he replied, "a man's marriage has to come first."

I called up Bill . . . and asked him if his wife was giving him any trouble about the weekend. "Hell, no," he said, "she just packed up and left."

"Left? Where did she go?"

"I don't know. She said something about Reno and getting a divorce. . . ."

A final telephone call illustrates what great turmoil this country is in. I called my friend Carey and asked him how his wife felt about the long weekend. He said sadly, "She's going to watch all the games with me. She said it's the wife's duty to stay at her husband's side, no matter how rough the going gets. . . ."

"What are you going to do?"

"What am I going to do? I'm going out to the movies by myself. . . ."

—Art Buchwald, "The Loneliest Weekend"

There is a male subculture in every society, including our own, and . . . women will understand men in general, and their husbands in particular, much better if they have some realistic knowledge of and insight into this subculture. . . . There are essentially two different social worlds, that of the male and that of the female in our society. . . . Tavern society is still basically a man's world. The world of the Elks Club, the American Legion, the Moose, are basically male worlds. Luncheon clubs, athletic clubs, veterans' organizations, hunting clubs—all these, within limits, illustrate a way of life that is essentially masculine in our society.

—E. E. LeMasters, *Modern Courtship and Marriage*

Buchwald's sad little fable of the four husbands and LeMasters's didactic lesson for women which rests on its moral, illustrate in the vividest manner how women have more than a man's work to compete with for his time and attention—and how little they can do except grin and bear it.

Plato, who probably knew the mind of the gods as well as any other man, is authority for the statement that "the gods took pity on the tedious life of mortals, wearied with never-ending tasks and labors, and that they might not lack recreations and that they take heart again, the gods established festivals, banquets, and games."[1] Among the festivals were the Dionysian and among the games, the combative and the competitive.

The Dionysian quest for excitement and adventure has taken many forms in human history: battle, conquest, dueling, jousting, exploring, climbing mountains because they were there, exploit, sky-diving, pioneering, rioting, gambling, LSD trips, drinking. . . . The catalogue could be greatly extended. Some, like the fertility orgies of Greece or the sex chase, have involved sex. But by and large these activities have been one-sex in nature, and somewhat different for men and for women.

A major form of this quest for excitement and challenge by men in the modern world is that of competitive sports, either as participant or vicariously as spectator. For the individual man they supply an antidote, as the gods intended, for the tediousness of life for mortals. For our society as a whole they have performed a quite different and unanticipated function also, that of ethnic integration. One of the key facets of the immigrant's story in the United States was the part that organized sports played in the integration of differing ethnic and racial groups. A favorite and much-loved device illustrating this is to list the foreign-sounding names of, let us say, the Notre Dame football team, and, more recently, to play up the sports area as the scene for the integration of Negroes. This socially homogenizing effect of sports has been hailed as one of their major contributions.

Not so with respect to men and women. It is not likely that competitive sports like football and baseball will ever offer the sexes a chance to achieve "assimilation" or "integration." As soon as Art Buchwald's fourth friend, Carey, learned that his wife was going to watch the games with him, he left for the movies. And when "a woman watching a football game on a miserably cold day, through snow and sleet, said to her husband, 'Why don't we go home?' she answered her own question with 'This is probably another one of my silly questions.' "[2]

Even aside from Dionysian activities, a very considerable proportion of the recreation of men and women is one-sex in nature. In part this is an accidental result of timing; women are more likely than men to have their afternoons free. Thus many bridge clubs are one-sex in composition and the audience at matinees is heavily weighted in favor of women. In part, it is due to different tastes; the girlie show is less likely to appeal to women than to men. But in part the sexual segregation in recreation is by design. As in the case of the work group, men seem to want it that way. They do not want women in their taverns or in their lodges; they do not want them in their clubs. They do not want them at the poker table. They would prefer them off the golf course when they are playing. If women insist on sharing some of these activities, it must be on the terms set by men, as auxiliaries. Or they must surrender any consideration as women. A woman may want to climb mountains; hunting may—just may—be her forte. If so, she can expect no concessions, for "a woman who shoots is just one of the boys, entitled to no special privileges or courtesies."[3]

In the case of some men, this flight from women may have homosexual overtones, although Fiedler, it will be remembered, discounted this explanation; in others, it is simply, as in the case of the work group, a desire to get away from everything women stand for in their minds, whatever it is. In some men this desire is pervasive; they want as little to do with women as possible in their recreational life. In others, though, it is only partial; they do not flee women in all kinds of situations but only in some. They may even relish the presence of women in part of their recreational life; they just like a breather now and then.

◆◆◆◆◆

The playing field *can* be a place where men and women learn to enjoy one another's company, learn to appreciate one another's skills, talents, and differences, and learn how pleasant one another's company can be, quite aside from the physical attraction they exert on one another. Some universities have experimented with what is known as co-recreation programs.

Usually the reason is primarily administrative; co-recreation is cheaper and makes possible a better use of scarce facilities. But the side effects reported are also intriguing. At the University of Kansas, for example, about half of both men and women chose co-recreational classes, the men preferring dance and the women, individual sports. At the University of Kentucky, mixed classes had the effect of eliminating swearing among the men and of stimulating them to come to class with clean clothes and clean bodies.[4] Other studies also show that students of both sexes like co-recreation classes.[5]

The reasons given by women for liking co-recreation have been: it was a natural situation; it enhanced competition and hence effort; it provided divergent outlooks which was conducive to better learning; it was an aid to social development; and it was more interesting and enjoyable. The men gave similar reasons, though in a somewhat modified order: it aided social development; it was more interesting and enjoyable; it improved sportsmanship and personal appearance; it was a more natural situation; and it was more conducive to learning. Six men gave as their reason simply, "I like girls."

Reasons for not liking co-recreational classes as given by the girls were: it made for embarrassment and self-consciousness; the men had superior ability and experience; it made for distractions; both sexes tried to impress one another; they felt reluctant to compete with men; they felt uncomfortable in shorts(!); and they felt inferior. The men: both sexes tried too hard to impress one another; the women were inferior; the stimulation of competition was missing; they felt embarrassed; clothing was a problem; and too much time was wasted.[6]

In general, men and women tended to have different reasons for liking co-recreation, but more nearly similar reasons for not liking it. They shared their mutual dislike of one another's company; they diverged in reasons for liking it.

The general conclusion from the research studies was that if the development of skills was the objective of the program, then co-recreation was definitely not indicated, but if social development was, then it was clearly desirable.[7] So far as actual practice is concerned, the negative factors seem to have had greater influence on policy than the positive. It has even been argued that such programs may contribute to the role confusion commonly complained about in modern men and women.

Co-recreation under college auspices is one thing. Genuinely competitive sports are something else again. In the early 1960's there were a number of outstanding women in the university sports field. And it is interesting to note that the reaction against women on competitive teams was very much like the reaction of southern teams in the past when faced with teams which included Negroes. Two women were outstanding in varsity tennis, one at Washington University and one at the University of Alabama; both teams met opposition from other schools, who refused to play against them.[8] "The University of Illinois tennis team refused to play Washington University because Carol Hanks was on the team. The men from Indiana University said they would only step out onto the tennis court against Washington if Carol was kept off it. Reluctantly, Washington agreed to play without Carol—and lost." Mississippi State forfeited matches against Alabama in which a young woman was scheduled to play.[9]

One reason given by a university tennis coach for rejecting competition with women in tennis was that it was a heads-I-lose-tails-you-win proposition for the men. "Playing competitive tennis is an eyeball-to-eyeball death struggle. But no man is going to battle that hard against a woman. Look at the pressure on the man: if he wins, he gets no honor, but if he loses, he is humiliated." Another reason offered by one young man was, "I was afraid I'd hit the ball too hard and hurt her." Still another young man, defeated by a feminine opponent, concluded philosophically that it was good for a man's humility.[10]

The case of swimming seems to be different. The presence of two women on the Tulane University swimming team, by way of contrast, was said to have given the team a lift. Here, apparently, the girls are on their way to catching up with the boys. In 1896, we are told, the Olympic 100-meter swim was completed in 12 seconds; in 1960, a young woman did it in 11.3 seconds. One physical fitness expert has stated that "if a woman starts early enough and gets proper training there is no reason why she can't be as good as a man in a great many sports" and in swimming distances over 200 yards, she has an advantage in greater buoyancy.[11]

The girls on the tennis teams denied any aggressive motivations. The outstanding woman golfer did, too. She did not think it a "good idea for girls to compete against men in varsity sports. . . . But by competing on men's teams, we're stirring up interest in varsity sports for women." The logic of this roundabout approach to their goal is not wholly clear to an outsider. More understandable was the logic of the girl who had a somewhat different explanation for her participation. "Now maybe the men will wake up and realize that we girls can do a few things besides cook and sew."[12] It seems to a sedentary adult that this was surely a hard way to do it.

❖❖❖❖❖

Even private athletic games between the sexes have their peculiar hazards. The case of tennis again offers an interesting example. Mirra Komarovsky has reported—and it is commonly accepted as a truism—that girls do not like to win over men opponents. Not in tennis or swimming or in other activities in which physical differences do not entirely preclude success to women.[13] "Outside the office many eligible men can be found trapshooting, skiing, sailing, surfing, spear fishing, sky diving, playing tennis or golf, and riding bikes. . . . [But] if you're good at a particular sport, don't be better than he is—or braver either."[14] The advice is understandable, for "dating doesn't seem to follow playing together. Could it be because boys are reluctant to date a girl in the evening who beat them that afternoon on the tennis court?" asks one observer.[15] Probably so.

By and large, for whatever reason, for most athletic games and sports for most players most of the time, the sexes will tend to play with partners of their own sex. The physiques of men and women are different enough to make bisexual participation less fun as sport, however much fun it may be as a setting for sexual byplay.

❖❖❖❖❖

The kind of communication and the messages suitable between men and women at play seem to vary according to the situation. If they are skiing, we are told, "the 'date' relationship continues on out to the ski slopes, in that you look out for her and keep her company as her ski skill requires. . . . It's wise not to make big talk."[16] When skating, the man should not hold even the woman's hand; "you can always go 'sparking' in a nice dark movie instead of skating at the club!"[17] In primarily male activities, such as hunting and fishing, she is strictly on her own, one of the boys, entitled to no special courtesies. She wants assimilation? This is it.

The communication required or permitted on the dance floor varies from time to time and place to place. Sometimes it is ritualistic or pantomimic. Sometimes it permits of idiosyncrasy. Sometimes men and women do about the same thing; sometimes they do complementary things. In folk or square dancing the sexes seem to be equal; in nineteenth-century ballroom dancing, on the other hand, men were boss; they led and were masters. Since they were in a face-to-face position—in fact, in twentieth-century versions, cheek-to-cheek—verbal as well as gestural communication was possible. Currently there is an enormous amount of improvisation; in fact, most dancing seems to observers to be by individuals alone, almost without regard to one another. The individuals seem to know whom they are dancing "with"; an observer can hardly tell. The communication is arcane. The message in any event is almost primitively sexual.

Games represent a very special kind of interaction. Not all parlor games are child's play, as anyone who has watched them in process may well have noticed; a set of circumstances is designed, rules are laid down, and subjects go about fighting it out, that is, playing the game.

Different players play differently. Whatever the game, women tend to play differently from men. In a competitive situation they are more likely than men to arrive at a compromise-type solution. But in a conflict-type situation, they tend to be less cooperative than men. It makes a difference, however, whether they are playing against men or against women. They tend to be more cooperative playing against men than against women. The opposite is reported for men. These are surely among the most revealing results of this kind of research.

Games are, of course, of many kinds. Some, like throwing dice, are purely chance games; no skill is involved. Some, like athletic games, are games of skill; chance is at a minimum. Some combine a measure of both, as in poker: chance determines the cards one is dealt, but how they are played depends on skill. Skill often involves strategy and strategy often involves forcing another person's hand. Manipulation. Bluffing. Feints. As one woman put it, you have to be mean to win.

In some social circles, it has been noted, "organized games provide a cloak for, or defense against, personal contact," whereas in others they are seen as "routes toward contact and conversation," while in still others, "struggles . . . go on as to which version should have hegemony at any given time."[18] If there is a class differential in attitude toward games it may reflect the amount of time people have for perfecting their skills. Women whose time is all taken up with their household or professional chores would probably have less interest in playing bridge than women who, in effect, make a career of playing bridge.

There is, too, in addition to a class differential, certainly a personality difference in preference for or against organized games. Some people find enormous satisfaction in playing games, especially highly competitive games and games which pit one player against another aggressively, as in poker. Others loathe that kind of game but find word games fun. Some prefer games in which chance plays a determining role; others prefer games in which skill is important; and still others enjoy games where it is possible to outwit chance by manipulating an opponent. An insightful test of personality might well be constructed around preferences in games.

Finally, there may be a sex difference also in game preferences. Although both sexes are capable of playing all kinds of games, one hears of few women who regularly meet to play poker—though one woman was once reported to find poker an acceptable substitute for orgasm[19]—or of men who meet to play bridge. When men and women play together, the game is more likely to be bridge than poker. At the gambling casinos one sees both men and women playing games in which chance alone determines the outcome; but a detailed analysis might find sex differences in the popularity of the several kinds of devices.

Games change their patronage from time to time. Bowling, which was once a masculine activity, has now become a family game. Billiards at home may be engaged in by women—the Queen Mother of England is reportedly an expert—but public pool halls attract very few women, even when admission is free.

Games have the advantage of clear-cut rules. If there is any question about the correctness of a move or play, there is an authoritative guide to interpret the situation. Handicaps are recognized. The kinds of communication between or among players are clearly specified; this is permissible, this is not. Such a neat and firm structure offers security; men and women at the bridge table are protected by it. Husbands and wives do not have to worry when their spouses team up with other people.

To be sure, the rules about information in games refer only to instrumental information; they cannot protect against expressive communication. The man and woman may be adhering meticulously to the official rules and so far as the game itself is concerned, their messages are strictly legal. But in that other game, the one they are playing together by themselves, the messages they are sending back and forth may be of quite a different order. Not legitimate at all, the angry spouses remind them on the way home.

Fun and games may be extremely serious. The messages are very clear, if implicit, in the situation. Jennie Grossinger, for example, was unabashedly candid about the program at Grossinger's Hotel in the Adirondacks. She was interested in helping marriage-minded women find marriage-minded men. The so-called bachelor-cruises in effect institutionalize a function long implicit in "travel," that of finding a mate, if not romance. The shipboard or the summer romance might be just a fun thing for the man; it might be deadly serious for the woman. The problem is that all too often the sex ratio is so low as to disappoint a large contingent of women.

An innovation in the fun-and-games form of sex play has

been reported for a somewhat more sophisticated set in New York, the so-called singles party. Guests are assembled either by advertising or by invitation at a bar, club, other public facility, or at someone's apartment, and they come one-by-one—separately, not as couples. Ostensibly they come "looking for a temporary companion, not a mate," so that "even if a girl is dead set on husband hunting, she is wiser if she plays it cool at singles affairs." Sometimes the girl "single" succeeds, for sometimes "marriages have come from singles parties."[20]

❖❖❖❖❖

All games played by both sexes are, in a general sense, sex games. But there are some which are specifically sex games. At a fairly young age children begin to play them. Among the earliest are post office and spin the bottle. These are games which relieve individuals of having to take the initiative in a sexual episode; they supply the setting in which a boy and girl may have a brief encounter strictly according to rule. An opportunity is provided to engage in sex play on a chance basis. Youngsters who would not dare to ask a girl for a kiss have the privilege granted to them on a playful basis. Because they are so young, it makes little difference who the partner is; almost anyone would do. The communication is uncomplicated, the message simple. No one need feel jealous; no one need feel left out since partners are determined by chance. These games are outgrown in later adolescence, replaced by others.[21]

Most of the Dionysian activities discussed above are not suitable for women or appealing to them. When women seek excitement, risk, adventure, it often takes the form of a sexual game. They "play with fire" or with "dynamite." They see how far they can go without yielding. The sex chase is one of the most exciting games. And one of the oldest. The medieval courts of love enforced the rules of the game as it was played in those days. It has somewhat different rules today. But though the rules are not codified, everyone seems to know when a girl is said to have cheated or when a boy has taken unfair advantage. In Eskilstuna, Sweden, in 1966, a court fined a gypsy girl for fraudulent behavior when she refused to prostitute herself after accepting money from a man. "The plaintiff claimed that he was cheated when he paid the girl $20 for a 'sex date' which she failed to keep."²² The "Rapo" game described in Chapter Eight might also be interpreted as a form of cheating in a sex game.

Sex as a purely playful activity has only recently been emphasized in our society, but it is increasingly so viewed. We have noted that sexual intercourse can be used in scores of ways, can convey scores of messages. In marriage, it may be used in a simple, biological way, to have babies; in or out of marriage it may be an expression of hostile aggression, of conquest, of triumph, of victory; it may be viewed as submission to duty; it has been studied as a biological "outlet," one among several; it is veiwed by some as a way of relieving tension; it was once viewed in the same light as a drink of water, a simple solution to a simple need; it is seen as a prescription against alienation, as a form of togetherness, as punishment, as reward, as proof of maleness or of femaleness or of adulthood or of emancipation, or as rebellion, as, in fact, almost anything one can imagine. But sex as fun or as play is none of the above. Definitely not a way to have babies, to express hostile aggression, a duty, outlet, tension releaser, protection against alienation, merely togetherness, punishment, reward, proof of anything at all, act of rebellion. . . . It is just fun, a game, play.

The name of the game is touch-and-go. For sex just for fun cannot be serious; it cannot require a lifelong commitment; it implies no responsibility. The sex-as-play concept constitutes the central core of much erotic or pornographic writing. One commentator, discussing a major classic of nineteenth-century pornography, *My Secret Life,* notes the inability of the author to enter into, let alone maintain, a genuine human relationship with a woman. Something is missing from his makeup, there is a "large hole or vacuum somewhere in him." He literally does not know what such words as "like" and "affection" mean, for "such words describe the quality of one's feelings in *relation* to other persons, and it is at precisely this juncture that the author is most clearly defective."²³ He is always glad when an affair is over because such ties worried him. Such antipathy to ties characterizes pornographic writing in general.²⁴

Sex as fun, one commentator notes, may be intrinsically in conflict with civilized sexuality. "Before we criticize this mode of experience for its shallowness and inadequacy," Steven Marcus says, "we might suggest that in it is expressed one of the fundamental contradictions of human sexual life. For there can be little doubt that full aggressive potency, demonic genitality is permanently at odds with that elaborately developed life of the emotions which is our civilized heritage—and burden."[25]

Still, it persists in one form or another. In its current form, it is at least a social, if not truly an emotional, relationship. It must even be mutual. For sexual relationships cannot be fun for either partner, in the contemporary version of the sex-as-fun game, unless it is fun for both. It does not permit of super- or subordination; no one is giving in, no one is winning over the other; it is, theoretically, a game strictly between equals. Each, according to the modern rules, gives as much as he receives. But, as in the classic—pornographic—form, sex as fun still has to be temporary and short-lived. This is the rock-bottom character-izing nature of the sex-as-fun game: no ties. If it lasts too long, one of the players is almost sure to become bored, or both may; this has long been known to be the natural course of events. Or one partner falls in love with the other, or they both do. And love is serious. Sex becomes much more than fun. Love spoils the game.

Sex as fun can thrive only under rather special circumstances: chance or occasional encounters at conventions or accidental rendezvous; strangers who just happen to be in the same place at the same time under auspicious circumstances; ships-that-pass-in-the-night type of hail-and-farewell meetings. Even under these conditions, the relationship may be quite different from sheer fun; it may be a refuge from loneliness, an antidote to alienation, reassurance for some ego hurt—almost any seeking for reassurance. But it *looks* like sheer fun and either or both may insist that it is, and reassure themselves that it is. It *has* to be. (Note: if they remain as lonely afterwards as before or if the experience leaves a bitter taste, it was not fun.)

The rules as institutionalized for this touch-and-go, sex-as-fun game have been reported by Helen Gurley Brown. The

"Matinee" or two-hour "little affair" form, on the basis of an informant, has two basic conditions: one of the parties has to be married and the times together have to be restricted to lunch hours. It is definitely not for deep emotional involvement. There is positively no room for the normal demands which those in love make on one another. They can do nothing but spoil the relationship and make one or the other feel guilty. The partners may be good friends, but if they are looking for someone to fall in love with, they would do well to give up the Matinee and look for "a more expensive ticket for evening performances."[26] A woman looking for a playmate for this game should find someone she knows and likes very much, is physically attractive, and above all, someone who is happily married. The Matinee requires secrecy; it must be clandestine. Standard operational procedure, therefore, requires not being seen together too much, not wearing identifiable perfume or lipstick that might leave a trace on the man, never telephoning him at home under any circumstances. In brief, utmost discretion.[27]

A similar codification of the rules of the touch-and-go, sex-as-fun game from the male point of view is presented by Hugh Hefner, the major exponent of the theory and practice of the game. Harvey Cox has summarized it for us. Sex is to be viewed as a leisure-time activity which one must handle with skill and detachment. The girl is a "playboy accessory," both desirable and dispensable. But the relationship must be kept within the area of entertainment and recreation. "Don't let her get 'serious.' " When the game is over, her function stops and she must be made to understand this rule. "As the crew-cut young man in a *Playboy* cartoon says to the rumpled and disarrayed girl he is passionately embracing, 'Why speak of love at a time like this?' " The fiction in this magazine conveys the same lesson for the young-men readership. They are taught that sex is to be severely departmentalized. The gorgeous and seductive women make no demands on the young man the story is about (he is rarely a hero). There is a casual but satisfying experience "with no entangling alliances whatever." These feminine fictional characters know the rules; they know their place and ask for nothing more. Certainly no permanent involvement. "Like any good accessory, they are detachable and disposable." Just as children outgrow post office and spin the bottle, so, apparently, do men outgrow the touch-and-go, sex-as-fun game. At any rate, the readers of *Playboy* decline in number when in their thirties.[28]

We used to think of the touch-and-go, sex-as-fun game as more appealing to men than to women. Women were supposed to demand a more secure and permanent relationship. They tended to spoil the game by wanting marriage. At least love. But if Helen Gurley Brown's informant is correct, we may be creating a kind of woman who is satisfied with the touch-and-go, sex-as-fun game. If we are, she is a phenomenon so new that we can hardly even begin to trace the implications either for her or for the family or for the social order. Or, for that matter, for men. We'll have to wait and see. When it is playboy who is the disposable accessory and playmate the detached disposer; when it is playboy who knows his place and asks for nothing more and playmate who decides when playtime is over; when it is playboy who is rebuked by playmate because he wants to talk of love during a passionate embrace. . . .

Well, *what* then?

CHAPTER THIRTEEN

Social Life

The worst effect [of smoking] is banishing for hours
The sex whose presence civilises ours.

—William Cowper, *Conversation*

It is noteworthy . . . how seldom the party-goers in our observation
went anticipating a good time.

—David Riesman and Associates, "Sociability, Permissiveness, and Equality"

Inasmuch as sociability "at its best" serves to lend "drama to
life, intensifying reality,"[1] its frequent failure to supply even
a good time, documented in the research quoted above, is
puzzling and certainly worth exploring. Reliance on alcohol is
another commonly cited evidence of the failure of social life.

Evaluation of social life is not easy. "Sociability is the interaction which occurs between people who have come together
to enjoy each others' company; or between people who are trying to enjoy each others' company because they have been
brought together."[2] But how to judge such interaction? "As

compared with the spheres of work, sex, and sports, there are no clear standards as to what constitutes adequate performance."[3] There is no dearth of rules and advice in etiquette and cook books for staging parties and for entertaining successfully. Still every hostess knows that despite every effort, the enterprise is all-too-often a flop.

◇◇◇◇◇

The decline of the host or leadership role is one reason that has been suggested for the failure of so much sociability. "More and more, our observations have led us to conclude that sociability remains inadequate without the guidance of leaders sensitive not only to a group's moods but [also] to things and values outside the group."[4] Social gatherings are not automatically successful; "leadership and invention are required."[5] A social gathering represents a rather complex kind of organization. It can take the form of amorphous milling about by individuals, as at a large cocktail party where there may be a lot of noise and pseudocommunication, but little else. It can take the form of a random set of one-sex or mixed-sex dyads. It may break up into one-sex or mixed-sex cliques. It may be extremely fluid, forming into one pattern and then another. Riesman and his associates note a decline in the "lion" concept in which one person commanded homage from all; they also contrast the older European model in which there were soloists who sought to shine as individuals, to be brilliant and clever with the newer, more communal American model which seems to be both anti-star and still highly permissive to individualism. There is no place in this model for the life-of-the-party role.

The abdication of the leadership role may be related, among other things, to the trend toward equality of the sexes. For the most part entertaining is a woman's world. She runs it. It is one administrative role that hardly any men ever challenge. Whether it is a decision about admission to the 400 or an exclusive social circle or whether it is planning a large charity ball, open to anyone who can afford a ticket, women are likely to be at or near the helm.

Entertaining is an active, aggressive enterprise. The hosts

[310]

make a commitment: they promise to give guests a pleasant time. The hostess who entertains is boss. She has made the plans. She is permitted to order people around to an extent that would never be tolerated in other circumstances. Delightfully, of course, but no less firmly. "Won't you please sit next to Charles, Helen? You'll enjoy his story about Nigeria." "Oh, come, gentlemen; please, no shoptalk now!" "Everyone line up, please, for dinner." No matter if the message is instrumental; the manner must be appeasing. The guests do not begrudge her her polished bossiness. Entertaining is one segment of life in which women are permitted, even charged with, a masculine or task-leader role.

When equalitarianism invades this area of life, women are no longer in exclusive charge. Entertaining becomes a shared activity. In one study of some eighty parties, for example, it was found that, contrary to expectations, men and women showed almost identical amounts of "hosting" behavior, that is: encouraging shy guests, inducting newcomers, stimulating performers, conciliating arguers, or making sure that the quiet ones were not excluded; about a tenth of the behavior of both men and women consisted of hosting and subhosting.[6] With no strong hand on the reins, the party disintegrates. Exaggerated permissiveness means that some guests are so little engaged that they may even fall asleep. Such laissez-faire is in part a response to guests' resistance to any kind of authority, but it is fatal to a good party. Riesman and his associates suggest that the failure they observed was often due to the absence of a strong host role performance. If the hostess had been on the ball, they would have judiciously broken up "in" groups and conversations and seen to it that participation was general. Sometimes hostesses complained that the guests took the party away from them. They could have left and no one would have noticed.

A distinction should be made between entertaining and hospitality. People who are hospitable may never entertain in the sense of giving parties. But they do enjoy company. They may love to have people drop by; they may love to have house guests. They make their guests feel wonderfully comfortable and at ease. Their hospitality may be a byword among their friends. The hostess is in a suitably feminine role; she does all she can to see that her guests enjoy their stay; but it is always unobtrusively. Her guests should never know. Hospitality is a state of being. There is no verb to express being hospitable. To entertain means *doing* something. To be hospitable means just that, *being* something. Riesman and his associates are of the opinion that there is a trend toward confusing the two. The hospitable person permits a great deal of freedom to his guest; but what is suitable for hospitality may not be suitable for entertaining.

Since the structure of a party depends in large part on the sex composition, the sex ratio in social gatherings is a major concern of the hostess. The invitation list for a traditional coming-out party will be heavily weighted in the direction of young men. There should be, the hostess knows, a long stag line to ensure every young woman a wide choice of dancing partners. A sex ratio of two or three—even more—to one is considered desirable. To make the party worth the young man's time, he is assured of plenty to eat and drink. But for the usual dance or dinner party or just an ordinary party, at a one-generation level, the hostess aims at sex parity. She may or may not pair people off, but she wants to be sure there is a woman for every man or, rather, a man for every woman. Even here, if there has to be an odd person she prefers that it be a man rather than a woman. There is hardly anything more awkward socially than an extra woman. Indeed, the fate of being an extra woman socially is a fate not much better than social death; it is openly recognized as one of the most serious consequences of bereavement or divorce.

Any of all kinds of communication may occur. If the people are unacquainted with one another, there may be a great deal of protocommunication between them, "prospecting" for more information than the hostess supplies in her introduction. Behind the simple job, residence, and family information which she gives, the guests have to do their own probing. If the guests know one another intimately, the communication may be largely of one or another shared-experience type. Indeed, it may be so in-group in nature as to repel others and thus detract from the success of the party as a whole. If the hostess is herself guilty of such *faux pas*, the party may disintegrate.[7] Sometimes, though, a gathering "catches" one person's emotions, or several persons', and they begin to sing or laugh together; the party solidifies into a unified group.

Whatever structure the group falls into, whatever the medium used among the communicators at a social gathering, and whatever the instrumental contents may be, the messages conveyed are supposed to be stroking in nature. The purpose of a dinner party, for example, is "to put you in company with persons of consideration, and to give you an opportunity to display your intelligence, or cause your good qualities to be appreciated in the . . . semi-intimacy which may result from it."[8] The term "polite society" has become an anachronism, but much of what was included in the concept remains. It was, in effect, a bourgeois version of an aristocratic or leisure-class tradition. Ladies and gentlemen, serene and above the mundane battles of survival, could cultivate a style of interaction ostensibly noncombative and insulated from the world of competition, lust and violence.[9] The rules were designed to prevent controversy. But repartee, the battle of wits, the verbal duel, were permitted. Also coquetry—anything, so long as it was polite and polished. The rules have been relaxed; but one remains. The message must still be stroking in character. The interaction should be enjoyable. The good hostess tries.

But despite the fact that women "want talk that is actively general, neither the exclusive shoptalk of the men, nor the comparable 'shoptalk' of the women, namely, children, shopping, the neighborhood," most social gatherings fail to achieve it for them. This is one battle that hostesses lose with monotonous, almost predictable, regularity. Do what they may, they find their party simply bifurcating, one sex at the front of the living room, the other at the rear.

Women who have known what fun good talk between the sexes can be sometimes wonder why it is so rare. Why do so few men ever learn about this delightful leisure-time activity, let alone how to engage in it? And why don't those who know tell others? Why, in brief, is there so little of it? And why are so many women equally unprepared for it?

✦✦✦✦✦

Sexual apartheid is so ubiquitous and persistent as to suggest that it is almost, at least figuratively speaking, a "natural law." There seems to be an almost inescapable tendency for the sexes to separate into one-sex groups unless ways to avoid it are institutionalized. Except when the sexes pair off socially as at dances, they seem, indeed, to have a "natural" tendency to separate from one another. Even preliterate societies have their bachelor houses. This kind of social apartheid of the sexes is so old, so omnipresent, crossing all class lines and local boundaries, that illustration is hardly necessary. There is probably no middle-class hostess who has not at some time or other, or until she admitted defeat and gave up, chewed her nails trying to prevent the women from congregating at one end of her living room and the men at the other. Still, sheerly for intrinsic interest, if not for documentary purposes, it is sadly amusing to review the long and dismal story.

In eighteenth-century England, for example, except for the well-organized salons, a party of men and women was a mechanical mixture, tending always to break down into the original elements. A contemporary describes one:

> As if the two sexes had been in a state of war, the gentlemen ranged themselves on one side of the room, where they talked their own talk, and left us poor ladies to twirl our shuttles and amuse each other by conversing as we could. By what little I could hear, our opposites were discursing on the old English poets, and this subject did not seem so much beyond a female capacity, but that we might have been indulged with a share in it.[10]

With dreary repetitiveness the same kind of sexual apartheid was reported in the United States. In 1828, Captain Basil Hall noted that the sexes had "such different classes of occupations, that they seldom act together; and this naturally prevents the growth of that intimate companionship, which nothing can establish but the habitual interchange of opinions and sentiments upon topics of common employment."[11] Mrs. Trollope in 1832 reported that at several lavish balls she attended "the gentlemen sat down to supper in one room, while the ladies took theirs, standing, in another."[12] And she told of a young German who wanted to organize a picnic of young people but was told by the girl he suggested it to that they were "not used to such sort of things here, and I know it is considered very indelicate for ladies and gentlemen to sit down together on the grass." Men and women could not even go to the art gallery in Philadelphia together but had to go in separate groups.

In America, with the exception of dancing, which is almost wholly confined to the unmarried of both sexes, all the enjoyments of the men are found in the absence of the women. They dine, they play cards, they have musical meetings, they have suppers, all in large parties, but all without women. . . . The two sexes can hardly mix for the greater part of a day without great restraint and ennui.[13]

A German observer of the American scene in 1839 commented that "at a party the women [were] quietly sequestered near the wall, or in some corner of the room, talking amongst themselves."[14] Here is how Henry Seidel Canby remembered social life in the 1890's:

At dinner the sexes were adequately mingled, the conversation playing upon the surface of easy banter. Afterwards, without that separation for coffee practiced in more formal societies, the guests flowed into the living room and even in flowing separated into austral and oriental currents while the tides of talk rose and took on different notes. With an obvious relief the men gathered around the fireplace dropping facetiousness, while the women's conversation (much the better) sought human values around my mother's coffee table.[15]

Canby concluded that both sexes lost, but women more than the men. "Women suffered most, for the male intellect in an age busy with things had plenty of satisfying fact to talk about. . . . But men suffered too by a kind of vivacious dullness which was the note of the period."[16] Something was missing there and still is.

Almost half a century later, precisely the same kind of sexual apartheid was reported by other observers of the American scene, notably the Lynds. "The men and women frequently either gravitate apart into separate groups to talk men's talk and women's talk, or the men do most of the talking and the women largely listen."[17] Feminine listeners or none was the only choice available to the women.

Again in the 1940's.

. . . predinner cocktails are usually served in sufficient quantity and strength to make the man talkative or even gay during much of the time at table, but as the minutes pass and the wines aren't potent enough to take up the slack of the waning cocktails, the talk and the men tend to slow down. But when the company separates after dinner, the men act as though released from a heavy burden. Somebody says, "Have you heard the one about the twelve men and the girl in the sleeping car leaving for Denver?" Others talk about business, football, politics, Joe Matthews (Yale, '19) who struck it rich out west, and they thoroughly enjoy themselves. The stag party continues until the hostess asks the men to rejoin the women, but often it is prolonged almost until it is time to go home. In small towns the process is little different. There, after dinner, the men huddle in one corner of the living room, talking to one another about things that really concern them—crops, weather, business, politics—while the women sit in another corner, discussing children, servants, clothes, gardens, or retailing local gossip.[18]

Finally, as though further demonstration were required, the study of eighty parties, cited earlier, found "without exception, at the parties which we have observed, efforts by the hostess . . . to forcefully prevent men and women from separating proved self-defeating."[19]

The Renaissance succeeded in working out a two-sex pattern of social life more spontaneous than that of the Middle Ages. If communication between a knight and his lady in the Middle Ages had tended to be highly stylized, even ritualistic, communication between a courtier and a lady during the Renaissance was personalized and individualized, with the result that

the talk of the Renaissance was one of the finest products of a period which in literature was not great, and in talk the lady shone, as she is always able to do when she will take the trouble. . . . Only at certain times [however] of which perhaps the Renaissance is thus far the most noteworthy, will men join in the pursuit of an art of life. The men of the Renaissance themselves started the game, and they found at once that the women were indispensable partners.[20]

The great salonnières of the eighteenth century in Paris also succeeded in the difficult sociochemical task of making men and women mix freely in a social situation. But they had to make a career of it and their success was not duplicated widely in other times or places. It took a great talent even then to succeed; those who did were exceptional women. In their great salons good talk between the sexes was cultivated as a very fine art. The most dazzling exponent of all was Madame de Staël, for whom "conversation was, next to love, the principal *raison d'être*."[21] Of conversation in France, she noted:

Words are not merely, as they are in all other countries, a means to communicate ideas, feelings, and needs, but an instrument one likes to play and which revives the spirit, just as does music in some nations, and strong liquors in others. [It is] a certain way in which people act upon one another, a quick give-and-take of pleasure, a way of speaking as soon as one thinks, of rejoicing in oneself in the immediate present, of being applauded without making an effort, of displaying one's intelligence by every nuance of intention, gesture, and looks—in short, the ability to produce at will a kind of electricity which, emitting a shower of sparks, relieves the excess of liveliness in some and rouses others from their painful apathy.[22]

Germaine de Staël, her biographer tells us, needed conversation as much as she neded air. She was witty, could talk on the court, the theater, and convey social gossip with equal charm; but she was at her best when talking about topics that she felt passionately about. She communicated an effect like that of music on her hearers, an "intellectual melody." "When she had her inspired moments, which could last for nearly an hour, her listeners were absolutely under her spell, sometimes even reacting physically, so tense was the excitement she generated. And yet she conversed; she did not orate."[23]

If overcoming sexual apartheid depended on such extraordinary genius on the part of women as that of Germaine de Staël's, it would be a lost cause. Not many people, men or women, can give such virtuoso performances. All that Madame de Staël proves is that this kind of talent is not the monopoly of the male sex. And the *savantes* show that given the proper milieu, many woman can achieve distinction.

In England the Blue Stockings seem to have worked through organization rather than to have depended on individual stars. They leaned more heavily on proper structuring of the group than on such a rare commodity as talented personalities. Two schools of thought evolved, each led by an important hostess. One of them, Mrs. Montagu, operated on the theory that the hostess was a teacher; the other, Mrs. Vesey, followed a more permissive line.

Mrs. Montagu was all for organization. She seated her guests in a circle around her, those with highest rank on one side and the most talented on the other, in order. She conceived her role as that of, in effect, a teacher. As such she graded them. She suggested the topic to be talked about, recognized those who were to be permitted to contribute, and at the end summed up the whole discussion, with eighteenth-century dogmatic finality. Despite the arrogation of this discussion-leader role to herself, she was actually quite uncertain of herself and rather afraid of her guests. And well she might be, considering that men like Horace Walpole were among them. She waited until she had been applauded before she got over her anxiety. It sounds rather grim from this distance. But her guests must have enjoyed it—at least enough to respond to her appeals for reassurance.

Mrs. Vesey was different. She had a horror of the circle and all the ceremony and awe that went with it. She leaned over backward to prevent a circle from forming, even naturally. She scattered the furniture around so that a circle would be impossible. Her guests came not to talk to or with her but with each other. And that suited Mrs. Vesey just fine. "It was sufficient satisfaction to her that they came at all."[24]

Of the several ways to encourage sociosexual integration—the captivating star, the circular seminar, or the small-group pattern—none seems to be the American solution. But for Americans, apparently, the trend seems to follow the Blue Stocking rather than the de Staël model, and it is more like Mrs. Montagu's than like Mrs. Vesey's. It is in the direction of serious round-table discussion rather than of random persiflage; and it is not in the tradition of social life but, rather, in that of education.

It should be noted that even when apartheid is most blatant, the sexual phalanxes are not always solid. There may be one or two defectors: men who line up gallantly with the women—"the hee-hawers of static gallantry"—and the women "gigglers and teasers"[25] who show solidarity with the men. In such mixed company the topics to talk about are limited by the range of shared interests. But the tendency which, as related to race relations, is called "tipping" takes place. Up to a point the topic invites participation by both sexes. If there are more women than men in the group, the men may not be able to hold their own. The balance is upset and the group tips in favor of woman-talk; the men are silenced; they withdraw. One sensitive man commented that he enjoyed the company of one woman, even of two, but rarely of more than that number at any one time.

❖❖❖❖❖

One alternative to sexual apartheid is a structure of paired couples. One of the functions of two-sex social life is to enhance the couple's sense of unity and solidarity. It is we versus they. The couple come as a unit. They are viewed as a unit. They see themselves reflected back from others as a unit. No matter how far apart they may be actually, until they are ready to admit a break, they must put up a united front. They have to act as though they were a unit. So far so good. But according to one analyst, there has to be a limit. If encouraged too far, "the competitive conversation centering around children and material possessions (such as houses, furnishings, cars, lawn, and gardens)" would be too divisive of the group as a whole.[26] The party would tend to break down into husband-wife teams or coalitions, competing or in conflict with one another. There would be no party.

To counteract this possibility, hostesses separate husbands and wives. They are not allowed to sit next to one another at the dinner table, and it would—in middle-class parties, at any rate—be awkward if spouses remained together afterward. Each is supposed to circulate freely. Instead, however, of a general mixed group, in which superficial persiflage is exchanged, what usually happens is either the usual social apartheid we have been illustrating or a number of paired flirtation encounters.

This "adulterous flirtation" which characterizes much social life that is not segregated, has been interpreted by Philip Slater as one among a number of techniques for preventing spouses from becoming too wrapped up in one another to the detriment of community solidarity. Theoretically the norm for the re-

[319]

lations of husband and wife in our society is one in which the husband cleaves to his wife and the wife clings to her husband; in which they become a union. Actually, however, an analyst suggests, this kind of pattern of relationships, if followed meticulously, would be socially subversive. He speaks, following Freud, of what he calls "dyadic withdrawal" which, if permitted, would render the couple too self-sufficing and hence independent of the social world.[27] The community does not want two people to become "all wrapped up in one another"; it does not want dyadic intimacy to become an end in itself, the "world-well-lost" sort of thing. It does everything it can to intrude upon such intimacy. The whole wedding complex, Slater concludes, is an intrusion ritual to draw families, peer groups, and community into the act, to seize the initiative, so to speak, from the couple and, in effect, socialize the relationship. Even the honeymoon is playfully and symbolically impeded by pranks of one kind or another. The general function of all these intrusions, he argues, is to prevent the dyadic relationship from absorbing the couple completely, leaving no need for the wider social groups, rendering them independent of it and hence not subject to its controls.

Adulterous or extramarital flirtation, which is a possible alternative to sociosexual apartheid, is, according to this point of view "a cohesive force which prevents the marital bond from atomizing the community."[28] It counteracts invidious competitive conversation and "tends to vitiate the divisive effect of such invidious comparisons."[29] However valid this particular interpretation may be, it is probable that most wives would prefer apartheid to adulterous flirtation. If they cannot have the exclusive company of their husbands, they certainly do not want other women to have it.

As a matter of fact, it is much more usual to explain the universality of sociosexual apartheid as precisely a device to prevent such illegitimate attractions. We noted in connection with working groups that "practically speaking, it may be predicted that sexual or quasi-sexual relationships of some importance will develop in most mixed working groups. Insofar as this introduces extraneous conflicts, it represents a direct threat to the group."[30] Not all social groups are daily, ongoing, and as involving as work groups are, but the general conclusion about them is relevant here; the same logic may be applied to social as to work groups. Thus the social apartheid of the sexes may be simply a protection against a threat. If they were not segregated from one another, there would be altogether too much expressive communication between the men and the women to suit at least the less secure spouses. Apartheid is a safer antidote to Slater's excessive marital togetherness than adulterous flirtation. By maintaining a social curtain between the sexes, forbidden attractions are minimized, if not wholly prevented.

In the case of adolescents, a great deal of distance is, often enough, necessary to protect them from their own powerful drives. But adults? Even *old* adults? The patterns of sociosexual apartheid are so strong that even in old age, when both men and women have time on their hands and the threat of wayward sexual passion is not great, the tendency is for the old men and the old women to pursue their segregated social life.[31] Recent attention to geriatrics has tended to encourage efforts to make social contact among the elderly more feasible. The delights of sex—if not of sexual—relations remain long past the damping of glandular fires.

Sometimes even under the apartheid system there is interaction between the men and the women, not as individuals, either in dyads or in groups, but as coalitions in the battle of the sexes. The speakers address themselves to the assembled company, airing their grievances against the other sex, knowing well that they have the support of their sex peers. "Men always . . ." or "Women never . . ." and the battle is on. In the anonymity of the collective attack, individual men and women may air grievances against specific spouses, protected by the presence of others. Messages are communicated that astonish the spouse; he (she) never dreamed the other felt that way about. . . .

The shared-experience forms of communication depend, as we saw, on at least a modicum of similarity. J. C. Fluegel speaks of what he calls homosociality, a sort of psychological tendency for like to seek like. And Simone de Beauvoir complains that women are always uncomfortable with men, always having to act when in mixed groups, pretending to accept their inferior status as the second sex. Thus wherever the division of labor between the sexes augments likeness among men and differences between them and women, the conditions for apartheid are fostered. If the men share occupational or professional interest and concerns, they are likely to find shoptalk more interesting than other kinds. And shoptalk is a large component of interesting talk, often the most engaging kind to most people. In the eighty parties studied by Riesman and his associates, it was almost impossible to prevent shoptalk, especially among the men.

The shoptalk of women, because of the way they spend their time, is—let's face it—often as boring as it is reported to be. In the eighty parties, most of the two thousand episodes recorded for women were "routine in perspective and flat in artistry." Riesman and his associates comment that although femininity permits of more fantasy than does masculinity, and although women read more novels than men and watch more soap operas, they have less direct experience to bring to social talk; they exist too much "on borrowed experience" to be interesting.[32] The women they observed were, therefore, unimaginative, literal-minded, and seldom rose to the fanciful.

Pearl Buck corroborates the general tenor of these findings. She is of the opinion that if men do not enjoy the company of women it is the fault of the women. They have, she believes, convinced themselves that men do not like intelligent women and therefore that they must not seem intelligent. Not so at all, says Pearl Buck. The American man, at any rate, now finds that he does like to talk with women intelligently. "He is," in fact, "impatient when her conversation is limited to trivialities and daily humdrum and gossip. Never before has the intelligent and well-educated woman had so much good male companionship as she has now. I am impressed by the fact that while American men are hungry for a fuller companionship with women sexually, they are even more hungry for her intellectual and spiritual companionship."[33] Nobody, she concludes, is holding women back except the women themselves.

The point Miss Buck is making is given a somewhat different twist by the findings of Riesman and his associates. Not only were the women they observed unimaginative themselves, but they were also resentful of the more intelligent women. Since in any given party, especially if the guests were selected on the basis of the men's occupational contacts, the women will be from a more diversified background and have more diverse interests than the men, the distance between the most and the least successful will be greater than it is among men. The less intellectual women may even ruin the party for the more intellectual ones. "Some wives," report Riesman and his associates, "at parties we observed actively resented the 'intellectual' talk of other women—and frequently managed to sabotage it, either directly by facilitating a separation of the sexes or indirectly by literal-minded interruption of any sequence involving another woman."[34] In frustrated indignation one academic woman cried, "I wish hostesses would let me stay with the men, whose talk is interesting . . . rather than insist on including me among the women, most of whose talk is not interesting to me!"[35]

Not everyone agrees in attributing the separation of the sexes to defects in women. Thackeray attributed it in part to the grossness of men: "All men who avoid female society have dull perceptions and are stupid, or have gross tastes and revolt against what is pure." Henry Seidel Canby believed that it was the desexing of women which robbed them of their appeal.

Their imagination . . . suffered from the restraint of something vital. For these men and women (good friends all) had tacitly agreed to look upon each other as sexless, and that was . . . fatal to their companionship. By convention as strong as faith they left out of their relationship precisely that which might have made it as stimulating as a meeting between man and congenial man or woman and sympathetic woman. . . . Every man was all man in his club or business or at the saloon bar (and this is one reason for the popularity of the old saloon), but less than man in the company of any respectable woman but his mother or his wife. And every married woman was less than woman in mixed society because her sex was dormant, canalized, inhibited, because no male present . . . imagined her as she was.[36]

There was no tradition of the enjoyment of the conversation of women to set the stage. If it is, alas, in fact true that women are socially boring, it is certainly not due to lack of education or to intrinsic dullness. In an appropriate setting and in a role recognized by men their performance, as shown by the salonnières, has been brilliant, nothing short, in some cases, of prodigious. So far from boring men, these great women attracted the outstanding geniuses of their time. Dull women could not have enticed them.

Today when women are, indeed, recognized as sexual creatures, the approach of many men to women puts women at once on the defensive. It is either one of sexual aggression—well-mannered or crude or even phony—or of minimal contact, pseudocommunication. They want or pretend to want a sexual encounter or they want not to be bothered. They come with an image of women as delightful sexual partners or as impossible bores or as threatening ogres.

In any event, for whatever reason or cause and whether he or she is "to blame," very few men really enjoy the company of women. And, considering the social matrix in which they operate, few women as a result are good company. But with men who know how to approach them, who know how to bring out the best rather than the worst in them, who are appreciative, gentle, and genuinely interested in learning how the world looks to women, with men, in brief, who enjoy the pleasure of their company, women—even the only-a-housewife women—can be, or become, interesting companions. Men, in effect, have the kind of feminine company they deserve.

Some people argue that sociosexual apartheid needs no defense. So far from blame being assessed, credit is due to those who uphold it. One-sex groupings, they maintain, are necessary in order for the sexes to validate their own sex roles. The point is made that the alleged role confusion of the sexes today is a result of the togetherness drive of recent years, including the development of recreational programs designed for both sexes.

It would be strange indeed if the best way for a man to define his role vis-à-vis women were to avoid them—to associate only with men. The assumption that mixing the sexes necessarily desexes them is just the reverse of Canby's conclusion that it was the social separation of the sexes that desexed them. We are speaking, of course, with great imprecision, in an idiom hard to apply accurately. But in general the man who is secure enough in his maleness to enjoy the company of women seems much more of a man than the one who feels himself a man only away from women. One could say the same of Simone de Beauvoir's theory. Women who are uncomfortable with men or who resent them are less secure in their own femininity than women who enjoy men. In fact, it is possible for the sexes to enjoy one another socially only when both are so secure in their own sexual identity that the other is neither threatening nor invidious. When men and women can confront one another so confident of their own sexual identities that they can "glory"—to use an old-fashioned phrase—in their differences, knowing that the differences do not mean superiority or inferiority, problems of role confusion tend to recede rather than proliferate. Such a goal is not likely to be achieved, though, if either sex recoils from the other.

To say this, though, is not the same as saying that there is no room for the comfort and pleasure that each of the two great collectivities derives from the companionship of its fellow members. The woman who never enjoys participation in a woman's group or who brags of her lack of women friends may be having as much difficulty with her sex identity as the woman who is never at home in a mixed group.

❖❖❖❖❖

The hunger for interesting conversation in mixed company, unsatisfied in so much social life as presently organized, is being met in different ways. Adult education, continuing education, the Great Books Program—twentieth-century analogues of the eighteenth-century salon—are among the experiments in process. There will doubtless be more. For good talk, hopefully, is to be one of the most important leisure-time activities of the future, preferably intersex in nature. But good talk or interesting conversation, as we have had occasion to note, does not just happen. In fact, it hardly ever just happens; it has to be cultivated.

Good talk or conversation will probably always be the prerogative of the higher socioeconomic classes. They are more interested in the things that make for good talk and conversation and they tend to be more articulate. The one study that has evaluated those who participate in at least one of these modern counterparts to the eighteenth-century salons—the Great Books Program—corroborates this expectation. They are well-educated, high-status, socially active young adults. "They are not 'ivory-tower' intellectuals, but rather . . . 'middle-brow.' "[37] They are not at all alienated; they share middle-class values and norms of community participation. The Great Books Program is only one of many social groups, formal and informal, they belong to.

The researchers show their own biases when they report that these men and women are not " 'social misfits,' for the old and the unmarried . . . are underrepresented."[38] Still, the women were more likely to be "misfits," as the researchers conceived the term, than were the men. Twice as likely, in fact. About 13 percent of them were not married (either never-married or ex-married) compared to only 7 percent of the men.[39] The fact that there were about twice as many unattached women as unattached men suggests that these "salons" were not primarily mating institutions.

The sex ratio, expectedly, favors women. Almost two-thirds of the participants were women. If all the women's husbands had participated and all of the men's wives, the sex ratio would have been more nearly equal; then there would have been only 54 percent who were women.

The sex composition of these "salons" made a difference in the way they operated and in their viability. Men tended to be more active participants, and groups in which activity was high tended to hold their members better. Some of these "salons" were led by women; in one study, about two-fifths of the leaders were women,[40] but these tended to be less successful than those led by men. The groups in which women predominated, even though led by men, were less successful than those in which men predominated. The women tended to prefer the lecture method more than the men did; the men tended to prefer the discussion method more than the women did.[41]

Both men and women participated for a variety of reasons. They came because they were hungry for intellectual contacts which were not being supplied by their social life. "They were concerned about the intellectual narrowness of their lives and wanted not just knowledge of great authors but also contact with other group members who shared their intellectual orientation."[42]

It is an interesting commentary on the values of our society, still tinged as it is with the Protestant ethic, that the sponsors of the program did not seem to think that the fun, pleasure, excitement, and self-enlargement supplied by their "salons" were sufficient justification for them. The participants did, though. "We noted," says the program's report, "that those things which 'pay off' right away in the discussion group (e.g., 'getting a chance to express ideas I had been thinking and reading about') seemed much more effective than those things which required applications to the resistant world outside the immediate program (e.g., 'finding solutions to contemporary social problems')."[43] One is reminded of Mrs. Chapone's salon. "Her coteries, which though not sought by the young and perhaps fled from by the gay, were rational, instructive and social; and it was not with self-approbation that they could ever be deserted."[44] As one author comments, "the appeal to the conscience . . . would perhaps suggest itself to no hostess in the world outside of England and New England."[45] Or the sponsors of the Great Books Program.

It was important that these discussion groups were held in private homes, for "people who previously had not tended to do so got accustomed to having serious discussions in living rooms. Several reported that this carried over into their normal social relationships, and where previously they did not think it courteous to get into arguments about serious matters with friends, they now realized that it was perfectly possible to have friendly discussions on serious matters and that it was possible to disagree with friends in an amiable way."[46] In addition it was found also that "the discussion group experience stimulates discussion of serious problems between husbands and wives at home and carries over into their social relationships."[47] If these "salons" improved conversation between spouses and gave the women more interesting things to talk about at social gatherings, why should they also be expected to find solutions to contemporary social problems?

Maybe they did help find solutions to one kind of social problem after all. The problem, that is, of implementing the change from the parallelist, or institutional, conception of marriage to that of the interactional, or companionship, conception.

EPILOGUE

✧✧✧

What does it all add up to? What direction does it all point to for the future?

No one who has lived through the many social revolutions and reactions of the twentieth century is going to predict with assurance about the future. Like the chastened weatherman, chagrined by many misses, all he will be willing to do is speak in probabilities. Sudden meteorological changes can invalidate all predictions. No one wants to be caught in the position of the newscaster reading blithely from his script that today will be clear and fair, while outside a blizzard rages.

Between the collectivities there appear to be no signs of blizzards. We are not heading pell-mell into a great apocalyptic Götterdämmerung. Continuing change, of course, but not catastrophic change. Sociologists never weary of reminding us of the interconnectedness of things. Change one and everything else changes too. In any direction. It does not take sophisticated sociological theory to observe that when any one set of institutions changes, ʳeverberations are set in motion which produce changes in all related sets of institutions. Like sleepers in a bed or puppies in a litter, if one changes his position, so must all the others. Change the nature of work and a dozen other things have to change, including the relations between the sexes. Learn how to control conception and a vastly complex structure controlling the relations of the sexes begins to crumble.

✧✧✧✧✧

Among the many new circumstances that have to be accommodated to today is the homogenizing effect of modern life, especially of modern work. Modern technology vastly proliferates the kinds of work that have to be done. But they are mainly the kinds of work that sex makes little difference in. The kinds of work at which men have had an advantage—work requiring heavy muscles—are going out; men's bodies have no particular advantage in the new kinds of work like, for example, the care and feeding of computers or the professional stroking of human beings. They can be done by either men or women and the endless amount of talking and reporting that modern productive systems require can also be done by both collectivities. Entrepreneurial work is still largely men's; but bureaucratic work is more voluminous and engages far more people. More and more of the work of a modern society is done in a one-world setting, men and women together, even when they are doing different kinds of work. The mystique of the great, powerful, fighting male is one of the casualties of modern technology.

So, too, is the mystique of the great earth mother, the "nestling" subsex who found fulfillment only in motherhood. This subsex was an anachronism even in its artificially cultivated form of the 1940's, documented so savagely by Betty Friedan. Not only was it not a suitable sex for modern times; it was a positive menace. Thinking about the unthinkable is not limited to thinking about nuclear war. There was a time, for example, when it was unthinkable to be—or, at least, to admit being—against motherhood. Understandably, for motherhood was once so important to species survival that it had to be accorded almost a sacred status. A woman could expect homage for motherhood alone. For many millennia women could always count on motherhood as an honored vocation. Not much more was demanded of her. And many men were satisfied to be freed from psychological demands on them by women completely occupied with their segregated maternal life.

But the unthinkable has become thinkable. There has been a change from near-worship of motherhood to near-denigration. It began with disapproval of uncontrolled maternity among the poor—especially in recent years, the Negro poor. But it is not unknown in recent years that even people in new middle-class communities, struggling to provide facilities for children, look with consternation on the family that contributes yet another child to the overflowing school population. The family that, in Reuben Hill's words, chooses children rather than other consumer goods will not be admired for its choice. And now with feasible contraception, it has a choice. Just as the nature of work tended to separate the collectivities in the past, so did concentration on motherhood. "The earth goddess communing only with her foetus excludes the male rather than complementing him."[1]

✧✧✧✧✧

Every generation has to work out its own sexual destiny, its own accommodation to the circumstances it must live in. Like all those who have preceded us, we have to learn how to live in a world we never made. Old myths which served well in the past get in the way rather than facilitate what needs to be done. New ones have to be evolved. Different conditions create different kinds of people, for people, too, change to suit the times. Relationships which suited the past do not fit today. We are in the throes of working out relationships which fit the kinds of people today's living conditions create. All kinds of collectivities are in process of revamping their relations with one another: old and young, rich and poor, white and colored. And men and women.

As long as the work of the world was organized in a way that fostered a parallel kind of relationship between the sexes and as long as motherhood absorbed most of a woman's attention, a minimum amount of communication between the collectivities was called for. Each did what was assigned to it and depended on custom to coordinate their efforts. Even sexual interaction, as John Gagnon has noted, could be managed without too much communication. With notable but minor exceptions the parallel pattern has characterized the relationships between the two collectivities for millennia. Until now. They have lived their more or less segregated lives together. Despite the remnants of this pattern—in marriage, at work, at play, and in social life—illustrated almost *ad nauseam* in the preceding chapters, it appears to be on its way out. The conditions of modern life do not support it and the kind of women our times create do not like it.

Women welcome the new companionate model of relations between the sexes; men tend to resist it. In marriage, at work, at play, in social life, it is the women who long for it and the men who tend to hold back. A companionate, social relationship is psychologically more difficult than an institutionalized one. It makes for more interaction and hence for greater psychological interdependence. We speak of the independence of modern women because they can earn money and support themselves, but in a psychological, if not an economic, sense, women in the traditional relationship to men were more independent of them. They did not need men in the same way as do women in companionate relationships.

Because there is more interaction in the new model of relationships there are more opportunities for differences to become abrasive. There is a never-ending need to reconcile and accommodate differences in suitable and, hopefully, satisfying ways. What we can legitimately look forward to is not the elimination of differences, or even of conflict, but a better appreciation of the nature of the game—in the technical rather than in the psychiatric sense—the sexes are engaged in. It is not a "zero-sum" game they are destined to go on endlessly and mechanically playing, in which one must lose what the other gains, but rather a "cooperative" game in which both may win, if properly played, or, unfortunately, both may lose. This kind of game involves communication if each player—individual or team—is to optimize the payoffs for both, or at least to avoid pitfalls which result in defeat for both. Since the conditions of modern life move in the direction of homogenizing the experiences of the two collectivities, it may become increasingly possible for them to communicate not only by way of the "Wowser-Holmes" model but also by way of the shared-experience models.

❖❖❖❖❖

There is no one all-purpose model for the relations between the two collectivities which is equally satisfactory at all times and at all places. A way that suits one age will not suit another; the fifteenth-century model did not suit the nineteenth century, nor the nineteenth, the twentieth. Or, even, the twentieth, the twenty-first. A way that suits one sex may not suit the other.[2] There does *not* exist somewhere, if we could only find it, a

Platonic ideal of sex relations, a correct, suitable, problemless way of solving the difficulties that their differences inevitably create.

It is never easy to move from one cultural style to another. It is not easy to give up myths and old securities. It is not easy to work out new ways of relating to one another. There are many casualties in the process of working out the relationships suitable for this day and age, many experiments that prove lethal. Coping with challenges new to the human species is, we repeat, not easy. But who ever said that the human condition was painless? Who ever said it was easy to be a human being? Of either sex?

NOTES

◇◇◇

Prologue

1. Sally Carrighar, *Wild Heritage* (Houghton Mifflin Company, 1965), p. 111.

2. *Ibid.*, p. 111.

3. Konrad Lorenz, *On Aggression* (Harcourt, Brace & World, Inc., 1966), p. 194.

4. *Ibid.*, pp.192–95.

5. Carrighar, *Wild Heritage*, p. 95.

6. *Ibid.*, p. 95.

7. *Ibid.*, p. 95.

8. *Ibid.*, pp. 102–4.

9. *Ibid.*, p. 105.

10. *Ibid.*, p. 112.

11. The loss of sexual seasonality based on female estrus came rather late in evolution; it may not yet have come to all the primates. There is, therefore, considerable controversy in the scientific literature on the subject. A recent survey of all field studies of primates reports equivocal results. Using the seasonal pattern of births as an index, the authors concluded that "seasonal differences in births are characteristic of most and possibly of all the monkey populations in the present sample. . . . [But] birth periodicity among the African apes remains an open question." A second index of seasonality, observed copulation, showed a close but not exact correspondence with birth data. Among some macaques, female estrus and coitus stop at the birth season and resume five months later. But "in the Indian macaques, rhesus and bonnet, there are some copulations during most of the year, even in some months of the birth season. Southwick *et al.* observed mountings in all months . . . except March, with a marked peak . . . from October through January, which corresponds to the season during which conceptions occur." In two baboon populations, seasonal differences in copulation were reported, but in all other studies, "copulations were observed in all the months of the study periods, including the months of the birth peaks." (Jane B. Lancaster and Richard B. Lee, "The Annual Reproductive Cycle in Monkeys and Apes," in Irven DeVore, ed., *Primate Behavior:*

Field Studies of Monkeys and Apes (Holt, Rinehart and Winston, Inc., 1965), pp. 511–12.

12. Carrighar, *Wild Heritage*, p. 110.

13. *Ibid.*, p. 122.

14. *Ibid.*, pp. 115, 116.

15. A. C. Kinsey and Associates, *Sexual Behavior in the Human Male* (W. B. Saunders Company, 1948), p. 234.

16. Carrighar, *Wild Heritage*, pp. 117, 118.

17. *Ibid.*, pp. 116, 118, 119, 121, 122.

18. *Ibid.*, p. 132.

19. *Ibid.*, p. 122.

20. *Ibid.*, p. 114.

21. *Ibid.*, pp. 132–33.

22. *Ibid.*, p. 133.

23. Konrad Lorenz speaks of rituals, of ceremonies, and of norms among animals, especially his Greylag Goose, and these are basic components in human culture. But he does not report other characteristics of culture, such as attempts by outsiders at enforcement of norms, of punishment by the group for nonconformity, and the like. The animal model may be a prototype of human culture but it is too rudimentary to be comparable in more than an analogical sense.

✦✦✦✦✦

Chapter One

1. Clifford Kirkpatrick, *The Family as Process and Institution* (The Ronald Press Company, 1955), pp. 162ff.

2. Leslie A. Fiedler, *Love and Death in the American Novel* (Meridian, 1962), pp. 274, 275.

3. *Ibid.*, pp. 275, 285.

4. *Ibid.*, pp. 275–76.

5. *Ibid.*, pp. 286–87, 300, 302.

6. M. R. Sapirstein, *Emotional Security* (Crown Press, 1948), Chap. 13.

7. A. C. Kinsey and Associates, *Sexual Behavior in the Human Female* (W. B. Saunders Company, 1953).

8. Fiedler, *Love and Death*, p. 322.

9. Mario Praz, *The Romantic Agony* (Meridian Books, 1963), p. 206.

10. Fiedler, *Love and Death*, p. xx.

11. Kinsey and Associates, *Sexual Behavior in the Human Female*, pp. 526–27.

12. Robert Blood, Jr., and Donald M. Wolfe, *Husbands and Wives, The Dynamics of Married Living* (Free Press, 1960), pp. 11–46.

13. Lee Rainwater and Karol Kane Weinstein, *And the Poor Get Children* (Quadrangle Books, 1960), pp. 98–121.

14. *Ibid.*, p. 121.

15. Henry Seidel Canby, *The Age of Confidence* (Farrar and Rinehart, 1934), p. 173.

16. *Ibid.*, p. 117.

17. George Farquhar, *The Beaux' Strategem*, Act IV, Sc. 1.

18. Jessie Bernard, *Remarriage, A Study of Marriage* (Dryden Press, 1956), p. 184.

19. Kinsey and Associates, *Sexual Behavior in the Human Female*, p. 549, and *Sexual Behavior in the Human Male*, p. 226.

20. Madeline Macdonald in the *London Observer*, reproduced in the *Washington Post*, September 21, 1966.

21. Eli Ginzberg and Associates, *Life Styles of Educated Women* (Columbia University Press, 1966), Chap. 10.

22. Praz, *The Romantic Agony*, p. 206.

23. Steven Marcus, *The Other Victorians* (Basic Books, 1966), p. 180.

24. R. E. L. Masters, Introduction to John Philip Lundin, *Women* (Lancer, 1965), p. xvi.

25. Erving Goffman, *The Presentation of the Self in Everyday Life* (Anchor Books, 1959), pp. 128, 130.

26. David Riesman has reminded us of our dependence on a well-functioning infrastructure of services which we take for granted but without which the superstructure would be impossible. "Thus, 'free enterprise' depends on a host of services which the community provides and which businessmen are often ignorant of, or antagonistic toward,

until they have to manage without them." ("Sociability, Permissiveness, and Equality," *Psychiatry*, 23 (Nov., 1960), 333.) Again, more specifically with respect to women: "There is among . . . men . . . a kind of rosy individualism which consciously asserts one's self-made status, neglectful of the infrastructure—governmental, societal, and often female—which makes the visible show possible." (Jessie Bernard, *Academic Women* (Pennsylvania State University Press, 1964), p. xxiv.)

27. Sapirstein, *Emotional Security*, p. 187.

28. Crane Brinton, *Nietzsche* (Harvard University Press, 1941), p. 134. See also Chapter Twelve below for further characterization of the Dionysian male.

29. Shakespeare, *Love's Labour's Lost*, Act I, Sc. 2.

30. Coventry Kersey Dighton Patmore, *Olympus*, l. 15.

31. Fiedler, *Love and Death*, p. xx.

32. *Ibid.*, p. 365.

33. Frederick Feied, *No Pie in the Sky* (Citadel Press, 1964), quoting Dan O'Brien, pp. 17–18.

34. Jack Kerouac, *Big Sur* (Farrar, Straus and Giroux, Inc., 1962), p. 189.

35. *Ibid.*, p. 191.

36. Hunter S. Thompson, "Life Styles: The Cyclist," *Esquire*, 67 (Jan., 1967), 135.

37. David P. Campbell, "The Vocational Interests of Beautiful Women," paper given at the Midwestern Psychological Association, May, 1966. This reports a study of one hundred models among whom the author distinguished a James Bond type, who expressed a strong preference for "exciting, adventuresome activities, including those with the abstract feel of danger" (mimeographed copy, p. 3).

38. James David Horan, *Desperate Women* (Putnam & Company, Ltd., 1952), p. vii.

39. *Ibid.*, p. vii.

40. Robert Lynd and Helen Merrill Lynd, *Middletown* (Harcourt, Brace, 1929), p. 117.

41. Vincent Nowlis, "Critique and Discussion," in John Money, ed., *Sex Research, New Developments* (Holt, Rinehart and Winston, 1965), pp. 151–52.

42. David A. Hamburg and Donald T. Lunde, "Sex Hormones in the Development of Sex Differences in Human Behavior," in Eleanor

Maccoby, ed., *The Development of Sex Differences* (Stanford University Press, 1966), pp. 1–24.

43. Donald K. Pumroy, "Advances in Research on Sex Differences in Childhood," review of Martin L. and Lois W. Hoffman's Child Development Research, in *Women's Education*, Dec., 1964, p. 8. See also Eleanor Maccoby, *The Development of Sex Differences*.

44. James H. S. Bossard, *The Sociology of Child Development* (Harper and Brothers, 1954), p. 187.

45. Donald K. Pumroy, *loc. cit.*, p. 8.

46. Edward T. Hall, *The Silent Language* (Premier Books, 1963), p. 10.

47. Clifford Kirkpatrick, *The Family as Process*, pp. 161–62.

48. Margaret Mead, *Sex and Temperament in Three Primitive Societies* (William Morrow and Company, 1935).

49. L. M. Terman and others, *Sex and Personality* (McGraw-Hill, 1936), pp. 209–10.

50. Clark E. Vincent, "Implications of Change in Male-Female Role Expectations for Interpreting M-F Scores," *Jour. Marriage and Family*, 28 (May, 1966), 199.

✦✦✦✦✦

Chapter Two

1. See Eleanor E. Maccoby, ed., *The Development of Sex Differences* (Stanford University Press, 1966), for a survey of the research in the area of sex differences.

2. Larry T. Reynolds, "A Note on the Perpetuation of a 'Scientific' Fiction," *Sociometry*, 29 (March, 1966), 85–88. The fiction was that women can make finer color discriminations than men.

3. John Philip Lundin, *Women* (Lancer, 1965), pp. 333–36. This passage is quoted in Chapter Five below.

4. Margaret Mead, *Sex and Temperament;* Jessie Bernard, "Observation and Generalization in Anthropology," *Amer. Jour. Sociol.*, 50 (July, 1945), 284–91.

5. Hall, *The Silent Language*, p. 10.

6. Jon Eisenson, *The Psychology of Communication* (Appleton-Century-Crofts, 1963), p. 220.

7. M. Templin, *Certain Language Skills in Children* (University of Minnesota Press, 1957).

8. Margaret Mead, "Gender in the Honors Program," *Newsletter of the Inter-University Committee on the Superior Student*, May, 1961, pp. 2–5.

9. Otto L. Sonder, "An Experimental Study of the Identification of the Sex of Discussion Group Participants" (Doctoral dissertation, The Pennsylvania State University, 1964).

10. Jessie Bernard, *Academic Women* (The Pennsylvania State University Press, 1964), p. 168.

11. Edward M. Bennet and Larry R. Cohen, "Men and Women: Personality Patterns and Contrasts," *Genetic Psychology Monographs*, 59 (The Journal Press, 1959), pp. 101–155.

12. *Ibid.*, p. 149.

13. Paul H. Gebhard and Associates, *Sex Offenders: An Analysis of Types* (Harper & Row, 1965), pp. 380–81.

14. Group interview.

15. Kinsey and Associates, *Sexual Behavior in the Human Female*, Chap. 16.

16. *Ibid.*, pp. 681, 682.

17. This generalization may seem to contradict the findings of Kinsey and his associates with respect to sex differences in the effect of social factors (education, decade of birth, and religion) on patterns of sexual behavior as reported in *Sexual Behavior in the Human Female*, pp. 685–86. Of 93 items specified, 54 among the women and 58 among the men showed some relationship, however small, to education, decade of birth, and religion. This would seem to suggest no sex differences with respect to sexual behavior and social factors. But these figures refer to *patterns* of sexual behavior (e.g., masturbation, petting, etc.) and not to total outlet. If one restricts the discussion to total outlet, the females show much greater susceptibility than males to outside influences. Of the nine items under total outlet, all showed a relationship between total outlet and social factors in the case of the females, only three in the case of the males. Ovulation, which is the female analogue of ejaculation, on the other hand, has been as resistant to cultural controls as ejaculation. Indeed, since it is so unrelated to orgasm, there have been no norms governing it. Not until the 1960's did ovulation even become subject to control and as yet the norms to govern it have not crystallized if, in fact, they ever can be.

18. "Three Essays on the Theory of Sexuality." Present citation from Marcus, *The Other Victorians*.

19. Marcus, *The Other Victorians*, p. 178.

20. *Ibid.*, p. 177.

21. *Ibid.*, p. 212.

22. Praz, *The Romantic Agony*, p. 206.

23. *Ibid.*, p. 206.

24. *Ibid.*, p. 206.

25. Lorenz, *On Aggression*, p. 103.

26. *Ibid.*, p. 103, 104.

27. Walter Mischel, "A Social-Learning View of Sex Differences in Behavior," in Maccoby, ed., *The Development of Sex Differences*, pp. 73ff.

28. J. I. Case Co. v. National Labor Relations Board, 321 U.S. 332.

29. Sapirstein, *Emotional Security*, p. 188.

30. William H. Masters and Virginia E. Johnson, *Human Sexual Response* (Little, Brown and Company, 1966), p. 133.

31. Sylvia Reice, "The Chase Is Dynamite," syndicated newspaper column, July 24, 1966.

32. Ralph Greenson (clinical professor of psychiatry, the University of California at Los Angeles), quoted in the *Washington Post*, Dec. 1, 1966.

33. Kinsey and Associates, *Sexual Behavior in the Human Female*, pp. 688–89.

❖❖❖❖❖

Chapter Three

1. There is an impressive technical literature on signs, signals, and symbols which need not preoccupy us here. A discussion in depth can become very deep indeed. Nominalism, realism, the meaning of meaning, operationalism, the *Ding-an-Sich* concept, semantics, and reductionism are only a few of the many abstruse topics that soon become involved. They are far beyond our depth and distracting from our major interest.

2. Sir Arthur Conan Doyle, "A Study in Scarlet," in *The Complete Sherlock Holmes* (Doubleday and Company, n.d.), p. 13.

3. Georg Simmel, "Aesthetic Significance of the Face," in Kurt H. Wolff, ed., *Georg Simmel, 1858–1918* (Ohio State University Press, 1959), p. 279.

4. F. Feldenkreis, *Body and Mature Behavior* (International Universities Press, 1949), p. 35. The subtitle of this volume is also relevant: "An examination of the influence of the carriage, posture and movement of the body and of muscular perception on certain patterns of behavior; e.g., facility in learning and doing, anxiety and worry, and mental-physical co-ordination."

5. See Chapter Nine.

6. All sensory modes may be used; taste and touch require physical contact. Audition and olfaction are alternatives, the first useful for distant communication, the second, for short-range (Peter Marler, "Communication in Monkeys and Apes," in DeVore, ed., *Primate Behavior*, p. 350). Among insects, either sex may exude a chemical attractant. One virgin female pine saw-fly is reported to have lured 7,000 males within five hours and thereafter, 1,000 per day from distances of 200 feet. In 1960 species, the female is known to exude such attractants, sometimes as far as two miles downward; in 55 species, the males attract females by such excitants. The researchers hope in time to substitute these attractants for chemical pesticides to control insect populations (Nate Haseltine, "Virgin Pine Saw-Fly is Cleopatra of Insects," *Washington Post*, September 14, 1965). Social organization among rats seems to depend on a clan smell, as it does also among bees (Lorenz, *On Aggression*, p. 62).

7. "Avoid Being a Flop," *Potomac Magazine*, April 25, 1965.

8. Philippe Halsman, "Reflections in a Woman's Mirror, Her Face," *Cosmopolitan*, June, 1963, p. 48.

9. Editors of *Esquire, Esquire Book of Etiquette* (J. B. Lippincott Company, 1953), pp. 265–67, 268–69.

10. *Washington Post*, Jan. 14, 1967.

11. St. John Chrysostom, *Baptismal Instructions*, trans. and annotated by Paul Harkins (Newton Press, 1963), p. 187.

12. Bliss Perry, ed., *The Heart of Emerson's Journal* (Houghton Mifflin, 1926), p. 241.

13. Edmond Rostand, *Cyrano de Bergerac*, Act III.

14. Simone de Beauvoir, "The Question of Fidelity," *Atlantic Monthly*, Nov., 1964, p. 61.

15. Letter to *Playboy*, Sept., 1964, p. 62.

16. Harold Feldman, *Development of the Husband-Wife Relationship* (Cornell University, 1965), p. 28.

17. Marcus, *The Other Victorians*, p. 178.

18. Editors of *Esquire*, *Etiquette*, p. 261.

19. In a study of complaints made in six hundred divorcing couples in Cleveland, George Levinger found physical abuse reported by eleven times more wives than husbands (paper given at meetings of American Orthopsychiatric Association, New York, 1965, Table 1).

20. Kinsey and Associates, *Sexual Behavior in the Human Female*, Chap. 16.

21. *Playboy*, Jan., 1965, pp. 21–22.

22. Frances Angell, *Compete!* (Dorrance, 1935), p. 39.

23. It is curious that many languages—all, some say—have two sets of words referring to sexuality, one respectable and decent and one indecent. The very sound of the indecent words may be sexually exciting to men. Saying them or hearing them is an act itself; the communication is immediate, not symbolic. This is a special case and not relevant for our discussion of the use of words. See Duncan Macdougald, Jr., "Language and Sex," *Encyclopedia of Sexual Behavior* (Hawthorn Books, 1961), II, 599.

24. J. Christopher Herold, *Mistress to an Age, A Life of Madame de Staël* (Bobbs-Merrill Company, Inc., 1958), pp. 72–73. See Chapter Thirteen below for a description of Madame de Staël's talking style.

25. Eric Berne, *Games People Play, The Psychology of Human Relationships* (Grove Press, 1964), pp. 13–15.

26. A male student at Berkeley, quoted by Betty Hannah Hoffman, in "How America Lives," *Ladies' Home Journal*, Oct., 1965, p. 167.

27. A correspondent in Mary Haworth's syndicated column, Aug. 12, 1965.

28. *Washington Post*, a correspondent in above column, Sept. 14, 1965.

29. Irving E. Alexander, "Family Therapy," *Marriage and Family Living*, 25 (May, 1963), 148.

❖❖❖❖❖

Chapter Four

1. The two kinds of communication here discussed—one based on similarities, one not—correspond to those discussed by Colin Cherry in *On Human Communication* (Wiley Science Editions, 1961), p. 89, one mediated by object-language, the other by meta-language.

2. Human beings are handicapped by their low olfactory sensitivity, according to Peter Marler. See "Communication in Monkeys and Apes," in DeVore, ed., *Primate Behavior*, p. 350.

3. Rainwater and Weinstein, *And the Poor Get Children*, pp. 16, 102, 104, 105, 113, 114, 116, 134, 137.

4. Mervin B. Freedman, *The College Experience* (Jossey-Bass, 1967), pp. 98ff.

5. Bernard, *Academic Women*, pp. 168–69.

6. Goffman, *The Presentation of the Self*, p. 251.

7. Juergen Ruesch, "The Tangential Reply," in Paul H. Hoch and Joseph Zubin, eds., *Psychopathology of Communication* (Grune and Stratton, 1958), p. 39.

8. James Lloyd Bowman and Margery Bianco, *Tales from a Finnish Tupa* (Albert Whitman, 1936).

Chapter Five

1. John Wilson, *Logic and Sexual Morality* (Pelican Books, 1965), p. 217.

2. *Ibid.*, p. 219.

3. Edwin C. Hall, *The Silent Language* (Premier Books, 1963), p. 10.

4. Susan Filson, "Sex Education's Game Far from Birds and Bees," *Washington Post*, Dec. 26, 1965. Even serious students find themselves as puzzled as the schoolboys. "I have been impressed in the course of my research," says the author of one of the most exhaustive studies of college women, "by the capacity of young women to carry on very well without any physical sexual activity whatsoever—including masturbation" (Freedam, *The College Experience*, p. 98).

5. Lundin, *Women*, pp. 333–34.

6. Marcus, *The Other Victorians*, p. 194.

7. Herodotus, *The Histories,* trans. Aubrey de Selincourt (Penguin Books, 1954), p. 34.

8. Kinsey and Associates, *Sexual Behavior in the Human Male,* p. 199.

9. Kinsey and Associates, *Sexual Behavior in the Human Female,* p. 539.

10. *Ibid.,* p. 538.

11. *Ibid.,* p. 687.

12. *Ibid.,* p. 657.

13. *Ibid.,* pp. 657–58.

14. *Ibid.,* pp. 526–27.

15. *Ibid.,* p. 527.

16. Hall, *The Silent Language,* Chap. 1.

17. Nathaniel Hawthorne, *The Blithedale Romance* (Donahue, 1852), p. 113.

18. *Appian,* trans. Horace White. Present citation from Emily James Putnam, *The Lady, Studies of Certain Significant Phases of Her History* (Sturgis and Walton, 1910), pp. 61–62.

19. Livy, *Cato on Extravagance,* trans. Cyrus Edwards, in Basil Davenport, ed., *The Portable Roman Reader* (Viking Press, 1951), p. 440.

20. *Ibid.,* p. 443.

21. Gershon Scholem, "Jews and Germans," *Commentary,* Nov., 1966, pp. 31–38.

Chapter Six

1. *Oxford Universal Dictionary* (Oxford University Press, 1955), p. 2126.

2. *Ibid.,* p. 2126.

3. Walter Bagehot, *Physics and Politics* (Appleton, 1873), pp. 165–204.

4. Robert F. Bales, *Interaction Process Analysis: A Method for the Study of Small Groups* (Addison-Wesley Publishing Company, Inc., 1950). Robert F. Bales, who pioneered this kind of laboratory research, found six common problems in all task-oriented small groups: problems of communication, of evaluation, of control, of decision, of tension-

management, and of group integration. Since there were two dimensions to each of the six problems, the Bales behavior schema had twelve categories, as follows: (1) shows solidarity, that is, raises the status of the other, gives help, rewards; (2) shows tension-release by joking, laughing, showing satisfaction; (3) agrees, concurs, complies, understands, passively accepts; (4) gives suggestions or directions, implies autonomy of others; (5) gives opinion, evaluation, analysis, expressing feelings or wishes; (6) gives orientation or information or clarifications. Then, reversing, (7) asks for orientation, information, or clarification; (8) asks for opinion, evaluation, analysis, expression of feelings or wishes; (9) asks for suggestions or directions; (10) disagrees, shows passive rejection, withholds help; (11) shows tension, asks for help, withdraws from field; and (12) shows antagonism, deflates other's status, is defensive or assertive. On the basis of Bales's pioneer work a number of other schemas have been developed for the study of therapeutic interaction, mother-child interaction, teacher-pupil interaction, etc. See Edgar F. Borgatta and Betty Crowther, *A Workbook for the Study of Social Interaction Processes* (Rand McNally & Company, 1965).

5. Morris Zelditch, "Role Differentiation in the Nuclear Family: A Comparative Study," in Talcott Parsons and Robert F. Bales, eds., *Family, Socialization and Interaction Process* (Free Press, 1955), pp. 307–52.

6. Fred L. Strodtbeck and Richard D. Marm, "Sex Role Differentiation in Jury Deliberations," *Sociometry*, 19 (March, 1956), 9–10.

7. Herold, *Madame de Staël*, p. 71.

8. E. F. Borgatta and J. Stimson, "Sex Differences in Interaction Characteristics," *Jour. Social Psychology*, 60 (1963), 89–100.

9. Anatol Rapoport and Albert M. Chammah, *Prisoner's Dilemma, A Study in Conflict and Cooperation* (University of Michigan Press, 1965), pp. 191, 192.

10. Edward E. Sampson and Marcelle Kardush, "Age, Sex, Class, and Race Differences in Response to a Two-Person Non-Zero Sum Game," *Jour. Conflict Resolution*, 9 (June 1965), pp. 212–20.

11. Anon., *Handbook of Good Society: The Art of Conversation* (Carleton, 1883), p. 119.

12. James Bryce, *Reflections on American Institutions.* (Fawcett, 1961), p. 155.

13. Jurgen Ruesch, "The Tangential Response," in Hoch and Zubin, eds., *Psychopathology of Communication*, p. 40.

14. *Ibid*, pp. 47–48.

15. *Ibid.*, p. 44. Unpublished studies at Cornell report that women tend to complete other people's sentences more than men do.

16. Sir William Cowper, *Conversation*, ll. 235ff.

17. P. 93.

18. *Ibid.*, p. 90.

19. Cowper, *Conversation*, ll. 93ff.

20. Oliver Wendell Holmes, *The Autocrat at the Breakfast Table* (Houghton Mifflin Company, 1882), p. 52.

21. W. Edgar Vinacke, "Sex Roles in a Three-Person Game," *Sociometry*, 22 (Dec., 1959), 359. See also: John R. Bond and W. E. Vinacke, "Coalitions in Mixed Set Trends," *Sociometry*, 24 (March, 1961), 61–75, and Thomas C. Uesugi and W. Edgar Vinacke, "Strategy in a Feminine Game," *Sociometry*, 26 (March, 1963), 75–88.

22. Aileen D. Ross, "Control and Leadership in Women's Groups: An Analysis of Philanthropic Money-Raising Activity," *Social Forces*, 26 (Dec., 1958), 130.

23. Fred L. Strodtbeck, "Husband-Wife Interaction over Revealed Differences," *Amer. Sociol. Review*, 16 (1951), 472.

24. Bernard, *Academic Women*, pp. 255–57.

25. Kurt H. Wolff, *The Sociology of Georg Simmel* (Free Press, 1950), p. 52.

26. Berne, *Games People Play*, p. 30.

27. James Bryce, *Reflections*, p. 155.

28. Jurgen Ruesch and Weldon Kees, *Nonverbal Communication. Notes on the Visual Perception of Human Relations* (University of California Press, 1956), p. 21. This is a picture book of exceptional charm as well as of illumination.

29. Wolff, *The Sociology of Georg Simmel*, p. 328.

30. *Ibid.*, p. 53.

31. Editors of *Esquire*, *Etiquette*, p. 302.

32. John H. Gagnon, "Sexuality and Sexual Learning in the Child," *Psychiatry*, 28 (Aug., 1965), 214.

33. Editors of *Esquire*, *Etiquette*, p. 295.

34. Murrey Marder, "U.S. Foreign Policy Fares Poorly on TV Panel," *Washington Post*, Oct. 28, 1965.

35. Holmes, *The Autocrat*, p. 52.

36. Lindsey Churchill, "On Everyday Quantitative Practices" (mimeographed paper), p. 19.

37. *Ibid.*, p. 7.

38. *Ibid.*, p. 20.

39. Holmes, *The Autocrat*, p. 52.

40. Emily James Putnam, *The Lady, Studies of Certain Significant Phases of Her History* (Sturgis and Walton, 1910), pp. 183–85.

41. *Ibid.*, p. 185.

42. Willard Waller and Reuben Hill, *The Family, A Dynamic Interpretation* (Dryden Press, 1951), p. 177.

43. Editors of *Esquire, Etiquette*, p. 301.

44. Geoffrey Gorer, *The American People* (W. W. Norton & Company, Inc., 1948), pp. 116–17.

45. Mirra Komarovsky, "Cultural Contradictions and Sex Roles," *Amer. Jour. Sociol.*, 52 (July, 1946), 186–88. But note also that the *Esquire Book of Etiquette* instructs tennis-playing men to play down to women also (p. 179).

46. Komarovsky, *loc. cit.*, pp. 186–88.

47. Berne, *Games People Play*, p. 15.

48. Christopher Isherwood, *The Observer*, May 13, 1951.

49. Hawthorne, *The Blithedale Romance*, p. 115.

50. Reuben Hill and others, *The Family and Population Control* (University of North Carolina Press, 1959), p. 59.

51. Waller and Hill, *The Family*, p. 182–83.

❖❖❖❖❖

Chapter Seven

1. Thomas C. Schelling, *The Strategy of Conflict* (Harvard University Press, 1960), pp. 139ff., 145.

2. Harry Nelson, " 'New Morality' at Issue, Birth Pills for Unwed [Co-eds] Perplex Colleges," *Washington Post*, Nov. 27, 1966.

3. "Stockholm Creates All Women Equal," *Ibid.*, September 11, 1965.

4. David Riesman, Robert J. Potter, and Jeanne Watson, "Sociability, Permissiveness, and Equality," *Psychiatry*, 23 (Nov., 1960), 327.

5. See Gen. 4:1; Gen. 4:17; Gen. 4:25; Judg. 19:25; I Sam. 1:19; Matt. 1:25.

6. Editors of *Esquire, Etiquette*, pp. 298–99.

7. Rebecca Birth Stirling, "Some Psychological Mechanisms Operative in Gossip," *Social Forces*, 34 (March, 1965), 262.

8. Sidney M. Jourard, *The Transparent Self* (D. Van Nostrand Company, Inc., 1964), p. 15.

9. Rostand, *Cyrano de Bergerac*, Act II.

10. Goffman, *Presentation of the Self*, Chap. 4.

11. Kinsey and Associates, *Sexual Behavior in the Human Female*, pp. 138, 165.

12. John H. Gagnon, "Sexuality and Sexual Learning in the Child," *Psychiatry*, 28 (Aug., 1965), 214.

13. Waller and Hill, *The Family*, p. 178.

14. *Ibid.*, p. 180.

15. C. V. Wedgwood, "The Cause of the Empress," review of *Empress Maria Theresa*, in *Book Week*, July 31, 1966, p. 10.

16. Waller and Hill, *The Family*, pp. 188–89.

17. *Ibid.*, p. 188.

18. Lynd and Lynd, *Middletown*, p. 120. The statement is quoted from a minister.

19. *Ibid.*, p. 120. This statement is quoted from Dorothy Dix.

20. William Schofield, *Psychotherapy, The Purchase of Friendship* (Spectrum Books, 1964), p. 161.

21. Jourard, *The Transparent Self*, p. 13.

22. *Ibid.*, p. 14.

23. *Ibid.*, pp. iii, 15–16.

24. George Levinger, "Task and Social Behavior in Marriage," *Sociometry*, 27 (Dec., 1964), p. 447.

25. Sheldon Stryker, "Conditions of Accurate Role-Taking: A Test of Mead's Theory," in Arnold Rose, ed., *Human Behavior and Social Processes* (Houghton Mifflin Company, 1962), p. 60.

26. Jourard, *The Transparent Self*, pp. 15–16.

27. Schelling, *The Strategy of Conflict*, p. 17.

28. Mirra Komarovsky, "Sex Differences in Dissatisfaction with Marriage Communication: A Study of 58 Working-Class Marriages" (paper read at National Council of Family Relations, April, 1962). See also *Blue-Collar Marriage* (Random House, Inc., 1964), Chaps. 6 and 7.

29. Jessie Bernard, *American Community Behavior* (Holt, Rinehart and Winston, Inc., 1962), pp. 407–8.

❖❖❖❖❖

Chapter Eight

1. Joseph Fletcher, *Situation Ethics: The New Morality* (Westminister Press, 1966), pp. 11, 64–65.

2. Waller and Hill, *The Family*, p. 171.

3. Berne, *Games People Play*, pp. 126–29.

4. Robert G. Ryder and D. Wells Goodrich, "Married Couples' Responses to Disagreement," *Family Process*, 5 (March, 1966), 41.

5. For the relation between marital satisfaction and perceived consensus, see George Levinger and James Breedlove, "Interpersonal Attraction and Agreement: A Study of Marriage Partners," *Jour. of Personality and Social Psychology*, 3 (1966), 367–72. For the greater importance of perceived over actual consensus, see Boyd C. Rollins, "Consensus of Husband and Wife on Companionship Values and Marital Satisfaction: Some Theoretical Implications" (paper given at meeting of National Council on Family Relations, Oct. 29, 1966).

6. A. George Gitter, "Studies on Hypocrisy" (paper given at District of Columbia Sociological Society, April, 1966).

7. Shakespeare, *Much Ado About Nothing*, Act III, Sc. 3.

8. Rainwater and Weinstein, *And the Poor Get Children*, pp. 99, 110.

9. *Universal Oxford Dictionary*, p. 463.

10. Masters and Johnson, *Human Sexual Response*, p. 134.

11. Mary Beard, *Woman as Force in History* (The Macmillan Company, 1946), p. 327.

12. Mirra Komarovsky, "Cultural Contradictions and Sex Roles," *Amer. Jour. Sociol.*, 52 (July, 1946), 188.

13. John Greenleaf Whittier, "In School Days."

14. Quoted by Steven M. Spencer, "The Birth Control Revolution," *Sat. Eve. Post*, Jan. 14, 1966, p. 67.

15. Leo Tolstoy, *War and Peace* (Dell Books, 1955), pp. 146–49.

✦✦✦✦✦✦

Chapter Nine

1. Thomas C. Schelling, *Arms and Influence* (Yale University Press, 1966).

2. Harold V. Routh, "The Progress of Social Literature in Tudor Times," in A. W. Ward and A. R. Waller, *Cambridge History of English Literature* (The Macmillan Company, 1933), III, 98ff.

3. The Second Fable from Night VIII of The Nights of Straparola, a translation by W. G. Waters of *Piacevoli Notti* of Giovanni Francesco Straparola (London, privately printed, 1894); present citation from Milton Rugoff, ed., *A Harvest of World Folk Tales* (Viking Press, 1949), p. 517.

4. Frederick Morgan Padelford, "Transition English Song Collections" in Ward and Waller, *Cambridge History*, II, 437.

5. Harold V. Routh, *loc. cit.*, p. 99.

6. *Playboy*, March, 1966, pp. 135–37.

7. Harold V. Routh, *loc. cit.*, p. 99.

8. George Levinger, "Marital Satisfaction and Complaint" (paper given at meeting of American Orthopsychiatric Association, 1965), Table 1, p. 6. Despite the reputation of women for shrewishness, it is not something they have a monopoly on; men are by no means lacking in it. In a study of the complaints made by six hundred couples seeking divorce in Cleveland, it was found that verbal abuse by spouse was mentioned far more often by women than by men in both the middle and the lower socioeconomic classes. This suggests that though women may nag and scold more, men may engage in vituperative assault more. Or could it mean that the men were more long-suffering?

9. E. S. Stevens, *Folk Tales of Iraq* (Clarendon Press, 1941). Present citation, Rugoff, ed., *Folk Tales*, p. 160.

10. *Ibid.*, p. 164.

11. H. Munro Chadwick, "Early National Poetry," in Ward and Waller, *Cambridge History*, I, 42.

12. Geoffrey Chaucer, *Prologue to the Wife of Bath's Tale*, translated into modern prose by David Wright (London: Barrier and Rockliff, 1964), pp. 159–62.

13. Stith Thompson, *The Folktale* (Dryden, 1946), p. 105.

14. Letter to Mary Haworth, syndicated column, Sept. 27, 1965.

15. Schelling, *Arms and Influence*, p. 2.

16. My discussion of strategy in this chapter is based on Schelling, *The Strategy of Conflict*.

17. *Ibid.*, p. 6.

18. Robert G. Ryder and D. Wells Goodrich, "Married Couples' Responses to Disagreement," *Family Process*, 5 (March, 1966), 41.

19. William J. Goode, "Illegitimacy in the Caribbean," *Amer. Sociol. Rev.*, 25 (Feb., 1960), 28.

20. Samuel T. Coleridge, *Table Talk*, July 23, 1827.

21. Leo Srole and Associates, *Mental Health in the Metropolis: The Midtown Manhattan Study* (McGraw-Hill, Inc., 1962), p. 178.

22. Waller and Hill, *The Family*, pp. 191–92.

23. Berne, *Games People Play*.

❖❖❖❖❖

Chapter Ten

1. Feldman, *Husband-Wife Relationship*, p. 28.

2. E. W. Burgess and Paul Wallin, *Engagement and Marriage* (J. B. Lippincott Company, 1953), p. 504.

3. George Levinger, "A Comparative Study of Marital Communication" (mimeographed paper, 1965), p. 3.

4. Boyd C. Rollins, "Consensus of Husband and Wife on Companionship Values and Marital Satisfaction: Some Theoretical Implications" (paper given at meetings of National Council on Family Relations, Oct. 29, 1966), p. 12.

5. Jourard, *The Transparent Self*, p. 37.

6. E. W. Burgess, H. J. Locke, and Mary Margaret Thomes, *The Family, From Institution to Companionship* (American Book Co., 1963), p. vii. It is technically inaccurate to contrast "institution" and "com-

panionship" since the companionship is really another way to institutionalize the relations between the spouses.

7. George Levinger, "Task and Social Behavior in Marriage," *Sociometry*, 27 (Dec., 1964), 441.

8. Harvey J. Locke and Mary Margaret Thomes, "Communication and Unity of the Husband-Wife Dyad" (mimeographed, no date), p. 3; Harvey J. Locke, *Predicting Adjustment in Marriage: A Comparison of a Divorced and a Happily Married Group* (Holt, 1951), p. 246; Georg Karlsson, *Adaptability and Communication in Marriage: A Swedish Predictive Study of Marital Satisfaction* (Uppsala, Almqvist and Wiksells Boktrycheri Actiebolag, 1951); Harvey J. Locke, George Sabagh, and Mary Margaret Thomes, "Correlates of Primary Communication and Empathy," *Research Studies of the State College of Washington*, 24 (1956), pp. 116–24; C. W. Hobart and W. J. Klausner, "Some Interactional Correlates of Marital Role Disagreement and Marital Adjustment," *Marriage and Family Living*, 21 (1959), pp. 256–63; S. A. Brody, "Husband-Wife Communication Patterns Related to Marital Adjustment" (Doctoral dissertation, University of Southern California, 1963), present citation, Locke and Thomes, "Communication and Unity," pp. 10–11.

9. Burgess and Wallin, *Engagement and Marriage*, p. 504.

10. Levinger, "Marital Communication," p. 2.

11. *Ibid.*, p. 3.

12. Jourard, *The Transparent Self*, p. 177.

13. Feldman, *Husband-Wife Relationship*, p. 43.

14. Jourard, *The Transparent Self*, pp. 36, 177.

15. Levinger, "Marital Communication," p. 2.

16. Roland G. Tharp, "Dimensions of Marriage Role," *Marriage and Family*, 25 (Nov., 1963), 389–404. Among Tharp's male subjects, intimacy was weighted in the direction of sexual pleasure; among the wives, in the direction of understanding.

17. Locke and Thomas, *loc. cit.*, p. 11.

18. Levinger, "Marital Communication," p. 2.

19. Mirra Komarovsky, *Blue-Collar Marriage* (Random House, Inc., 1964), Chap. 9.

20. John E. Meyer, *The Disclosure of Marital Problems, An Exploratory Study of Lower and Middle Class Wives* (Institute of Welfare Research, Community Service Society of New York, 1966), pp. 104–16.

21. Francis Joseph Grund, *Aristocracy in America* (London: Bentley, 1839), pp. 88–89.

22. Lynd and Lynd, *Middletown*, p. 118.

23. *Ibid*, pp. 119–20.

24. David L. Cohn, *Love in America, An Informal Study of Manners and Morals in American Marriage* (Simon and Schuster, Inc., 1943), p. 31.

25. Mortimer Feinberg, "Confidential Memo to Busy Husbands: Ten Ways to Satisfy a Neglected Wife," *Ladies' Home Journal*, Oct., 1965, p. 69.

26. Mary Haworth's syndicated column, Jan. 25, 1966.

27. Lee Rainwater, Richard P. Coleman, and Gerald Handel, *Workingman's Wife, Her Personality, World and Life Style* (Macfadden, 1959), p. 88.

28. Mirra Komarovsky, paper read before National Council Family Relations, 1962. About a fifth of the wives complained to the researcher, if not to their husbands, that their husbands did not talk to them enough to suit them.

29. John F. Cuber and Peggy B. Harroff, "The More Total View: Relationships among Men and Women of the Upper Middle Class," *Marriage and Family Living*, 25 (May, 1963), 140–45.

30. J. Richard Udry, Harold A. Nelson, and Ruth Nelson, "An Empirical Investigation of Some Widely Held Beliefs about Marital Interaction," *Marriage and Family Living*, 23 (Nov., 1961), 388–90. See also Clifford Kirkpatrick and Charles Hobart, "Disagreement, Disagreement Estimate, and Non-Empathic Imputations for Intimacy Groups Varying from Favorite Date to Married," *Amer. Sociol. Rev.*, 19 (Feb., 1954), 10–19.

31. Jourard, *The Transparent Self*, p. 177.

32. Komarovsky, paper, 1962.

33. Lynd and Lynd, *Middletown*, p. 117.

34. Komarovsky, *Blue-Collar Marriage*, pp. 29–30.

35. *Ibid.*, p. 198.

36. *Ibid.*, p. 29.

37. Philip E. Slater, "On Social Regression," *Amer. Sociol. Rev.*, 28 (June, 1963), 339–64. This point is elaborated in Chap. Thirteen.

38. Feldman, *Husband-Wife Relationship*, pp. 19–20.

39. *Ibid.*, pp. 35–36.

40. *Ibid.*, pp. 99, 101.

41. Locke, Sabagh, and Thomes, "Communication and Empathy."

42. Blood and Wolfe, *Husbands and Wives*, p. 158.

43. Feldman, *Husband-Wife Relationship*, p. 119.

44. *Ibid.*, p. 122.

45. James H. S. Bossard, *The Sociology of Child Development* (Harper and Brothers, 1934), pp. 195–96.

46. Lynd and Lynd, *Middletown*, p. 119.

47. Feldman, *Husband-Wife Relationship*, p. 14.

48. John H. Gagnon, "Sexuality and Sexual Learning in the Child," *Psychiatry*, 28 (Aug., 1966), 214.

49. *Ibid.*, p. 214.

50. Feldman, *Husband-Wife Relationship*, p. 16.

51. *Ibid.*, pp. 134–37.

52. Levinger, "Marital Communication," p. 2.

53. Bossard, *Child Development*, p. 196.

54. W. J. Goode, "Family Disorganization," in Merton and Nisbet, *Contemporary Social Problems* (Harcourt, Brace & World, Inc., 1961), p. 392.

55. *Ibid.*, p. 393.

56. Blood and Wolfe, *Husbands and Wives*, Chap. 7.

57. Clark Vincent, "Sex and Marital Communication" (paper read at Groves Conference, 1966), p. 11.

58. W. F. Kenkel and Dean K. Hoffman, "Real and Conceived Roles in Family Decision Making," *Marriage and Family Living*, 18 (Nov., 1956), 314. Unpublished studies at Cornell show that women talk faster than men. This fact may confuse the observer, self or other. Women may, that is, "talk more" than men in the same amount of time. If amount of talking is measured in terms of time, the men may talk more; but if measured in terms of number of words, perhaps, the women talk more.

59. Mary Wilkov, "Experimental Study of Spouses' Ability To Predict One Another's Choices" (Master's thesis, The Pennsylvania State University, 1964).

60. Nicholas Babchuk and Alan P. Bates, "The Primary Relations of Middle-Class Couples: A Study of Male Dominance," *Amer. Sociol. Rev.*, 28 (June, 1963), 378.

61. Locke, Sabagh, and Thomes, "Communication and Empathy," p. 119.

62. Eleanor Braun Luckey, "Marital Satisfaction and Its Association with Congruence of Perception," *Marriage and Family Living*, 22 (Feb., 1960), 49–54. See also her "Marital Satisfaction and Congruent Self-Spouse Concepts," *Social Forces*, 39 (Dec., 1960), 153–57.

63. R. D. Laing, H. Phillipson, and A. R. Lee, *Interpersonal Perception, A Theory and a Method of Research* (Springer Publishing Co., 1966), Chap. 6.

64. Sanford Brown, "May I Ask You a Few Questions About Love?" *Sat. Eve. Post*, Dec. 31, 1966, p. 27,

65. Feldman, *Husband-Wife Relationship*, pp. 116, 117.

66. ABC-TV, Spring, 1966.

67. Thomas Usk, *Wall Street Journal*, Dec. 5, 1965.

68. Hobart and Klausner, "Interactional Correlates," p. 261.

69. Kinsey and Associates, *Sexual Behavior in the Human Male*, p. 199.

70. *Ibid.*, pp. 127, 128.

71. George Levinger, "Systematic Distortion in Spouses' Reports of Preferred and Actual Sexual Behavior," *Sociometry*, 29 (Sept., 1966), 291–99.

72. *Ibid.*

73. *Ibid.*

74. Bernard, *Remarriage*, pp. 186–87.

75. Kinsey and Associates, *Sexual Behavior in the Human Male*, pp. 127–28. Lee Rainwater did not find this spousal disagreement among the middle class, but he did among the lower class. See *Family Design, Marital Sexuality, Family Size, and Contraception* (Aldine Publishing Company, 1965), pp. 71–72.

76. John H. Gagnon, *loc. cit.*, p. 214.

77. Vincent, "Sex and Marital Communication," pp. 8–9.

78. *Ibid.*, pp. 8–9.

79. *Ibid.*, p. 13.

80. Joseph C. Reingold, *The Fear of Being a Woman* (Grune and Stratton, 1964), p. 419.

❖❖❖❖❖

Chapter Eleven

1. George P. Murdock, "Comparative Data on the Division of Labor by Sex," *Social Forces*, 15 (1937), 551–53.

2. Talcott Parsons, "The American Family: Its Relations to Personality and to the Social Structure," in Parsons and Bales, eds., *Family, Socialization and Interaction Process*, p. 15.

3. Theodore Caplow, *The Sociology of Work* (McGraw-Hill, Inc., 1964), p. 237.

4. *Ibid.*, p. 239.

5. *Ibid.*, p. 239.

6. *Ibid.*, p. 239.

7. Elizabeth Faulkner Baker, *Technology and Woman's Work* (Columbia University Press, 1964), p. 158.

8. Robert W. Smuts, *Women and Work in America* (Columbia University Press, 1959), p. 88.

9. *Ibid.*, p. 89.

10. *Ibid.*, p. 89.

11. Gerhard E. Lenski, "Social Participation and Status Crystallization," *Amer. Sociol. Rev.*, 21 (Aug., 1956), 458–64.

12. Bernard, *Academic Women*, pp. 185–88.

13. Editors of *Esquire*, *Etiquette*, p. 4.

14. Helen Gurley Brown, *Sex and the Office* (Pocket Books, 1965), p. 105.

15. Caplow, *The Sociology of Work*, p. 243.

16. Brown, *Sex and the Office*, pp. 65–66.

17. Caplow, *The Sociology of Work*, p. 238.

18. Margaret Cussler, *The Woman Executive* (Harcourt, Brace & World, Inc., 1958), p. 74.

19. *Ibid.*, p. 65.

20. "How Good Are Women Bosses?" in *Changing Times*, April, 1967, p. 16.

21. William Foote Whyte, *Men at Work* (Dorsey Press and Richard D. Irwin, 1961), pp. 128–29.

22. "Women in Business," *Fortune Magazine*, August, 1935, p. 50.

23. Clark Vincent, *Unmarried Mothers* (Free Press, 1961), p. 9.

24. *Ibid.*, p. 9.

25. Katharine Archibald, *War Time Shipyard* (University of California Press, 1947), pp. 18–20.

26. See William Form and Delbert Miller, *Industrial Sociology* (Harper and Brothers, 1951), pp. 279–81, 294–95, for a discussion of the importance of talking in the informal work group. Women workers also like to talk about sex, Helen Gurley Brown is quoted as saying (*Washington Post*, Sept. 19, 1965), but they are more likely to talk about dates, theirs and others' and who's going with whom, and the like.

27. *Esquire*, Jan. 1967, p. 86.

28. C. Wright Mills, *White Collar* (Oxford University Press, 1951), pp. 202–3.

29. Frances Benton, *Etiquette* (Random House, Inc., 1956), pp. 209, 378.

30. "How Good Are Women Bosses?" in *Changing Times*, April, 1967, p. 16.

31. Brown, *Sex and the Office*, p. 57.

32. *Ibid.*, p. 106.

33. *Ibid.*, p. 53.

34. *Ibid.*, p. 53.

35. Midge Decter, "The Ivy League Girls on the Road," *Esquire*, Sept., 1965, pp. 183ff.

36. Mills, *White Collar*, pp. 175–78.

37. Virginia Gildersleeve, *Many a Good Crusade* (The Macmillan Company, 1954), p. 98.

38. Brown, *Sex and the Office*, pp. 66–67.

39. Burgess, Locke, and Thomes, *The Family*, p. 250.

40. Angell, *Compete!*, p. 22.

41. Frances Benton, *Etiquette*, p. 378.

42. Patricia McCormack, *Washington Post*, Dec. 5, 1965.

43. Deputy Assistant Secretary of State Katie Louchheim, quoted by Dorothy McCardle, "For War between the Sexes She Maps Out Strategy," *Washington Post*, May 26, 1967.

44. Cussler, *The Woman Executive*, pp. 66–67.

45. *Ibid.*, p. 74.

46. Kathryn Clarenbach, quoted by Elizabeth Shelton, "'Knit Gnawing' Rankles Women Summit Thinkers," *Washington Post*, June 30, 1966.

47. Bernard, *Academic Women*, pp. 204–5.

48. Nancy Koplin Jack and Betty Schiffer, "The Limits of Fashion Control," *Amer. Sociol. Rev.*, 13 (Dec., 1948), 730–38.

Chapter Twelve

1. Barrett H. Clark, *European Theories of the Drama* (Crown, 1965), p. 44.

2. *Washington Post*, Dec. 11, 1965.

3. Editors of *Esquire*, *Etiquette*, p. 179.

4. Henry Shenk, "Co-education in the Service of Curriculum for College Students under an Elective Program," *Annual Proceedings of the College Physical Education Association*, 60 (1957), 275, 276.

5. G. F. Cousins, "Co-educational Physical Education for the College Level?" *Ibid.*, p. 282.

6. *Ibid.*, pp. 282–83.

7. *Ibid.*, p. 283.

8. John and Barbara Devaney, "It's the Girls Against the Boys!" *This Week*, July 28, 1963, p. 7.

9. *Ibid.*, p. 7.

10. *Ibid.*, p. 6.

11. *Ibid.*, p. 7.

12. *Ibid.*, p. 8.

13. Mirra Komarovsky, "Cultural Contradictions and Sex Roles," *Amer. Jour. Sociol.*, 52 (July, 1946), pp. 186–88.

14. Patricia McCormack, "A 'Work and Prey' Plan," *Washington Post*, Dec. 5, 1965.

15. Devaney and Devaney, *loc. cit.*, p. 7.

16. Editors of *Esquire, Etiquette*, p. 168.

17. *Ibid.*, p. 172.

18. Riesman, Potter, and Watson, "Sociability, Permissiveness, and Equality," *Psychiatry*, 23 (Nov., 1960), 327. We are not talking about the special kinds of "psychiatric games" discussed by Eric Berne in his *Games People Play* and illustrated by Edward Albee in the play *Who's Afraid of Virginia Woolf?*

19. E. Franklin Frazier reported the case of a woman who found poker a substitute for orgasm. See *Black Bourgeoisie* (Collier Books, 1962), p. 183.

20. "Young, Single, and Stranger in New York," *Look Magazine*, August 23, 1966, pp. 93, 94.

21. Jessie Bernard, Helen Buchanan, and William Smith, *Dating, Mating, and Marriage* (Howard Allen, 1958), Chap. 2.

22. Wilfred Fleisher, "Girl Fined as Cheat in Sweden for Reneging on 'Sex Date,'" *Washington Post*, July 17, 1966.

23. Marcus, *The Other Victorians*, p. 179.

24. *Ibid.*, p. 180.

25. *Ibid.*, p. 180.

26. Brown, *Sex and the Office*, pp. 117, 118.

27. *Ibid.*, pp. 119–21.

28. Harvey Cox, *The Secular City, Secularization and Urbanization in Theological Perspective* (The Macmillan Company, 1965), pp. 201ff.

❖❖❖❖❖

Chapter Thirteen

1. David Riesman, Robert J. Potter, and Jeanne Watson, "Sociability, Permissiveness, and Equality," *Psychiatry*, 23 (Nov., 1960), 324.

2. *Ibid.*, p. 326.

3. *Ibid.*, p. 330.

4. *Ibid.*, p. 340.

5. *Ibid.*, p. 331.

6. David Riesman, Robert J. Potter, and Jeanne Watson, "The Vanishing Host," *Human Organization*, 19 (Spring, 1960), 26.

7. *Ibid.*, p. 21.

8. *Handbook of Good Society: The Art of Conversation*, p. 117.

9. Riesman, Potter, and Watson, quoting Georg Simmel on sociability, "Sociability, Permissiveness, and Equality," *loc. cit.*, p. 324.

10. Emily James Putnam, *The Lady, Studies of Certain Significant Phases of Her History* (Sturgis and Walton, 1910), p. 264.

11. Captain Basil Hall, *Travels in North America*, II, 1827–1828, pp. 150, 153.

12. Frances Trollope, *Domestic Manners of the Americans*, 1832. Present citation, John Graham Brooks, *As Others See Us* (The Macmillan Company, 1909), p. 10.

13. Trollope, *Ibid.* Present citation, Arthur Schlesinger, Jr., "An Informal History of Love U.S.A.," *Sat. Eve. Post*, Jan. 7, 1967, p. 32.

14. Thomas Joseph Grund, *Aristocracy in America, From the Sketch-Book of a German Nobleman* (London: Bentley, 1839), p. 273.

15. Canby, *The Age of Confidence*, p. 173.

16. *Ibid.*, p. 177.

17. Lynd and Lynd, *Middletown*, p. 118.

18. David L. Cohn, *Love in America, An Informal Study of Manners and Morals in American Marriage* (Simon and Schuster, Inc., 1943), pp. 49–50.

19. Riesman, Potter, and Watson, "The Vanishing Host," *loc. cit.*, p. 23.

20. Putnam, *The Lady*, pp. 183, 185.

21. Herold, *Madame de Staël*, p. 70.

22. *Ibid.*, p. 71.

23. *Ibid.*, p. 71.

24. Putnam, *The Lady*, p. 270.

25. Canby, *The Age of Confidence*, p. 175.

26. Philip E. Slater, "On Social Regression," *American Sociol. Rev.*, 28 (June, 1963), 357.

27. *Ibid.*, pp. 348–61.

28. *Ibid.*, p. 357.

29. *Ibid.*, p. 357.

30. Caplow, *The Sociology of Work*, p. 239.

31. James West, *Plainville, U.S.A.* (Columbia University Press, 1945), pp. 100–104.

32. Riesman, Potter, and Watson, "Sociability, Permissiveness, and Equality," *loc. cit.*, p. 339.

33. Pearl Buck, "Changing Relationships between Men and Women," in Beverly Benner Cassara, ed., *American Women: The Changing Image* (Beacon Press, 1962), pp. 7–8.

34. Riesman, Potter, and Watson, "The Vanishing Host," *loc. cit.*, p. 24.

35. Bernard, *Academic Women*, p. 188.

36. Canby, *The Age of Confidence*, p. 176.

37. James A. Davis, *A Study of Participants in the Great Books Program* (National Opinion Research Center, 1957), p. 112.

38. *Ibid.*, p. 113.

39. *Ibid.*, p. 15.

40. Abbot Kaplan, *Study-Discussion in the Liberal Arts* (Fund for Adult Education, 1960), pp. 97–112.

41. Richard J. Hill, *A Comparative Study of Lecture and Discussion Methods* (Fund for Adult Education, 1960), p. 125.

42. James A. Davis, *Great Books Program*, p. 113.

43. *Ibid.*, p. 113.

44. Putnam, *The Lady*, p. 270.

45. *Ibid.*, p. 270.

46. James A. Davis, *Great Books Program*, p. 124.

47. *Ibid.*, p. 131.

❖❖❖❖❖

1. Katharine Whitehorn in the *London Observer*, reproduced in the *Washington Post*, September 21, 1966.

2. The trauma associated with the new relationships for men are documented in M. R. Sapirstein, *Emotional Security* (Crown Press, 1948), pp. 188ff., and Myron Brenton, *The American Male* (Coward-McCann, 1966), pp. 165ff.

BIBLIOGRAPHY

Aberle, Sophie D., and Corner, George W., *Twenty-Five Years of Sex Research*. Philadelphia, W. B. Saunders Company, 1953.

Allen, Frederick Lewis, *Only Yesterday*. New York, Bantam Books, Inc., 1959.

Bales, Robert F., *Interaction Process Analysis: A Method for the Study of Small Groups*. Reading, Mass., Addison-Wesley Publishing Company, Inc., 1950.

Beauvoir, Simone de, *The Second Sex*. New York, Bantam Books, 1961.

Bennet, Edward M., and Cohen, Larry R., *Men and Women: Personality Patterns and Contrasts*. Genetic Psychology Monographs, 59, 1959.

Bernard, Jessie, *Academic Women*. University Park, Pa., The Pennsylvania State University Press, 1964.

Bernard, Jessie, *Remarriage, A Study of Marriage*. New York, Dryden Press, 1956.

Berne, Eric, *Games People Play, The Psychology of Human Relationships*. New York, Grove Press, 1964.

Blood, Robert O. Jr., and Wolfe, Donald M., *Husbands and Wives, The Dynamics of Married Living*. Chicago, Free Press, 1960.

Brenton, Myron, *The American Male, A Penetrating Look at the Masculinity Crisis*. New York, Coward-McCann, Inc., 1966.

Brown, Helen Gurley, *Sex and the Office*. New York, Pocket Books, Inc., 1965.

Buck, Pearl, *Of Men and Women*. New York, The John Day Company, Inc., 1941.

Burgess, Ernest Watson, Locke, Harvey J., and Thomes, Mary Margaret, *The Family, From Institution to Companionship*. New York, American Book Company, 1963.

Canby, Henry Seidel, *The Age of Confidence*. New York, Farrar and Rinehart, 1934.

Caplow, Theodore, *The Sociology of Work*. New York, McGraw-Hill, Inc., 1964.

Carrighar, Sally, *Wild Heritage*. Boston, Houghton Mifflin Company, 1965.

Cassara, Beverly Benner, ed., *American Women: The Changing Image*. New York, The Beacon Press, Inc., 1962.

Cherry, Colin, *On Human Communication, A Review, a Survey, and a Criticism.* New York, Wiley Science Editions, 1961.

Cohn, David L., *Love in America, An Informal Study of Manners and Morals in American Marriage.* New York, Simon and Schuster, Inc., 1943.

Coolidge, Mary, *Why Women Are So.* New York, Henry Holt, 1912.

Cussler, Margaret, *The Woman Executive.* New York, Harcourt, Brace & World, Inc., 1958.

David, James A., *A Study of Participants in the Great Books Program.* National Opinion Research Center, 1957.

DeVore, Irven, ed., *Primate Behavior: Field Studies of Monkeys and Apes.* New York, Holt, Rinehart and Winston, Inc., 1965.

Eisenson, Jon, *The Psychology of Communication.* New York, Appleton-Century-Crofts, 1963.

Farnham, Marynia, and Lundberg, Ferdinand, *Modern Woman: The Lost Sex.* New York, Harper and Brothers, 1947.

Feldenkreis, F., *Body and Mature Behavior.* New York, International Universities Press, Inc., 1949.

Feldman, Harold, *Development of the Husband-Wife Relationship.* Ithaca, N.Y., Cornell University Press, 1965.

Fiedler, Leslie, *Love and Death in the American Novel.* New York, Meridian Books, 1962.

Ford, Clennan S., and Beach, Frank A., *Patterns of Sexual Behavior.* New York, Ace Books, 1951.

Friedan, Betty, *The Feminine Mystique.* New York, W. W. Norton & Company, Inc., 1963.

Gagnon, John H., "Sexuality and Sexual Learning in the Child." *Psychiatry,* 8 (Aug., 1965), 212–28.

Goffman, Erving, *The Presentation of the Self in Everyday Life.* New York, Anchor Books, 1959.

Hall, Edward T., *The Silent Language.* New York, Premier Books, 1963.

Herold, J. Christopher, *Mistress to an Age, A Life of Madame de Staël.* Indianapolis, Ind., The Bobbs-Merrill Company, Inc., 1958.

Hoch, Paul H., and Zublin, Joseph, eds., *Psychopathology of Communication.* New York, Grune & Stratton, Inc., 1958.

Hunt, Morton M., *The Natural History of Love.* New York, Alfred A. Knopf, Inc., 1959.

Jourard, Sidney, *The Transparent Self.* New York, D. Van Nostrand Company, Inc., 1964.

Kaplan, Abbott, *Study-Discussion in the Liberal Arts.* Fund for Adult Education, 1960.

Karlsson, Georg, *Adaptability and Communication in Marriage: A Swedish Predictive Study of Marital Satisfaction.* Uppsala, Almqvist and Wiksells Boktrycheri Actiebolag, 1951.

Kinsey, Alfred C., and Associates, *Sexual Behavior in the Human Female*. Philadelphia, W. B. Saunders Company, 1953.

Kinsey, Alfred C., and Associates, *Sexual Behavior in the Human Male*. Philadelphia, W. B. Saunders Company, 1948.

Komarovsky, Mirra, *Blue-Collar Marriage*. New York, Random House, Inc., 1962.

Komarovsky, Mirra, *Women in the Modern World, Their Education and Their Dilemmas*. Boston, Little, Brown and Company, 1953.

Lifton, Robert Jay, ed., *The Woman in America*. New York, Houghton Mifflin Company, 1965.

Lorenz, Konrad, *On Aggression*. New York, Harcourt, Brace & World, Inc., 1963.

Maccoby, Eleanor E., ed., *The Development of Sex Differences*. Stanford, Calif., Stanford University Press, 1966.

Marcus, Steven, *The Other Victorians*. New York, Basic Books, 1966.

Masters, William H., and Johnson, Virginia, *Human Sexual Response*. Boston, Little, Brown and Company, 1966.

Mead, Margaret, *Male and Female*. New York, New American Library, 1955.

Mead, Margaret, *Sex and Temperament in Three Primitive Societies*. New York, William Morrow and Company, Inc., 1935.

Mills, C. Wright, *White Collar*. New York, Oxford University Press, Inc., 1951.

Money, John, ed., *Sex Research, New Developments*. New York, Holt, Rinehart and Winston, Inc., 1965.

Parsons, Talcott, and Bales, Robert F., *Family, Socialization, and Interaction Process*. Chicago, Free Press, 1955.

Praz, Mario, *The Romantic Agony*. New York, Meridian Books, 1963.

Putnam, Emily James, *The Lady, Studies of Certain Significant Phases of Her History*. Sturgis and Walton, 1910.

Rainwater, Lee, *Family Design*. Chicago, Aldine Publishing Company, 1965.

Rainwater, Lee, and Weinstein, Karol Kane, *And the Poor Get Children*. Chicago, Quadrangle Books, Inc., 1960.

Rainwater, Lee, Coleman, Richard P., and Handel, Gerald, *Workingman's Wife, Her Personality, World and Life Style*. New York, Macfadden Bartell Corp., 1959.

Rapoport, Anatol, and Chammah, Albert M., *Prisoner's Dilemma, A Study in Conflict and Cooperation*. Ann Arbor, Mich., University of Michigan Press, 1965.

Reingold, Joseph C., *The Fear of Being a Woman*. New York, Grune & Stratton, Inc., 1964.

Riesman, David, Potter, Robert J., and Watson, Jeanne, "Sociability, Permissiveness, and Equality." *Psychiatry*, 23 (Nov., 1960), 323–40.

Riesman, David, Potter, Robert J., and Watson, Jeanne, "The Vanishing Host." *Human Organization*, 19 (Spring, 1960), 17–27.

Rougemont, Denis de, *Love in the Western World*. New York, Pantheon Books, 1956.

Sapirstein, M. R., *Emotional Security*. New York, Crown Publishers, 1948.

Schelling, Thomas C., *The Strategy of Conflict*. Cambridge, Mass., Harvard University Press, 1960.

Scott-Maxwell, Florida, *Women and Sometimes Men*. New York, Alfred A. Knopf, Inc., 1957.

Seward, Georgene, *Sex and the Social Order*. New York, McGraw-Hill, Inc., 1946.

Slater, Philip, "On Social Regression." *Amer. Sociol. Rev.*, 28 (June, 1963), 339–64.

Smuts, Robert W., *Women and Work in America*. New York, Columbia University Press, 1959.

Thomas, William Isaac, *Sex and Society*. Chicago, University of Chicago Press, 1906.

Thompson, Stith, *The Folktale*. New York, Dryden Press, 1946.

Uesugi, Thomas C., and Vinacke, W. Edgar, "Strategy in a Feminine Game." *Sociometry*, 26 (March, 1963), 75–88.

Vinacke, W. Edgar, "Sex Roles in a Three-Person Game." *Sociometry*, 22 (Dec., 1959), 343–59.

Waller, A. R., and Ward, A. W., eds., *Cambridge History of English Literature*, II, 422–48, III, 93–129. New York, The Macmillan Company, 1933.

Waller, Willard, and Hill, Reuben, *The Family, A Dynamic Interpretation*. New York, Dryden Press, 1951.

Wilson, John, *Logic and Sexual Morality*, Baltimore, Penguin Books, 1965.

INDEX

Assimilationist male subsex, 36, 48, 207

Bacon, Francis, 153
barriers to communication
  age differences as, 119; cultural stereotypes as, 256–57; culture differences as, 118–19; differences in experiences as, 99–100, 101–2; individual differences in sexuality as, 101, 121–22; race differences as, 119; sex differences as, 83–85, 100, 116, 119, 255–57
Beard, Mary, 135
Beauvoir, Simone de, 87, 155, 189, 190, 196, 321, 325
bitch, 20, 266
Blood, Robert O., Jr., 245, 249
Bossard, James H. S., 247, 248
Bracken, Peg, 73
Broderick, Carlfred, 173
Brontë, Charlotte, 236
Brown, Helen Gurley, 272, 279, 280, 281, 283, 285, 306, 308
Buchwald, Art, 294–95, 296
Buck, Pearl, 322
buck-passing strategies, 219, 223–24
Burgess, E. W., 232, 234
Bryce, Lord James, 147

Canby, Henry Siedel, 315, 323, 324
Caplow, Theodore, 272, 273
Carrighar, Sally, 6, 7, 8, 9, 59
Chaucer, Geoffrey, 212
Cherry, Colin, 116, 135
cichlid-effect, 59–64
  and sacrifice of achievement by women, 285–87; at work, 285–87; expressive talk as, 138; humiliating effects of, on women, 61; in marriage, 244; rejection of, by shrew, 210
Civil Rights Act of 1964, 293
Coleridge, Samuel, 173
collective communication between the sexes
  the arts as, 127–28; culture as silent language in, 127; direct action as, 128–29; illness as, 129; societal norms as, 127
commitment strategies in sex conflict
  first move as, 219–20; strategic promises as, 220–21; strategic threat as, 221–23
communication, Chapter Four

and sexuality in marriage, 235; as control, 213–14; barriers to, see barriers to communication; based on assumed similarities between communicators, shared-experience models, 99ff., empathic model, 103–5, inferential model, 101–2, sympathetic model, 105–6; importance of, in modern approach to strategy, 217; not based on assumed similarities between communicators, the Wowser-Holmes model, 97–99; quantitative aspects of, 96–97; success of, 110; degrees of, 110–15
communication between the sexes
  and rapprochment of sexes with age, 67; barriers to, see barriers to communication; media of, see signals, signs, strategy, words; required by inbody fertilization, 3; verbal, 9, Chapter Three
communication between the sexes at play, Chapter Twelve
  competitive sports and, 299–300; co-recreation and, 298–99; games and, 301; kinds of, related to situation, 301; minimized by exclusion of women from male activities, 297
communication between the sexes in social life, Chapter Thirteen
  as prospecting for information, 312; stroking nature of, 313
communication between the sexes at work, Chapter Eleven
  and cichlid-effect, 285; and male mystique, 271, 273; and status inconsistency, 272–74, 287; and stroking, 279–84; change over time, 268–70; expressive character of, 276–77, 279–80, 284; in bureaucratic settings, 269–87; in doctor-nurse relationship, 288; in doctor-patient relationship, 288; in engineering profession, 289–90; in the fashion world, 291–92; in the home, 293; in lawyer-client relationship, 289; in libraries, 290–91; in minister-parishioner relationship, 289; in new professions, 279, 283; in sales work, 281–83; instrumental character of, 275–76; in teacher-pupil relationship, 289; in theater and entertainment world, 291; older women and, 266; younger women and, 267

[367]